The New York Times

CROSSWORDS FOR A HOLIDAY WEEKEND

Published in the United States by St. Martin's Griffin,
an imprint of St. Martin's Publishing Group

THE NEW YORK TIMES CROSSWORDS FOR A HOLIDAY WEEKEND.
Copyright © 2023 by The New York Times Company. All rights reserved.
Printed in the United States of America. For information, address St. Martin's
Publishing Group, 120 Broadway, New York, NY 10271.

www.stmartins.com

All of the puzzles that appear in this work were originally published in
The New York Times from October 22, 2018, to December 31, 2018; April 1, 2019, to September 2, 2019;
January 1, 2020, to April 9, 2020; or May 5, 2021, to April 22, 2022.
Copyright © 2018, 2019, 2020, 2021, 2022 by The New York Times Company.
All rights reserved. Reprinted by permission.

ISBN 978-1-250-89605-6

Our books may be purchased in bulk for promotional, educational, or business use.
Please contact your local bookseller or the Macmillan Corporate
and Premium Sales Department at 1-800-221-7945, extension 5442, or
by email at MacmillanSpecialMarkets@macmillan.com.

First Edition: 2023

10 9 8 7 6 5 4 3 2 1

The New York Times

CROSSWORDS FOR A HOLIDAY WEEKEND
200 Easy to Hard Crossword Puzzles

Edited by Will Shortz

ST. MARTIN'S GRIFFIN
NEW YORK

Looking for more Easy Crosswords?

The New York Times

The #1 Name in Crosswords

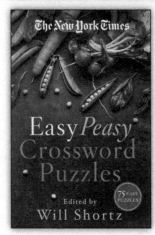
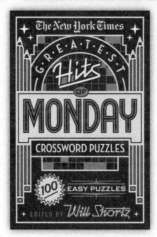
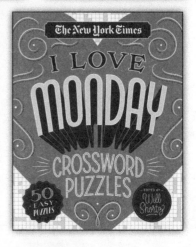

ACROSS

1 Base after third base
5 Flows back
9 1, 8, 27, 64, etc.
14 The "U" of B.T.U.
15 1982 movie inspired by Pong
16 Yoga posture
17 *Capricious
19 French "thank you"
20 ". . . man __ mouse?"
21 Jokester's jokes
22 *Forgivable
23 __ McDonald (clown)
25 Additionally
27 Gas brand whose logo has a blue oval
28 "Desserts" made from wet dirt
30 Pupu __
32 Isaac's elder son
33 Gas brand whose logo has a red triangle
35 What free apps often come with
36 *Warlike
38 Little rapscallion
41 Glass that makes a rainbow
42 Website for crowdsourced reviews
46 Church activity
48 Clothing
51 "Will do!"
52 "The War of the Worlds" villains, briefly
54 Sitting Bull's people
55 *Jolly
57 Meriting a "D," say
59 Figure in the form 123-45-6789, e.g.: Abbr.
60 "__ ears!" ("Listening!")
61 *Gloomy
63 Portions (out)
64 Vaper's device
65 Italy's shape
66 "You __ right!"
67 Composer John with six Emmys
68 Tiny hill builders

DOWN

1 "Just play along, please"
2 Burdensome
3 "Hamilton" composer
4 List-ending abbr.
5 Brokerage with an asterisk in its name
6 Clink on the drink
7 Toot one's own horn
8 Weekly parody source, briefly
9 Arrived
10 Online discussion forum
11 Professional coffee server
12 Fully surrounded (by)
13 Ones under a captain's command
18 __ fruit (wrinkly citrus)
22 Europe's longest river
24 Kwik-E-Mart minder on "The Simpsons"
26 Kia model
29 What actors memorize
31 Alternative to Hotmail
34 "__ Not Unusual" (Tom Jones standard)
36 Car speed meas.
37 Shakespearean sprite
38 Site of a 1945 Allied victory in the Pacific
39 Amino acid vis-à-vis a protein, e.g.
40 Public's opposite
42 Tibetan beast
43 Beachfront property woe
44 "How about we forgo that"
45 Etymological origins of the answers to the five starred clues
47 Subway entrances
49 What oxen pull, in England
50 Catherine who married Henry VIII
53 The final frontier, per "Star Trek"
56 Additionally
58 Big name in elevators
61 Prepare, as a dinner table
62 Org. for the Sixers and Spurs

by Alex Eaton-Salners

ACROSS

1 Bob Marley, e.g.
6 J. ___ Hoover
11 Rainbow, for one
14 Choir voices
15 Band at a royal wedding
16 Elevator unit
17 Kid-lit character who travels via envelope
19 Ref's decision
20 ___ pad
21 Communists and capitalists, e.g.
23 Hot couple
24 Thelma's portrayer in "Thelma & Louise"
27 Trumped-up
29 Lobster ___ Newburg
30 Aloha State bird
31 Mexican Mrs.
32 Catastrophic
34 U.S.O. audience
36 Co-star of "Stranger Things"
40 Dapper fellow
41 U.S. city connected to the outside only by airplane, boat and sled
42 What debtors do
45 "Piece of cake"
48 Japanese garden fish
49 Tops
51 "I can't believe we both know him"
55 Charlie Brown expletive
56 Western ravines
57 Ideal places
59 What might bring you to a screeching halt
60 Protective sportswear . . . or a hint to the ends of 17-, 24-, 36- and 51-Across
64 Kimono tie
65 Choice for a prom
66 His and her
67 "Now where ___ I?"
68 French toast topper
69 Having some kick

DOWN

1 U.K. flying grp.
2 Standout player
3 What a governor enforces
4 Figures on poles
5 Org.
6 GPS display
7 Racket
8 Lead-bearing ore
9 Big concert venue
10 Like Lady Liberty's crown
11 Like the ingredient acetaminophen in Tylenol
12 Make hand over fist
13 Stick in a field game
18 Dude (up)
22 Cleric's house
23 Provisos
25 Become worthy of
26 Rigby who "waits at the window, wearing the face that she keeps in a jar by the door"
28 Poet ___ St. Vincent Millay
33 It's not free of charge
34 Trainer's workplace
35 Brainstorm
37 Short narrative poem
38 Stir up
39 Woos
43 Kayaker's attire
44 Double curve
45 Money held by a third party
46 Slide presentation?
47 Gulf War allies
48 On the up and up
50 Nativity scene
52 Performers who get top billing
53 Humble reply to "Great job, folks!"
54 The Pistons, on scoreboards
58 Airhead
61 The Fighting Tigers of the N.C.A.A.
62 Subj. of a test that might involve identifying playing cards
63 Get too personal

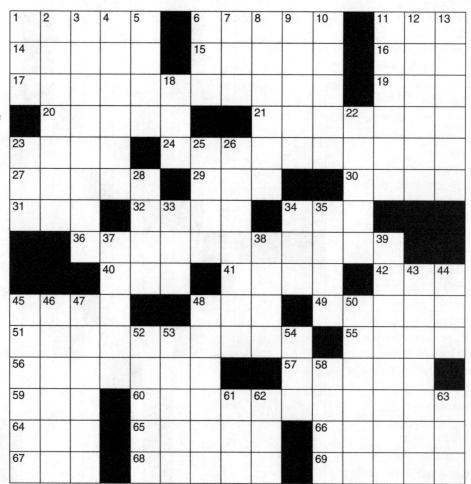

by Kathy Wienberg

ACROSS

1 Snatch
5 Mil. schools
10 Irritably impatient
15 Actress Dunham who wrote "Not That Kind of Girl"
16 What a designated driver should be
17 Where "I dos" are exchanged
18 Leave out
19 Children's publisher whose name includes a black-and-white animal
21 Home of Pago Pago
23 Moo goo ___ pan
24 Wonderland girl
25 Foul-smelling swamp plant whose name includes a black-and-white animal
28 Sent to the canvas, in brief
30 What "I do" means
31 Tavern
32 On, as a horse
34 Some small batteries
35 Volcanic residue
37 Samberg of "Brooklyn Nine-Nine"
38 Areas for pedestrians whose name includes a black-and-white animal
43 Hoedown seat
44 Schumer of "I Feel Pretty"
45 Relative of dynamite
46 Small sugar serving
49 Bread for a Reuben sandwich
50 Deg. from Wharton
53 Sharpshooter's asset
54 Restaurant chain whose name includes a black-and-white animal
58 Opposite of o'er
60 Sick
61 Line at an airport
62 Men's fancy duds whose name includes a black-and-white animal
65 Wait
66 Brand of blenders
67 High points
68 High cards
69 German steel city
70 Sheriff's group
71 Flip, as a coin

DOWN

1 Shiny photo
2 New version of an old film
3 Strong dislike
4 Relay race handoff
5 Nile biter
6 Mountain lion
7 Britcom of the 1990s, informally
8 E.M.T. procedure with electric paddles, for short
9 ___ Lanka
10 iPad, e.g.
11 Elite race in "The Time Machine"
12 Item hung on Christmas Eve
13 Accept a bet
14 100 in a century: Abbr.
20 Repeatedly scolds
22 "Allahu ___" (Muslim cry)
26 Spanish house
27 Sounds at spas
29 Susan of "L.A. Law"
33 Deliver a diatribe
34 Whom Cain slew in Genesis
35 Triceps locale
36 Sushi sauce
38 Buffoonery
39 Listings on the periodic table
40 ___ Crunch (cereal)
41 River of the underworld
42 Ham-handed
43 Drag queen's wrap
47 Economic improvement
48 When doubled, a dolphinfish
49 Depends (on)
50 Where Guadalajara is
51 Where less-played tunes can be found on old records
52 Levy, as taxes
55 Dance club that might have a rotating mirrored ball
56 Homecoming attendees, for short
57 Morocco's capital
59 James who wrote "A Death in the Family"
62 Poet who wrote "Once upon a midnight dreary . . ."
63 Midday snooze
64 Mao ___-tung

by Peter Gordon

ACROSS

1 Riding on
5 Place to get pampered
8 Summoned on an intercom, say
13 Witty comebacks
15 University town named for an Indian chief
16 Picture often used as an altarpiece
17 Combs (through)
18 Oozing
19 Word before status or studies
21 Golfer Ernie
23 Corruption from deep inside
24 Puppy's cry
27 "Talented" title character portrayed by Matt Damon
30 Lady of Spain
31 Assent at sea
32 Veer the other way
33 Swell
34 Late night for a working stiff . . . or a hint to the shaded squares
38 Came to the rescue
39 Help in finding buried treasure
40 "The __ of Pooh," 1982 best seller
41 It's prologue, they say
42 Put on a windowsill to mature, say
45 Author LeShan
46 Samovar, e.g.
47 Schubert's "The __ King"
48 Delaware Valley tribe
51 Too, in Toulouse
55 Like a river at its mouth, not at its head
57 Narcissists' excursions?
59 Coming in handy
60 Care about something, in slang
61 More curious
62 Government org. for retirees
63 Microscope part

DOWN

1 Theater, dance, etc.
2 Firestone product
3 Member of the Sons of Anarchy on FX's "Sons of Anarchy"
4 Device used with corn kernels
5 Hog heaven?
6 Bench presser's pride, informally
7 Off the main
8 Put forth
9 Met solo
10 "Get lost!"
11 "The Lord of the Rings" creature
12 First of two lists in fashion advice
14 Like the artists' names P!nk and Ke$ha
20 Playing hard to get, say
22 Neuter
25 "Your work is awesome!"
26 Words before a name on a check
27 Big number
28 Says the words on the page
29 JFK alternative
30 "Stupid me!"
31 Slack-jawed
33 Say the "h" in "historical," say
35 Dog doc
36 J.F.K. alternative in 1960
37 Venture
42 Lady of Spain: Abbr.
43 Removes, as from a fixed rate
44 Like ghosts and goblins?
46 Six feet __
49 Relaxation
50 Protection: Var.
52 Beget
53 What a pool shark puts on a ball
54 Comcast Xfinity and others, in brief
55 Halloween cry
56 Old postal letters
58 In vitro fertility needs

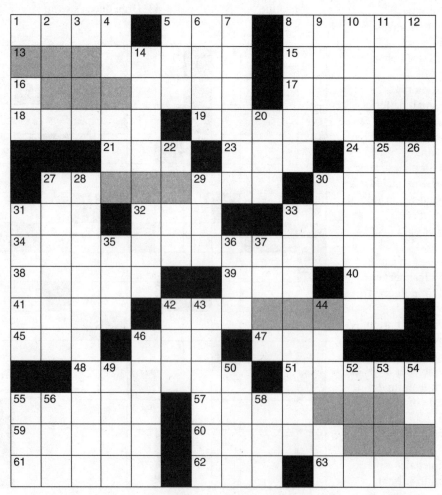

by Jules Markey

ACROSS

1 Pulsate, as with pain
6 What a red traffic light means
10 Container for soup or cereal
14 ___ acid (protein builder)
15 "Very funny!"
16 Eye layer
17 Chocolaty candy on a stick
19 500 sheets of paper
20 Realtors' showings
21 Endless, in poetry
23 Guard at an entrance
26 Length × width, for a rectangle
27 Desertlike
28 Breakfast cereal with a naval officer on its box
33 Put through a blast furnace, say
35 Dissolute sort
36 Rope-a-dope boxer
37 ___-relief
38 Two marks in "résumés"
41 Easy-to-chew food
42 It ends with diciembre
43 Danny who co-starred in "White Christmas"
44 Make red-faced
46 Brittle, spicy cookie
50 Besides
51 Hilarious person
52 Plan going forward, as for peace
54 As originally placed
57 Constantly rising things in gentrifying neighborhoods
58 Where Hartford is: Abbr.
59 Broadcast news snippets . . . or an apt description for 17-, 28- and 46-Across?
64 Grand-scale production
65 ___ Krabappel, teacher on "The Simpsons"
66 Love, love, love
67 Meyers of late-night
68 Most mammals have four of them
69 Core belief

DOWN

1 Tit for ___
2 Care provider, briefly
3 2016 Olympics host, informally
4 Hush-hush, slangily
5 ___ buddy
6 "For Your Eyes Only" singer Easton
7 Water spigots
8 "Look what I found!"
9 Slice from a book?
10 The "B" of F.B.I.
11 On top of
12 Withdraw gradually (from)
13 Unfunny, as a joke
18 Apple desktop
22 Mother canonized in 2016
23 Long-winded sort
24 Italian designer Giorgio
25 Attaches using string
26 Unknown author, for short
29 Fuss in front of the mirror
30 Incendiary weapon used in the Vietnam War
31 Category for a minor-league team
32 Rap, by another name
34 "Grab this!"
39 Amusement park ride that goes around and around
40 Growth under the skin
45 Unflattering angle of one's face
47 Christmas stealer in a Dr. Seuss book
48 Stadiums
49 Duck's habitat
53 Hitter's turn to hit
54 Helps reduce the swelling of, say
55 Slangy refusal
56 Foul mood
57 Step on a ladder
60 Poem of praise
61 2,000 pounds
62 Before, poetically
63 "On your mark, get ___ . . ."

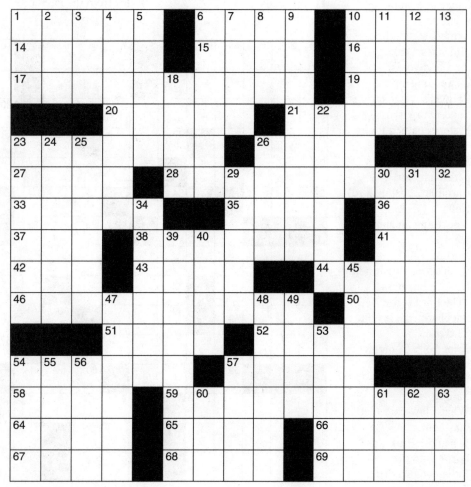

by Roland Huget

ACROSS

1 Like many internships
7 Place for a massage
10 Hybrid citrus fruits
15 "Just my luck!"
16 Ripken with a record 2,632 consecutive games played
17 Identify someone without speaking
18 Superman's fist?
20 Wee
21 Forever and a day
22 Yang's opposite
23 Forever and a day
25 Fortuneteller's deck
27 Iron Man without any clothes?
32 U.F.O. pilots
33 Sounds at doctors' checkups
35 Shape of a plunging neckline
36 Symbol of saintliness
37 Finish, as a cake
38 Profoundly wise
39 List-ending abbr.
40 Batman's water springs?
45 Lead-in to girl
46 Fastener named for its shape
47 Placed coins in, as a parking meter
48 Carolina ___ (state bird)
49 Bub
50 Something an apiphobe fears
51 Faux ___
54 Spider-Man not minding his own business?
57 "The Lord is my Shepherd" begins the 23rd one
59 Famed N.Y.C. nightclub, with "the"
60 Untrustworthy sort
62 Sailing
63 What a low-carb diet may ban
66 When the Hulk was born?
69 Indian yogurt drink
70 Things requested by bouncers
71 Partner on a talk show
72 Highly competitive, say
73 No-frills bed
74 Raises, as a flag

DOWN

1 New edition of software
2 Snickers bar filling
3 Hot rods?
4 "Am not!" reply
5 Text message qualifier
6 Go against
7 Aroma
8 Scathing review
9 Secondary identity . . . or what can be found in 18-, 27-, 40-, 54- and 66-Across
10 Wharton's school, familiarly
11 Proceeds
12 Broadway's ___-Manuel Miranda
13 Networkers' goals
14 Digs for pigs
19 Meet face to face?
24 "Cow's Skull: Red, White and Blue" artist
26 Phrasing so as not to offend, say
28 Nautical "Stop!"
29 Perry with the 2010 hit "Firework"
30 Flair
31 Loser to Clinton in 1996
34 Colorful image in a weather report
37 No matter what
38 Crept (out), informally
40 Baby deer
41 Spanish "other"
42 Pac-12 team about 625 miles from the Pacific
43 How the Quran is written
44 Cry
50 Kellogg's Raisin ___
51 Leisurely strolls
52 Yankees' division, in brief
53 Savviness
55 Lecterns
56 Young's partner in accounting
58 Greet someone cordially
61 Silicon Valley specialty
63 Lunch order that might be grilled
64 Title role for which Jamie Foxx won an Oscar for Best Actor
65 Paranormal ability, for short
67 Hoopla
68 Aussie animal

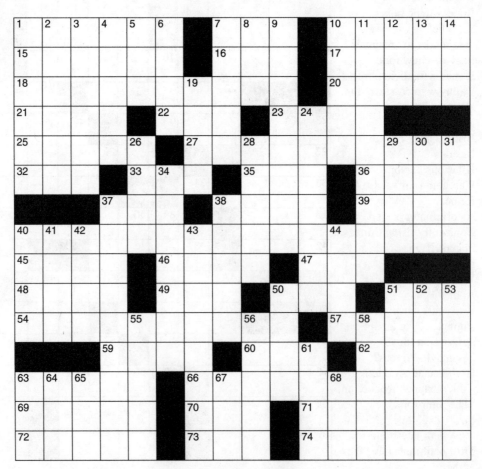

by Alan Southworth and Yacob Yonas

ACROSS

1 Walk in the kiddie pool
5 Org. for the Los Angeles Sparks and New York Liberty
9 Minor fight
14 Affordable German car
15 Garden worker
16 "Star Trek" lieutenant who speaks Swahili
17 Drops dead
19 Tilts
20 Declare something completely finished
22 Cain or Abel, to Adam and Eve
23 Tiny
24 "___ we can" (2008 campaign slogan)
25 Self-proclaimed greatest boxer
28 One-named soccer great
31 Sis's sibling
33 Expression of disgust in Valley Girl-speak
39 Give the glad eye
40 Grp. to call to get a tow
41 Site with a "Shop by category" button
42 Have surgery
47 Not worth a ___
48 One-named singer with the 1985 hit "Smooth Operator"
49 Concorde, e.g., for short
50 Ingested
53 Org. with the longtime leader Wayne LaPierre
55 QB's mistake: Abbr.
57 Show up for negotiations . . . or a hint for 20-, 33- and 42-Across
63 ___ Gay (W.W. II plane)
64 Act all hoity-toity
66 Indian princes
67 Felipe ___, first Dominican manager in M.L.B. history
68 Small construction unit?
69 Lose in a staring contest
70 Littlest in a litter
71 Sexual appetite

DOWN

1 Moo goo gai pan pan
2 Residents of a 1968 movie "planet"
3 Mosquito repellent brand
4 ___ Island, immigrants' landing spot, once
5 Comment after an amazing fact is stated
6 ___ Scotia
7 Meat in a burger
8 → or ←
9 Chumps
10 Spiced tea from the East
11 Like some noses and egg yolks
12 Bandleader Shaw
13 Histories
18 Listerine competitor
21 McEntire known as "The Queen of Country"
25 Eagerly expectant
26 Italian body of water
27 Inuit shelter: Var.
29 Pinocchio, notably
30 Les ___-Unis
32 Request from a dentist
34 Clothing department with jackets and ties
35 [LOL]
36 Japanese sashes
37 Clods
38 No, in Moscow
43 "You wouldn't believe it if I told you"
44 Currency unit usually worth a little more than a dollar
45 Delete from a manuscript
46 Longtime "S.N.L." cast member Thompson
50 Sour
51 Like music with traditional harmony
52 😍 or 👍
54 Equal to face value
56 Pre-Little League game
58 Panache
59 Giant in streaming video
60 School attended by princes William and Harry
61 In ___ of (replacing)
62 Units of work in physics
65 Drunkard

by Kathy Bloomer

ACROSS

1 Commercial prefix with Turf
6 Inspiring lust
10 Like about half the games on a team's schedule
14 First little pig's building material
15 Rouse
16 Snitched
17 Representatives Sessions (R-TX) and Aguilar (D-CA), for instance?
19 "Famous" cookie name
20 A pop
21 "Bali ___" (Rodgers and Hammerstein show tune)
22 Nauru's capital
24 Sault ___ Marie
25 Why many people visit Napa?
28 Key on the left side of a keyboard
29 "Handy" thing to know, for short?
30 RR stop
31 Nurseries?
36 Bud in baseball's Hall of Fame
38 A thou
39 Outlet from the left ventricle
41 "Je t'___" ("I love you": Fr.)
42 Fairy tale baddies
44 What ice trays typically do?
46 Its symbol is Sn
47 Western tribe
49 Overrule
50 President Herbert's wife and mother, e.g.?
54 Company with a mascot named Leo
57 ___ di Pietro, artist better known as Fra Angelico
58 "___ Majesty" (what to call a king)
59 De ___ (by law)
60 Singer Guthrie
61 Play "Name That Tune"?
64 Where Cinderella lost her slipper
65 Swarming pest
66 Biblical queendom
67 French buddies

68 They may cover a lot of ground
69 Mountain chain about 5,000 miles long . . . or a hint to 17-, 25-, 31-, 44-, 50- and 61-Across

DOWN

1 Fire remnants
2 Relative of a mink
3 Query after a knock-down-drag-out fight
4 Reckless, as a decision
5 Fall behind
6 Say on a stack of Bibles
7 Weird Al Yankovic's first hit
8 Classic Jaguar model
9 "Oh, absolutely!"
10 Game company that introduced Breakout
11 Movement that Ms. magazine developed out of
12 Period enjoyed by an introvert
13 Football stats: Abbr.
18 Irrational fear
23 Hole punches
25 Followers of mis
26 "___ mañana!"
27 Wise ones
28 Rug rat
31 Alternative to the counter at a diner
32 Cardiologist's X-ray
33 Mathematician Daniel after whom a principle is named
34 Words repeated by Lady Macbeth in Act V, Scene 1

35 Word following "Able was I . . ."
37 French waters
40 "Gunsmoke" star James
43 Went after, in a way
45 Modern prefix with gender
48 Band with the 1966 #1 hit "Wild Thing," with "the"
51 Baroque stringed instruments
52 In the lead
53 Vapors
54 Less bright, as colors
55 Diving bird
56 Monument Valley sights
59 Lav
60 Bygone court org.—or current court org.
62 Half of due
63 Org. based in Fort Meade, Md.

by John Ciolfi

ACROSS

1 Jack who starred on "Dragnet"
5 Percussion in a pagoda
9 Serves as a lookout for, say
14 Mata ___ (W.W. I spy)
15 Actress Perlman of "Cheers"
16 Tennis star Djokovic
17 Vaping device, informally
18 Skeptical comeback
19 Where pasta originated
20 "Green" 1986 film?
23 Word before Ghost or Grail
24 Not strict, as security
25 Defiant challenge to a bully
28 Singer McCartney
30 Resort with springs
33 Seller of TV spots, informally
34 Subject most familiar to a portrait painter
35 Roseanne who's not on "The Conners"
36 "Fluid" 2017 film?
39 Capital of 19-Across
40 Enter a pool headfirst
41 Streamer of "Game of Thrones," once
42 Rink surface
43 "O.K. by me"
44 "Whoa there!"
45 Ginger ___ (soft drink)
46 Light source that needs occasional replacement
47 "Noted" 1965 film?
55 Black ___ spider
56 Carl who composed "Carmina Burana"
57 Greek sandwich
58 Sheep-related
59 Teeming
60 Chew on like a beaver
61 Frighten off
62 Apple device with earbuds
63 Hankerings

DOWN

1 Sharpen
2 To ___ his own
3 Cracker topping spread with a knife
4 Grand pooh-bah
5 Car part between the headlights
6 "Yippee!"
7 ". . . and ___ the twain shall meet"
8 Feline: Sp.
9 Neither vegetable nor mineral, in a guessing game
10 Cosmetic injection
11 Welsh "John"
12 Story
13 Vodka in a blue bottle
21 Energy, informally
22 Trivial entertainment
25 Prefix with lineal
26 Like a committee formed for a special purpose
27 Krispy ___ doughnuts
28 Minor annoyance
29 Soothing plant extract
30 Withheld the publication of
31 Alternative to Ragú
32 Symbol on a one-way street sign
34 What planets do on their axes
35 Pram
37 Word of parting in Paris
38 Engulf, old-style
43 Blossom
44 Breathed heavily
45 In unison
46 Terrific, on Broadway
47 Lacking depth, informally
48 Hill : ants :: ___ : bees
49 Revise, as text
50 "Me neither," formally
51 Reason to call a plumber
52 "Auld Lang ___"
53 Longtime rival of Saudi Arabia
54 Anthropomorphic figures in many "Far Side" cartoons

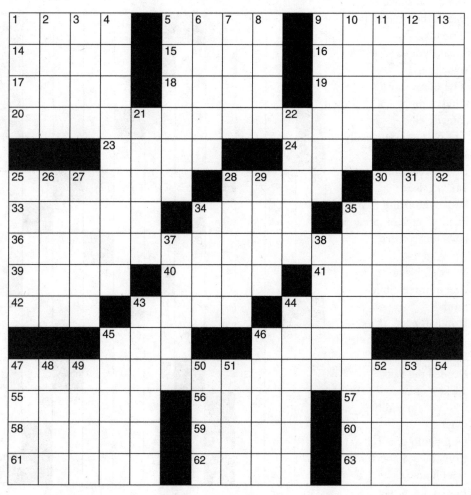

by Jim Hilger

ACROSS

1 Trajectories for fly balls
5 Bob of "Full House"
10 Tax prep pro
13 Sport shirts for golfers
15 Company with a spokesduck
16 Bud's bud in comedy
17 Turkey's place
19 Continent north of Afr.
20 Stiller's partner in comedy
21 Murals, sculptures, etc.
22 Mama's mama
23 Turkey's place
26 "OMG, 2 funny!"
29 D-worthy
30 Completely infatuated
31 Acted and spoke like
33 One of the friends on "Friends"
35 Speaks with a scratchy voice
38 "Out of my hair!"
40 Kind of night at a comedy club
42 One of the seven deadly sins
43 Family rec center
45 Take __ loan
46 Soda with fruity flavors
48 Family name of three lawmen brothers
50 Apply gently
51 Turkey's place
55 One of three biblical brothers
56 Paintball need
57 Host of "The Big Podcast With Shaq"
60 Headed the pack
61 Turkey's place
64 Chow mein additive, maybe
65 Dull photo finish
66 Compound in perfumes
67 "Get it now?"
68 Baby wipe target
69 Voice mail signal

DOWN

1 Program activated with a tap
2 Apartment unit
3 Crime scene find
4 Renewable kind of energy
5 For instance
6 Staples of soap operas
7 Harsh light
8 Wild animal tracking aid
9 Cable inits. for older films
10 Very confusing
11 Basic monetary unit of Egypt, Sudan and Syria
12 Heavenly glows
14 Helmet attachment
18 Shadow removers
22 Honshu city that hosted the 1998 Winter Olympics
24 Deschanel of "New Girl"
25 Suffix with glass or silver
26 W.C.s
27 Birthstone after sapphire
28 Garnish for a vodka tonic
32 "Let's hear more!"
34 Home of the Rams, for short
36 Gyro bread
37 Worker during a strike
39 "Didn't expect to run into you here!"
41 Place to get a tattoo or some ice cream
44 Had the intention of doing it
47 Ready to go, as a car
49 Tube-shaped pasta
51 Sunburn remedies
52 Busting the scales
53 Keen enjoyment
54 What Vegemite ultimately comes from
58 Regarding
59 Claim on a house
61 Nuclear bomb, for short
62 Elongated fish
63 "Why __ you asking?"

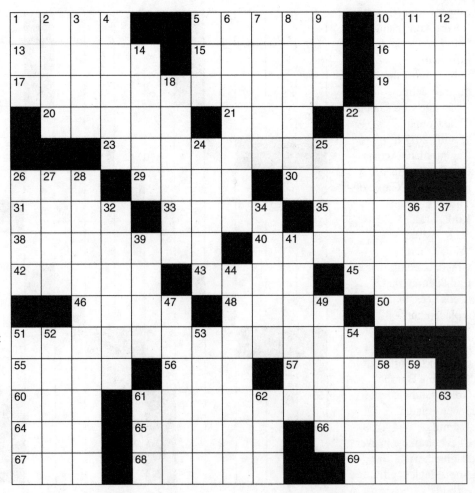

by Zhouqin Burnikel

ACROSS

1 Aware, in a modern way
5 Idris ___, People's 2018 Sexiest Man Alive
9 Abyss
14 "Man, I'm sorry to hear!"
15 Nursery rhyme word repeated before "go away"
16 "Social contract" philosopher John
17 Dachshund
19 Totally wipe out
20 Plant, as seeds
21 Our sun
22 Dress in Delhi
23 Copies of movies submitted to critics prior to release
28 ___ mark (#)
30 "Mazel ___!"
31 Witnessed
32 Partner at a table for two
35 Mideast grp. once headed by Yasir Arafat
36 Otherworldly
37 Big argument
38 Levin or Gershwin
40 The "L" of LSAT
41 Hawaiian necklace
42 Times when everything goes perfectly
45 Ambulance crew, for short
47 Words exchanged at an altar
48 Fellas
49 Genetically engineered, highly selective medical treatment
53 Modern food concerns, for short
54 Night before a holiday
55 Sack
58 Sing like Dean Martin
60 The secret geeky part of you . . . or a hint to 17-, 23-, 32-, 42- and 49-Across
63 Trailblazing Daniel
64 Modest poker holding
65 Et ___ (and others)
66 Jewish observance
67 Conveniences at many cash-only businesses
68 "Don't go!"

DOWN

1 Really impresses
2 Columbus's home
3 Was in the loop
4 Really, really long time
5 One might lead to an unearned run
6 Soup scoop
7 Book jacket bit
8 Director Lee of "Life of Pi"
9 Cloudless
10 Stockpiles
11 Running around during recess, e.g.
12 Bit of Winter Olympics equipment
13 Opera presenter, with "the"
18 Artist M. C. ___
22 Extreme
23 Nine-digit ID
24 When you'll likely reach your destination, for short
25 Away
26 Transportation problems caused by 27-Down, say
27 Winter precipitations
28 Plea from a fugitive
29 Announcer's cry after a successful field goal attempt
32 Handed (out)
33 Spring birds
34 Nickname for a 13-time N.B.A. All-Star
39 Attorney in court, e.g.
43 Neither's partner
44 Was really into
46 Olympic gold-medal gymnast Biles
50 Dead duck
51 Jean material
52 Camper enthusiasts, informally
55 Alternative to suspenders
56 Tune from "Turandot"
57 Greeting Down Under
58 "___ Evening News"
59 Fish eggs
60 Brewery output, for short
61 D.C. ballplayer
62 "Illmatic" rapper

by Evan Kalish

ACROSS

1 Swore
6 Kindergarten instruction
10 What may hold a bather or butter
13 Spring bloom
15 Casting director's assignment
16 Before, to poets
17 2018's "A Star Is Born," e.g.
18 It might accompany bacon and toast
20 "Well, ___ you special!"
22 Oscar hopeful
23 Political hopeful
26 Really good person, metaphorically
27 Bank job
28 Nike product
30 "I'm game!"
31 Mid-April addressee, for short
32 Like Cheerios
34 Homophone of "row"
36 You might learn a new language to write one
42 Sixth letter after alpha
43 Boot from power
44 Timeline swath
45 Pop flies?
48 What icicles do
50 Hilton or Marriott
52 Enterprise officer with an earpiece
54 Opinion piece
56 Unfamous sorts
58 What most college mottoes are in
59 Parting words from 18-, 23-, 36- and 54-Across?
61 Halloween creatures
64 Big name in nail polish
65 Fine sediment
66 Cirque du ___
67 Bit of board game equipment
68 Comic Rogen
69 Peevish

DOWN

1 Pre-TiVo device
2 Asset in the game The Settlers of Catan
3 Social theory popularized by Alice Walker
4 Virtual birthday greetings
5 Get into a fistfight
6 Doggie sound
7 Largest Asian island
8 Muse of history
9 Appears to be
10 ___-weenie
11 All-caps word in an email subject line
12 "Violence ___ violence"
14 Drop in the mailbox
19 Conversation
21 Fashion sense
23 Fashion-forward
24 Prefix with dynamic
25 Neck gland
29 Messes up
33 Slightly
35 1980s soca hit with the lyric "Me mind on fire, me soul on fire"
37 Rodent companion
38 Dilating eye part
39 Groups of advisers
40 The "A" in BART
41 Segway cop's workplace, maybe
45 Solar deity
46 Grammy-winning Goldberg
47 Term of respect for an older woman
49 Win, loss or draw
51 Baltimore athlete
53 Rack up
55 Identifiers at the bottom of a blog post
57 Lake named for a Pennsylvania people
60 Last degree, in math
62 Ignited
63 Foxlike

by Erik Agard

ACROSS

1 Expressions of amazement
6 Amaze
9 Illegal motions by pitchers
14 Houston player
15 Great Dane, e.g.
16 Notable happening
17 Great Dane of animated cartoons
19 Happen again
20 Immensely long stretches
21 Broke bread
22 Limited in number
23 Escalator feature
24 Result of overnight condensation
26 Lipton offerings
28 "Bus Stop" dramatist William
29 Nut often squirreled away
31 Basic trig ratio
33 Invitation request, in brief
37 Sound on a dairy farm
38 "Impossible for me!"
41 Harmful cigarette stuff
42 Equestrian's sport
44 Umpteen
45 Lessen
47 Fee payer, often
49 Londoner, e.g., informally
50 Words on returned mail
55 Vegetarian's no-no
58 Aviator Earhart
59 Cozy lodging
60 Ricelike pasta
61 Bring home, as a runner
62 Couple's ballet dance
64 Turn aside
65 Number replaced by "hup" by a drill sergeant
66 Resort island near Naples
67 Key Watergate evidence
68 72, maybe, on a golf course
69 Twin Mary-Kate or Ashley

DOWN

1 Oxygen and nitrogen
2 Racecourse near Windsor Castle
3 Implement for a Neanderthal
4 Thrive
5 Break down in tears
6 Make larger
7 Swain
8 Conscious self, to Freud
9 Explorer who lent his name to a strait off Alaska
10 Member of a Marvel superhero team
11 French play about a storied Spanish soldier
12 Gridiron legend Rockne
13 Spread here and there
18 Thanksgiving dishes
22 Made to pay as punishment
25 Dingbat
27 TV journalist Curry
29 Intensify, with "up"
30 Dove's sound
31 Fright
32 Knighted actor McKellen
34 Some down-ballot electees, informally
35 Big tub
36 Lead-in to occupy
39 From alpha to ___
40 Rowboat mover
43 Summary of key points
46 Like a probability curve with two peaks
48 New Orleans footballers
49 Flex
50 "Blue Ribbon" brew
51 Nebraska's largest city
52 Establish
53 Princess mourned in 1997
54 Indy racer Al or Bobby
56 Sky-blue
57 Snake venom, e.g.
62 Champagne-opening sound
63 Environment-related prefix

by Lynn Lempel

ACROSS

1 Commonly sprained joint
6 Smurf with a white beard
10 Sounds when settling into a hot bath
14 Good name for a dyslexic neurosurgeon?
15 Each
16 Four Corners state
17 Clothing store event to get rid of excess merchandise
19 Sitarist Shankar
20 French writer who refused the 1964 Nobel Prize in Literature
21 Evita of "Evita"
22 Government agency charged with protecting the first family
24 Tolerate
26 Prefix with -phyte
27 Participate in a prizefight
28 Nursery rhyme character who met a pieman
36 Old Russian autocrat
38 Prank
39 Steakhouse specification
40 In the near future
43 Word before sells or cells
44 Exclamation on "The Simpsons"
45 Admission of defeat
47 Brooke Shields sitcom set at a trendy magazine
54 "Hurray!" or "Olé!"
55 Really small, informally
56 Destruction
57 Nightclub singer who was given the nickname "Buddha" by Frank Sinatra
61 Strong desire
62 ___ Stanley Gardner of detective fiction
63 Christmas carols
64 Hot Chocolate or Vanilla Fudge
65 Professional org.
66 Plumber's device

DOWN

1 "Washboard" muscles
2 Org. opposed by Everytown for Gun Safety
3 North Korean leader
4 Expired, as a membership
5 Intertwines
6 Cut's partner in word processing
7 Separately
8 Firehouse fixtures
9 Orangutan, for one
10 Bye at the French Open?
11 Company that created Pong
12 Destruction
13 Bootblack's job
18 Drop the ball
21 Air Force One passenger: Abbr.
22 Schoolteacher's wake-up time, perhaps
23 First month of el año
24 Basic facts
25 Nincompoop
29 Billionaire Carl
30 Last full month of spring
31 Second addendum to a letter, for short
32 Summer zodiac sign
33 One who works with bricks
34 Bonanza discoveries
35 Barbershop call
37 Blushed or flushed
41 Active person
42 Popular Japanese cars
46 Applies, as a thick coat of paint
47 Second-stringer
48 Communications officer on the Enterprise
49 Condescend (to)
50 Distance units in astron.
51 Shouts
52 Commonest craps roll
53 Prefix with cellular
57 Where the buoys are
58 Affirmative vote
59 Jan. honoree
60 NNW's opposite

by Peter Gordon

ACROSS

1 Shoestrings
6 Cook in oil
9 Brewing giant originally based in Milwaukee
14 Roofing alternative to shingles
15 Whopper (but not the Burger King kind)
16 Hawaiian greeting
17 Extremely inexpensive
19 Things sometimes hidden behind paintings
20 Extinguish, as a fire
21 Cost of a bank transaction that's not with one's own bank
22 Confucian philosophy
24 Bottom-up, as a political movement
26 Runs away to marry
29 Like some winter highways
30 Perfect test grade
31 New Testament trio
33 Pop a fly?
37 "Now things are getting interesting" . . . or a hint to the first words of 17-, 24-, 45- and 57-Across
40 Gilbert of "Roseanne" and "The Conners"
41 Knots
42 Ship of 1492
43 High degree
44 Bub
45 Amateurish
51 GPS lines: Abbr.
52 Going from gig to gig
53 Texas city seen in many westerns
56 Hatred
57 Bars that kids go to?
60 Get a feeling
61 Iraq War danger, in brief
62 One of the Hawaiian Islands
63 Parts of a forest
64 "Here's something interesting," in brief
65 Got some Z's

DOWN

1 Timothy Leary's drug
2 "The Greatest" in the ring
3 One who doesn't travel to work alone
4 "___, Brute!"
5 Religious offshoot
6 ___-de-lis
7 Cowboy's rope
8 Informal affirmative
9 Danish or cream puff
10 Avis competitor
11 Highly successful, in theaterspeak
12 One of 500 in a ream
13 Zaps with a police gun
18 Harleys, in slang
21 PC character set
22 Milk dispensers
23 Leader of the pack
25 Sounds of resignation
27 Stage after larva
28 Bilingualism subj.
31 Sacred peak in Greek myth: Abbr.
32 Had one's fill
33 Equipment often transported on a car's roof
34 Was a maverick
35 Chipped in at a poker game
36 Old Russian royals
38 None of the above
39 Computer's "brain," for short
43 Clouds of smoke
44 What the Titanic had a disastrous encounter with
45 Give a lift
46 Beneath
47 "Goosebumps" writer R. L. ___
48 One of four purchased for a Monopoly property
49 Sticky
50 We, on a candy heart
54 Fraternal group
55 "You're on!"
57 Alternative to Skippy or Peter Pan
58 Big mouth
59 Cambridge sch. for budding engineers

by Alex Eylar

ACROSS

1 [It's gone!]
5 Visit on a whim
10 __-relief
13 Folk singer Mitchell
14 Heart chambers
15 Accessory for Sherlock Holmes
16 Combat trauma
18 Real estate measurement
19 Made more bearable
20 Center
21 Exam monitor
24 Leave quickly, as from a parking spot
26 Comedian who said "In America, anyone can become president. That's the problem."
27 Offended
28 Zilch
29 Dutch painter Jan
30 Indian wedding garb
31 "Great" boy detective
32 Baseball field maintainers
35 Run __
37 What the Roman goddess Fortuna controls
38 Nimble
41 Sweeping movie shot
42 Restaurant order specification
43 Hank of "The Simpsons"
44 Casino V.I.P.
46 Larghissimo, among all musical tempos
47 "The Smartest Guys in the Room" company
48 Tony winner McDonald
49 __ Clooney, lawyer often seen in tabloids
50 Place for kitchen scraps, such as those starting 16-, 24-, 32- and 44-Across
55 Apt rhyme for "invade"
56 Farewell in France
57 DVR pioneer
58 Weekly show broadcast from Rockefeller Center, for short
59 Jury members
60 Goulash, e.g.

DOWN

1 Sleepover attire, briefly
2 "Impressive!"
3 x's positive value in the equation $2x = 4x^2 - 2$
4 Low-level law firm employee
5 Forgo
6 Questionnaire choice
7 Egg on
8 Disposable lighter brand
9 Himalayan beast
10 Goldie Hawn comedy or Leonard Cohen documentary
11 Hairy Halloween costume
12 Where Boeing was founded
15 Water holder for a farm animal
17 Like Senators Marco Rubio and Ted Cruz
20 N.Y.C. museum, with "the"
21 Mac competitors
22 Snitch
23 Path for Western settlers
24 Prize money
25 Guitar legend Clapton
27 Couldn't say no
30 Slight problems
31 Units of power saved, in modern lingo
33 E.T. vehicles
34 Bathroom items that might be confiscated by the T.S.A.
35 Materializes
36 Go-to guy
39 Fleur-de-__
40 Break bread
42 Boatload
43 "Brave New World" author Huxley
45 Audacious
46 "Terrific!"
48 Female friend in France
50 Upper limit
51 Words of praise
52 Fell for a joke
53 "__ Got You Under My Skin"
54 Parent's emphatic order

by Amanda Chung and Karl Ni

ACROSS

1 Baseball's record-setting Ripken
4 Catches a touchdown pass, e.g.
10 Not much
14 Lead-in to carte or mode
15 Tel Aviv's land
16 Helen of __ (mythical beauty)
17 Flier that may carry rabies
18 Small bird of prey
20 French girlfriend
22 Ginger __ (soft drink)
23 Seaweed, e.g.
24 Something falling down, in a children's song
28 Lucy of 2000's "Charlie's Angels"
29 Summons, as strength
33 Put the kibosh on
36 Actor Efron of "High School Musical"
37 Sign by a fire escape
38 "Mazel __!"
39 Commandeers . . . or a friendly hello to the people starting 18-, 24-, 51- and 62-Across?
42 Inits. on an airport uniform
43 __ out a living (barely gets by)
45 Moonshine container
46 Carriage named for an English county
48 Careful reading
50 Farrow of "Hannah and Her Sisters"
51 Dorothy's footwear in "The Wizard of Oz"
57 White-faced
60 Bit of cookware
61 Biz bigwig
62 What follows Thanksgiving
66 "What __?!" (cry of surprise)
67 Volcanic flow
68 From not long ago
69 Was in charge of
70 In a dead heat
71 No longer shrink-wrapped
72 First Republican prez

DOWN

1 Group of schemers
2 Mission where Davy Crockett was killed
3 Don Juan sort
4 Bro's sibling
5 Network for political junkies
6 Big name in toothbrushes
7 Pinker in the middle, say
8 Always, in poetry
9 __-mo (replay option)
10 Olympics competitor
11 Toot one's own horn
12 Sioux City's state
13 Young 'un
19 Goes back and forth, as a tail
21 Revise copy
25 "That's gotta hurt!"
26 Big name in desktops
27 Teals and mallards
30 Start of a newsboy's cry
31 Move skyward
32 Obedience school command
33 "Watch your __!"
34 Soft drink choice
35 Muslim woman's head cover
36 Make a sharp turn back
40 Bastille Day's month
41 Kind of pump
44 "I'm up for doing the job!"
47 Like thumped watermelons making a deep sound
49 Like ships on the ocean floor
52 Pizazz
53 Filled with cargo
54 Harebrained
55 2007's Record of the Year by Amy Winehouse
56 Big public display
57 Up to the task
58 Czech or Croat
59 "Girls Just Want to __ Fun"
63 Jimi Hendrix's do, informally
64 Sen.'s counterpart
65 Paycheck stub abbr.

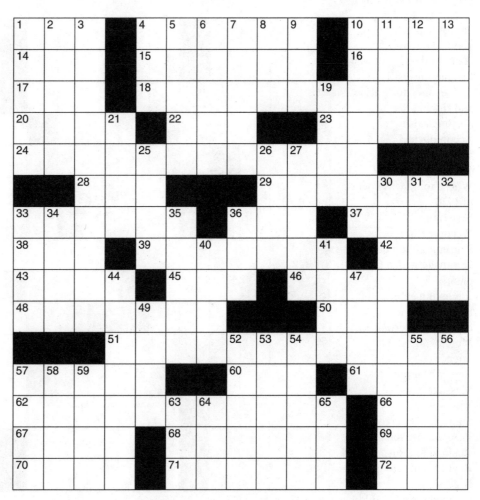

by Brian Thomas and Andrea Carla Michaels

ACROSS

1 Relative of Alt on a keyboard
5 Be part of, as a play
10 Pull-up muscles, briefly
14 Cookie with its name on it
15 One agreeing with everything you say
16 Sheltered at sea
17 Proper attire for taking fingerprints?
19 Enter
20 Dramatic "You too?"
21 Mauna ___
22 Bat for hitting practice fly balls
23 Red, white and blue team
24 Proper attire for picking up a series of clues?
27 Part of m.p.h.
28 Took a load off
29 Hicks and Judge of Major League Baseball
30 Conveyance for Calvin and Hobbes
32 Sushi garnish
34 Accomplished
35 Wearers of 17-, 24-, 50- and 59-Across?
40 Whose tomb was opened in 1923
41 Stop (up)
42 Weaponizes
44 Psychological wound
47 Cry made with a fist pump
49 Job listing abbr.
50 Proper attire for detaining a perp?
53 More of an ___ than a science
54 Barely beat (out)
55 Massage
56 Vittles
58 Sign gas
59 Proper attire for shadowing a suspect?
62 Reynolds of "Boogie Nights"
63 Gary who played Buddy Holly
64 Wedge, for one
65 "Planet of the ___"
66 "You can skip me"
67 Outbox folder

DOWN

1 Cousin of a pollock
2 Unvarnished identity
3 Pull-off spot
4 Former senator Trent
5 ___ loss
6 Parrot with a showy crest
7 George who played Sulu on "Star Trek"
8 It can't be improved upon
9 W.S.J. competitor
10 Alternative to John F. Kennedy
11 Basketball Hall-of-Famer Mourning
12 Model Chrissy who wrote the best seller "Cravings"
13 Titles with tildes
18 Sticks (out)
22 Thrash about
23 Co. with brown trucks
25 New Jersey river or bay
26 Black cat running across your path, it's said
31 Ones far from the honor roll
33 Caboose, e.g.
36 Like summers in Washington, D.C.
37 Balance sheet heading
38 Word with comfort or feature
39 Reappearance above water, as for a submarine
43 Wino, e.g.
44 Sports org. since 1946
45 Became uncomfortable, as some underwear
46 "An Inconvenient Truth" author
48 Distort
51 Put into categories
52 Arkansas River city
57 "No guarantees"
59 "Freeze! ___!"
60 Jewish cries
61 Prop for Wile E. Coyote

by Ross Trudeau

ACROSS

1 Kiss, in Spanish
5 Cooper of hard rock
10 "That was a bear!"
14 Reclined
15 Snake poison
16 Shovel's creation
17 Dog in "The Thin Man"
18 First ex-wife of Donald Trump
19 One of the Great Lakes
20 Features of some eco-friendly vehicles
23 Give the go-ahead
24 Comes to understand
26 ___ the chips fall where they may
28 City near Scottsdale
30 Dry region covering most of Botswana
36 Swamp
37 Similar
38 Battery for a remote
39 It may or may not correspond with one's birth sex
44 More crafty
45 "Delicious!"
46 Former attorney general Jeff
51 Involving warships
55 Getting picked up by the side of the road . . . or what 20-, 30- and 39-Across are literally doing?
57 Partly open, as a door
59 One way to commute
60 Jane Austen title woman
61 Broad valley
62 Clement C. ___, writer of "A Visit From St. Nicholas"
63 One twixt 12 and 20
64 Birds that hoot
65 In a pouty mood
66 George H. W. Bush had four

DOWN

1 Bored feeling, with "the"
2 Course you're almost guaranteed to get a good grade in
3 Not get involved while something's happening
4 Really cookin'
5 Rah-rah
6 Pry bar, e.g.
7 Silly
8 Dance done in a line
9 One might end "Sent from my iPhone"
10 Asthmatic noises
11 Taboo alternative to beef
12 Manning with a good throwing arm
13 Tiny
21 Furniture giant founded in Sweden
22 Time after dark, in commercials
25 Apply, as pesticides
27 Them ___ hills
29 Info on an airline website
30 Falls (over)
31 Woody Allen comedy that won Best Picture
32 Mahershala ___, co-star of 2018's "Green Book"
33 Cleanse (of)
34 Eisenhower, informally
35 Say it isn't so
36 Some fourth down scores: Abbr.
40 Wishes
41 Once, back in the day
42 Sandwich fish
43 Ottoman inns
47 Parts of a Cold War arsenal, for short
48 Words to a josher
49 Actor Williamson
50 Sarcastic comments
52 Alternative to YouTube
53 Some jingle writers
54 Favors one side
56 ___ Poupon mustard
57 Hullabaloo
58 Scary part of a T. rex

by Brendan Emmett Quigley

ACROSS

1 Speaker's spot
5 "Guess so"
11 Sister channel of Showtime
14 Novelist Ferber
15 Have relevance to
16 "Woo-hoo!"
17 First female recipient of the Cecil B. DeMille lifetime achievement award in film
19 Plastic pipe material, for short
20 Lobster ___ Newburg
21 Rural's opposite
22 Spa treatment
23 Become less dense, with "out"
25 Major crop of Brazil
28 "Hmm . . . I see now"
29 Another name for Cupid
30 Debauched sorts
32 Lyricist Cahn who wrote "Let It Snow! Let It Snow! Let It Snow!"
34 Wonderment
37 California baseball pro
40 Some words from Wordsworth
41 Like some cereals
42 Prerequisites for some college students
43 Funny Bombeck
44 Noted Art Deco artist
45 Washington, Jackson or Ford
50 Range for yodelers
51 Hebrew letter whose name is also a body part
52 Doctor Doom, to the Fantastic Four
54 Bagel go-with
56 Big Apple N.F.L. team, on scoreboards
57 Seasonal song with a hint to the last words in 17-, 25-, 37- and 45-Across
60 Ghost's cry
61 Retort to "No, you're not!"
62 Lead-in to girl or boy
63 Junkyard dog
64 Anastasia ___, woman in "Fifty Shades of Grey"
65 Sneaky laughs

DOWN

1 ___ vu
2 A step above the minors?
3 Here, as derived from hip-hop slang
4 Two cents' worth
5 Construction girder
6 People between Hungarians and Bulgarians
7 Pacific island nation
8 Supporters of England's King William III
9 Jesus, to Mary
10 Put the kibosh on
11 Like workaholics
12 Expert
13 Go biking
18 Rev, as an engine
22 Apples they're not
24 Home furnishings giant
26 Navy and Air Force vis-à-vis the military
27 "Once in ___ David's City" (carol)
28 "___ and Janis" (comic strip)
31 Saw logs
32 Reassure
33 Cakes and ___
34 Lab culture site
35 Deteriorated . . . or started out like Santa on December 24?
36 Word after who, what, when, where or why
38 Groups of whales
39 Seasonal song
43 German article
45 Rachel Maddow's network
46 "Stop being so silly!"
47 Pep
48 Hit musical with the song "Tomorrow"
49 Kidney-related
50 Author Rand
53 Something that goes viral
55 December 25, informally
57 Yiddish laments
58 Vietnamese festival
59 Cry from Scrooge

by Bruce Haight

ACROSS

1 Exchange after a lecture, informally
6 Room just under the roof
11 Sweetheart
14 Base just before home base
15 Postponed for later consideration
17 "You young people go ahead!"
19 Country between Ecuador and Bolivia
20 Part of a tree or a book
21 Lowest workers
22 G.I.'s ID
24 "That's so funny," in a text
25 Lack in energy
30 Dull, as a finish
33 Begged earnestly
35 Make a goof
36 Free-__ (like some chickens)
38 Punk offshoot
39 "Don't leave this spot"
42 Cairo's land
44 Force to exit, as a performer
47 Hosp. trauma centers
48 Broadway's __ O'Neill Theater
51 Puppeteer Lewis
54 __ Fein (Irish political party)
56 Either side of an airplane
58 Traffic reporter's comment
61 Plant-eating dino with spikes on its back
62 Discover almost by chance, as a solution
63 Hoppy brew, for short
64 Helper in an operating room
65 Another name for O₃ (as appropriate to 17-, 25-, 44- and 58-Across?)

DOWN

1 Brand of swabs
2 Man's name related to the name of Islam's founder
3 Lead-in to glycerin
4 Prolonged dry spell
5 "Much __ About Nothing"
6 Assert without proof
7 Cry of triumph
8 Spat
9 Last words before being pronounced husband and wife
10 Not drive by oneself to work
11 Cheery greeting
12 Ares : Greek :: __ : Norse
13 Loch __ monster
16 Patron of sailors
18 Kingly name in Norway
23 __ Bo (exercise system)
24 Make great strides?
26 Highest digits in sudoku
27 "Holy cow!," in a text
28 Quarry
29 Plant supplying burlap fiber
30 Kitten's sound
31 Spirited horse
32 Sextet halved
34 "i" or "j" topper
36 Dictionaries, almanacs, etc., in brief
37 Poodle's sound
40 Scoundrel, in British slang
41 What a setting sun dips below
42 Urge (on)
43 "Who'da thunk it?!"
45 Professor's goal, one day
46 __ Jemima
49 Mexican president Enrique Peña __
50 Company in a 2001–02 business scandal
51 Enthusiastic assent in Mexico
52 Web address starter
53 On the waves
54 Fly high
55 Notes from players who can't pay
57 Bit of inheritance?
59 The Buckeyes of the Big Ten, for short
60 However, briefly

by Brian Thomas

ACROSS

1 Part of a jacket where a hands-free mic is attached
6 Powder for a gymnast
10 Part of a constellation
14 Michelle with the 2018 hit memoir "Becoming"
15 Gymnast Korbut
16 Columbus's home
17 The end
18 Unruly crowds
19 Nevada casino city
20 Tea set?
23 __ Paulo, Brazil
24 Five cards of the same suit, in poker
25 Tune you just can't get out of your head
29 On fire
30 Suffragist __ B. Wells
33 Rice or wheat
34 Slowly swivel sideways, as a camera
35 Unknown author, for short
36 G-string?
40 French assents
41 Bit of financial planning for old age, in brief
42 "The Little Mermaid" princess
43 Cory Booker or Cory Gardner: Abbr.
44 Spanish article
45 All together, as a crowd
47 Like many people after eating beans
49 Main squeeze, modernly
50 Beeline?
57 Earsplitting
58 Peter Fonda title role of 1997
59 ". . . and sometimes y" preceder
60 Org. fighting for immigrants' rights
61 Lack of practice, metaphorically
62 Touches down on the tarmac
63 Corridor
64 Receives
65 Olympic sleds

DOWN

1 Apartment in an old warehouse district, say
2 Not much
3 Breathe like a tired runner
4 Give off
5 Band's closing number
6 Drum with a repetitive name
7 Tons and tons
8 Rainbow symbol of pride
9 Chess move involving the king and rook
10 Out of __ (discombobulated)
11 "Here's what you have to realize . . ."
12 Slangy negative contraction
13 Tree anchor
21 What cigarette filters are supposed to block
22 Egyptian boy king
25 Certain frozen waffles
26 Squabble
27 1980 Scorsese/De Niro classic
28 What many of the founding fathers wore
31 Old Venetian rulers
32 An obtuse one is more than 90°
34 Links org.
35 Home of the Taj Mahal
37 Supreme Court justice nicknamed "The Notorious R.B.G."
38 Shade similar to slate
39 N.B.A. souvenir
44 Thumb drive port, for short
45 __ Field, onetime home of the Brooklyn Dodgers
46 Catch red-handed
48 Paula who once judged on "American Idol"
50 When tripled, "and so on and so forth"
51 __ Raton, Fla.
52 Common email sign-off word
53 Lover
54 Microsoft search engine
55 Be an omen of
56 Kiss

by Joel Fagliano

ACROSS

1 Who says "Speak, hands, for me!" in "Julius Caesar"
6 Poehler vortex of funniness?
9 It might be on one's radar
13 Reward for Fido
14 Tiny
15 Where to enjoy a Goya
16 Queen's domain
17 N.Y.C. subway overseer
18 Wanders
19 Dressed like "a hundred-dollar millionaire"
22 Lo __ (Chinese noodle dish)
23 "Portlandia" airer
24 Glossy fabric
27 "I'll pass"
32 "__ bin ein Berliner"
33 It might have golden locks
35 Howe he could invent!
36 "I think I made a mistake here"
40 "Bedtime for __"
41 Celestial bear
42 Rage
43 Downward-Facing Dog, e.g.
45 Merchant
48 #Me__
49 Felt remorse for
50 "Add some throw pillows or a pop of color around here, why don't you!"
57 Parting words
58 Aah's partner
59 Words on some blood drive stickers
61 Is very fortunate, with "out"
62 Wharton grad
63 Creature to get down from
64 Polynesian carving
65 & 66 Choreographer whose life is depicted in the starts of 19-, 36- and 50-Across

DOWN

1 Middle: Abbr.
2 The "A" in BART
3 Animal having a ball at the circus?
4 1980 Blondie hit
5 Cost of withdrawing, say
6 "Gee, you're killin' me!"
7 Baseball's "Amazin's"
8 When sung three times, what follows "She loves you"
9 Vegetable with a head
10 Volcano's spew
11 Fateful day for Caesar
12 Deluxe
15 Present for acceptance
20 Actress Blair of "The Exorcist"
21 It can be picked
24 Remain idle
25 Sound during hay fever season
26 Dr. Dre's "Nuthin' but a 'G' __"
27 Our, in Orléans
28 Sun, moon and stars
29 Unbending
30 Phil __, slalom skiing gold medalist at the 1984 Olympics
31 Fragrant compound
34 Cross to bear
37 Greek sauce with yogurt and cucumbers
38 Bad rationalizations
39 Gobble
44 "Alley __!"
46 Analgesic's promise
47 Slow, in music
49 Where one might kick a habit, informally
50 Ghost at the altar?
51 Here, in Madrid
52 Facebook founder's nickname
53 Taj Mahal, e.g.
54 King of the road
55 Untrustworthy types
56 After-work times, in classifieds
60 "Able was I __ I saw Elba"

by Natasha Lyonne and Deb Amlen

ACROSS

1 Hit with a deft comeback
5 Greek T
8 Stuns, as with a phaser
12 Land unit
13 Subculture wearing a lot of black
15 Lighted sign by a stairwell
16 Chip dip, for short
17 Words on a pair of desk trays
18 Erotic
19 Comedian who co-starred in "Ride Along" and "The Upside"
22 Gloomy
25 Establishment that might have a rainbow flag in the window
29 "You may disagree," to texters
30 Wind instrument named after a Greek god
34 Regret
35 Eye of __ (part of a witch's brew)
37 Big to-do
38 "W" column in the standings
39 Gelatin substitute made from seaweed
40 Playful furry creature
41 Loathe
42 Anonymous woman
44 Initially
46 Trackside transactions
47 "Deadpool" actor Reynolds
48 Tom turkey or billy goat
50 Jack who played Sgt. Friday on "Dragnet"
53 Heterogeneous
56 Something a horse kicks with
59 Bitter beer
60 Marked, as a box
61 Big commotion
62 Rowboat propeller
63 Changing from time to time
65 "Mona Lisa" painter
67 Causing white knuckles, say
68 Leading
69 Medicinal amounts
70 Harass endlessly

DOWN

1 Zig's opposite
2 Critical hosp. ward
3 Second Amendment-supporting grp.
4 Geico spokeslizard
5 Author Morrison
6 Lots and lots
7 "Not gonna happen!"
8 Having a kick, as food
9 Lumberjack's tool
10 Photos, informally
11 Hog's home
13 Words from Woodsy Owl before "don't pollute!"
14 Gathering just for guys
20 Mind-reading ability, for short
21 "Insecure" actress Issa __
22 Rap star Nicki
23 Greek letter shaped like a horseshoe
24 __ Atkinson, portrayer of Mr. Bean
26 Prickly bush
27 Mothers of cousins
28 Stopwatch button
31 Do, re, mi, etc.
32 Middle of a poker table
33 Start of a rumor
36 Kind of musical clef
38 Complained
43 Road sign that hints at what can be found three times in this puzzle's grid
45 Lavish praise upon
48 Pepperidge Farm cookie with a geographical name
49 Wards off, as danger
51 Hair color that can be "dirty" or "platinum"
52 Lighthouse light
53 Bowie or Beckham
54 Smell, taste or touch
55 Eight things on an octagon
56 Assailed
57 Pocatello's state
58 Obtain money illegally
64 Supporting vote
66 "__ the Walrus" (Beatles song)

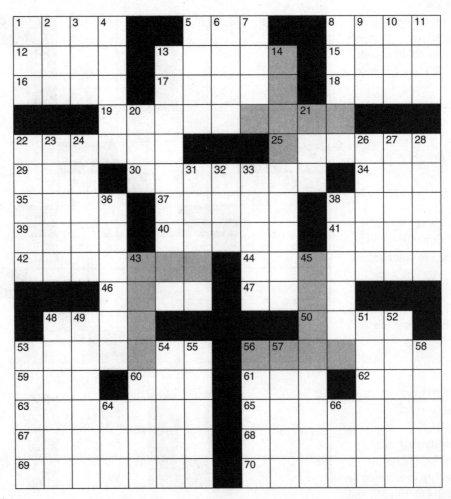

by Tracy Gray and Jeff Chen

Note: Each Across answer in this puzzle consists of a word spelled forward and another spelled backward. It's up to you to determine which clue goes with which word.

EASY 25

ACROSS

1 Can opener / Club
4 Charts / Inbox distraction
8 Apple varieties / Trick
12 Facts / Somewhat
14 Asian sea name / Journalist Logan
15 "Silas Marner" pen name / Upholstery fabric
16 Dubai dignitary / Winter coat
17 Colorado feeder / Sacha Baron Cohen character
18 Espies / Subway stations
19 Call ending a rugby match / Prolific inventor
21 Entertainer Marx / Entertainer Winfrey
23 Criticized / Save (from)
25 Cans / Letter flourish
27 Fix, as a driveway / Yelp reviewer, e.g.
29 Ice dancing gold medalist ___ Virtue / Plus
31 Ice hockey feint / Squeezed (out)
34 Bits of film tape / Film holder
36 Headline? / Snare
38 Ancient greeting / Señora Perón
39 Ram's sch. / Trojan's sch.
40 Exist / Reign denoter
41 Forever and a day / Genesis maker
43 Info, informally / Spirited mount
45 Beltway insiders / Spill (over)
46 Indy player / Summary
48 Green / Water from France
50 Fit for a king / Foamy draft
52 Guard / It might say "Hello"
56 Like Oxfords / Sticker
58 Aardvark or zebra / Thin layer
59 Arrive, as a cold front / Evenings, informally
62 Lionize / Twin
64 Go berserk / Some cookware
65 Jack of rhyme / Rain blockers
66 Cutting it / Mediterranean island
67 Hence / Monster
68 Daft / Daze
69 Elk, for one / Plant in a bog
70 Holy mlle. / Romulans, e.g., in brief

DOWN

1 Revealed
2 "There is ___ in the affairs of men . . .": Shak.
3 Sri Lankan tongue
4 Drawing things?
5 "Exodus" hero
6 ___ Alto, Calif.
7 Gives a hand?
8 Fallacious reasoner
9 Union letters
10 Computer key
11 Enero, por ejemplo
13 Yen
15 Bygone autocrats
20 Egg cells
22 Not made up
24 Pose again, as a question
26 Not tamed
28 Old-time slugger Al
30 Tahitian crop
31 Perp prosecutors
32 At any time
33 Kind of exercise that strengthens the pelvic muscles
35 Indian ___
37 Effervescence
42 Early settler of Nova Scotia
43 Kind of sheet
44 Phoned, to Brits
45 Appear to be correct
47 Salary negotiator
49 Annual cable channel prize for Song of the Year or Artist of the Year, in brief
51 Meteorologist's tool
53 Hint of color
54 "It's ___, not a science"
55 Reacts in disbelief, say
57 Job for a grease monkey
59 Sibilant sound
60 Competent, jocularly
61 One-man play about Capote
63 Draft selection

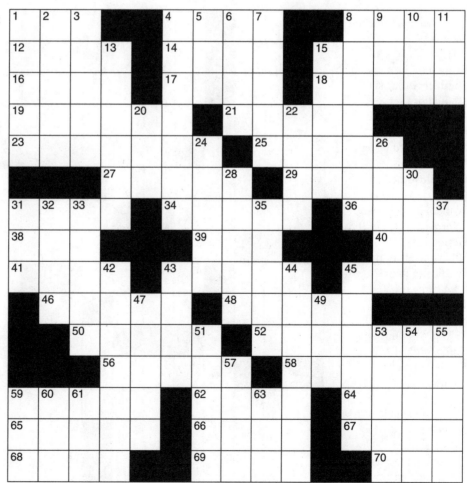

by Alex Eaton-Salners

ACROSS

1 Filming device, for short
4 Men's Health or Women's Health, for short
7 Sticks (to)
14 Mined rocks
15 Years that one has lived
16 Presidents and prime ministers
17 Gun advocacy grp.
18 It flows from the Himalayas to the Bay of Bengal
20 Piece of sports equipment with strings
22 First-___ (best)
23 Back-to-school mo.
24 Relaxation
28 Greek goddess of the hunt
30 Reference point during a piano lesson
33 Coke or 7Up
34 Bring into the company
35 Summer zodiac sign
36 "If memory serves . . ."
40 Nada
43 Black gemstone
44 Bulletin board fastener
47 Firm, as pasta
49 Fully illustrated, as a novel
52 Work of Shakespeare
53 "Norma ___" (1979 film)
54 German article
55 Where heads of the Pacific are found?
60 $ $ $
63 PBS-funding org.
64 Singer Flack with the 1973 hit "Killing Me Softly With His Song"
65 Serve that nicks the net
66 Paving goo
67 Reached the golf course standard
68 CPR sites
69 Tax org. undergoing some "reform" in this puzzle's circled squares

DOWN

1 Iran-___ (1980s scandal)
2 Behind in payments, after "in"
3 Did intentionally
4 O. Henry's "The Gift of the ___"
5 Court great Andre
6 Blues and rock, for two
7 Actor Guinness
8 Schoolroom assignment
9 Relative of a rabbit
10 Revised, as copy
11 Gun, as an engine
12 "But I heard him exclaim, ___ he drove out of sight . . ."
13 Byelorussia, e.g.: Abbr.
19 Cumberland ___
21 "Boy, do I ___ drink!"
25 Nothing's opposite
26 "Didn't I tell you?"
27 Green: Prefix
29 Worker with a trowel
30 Prop you might drop
31 Savings for the golden years, for short
32 Airline whose name is a Greek letter
34 Evil spell
37 QB miscue: Abbr.
38 Loaf that might have seeds
39 Place to pin a pink ribbon
40 Stick in the microwave
41 Sick
42 Holding hands or kissing on the street, for short
45 Italian red wine
46 Actor Greg of "Little Miss Sunshine"
48 Hole for a lace
49 Use mouthwash
50 Rob who directed "The Princess Bride"
51 Evergreens with fragrant wood
53 Big outdoor gear retailer
56 Senior party?
57 Mex. title that's an anagram of 58-Down
58 Old Russian title that's an anagram of 57-Down
59 Old Concordes, in brief
60 Hosp. V.I.P.s
61 Awed reaction
62 Certain Wall St. acquisition, for short

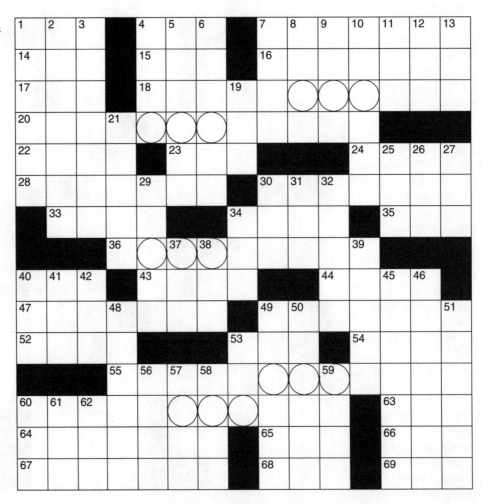

by Patrick Blindauer and Samuel A. Donaldson

ACROSS

1 One or two chips, maybe
5 Airer of N.C.A.A. March Madness games
8 Choctaw and Chickasaw
14 "Here's the ___ . . ."
15 Promise-to-pay note
16 Flower cluster whose name can also be read as a challenge
17 Deceive
18 Bulletin
20 Mob-busting law, for short
22 Get exactly
23 Single-minded religious group
24 Dental problem
26 Remini who co-starred on "The King of Queens"
27 Tax table figure
28 "Beau ___"
29 Romanov leader
30 Make tweaks to
35 Newsman Koppel
36 Nickname
39 "Life of Pi" director Lee
42 Ancestral ruler
43 Big tubs
47 Hired toughs
49 Elevated platforms for speakers
51 Big name in petrol
52 Noted 1950s–'70s D.J. dubbed a "fifth Beatle"
56 Basic idea
57 Start of "The Star-Spangled Banner"
58 Seeks legal recourse
59 "Is everything all right?"
62 Dahs' counterparts in Morse code
64 Dwindles, with "out"
65 L.A.-to-Denver dir.
66 Castaway's locale
67 Article of living room furniture
68 Denver-to-Albuquerque dir.
69 Sign for the superstitious

DOWN

1 Press "+" on a calculator
2 Cells separated by synaptic gaps
3 Starchy pudding
4 Some "college" participants
5 Idiosyncratic habit
6 Aaron ___, Yankees manager beginning in 2018
7 Shrub that might cause a rash
8 In all honesty
9 Scampered
10 One hanging around a house?
11 Inheritance, e.g.
12 Act like
13 Saw red
19 Unaccounted-for soldier, for short
21 Resistance unit
24 Relative of a chickadee
25 Annual horse race
28 "I'm speechless!"
31 Suffix with north- or south-
32 By way of
33 130 and 140 are high ones
34 Kama ___
37 Indulges too much, briefly
38 "APPLAUSE" sign locale
39 Features of May-December marriages
40 "Wrong you are!"
41 Actor Louis ___ Jr.
44 Non-prophet foundation?
45 Railroad bridge support
46 Cinch ___ (commercial trash bag name)
48 Still to come
50 Kvetchers' cries
52 Device that might have a trackball
53 Soldiers' support grp.
54 Does a bit of lawn work
55 "___ Hope" (classic soap opera)
60 Miner's haul
61 Plant in an English hedge
63 Politician with a six-year term: Abbr.

by Gary Cee

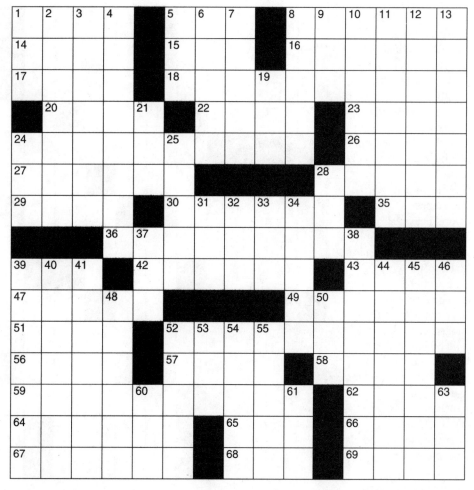

ACROSS

1 Turn away, as one's gaze
6 Bird's beak
10 Varieties
14 "Toy Story" studio
15 "Point taken"
16 Ne, on the periodic table
17 Tennis with dad?
19 With 8-Down, dessert brand that "nobody doesn't like"
20 Messy meal for pigs
21 Motorists' org.
22 "Not in a million years!"
23 Losing tennis player's prayer?
26 In a trite way
30 Exam for a future atty.
31 Wonderland girl
32 "__ making myself clear?"
33 Guzzle down
37 Dislike for tennis?
41 Sharp as a tack
42 ExxonMobil business
43 Jargon
44 Famous __ (cookie brand)
46 Things for cleaning dishes
48 "Wow, no wonder you're playing such great tennis!"?
52 Overdo, as a stage role
53 Assistance
54 "Good heavens!"
58 Letter-shaped beam
59 Lose every set of a tennis match 6-0?
62 Ship of 1492
63 "__ be over soon"
64 Take home from the shelter, say
65 And others: Abbr.
66 "Porgy and __"
67 Soda in an old blind taste test

DOWN

1 Smartphone downloads
2 Relative of a cello
3 Big fair
4 Speak with a gravelly voice
5 First "T" in TNT
6 Problem with more than one marriage?
7 Ayatollah's faith
8 See 19-Across
9 "__ Miz"
10 Arcade game instruction before playing
11 Depart
12 Locale for Pyongyang and Seoul
13 Snide remarks
18 Hammer's target
22 Org. for the Suns and the Heat
23 Tickled-pink feeling
24 Ticklish Muppet
25 "You wish!"
26 With 28-Down, part of a golf course
27 __ vera
28 See 26-Down
29 "Pretend nothing just happened"
32 Home to the world's busiest airport: Abbr.
34 Like Christmas decorations and some juries
35 Egg on
36 Sporty Pontiacs introduced in the '60s
38 Boggy wasteland
39 Italian city you might be "leaning" toward visiting?
40 Congeal, as blood
45 Something with a "You are here" arrow
46 Listings on a résumé
47 Mani-__ (spa offering)
48 Complain annoyingly
49 Nun's wear
50 Kitchen appliance brand
51 "Let" and "Fault," from a chair umpire
54 Quaint, as a shoppe
55 Circular kind of earring
56 Some postseason awardees, for short
57 Hairy Himalayan humanoid
59 Little lie
60 Gobbled up
61 Catch a few Z's

by Bruce Haight

ACROSS

1 Sound that a sound-absorbing chamber should eliminate
5 Mars candy bar with caramel and milk chocolate
9 Shrek's wife
14 "___ she blows!"
15 Go backpacking
16 Leader of the singing Chipmunks
17 One who may have a mortgage
19 Traction aid on a shoe
20 Race loser
21 Lipstick mishap
23 After all expenses
24 Nile reptile, for short
26 End result
29 Mine extractions
31 Twins
33 "___ Theme" from "Doctor Zhivago"
35 Indian flatbread
36 Your: Fr.
37 Liquid supply for body art
41 "Eww!"
44 Bird that usually mates for life
45 Word before fairy or decay
49 Message between two arrows on a shipping container
53 Prefix with -phobia
54 Popular European comic book hero
55 Old Russian ruler
57 Fryer contents
58 One who's doomed
60 Digitally endorsed
62 How a pirouette is done
64 Beach Boys album with the hit "Wouldn't It Be Nice" . . . or things hidden in 17-, 31-, 37- and 49-Across
66 Pharmacy stock
67 Get quickly, as lunch
68 Explorer Hernando de ___
69 7/4/1776 and 6/6/1944, e.g.
70 Alluring
71 Futuristic movie of 1982

DOWN

1 Gasoline additive
2 García Márquez's "Love in the Time of ___"
3 One with a squeaky wheel?
4 ___ Thins (cookies)
5 Upset, as plans
6 Narrow down
7 Singer Turner
8 Gen ___ (preceders of millennials)
9 Decoration for some die-hard sports fans
10 "Let me check"
11 Send beyond the green, say
12 Actress Long
13 Member of an underground colony
18 Member of a World of Warcraft race
22 Civilian clothes for a soldier
25 Noble person's headwear
27 Meaning of a raised index finger
28 Goals for QBs
30 Plopped down
32 Tic-tac-toe win
34 Cheek
38 String for a cake box
39 Smidge
40 RVer's stopover, for short
41 "The Addams Family" cousin
42 Tai ___ (martial art)
43 Jokey 1978 Steve Martin song
46 First female Supreme Court justice
47 Gave it a go
48 Waits a moment
50 Moe, Larry or Curly
51 Charge for some goods bought from out of state
52 Elapse
56 ___ Grande
59 Final Fantasy and others, in brief
61 Burst of wind
62 Not even
63 Big D.C. lobby
65 Before, in verse

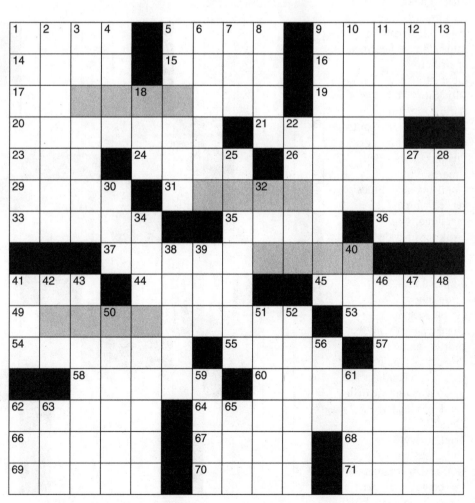

by Amanda Chung and Karl Ni

ACROSS

1 Where pumpkins grow
6 Count in Lemony Snicket books
10 Apex
14 Snoozer's sound
15 Prefix with -technology and -second
16 Greek earth goddess
17 Firefighter Red
18 Class stars
20 Misplaced
21 Suzuki with the M.L.B. record for hits in a single season (262)
22 To date
23 "The A-Team" actor with a mohawk
24 Initials meaning "I've heard enough"
25 Thread holder
27 ___ Lanka
28 Peter ___, Nixon impeachment hearings chairman
32 General vibe
33 "Toy Story" boy
35 Serta competitor
37 Hop to it . . . or what to do to the various eggs in this puzzle's shaded squares?
41 Hot drink sometimes served with a marshmallow
42 Explorer Ericson
44 Neighbor of Ghana
47 Cuban-born Grammy winner Jon
50 Little fellow
52 Go halfsies on
54 Disney dwarf with the shortest name
55 Pinocchio's undoing
56 One of the Kardashians
57 Spicy Korean side dish
61 Clark of the Daily Planet
62 Triangular Swiss chocolate bar
64 Coffee drink sometimes served with milk "art"
65 "Buy one, get one free" event
66 The "A" of U.S.A.: Abbr.
67 PC key above shift
68 Patella's joint
69 Polling expert Silver
70 Monopoly cards

DOWN

1 Biblical book of poems
2 181-square-mile country in the Pyrenees
3 Honoring, as at a wedding
4 Lit ___ (coll. course)
5 "On ___ Majesty's Secret Service"
6 Using LSD
7 Where mascara goes
8 Adamantly against
9 Number of Teenage Mutant Ninja Turtles
10 Get older
11 Words starting a request
12 Shooting star
13 SoCal area bordering the neighborhoods of El Sereno and Boyle Heights
19 Uno + uno
21 Texter's "if you ask me"
24 "___ see it my way"
26 Alexander who directed "Nebraska" and "Sideways"
29 Asimov or Newton
30 Japanese electronics giant
31 Sturdy wood
34 Interior design
36 Light purple
38 Includes when sending an email
39 ___ v. Wade
40 "The best a man can get" sloganeer
43 Blacked out
44 "Naughty, naughty"
45 Buckeye
46 Play the slots, e.g.
48 Stick like glue
49 Emphatic agreement
51 Discourages
53 Scrape (by)
58 Tehran's land
59 N.Y.C.'s home to Matisse's "The Dance"
60 Tech news site
61 "Citizen ___"
63 Ang who directed "Brokeback Mountain"
64 Pioneered

by Andrew Kingsley

ACROSS

1 Luau greeting
6 Feudal worker
10 City choker
14 Sights along lane closures
15 "The very __!"
16 Nickname for Dad
17 *Rock and Roll Hall of Fame band with the hits "The Flame" and "I Want You to Want Me"
19 Caustic solutions
20 South African money
21 Actress Witherspoon
22 "__ No Sunshine" (1971 hit for Bill Withers)
23 Et cetera
25 Hockey puck, e.g.
27 Install, as carpet
28 Spicy Chinese cuisine
32 Intimated
35 Where chewing tobacco is placed
36 "Eww, you've said quite enough!"
37 Lone Star State sch.
38 With 28-Down, multisubject photos . . . or a hint to the answers to the four starred clues
39 Den denizen
40 Had a little lamb, say?
41 What to call it when it's over
42 "Willy __ & the Chocolate Factory"
43 Seeks the opinion of
45 Adorer
46 Lab container
47 Rainbow mnemonic
51 Weaver's device
53 "That is to say . . ."
56 Patron saint of lost causes
57 "Othello" villain
58 *Actor's stand-in
60 Amaze
61 A panda, for the World Wildlife Fund
62 "Raw" or "burnt" hue
63 "America the Beautiful" pronoun
64 Bible garden
65 Tablets with Retina display

DOWN

1 Ghana's capital
2 Lindsay of "Mean Girls"
3 Upright
4 *Relative of a facepalm
5 Egyptian cobra
6 Ambulance sound
7 Falco of TV and film
8 Letters accompanying college applications, for short
9 Pretentious, in modern lingo
10 Cannonball dive effect
11 Dance floor request
12 Store window sign
13 Basic point
18 Setting for the "Iliad"
24 Cereal morsel
26 "Gross!"
28 See 38-Across
29 Greek counterpart of Jupiter
30 With frenzy
31 With 44-Down, jazz great who sang "I Put a Spell on You"
32 Green chip dip, informally
33 Palindromic boy's name
34 Youth-oriented Condé Nast publication
35 Reviews of books and such: Abbr.
38 Fall-for-anything
39 *Track-and-field event
41 Sine __ non
42 "Believe it," as a retort
44 See 31-Down
45 Enamored (of)
47 Synthetic fabric that feels like silk
48 Two-time Masters champion Watson
49 Did a whole lot of nothing
50 Swerves
51 Lean, as a ship
52 Solemn vow
54 What an emoji might reveal
55 Narrow advantage
59 "Most assuredly, monsieur!"

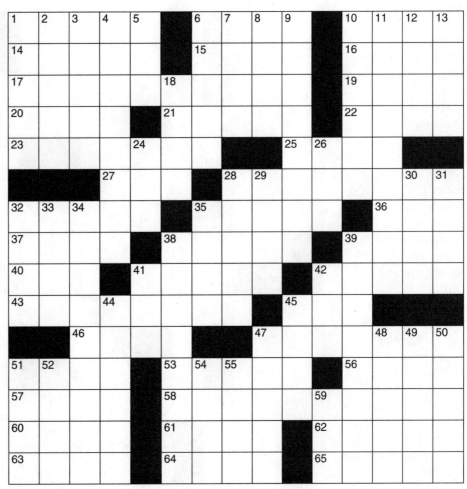

by Erik Agard

ACROSS

1 Poseidon's domain
4 Mortar accompanier
10 Swirl of smoke
14 Well-suited
15 Noah's landing place
16 Tennis's Kournikova
17 ___ for tat
18 Lone Star State baseball player
20 State whose license plates say "Famous Potatoes"
22 "That was a close one!"
23 "It's a mouse!"
24 Not national, as an airline
27 Fad
29 Gave off, as radiation
30 "Secret" person who writes a love note
32 What Marcie calls Peppermint Patty in "Peanuts"
33 Take unfair advantage of
35 What you might drape a dress or shirt on in a closet
40 Got ready to be operated on
41 Loud noise
43 Foreign ___ (international matters)
46 Fidgety
49 Hands out cards
50 Young gallant in "Romeo and Juliet"
51 Noah's craft
52 Drifter
55 Lumberjacks
56 Sandwich chain whose name is French for "ready to eat"
60 Time in history
61 Actress Hatcher of "Desperate Housewives"
62 Sailor's affirmative
63 Singer ___ King Cole
64 River of the underworld
65 See 59-Down
66 "What's the ___?" (pessimist's cry)

DOWN

1 Works like "Animal Farm" and "Gulliver's Travels"
2 Rapid spread of a disease
3 "Way to go, sister!"
4 Tushie
5 Bard's "before"
6 "Wailing" instrument
7 Fish by dragging a net
8 Place for mascara
9 Raison d'___
10 Pallid
11 Out of neutral, as a car
12 "Gesundheit!" elicitor
13 "Sex and the City" star Sarah Jessica ___
19 "You've got to be kidding me!"
21 Top 10 song
25 Lower in position
26 Ones selling commercial time, informally
28 Boxing venue
30 Cling (to)
31 ___ than a doornail
34 Egyptian cobra
36 October's birthstone
37 Country singer Yearwood
38 Where to find "Cut" and "Paste"
39 Coastal resort areas
42 Someone who was literally born yesterday
43 Makes a screenplay out of
44 Search (out)
45 Flimflam
47 Frightens
48 Men's formal attire, informally
50 "A blessing that is of no advantage to us excepting when we part with it," according to Ambrose Bierce
53 Minnesota representative Ilhan ___
54 1990s Indiana governor Evan
57 Box office purchases, for short
58 Pod of whales
59 With 65-Across, what the last words of 18-, 35- and 56-Across are to each other

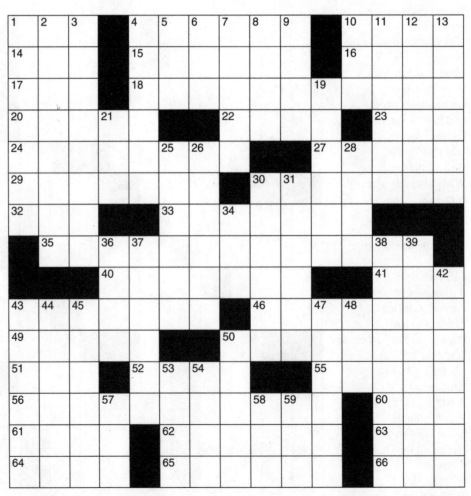

by Peter Gordon

ACROSS

1 Green carving stone
5 Execs who handle the green
9 Brunch item often topped with sugar or fruit
14 Alternatives to lagers
15 Aid to accessibility
16 Word before "the bar" or "the boom"
17 ___ Blanc
18 Ones making written comments on text
20 Purchase something sight unseen
22 Prosecutors, for short
23 Big wind
24 Chinchilla or macaw, e.g.
28 Snowfall unit
32 "Cousin" of 1960s TV
33 Not deceived by
34 Battlefield renown
35 1984 mockumentary with a lot of ad-libbed dialogue
39 Anti-rust coatings
40 Smell
41 Unified
42 Smoothie berry
43 Danger of laboring outdoors in the summer
46 Panache
48 ___ Lingus
49 Icing on the cake . . . or a hint to 20-, 24-, 35- and 43-Across
56 Brain region linked to speech
57 What someone who's never satisfied wants
58 Minaret, e.g.
59 "Me neither," formally
60 Qatari leader
61 Sch. whose athletes are the Minutemen and Minutewomen
62 Pest control brand
63 "My b"

DOWN

1 Frame component
2 Felipe or Moises of baseball
3 Refute
4 Nueva York or Dakota del Norte
5 Ocean Spray fruit snacks
6 Scary part of a wolf
7 Upscale hotel chain
8 Quick learner, say
9 Thunder sounds
10 Turn soil by machine
11 Furry "Star Wars" creature
12 Father, in France
13 Bustling hosp. locales
19 Stretched tight
21 Local dialect
24 System of moral values
25 Singer Aguilera's nickname
26 Abbr. for change
27 Quickly attach, as a top to a bottle
29 Taboo
30 Popular bird in origami
31 Promote excessively
32 Chichén ___ (Mayan ruins)
34 Attic
36 Arts and ___
37 Names, briefly
38 "[sigh] . . . We just dealt with this"
43 Say "Talk to the hand, 'cause the face ain't listenin'," say
44 Release from one's clutches
45 Theatrical cry from a balcony
47 Ones failing polygraphs
49 Native to
50 Hawkeye's home
51 Classic Camaro
52 Master detective Wolfe
53 Man, in Milan
54 Blood's foe
55 The wife's, e.g.
56 A/C stat

by Ross Trudeau

ACROSS

1 Drink, as water from a dish
4 Bits of broken glass
10 Locks in a barn?
14 Top card
15 How café may be served
16 ___ out (barely manages)
17 "Lady Chatterley's Lover" novelist
19 "Nervous" reactions
20 Goes down, as the sun
21 Change from the norm
23 Bart and Lisa's dad
27 King Arthur's home
30 Cigar residue
31 Flamenco cheer
32 Blow, as a volcano
35 Newspaper opinion piece
39 Early railroad tycoon whose nickname is a hint to the starts of 17-, 23-, 51- and 62-Across
43 James of jazz
44 Lauder of cosmetics
45 18 or so, for a typical first-year college student
46 "You don't mean me?!"
49 Made certain
51 Real-life lawman who lent his name to a 1950s–'60s TV western
56 Pilots
57 ___ car salesman
61 Appear
62 Utah senator who once ran for president
66 "Star Trek: T.N.G." counselor
67 Captivate
68 Noah's vessel
69 Europe's highest volcano
70 Getting up
71 "The Bells" poet

DOWN

1 Young chaps
2 Pain in a tooth or the heart
3 Hit repeatedly, as with snowballs
4 Viewed
5 Ben-___ (Charlton Heston role)
6 Pub offering
7 Time off, informally
8 Cuts into small cubes
9 Sugar substitute
10 Nerves of steel, e.g.
11 Actor Claude of old TV
12 Classic brand of candy wafers
13 German industrial city
18 Arthur of tennis fame
22 Gchats, e.g.
24 Bread spread
25 Time starting at dawn, to poets
26 Practice piece for a pianist
27 Secret message
28 Came down to earth
29 Vegetarian's no-no
33 Bedwear, briefly
34 Solution strength
36 Early talk show host Jack
37 Precipice
38 Like Easter eggs, colorwise
40 Abba song or musical
41 Department store department with shirts and slacks
42 Kiss: Sp.
47 Grain in Cheerios
48 Chemical cousin
50 "E pluribus ___"
51 Moisten, as a turkey
52 Deflect
53 Attach with a string, say
54 Singer Lopez
55 Form of the Spanish for "to be"
58 Become unhinged
59 Architect Saarinen
60 Comic actor Dick Van ___
63 "That's overly explicit," in textspeak
64 "Dianetics" author L. ___ Hubbard
65 Alternative to .com or .net

by Gary Larson

ACROSS

1 Rosters
6 Red ink
10 Showing the overall view
15 Enjoyed no end
16 Two-dimensional measure
17 "Tattered Tom" author Horatio
18 What the computer Deep Thought was programmed to figure out in "The Hitchhiker's Guide to the Galaxy"
21 Michael's wife in "The Godfather"
22 Give as an example
23 Life lines?
24 Environmental destruction
26 Spreading out
31 Mystiques
32 Common bar mixer
33 Wine glass part
34 "u r 2 funny"
35 In good shape
36 Pigeon sound
37 Hall-of-Fame player whose number has been retired by every team in Major League Baseball
41 Young 'un
42 ← What this is for this puzzle
43 Mer contents
44 Sharpen
46 Michael of "Superbad"
47 Safe place
49 Surges
51 Setter or retriever
53 TV's "Murder, ___ Wrote"
54 Line of clothing?
55 ___ Valley, neighborhood in San Francisco
56 He served between Bush 41 and Bush 43
62 Supermarket section
63 Bill
64 Cousin of a weasel

65 Uses performance-enhancing drugs
66 Quite gaunt
67 Sloughs off

DOWN

1 Part of a Hanukkah meal
2 "___ is Gorges" (T-shirt slogan)
3 "Peace out"
4 Belly, in babyspeak
5 Cereal brand with a weight-loss challenge
6 One hell of a writer?
7 Pennsylvania city
8 Economist Bernanke
9 Playground game
10 Michael's family in "The Godfather"
11 Sterling silver and such
12 Some movie f/x
13 Yellow card issuer
14 Rock band?
19 Buttresses
20 First half of a Beatles title
25 Swamp snapper
26 California wine region
27 Military academy freshman
28 "That's impossible!"
29 Bright night light
30 Non-___ (label on many organic foods)
32 Kitchen gadgets
35 Snicker sound
37 Place to solve a crossword, maybe
38 Had a hankering
39 Close one
40 Mideast royal name
41 Value of snake eyes

45 Skirmish
47 Serum container
48 Like a 14-year-old vis-à-vis the Little League World Series
50 Acts skittish
51 Tom's love in "The Adventures of Tom Sawyer"
52 Family inheritance
54 Obsessive fan, in modern slang
56 Something to jot notes on
57 Kia model
58 Skill tested by Zener cards, for short
59 Draw back
60 Prefix with -natal
61 "I don't think so"

by Damon Gulczynski

ACROSS

1 Wide open, as the mouth
6 Treaties
11 "What ___ I say?"
14 "Whoa, ease up!"
15 Stan's co-star in over 100 early film comedies
16 Made-up story
17 *Government's credit limit
19 Hubbub
20 Like many infield grounders
21 Lester Holt and Anderson Cooper
23 Issa ___ of HBO's "Insecure"
24 Smith or Scialfa of rock
27 Vienna's home: Abbr.
28 *Beanbag juggled with the feet
32 Massage intensely
36 Put on a black coat?
37 Guarantee
38 Great Plains tribe
39 "Start the music!" . . . or what one could do to the finish of the answer to each starred clue
41 Vaping device, informally
42 Full-time resident of a college community
44 "___ you through?"
45 Belles at balls, informally
46 ✓
48 "The ___ & Stimpy Show"
49 Labor organizer Chávez
52 Resort with mineral waters
55 Like a gift from above
58 Reproductive part of a flower
60 18+, e.g., in order to be able to vote
61 *Much-visited site in Jerusalem
64 Sleuth, in slang
65 Bury, as ashes
66 Girl Scout cookie with a geographical name
67 Cry of fright
68 Barely warm
69 "E" on a gas gauge

DOWN

1 Intense devotion
2 Actress Davis of "The Accidental Tourist"
3 Edward who wrote "Who's Afraid of Virginia Woolf?"
4 Trail
5 Onetime police officer
6 Dish made from taro root
7 None's opposite
8 Medical facility
9 Fork prong
10 Motorized two-wheelers
11 *Seafood topping that may be red or white
12 Assistant
13 Illuminating gas
18 Org. concerned with ecosystems
22 Figured (out)
25 Language in Bangkok
26 Served raw, as steak
29 McKinnon of "S.N.L."
30 Place for a baby to sleep
31 Beer barrels
32 Military program for coll. students
33 "Alternatively . . .," in texts
34 *Part of a ship just above the hold
35 Practices épée, e.g.
36 Not us
40 Ticks off
43 "No surprise to me!"
47 Develops a glitch
50 First full month of Major League Baseball, often: Abbr.
51 Get the suds out
52 Post office purchase
53 Person in a cockpit
54 Ease, as fears
55 Concert proceeds
56 Double-curved molding
57 State bird of Hawaii
59 Did a backstroke, say
62 Prefix with -state
63 Conclusion

by Gary Cee

ACROSS

1 Automaker with Supercharger stations
6 Quarreling
10 Identifies, as in a Facebook photo
14 "Peer Gynt" composer
15 Let go of
16 Word before "a hint," "a line" or "the ball"
17 "Oh, it's nothing to concern yourself with"
19 Rose with 4,256 major-league hits
20 __ machine (stage effect maker)
21 Cleveland's lake
22 "The Divine Comedy" writer
23 Omits mention of
26 Lethargy
29 Golden-years savings vehicles, for short
30 Strand, as during a winter storm
31 Australian boot brand
32 Abu Dhabi's land, for short
35 Has a huge impact . . . or a hint to this puzzle's circled letters
40 Cry when encountering 26-Down
41 Red 40 or Yellow 6
42 Made less strenuous
43 Profit
45 Genre for the Harry Potter books
47 Ones with private ambitions?
51 "Wait, you think I did that?"
52 PIN points?
53 Long March leader
56 Tie up, as a ship
57 Extra song on an album
60 Actress Paquin who won an Academy Award at age 11
61 Febreze target
62 Better trained
63 Twitter platform?
64 Chromosome component
65 Comic Radner of early "Saturday Night Live"

DOWN

1 End-of-the-week cheer
2 Therefore
3 Let secrets out
4 July–August sign
5 On the same page
6 Not idle
7 Little chuckle
8 State between Wash. and Mont.
9 Vietnamese New Year
10 Six-point accomplishment for a QB
11 Sports venue
12 Mobster John
13 Go 50 in a school zone, say
18 Notable times in history
22 Material in a cell's nucleus
23 Reclined
24 [Ah, me]
25 Desire
26 Little scurriers
27 Result of overexertion
28 Reason to replace a fuel line
31 Sport-__ (multiterrain vehicle)
32 __ Major
33 Some draft selections
34 Swirl above a drain
36 Actress Falco
37 Match up
38 Attended a party without a date
39 Some food for a horse
43 One doing heavy lifting, informally?
44 "__ you insane?"
45 Its time has not yet come
46 Goals
47 "Jeez Louise!"
48 Primary outflow of Lake Geneva
49 Jupiter's Ganymede and Europa
50 Kept going and going
53 Development that might compete with a downtown
54 Did an amazing job on
55 Gumbo green
57 Marsh
58 Laudatory poem
59 One of four for a grand slam, for short

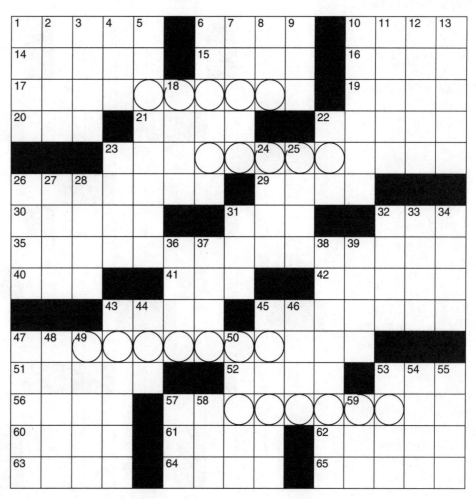

by Evan Kalish

ACROSS

1 ___-dandy
4 Tramps
9 Wild guess
13 "___ we having fun yet?"
14 Humdinger
15 BMW rival
16 What M.B.A.s enter upon graduation
19 On bended ___
20 Yoko who loved John Lennon
21 Spelling contest
22 Verbatim
27 Allows to expire
30 Slap the cuffs on
31 Prefix with -friendly
32 Extra energy
35 Upper floor of a barn
38 Canadian team in the N.B.A.
41 How music can be stored
42 Cause one's bedmate to use earplugs, say
43 "Moby-Dick" setting
44 Gluttonous type
46 Make a mess, as hot grease on a surface
48 Tale that might feature a haunted house
52 Christmas ___ (Dec. 24)
53 ___ constrictor
54 "Hey! Over here!"
58 Kind of test . . . and a hint to a word hidden three times each in 16-, 22-, 38- and 48-Across
63 "What a pity . . ."
64 Like a haunted house
65 Roof repair material
66 R&B singer with the 2006 #1 hit "So Sick"
67 Mascara misadventure
68 "I wonder . . ."

DOWN

1 Beanstalk climber in a children's story
2 Golf club that's not a wood
3 Simple
4 "Game of Thrones" airer
5 Opposite of 'neath
6 Sheep's plaint
7 No longer having in stock
8 Old office worker who took dictation
9 ___ Paulo, Brazil
10 Increase in engine power
11 Chicago's ___ Planetarium
12 Waited
17 Seats for parishioners
18 Frayed, as clothing
23 Stuff oneself with, briefly
24 Prison disturbances
25 Exorcism target
26 Poet Whitman
27 Actor Jared
28 Supply-and-demand subj.
29 Ceremonial pre-Olympic event
33 "Cheers!," in Berlin
34 A Marx brother
36 Complimentary
37 Pre-1917 ruler
39 Scent
40 Fruit that flavors liqueurs
45 Desert crossed by the ancient Silk Road
47 Spell-checker find
48 Virile one
49 Small egg
50 Word after "on the" and "learn the"
51 Site of 1690s witch trials
55 Jedi foe
56 Grifter's game
57 A U.S. senator's is six years
59 Chinese menu general
60 Poet's "before"
61 Org. where one needs a security clearance to work
62 That lady there

by Bruce Haight

ACROSS

1 Elizabeth of cosmetics
6 Residents of London's 10 Downing St.
9 Walk proudly
14 "Go now!"
15 Singer Carly __ Jepsen
16 __ bar (toffee candy)
17 Wander locally with no plans
19 Change
20 Blue Angels' org.
21 Basement of a castle, perhaps
23 Before, to bards
24 Little more than
26 Hitchcock movie with James Stewart and Grace Kelly
28 Purina alternative
30 Water under le pont
31 Unsettled feeling
33 "__ Stars" (long-running show in which experts appraise and buy antiques)
36 Tuna holders
40 Backstage
43 Suffix with bachelor- or kitchen-
44 Visit at 2 a.m., say, as a fridge
45 John who's the subject of 2019's "Rocketman"
46 Place to get pampered
48 Food company with a sunburst in its logo
49 Final amount
55 Asia's __ Sea
58 Opposite of WSW
59 Weather-related game cancellation
61 Rx watchdog
62 It's a good thing
64 Disagree . . . or a hint to the starts of 17-, 26-, 40- and 49-Across
66 Street in "Perry Mason"
67 Basket part grabbed after slam-dunking
68 Prince Harry, to Prince George and Princess Charlotte
69 Suddenly stop, as an engine
70 Downed, as a sandwich
71 Have the wheel

DOWN

1 Photo display option
2 Find a second function for
3 "Hell, yeah!"
4 Work done while tethered to a space station, for short
5 Superbrainy sort
6 Dried plum
7 Japanese comic art
8 Passover meal
9 Twain who sang "Man! I Feel Like a Woman!"
10 __ Aviv
11 Assigned stars to
12 In __ (unborn)
13 Intentionally lost
18 Not just mine
22 Jesse of the 1936 Olympics
25 Like bunny slopes, among all ski runs
27 Chocolaty spread
29 Everest, e.g.: Abbr.
31 Honest __
32 Final amount
33 Group whose activities pick up in Sept.
34 Tuna type
35 When U.S. election results are usually published: Abbr.
37 Communicate (with)
38 Prefix with -liberal
39 I.R.S. digits: Abbr.
41 Emmy genre
42 Co. leader
47 Website's access page
48 Book after Num.
49 Alternative to a door between rooms
50 Beginning
51 Nikola who invented the induction motor
52 Cooperative, balanced type, they say
53 Arctic people
54 Response to "Who broke this?!"
56 Confuse
57 Intense beam
60 Ergo
63 Right angle
65 Tonsillitis-treating doc

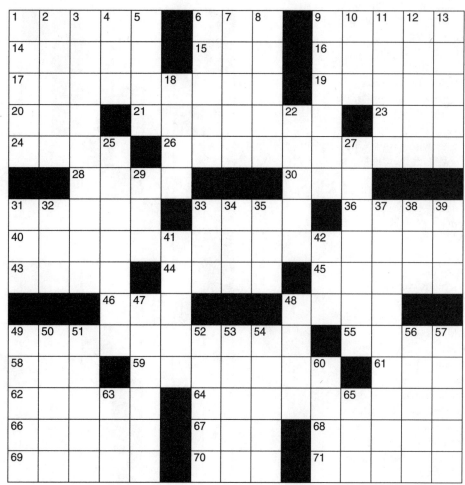

by Aimee Lucido

ACROSS

1 33⅓ r.p.m. records
4 Cher or Adele, musically
8 Allude (to)
13 Annoy
14 Building for bovines
15 Mogadishu native
16 *Chief source of support
18 Self-centeredness
19 ___ fixe (preoccupation)
20 General Mills puffed corn cereal
21 Distances in Britain
22 *Chapel Hill athlete
24 Pyromaniacs' pleasures
25 Monogram for Long John Silver's creator
26 Cut (off)
27 Outbuilding for storage
30 Quarrel
33 Yankee great Yogi
35 Park or Madison, on an N.Y.C. map
36 Bouncy youngster in Pooh's crowd
37 Praise after a proper response to the end of the answer to each starred clue
39 Kesey who wrote "One Flew Over the Cuckoo's Nest"
40 Vow sworn at the altar
41 Round Mongolian tents
42 Wary
44 Spot for a teacher's apple or Apple
46 Virtuous conduct, in Confucianism
47 Dot follower in a website address
48 Pass, as a law
50 *"Why?"
54 Saudi city where Muhammad is buried
56 One running for office, informally
57 Noteworthy periods
58 First king of the Franks (A.D. 481)
59 *Tend an absent resident's property

61 M.L.B. division that includes the Astros
62 Prefix with -tasse meaning "half"
63 Word before "blastoff"
64 Uptight
65 Harmonious, after "in"
66 Originally named

DOWN

1 Outer boundary
2 Devil's fashion choice, in a Meryl Streep film
3 Person on a slippery slope
4 Midsection muscles, briefly
5 Potato treats for Hanukkah
6 Backpacker's path
7 Black, banded gemstone
8 Radioer's "Got it"
9 Is melodramatic
10 *Equitable treatment
11 Otherwise
12 Edges, as of craters
15 Athlete getting part-time pay
17 India's first P.M.
23 Plaintive poem
24 Fiestas and Fusions
26 Resulted in
28 ___ and anon
29 Reject as false
30 Extremely dry
31 Went as a passenger
32 *Soft bedding material
33 Title character in a Sacha Baron Cohen mockumentary
34 Radiant
38 One rejected by a group
43 Roast host
45 Butchers' tools
47 Op-ed offering
49 Plant seed with a licoricelike flavor
50 Poppycock
51 "Citizen Kane" star Welles
52 State that's the largest U.S. producer of lobsters
53 Beauty mogul Lauder
54 Exam for a wannabe doc
55 Her: Fr.
56 Degrees after M.A.s
60 Error indicator in a quotation

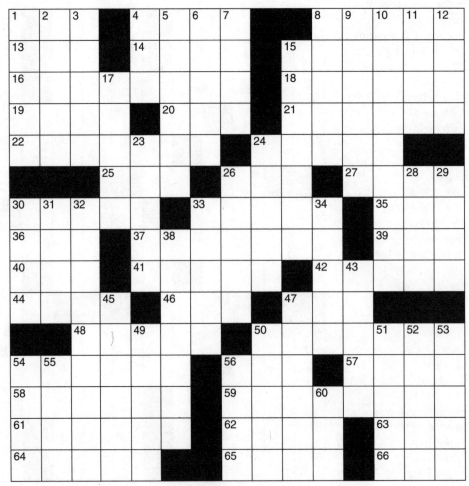

by Lynn Lempel

ACROSS

1 "We should totally do that!"
5 Key of Beethoven's Symphony No. 7: Abbr.
9 Ain't I a stinker?
14 Energy field, in holistic medicine
15 Made-up story
16 Rub the wrong way
17 Metal that rusts
18 Coup d'__
19 What a tabloid may be sued for
20 Need for targeted advertising
23 Medium for modern matchmaking
24 Ghost in a haunted house, e.g.
25 '60s conflict site
28 "That sounds painful"
30 Ozs. and lbs.
31 Danson of "The Good Place"
34 Birdlike
36 A very long time
38 Neighbor of Pennsylvania
39 Netflix or YouTube
42 Online option that turns into "show" when clicked
43 Absence of complication
44 Profess
45 Sun or moon
46 UPS competitor
47 The longer of the two Morse symbols
49 "Hey" alternatives
50 Restaurateur Lagasse
53 Part of a headset
55 It settles a case
61 Classic hit
62 Catcher of counterfeiters, in old lingo
63 Retort to "Are not!"
64 Investigator
65 [Same source as before]
66 Like drone bees
67 Pizza size
68 Disadvantages found in this puzzle's three longest Across answers . . .
69 . . . and advantages found in them

DOWN

1 Concerning the nonordained
2 $: dollar :: € : __
3 Disney sci-fi classic
4 Eldest Stark daughter on "Game of Thrones"
5 "Resume normal speed," in a score
6 Each animal in Noah's Ark had one
7 First thing in the morning?
8 Like 747s
9 Beauty parlors
10 Butter spreader
11 "Occasion" celebrated 364 times a year in Carroll's "Through the Looking Glass"
12 "The First __" (carol)
13 "South Park" boy
21 Leading by a single point
22 __ Rizzo, hustler in "Midnight Cowboy"
25 Cheesy snack
26 French "to have"
27 Tough puzzle
29 Accepting destiny
32 Mi-mi-re-re-do, in a children's song
33 College accommodations
35 Got full, say
37 How a smartphone knows where it is, for short
38 De-squeak
40 So-called "architect of India"
41 TV programming filter
46 Option with a trash can icon
48 Making __
51 Host's task, informally
52 Something to bend over backward for
54 Athlete's leg problem
55 West Virginia resource
56 Gymnast Korbut
57 Bigheaded
58 Actor Sharif
59 Scandinavian capital founded in the mid-11th century
60 Enemies

by Jake Halperin

ACROSS

1 Stitches
5 Old workplace sitcom with Danny DeVito as a dispatcher
9 Flashy effect
14 Honolulu's island
15 "Terrible" Russian despot
16 Many a New Year's resolution prescribes getting into it
17 Not strict adherence to what really happened, say
20 Convenience at a business that doesn't take credit cards
21 Confirmed the flavor of
22 Biblical garden
23 Surefire winner
25 Bewhiskered river swimmer
27 Touched down
29 "Be that as it may . . ."
33 When a fresh factory crew arrives
38 Singer Yoko
39 Elusive Tupperware components, often
40 Air quality watchdog created by the Nixon admin.
41 Norway's capital
42 Web address
43 Archipelago forming the southernmost part of the continental U.S.
47 Gloomy pal of Winnie-the-Pooh
49 Auditioner's goal
50 Newborn horses
53 Run for a long football pass
57 Singer Edith known as "The Little Sparrow"
60 Disappear
62 "Despicable Me" character voiced by Steve Carell
63 Member of an N.F.L. team transplanted to Los Angeles in 2017
66 "Could you, would you, with ___?" (Dr. Seuss line)
67 Black-and-white Nabisco cookie
68 Medics
69 Annual awards . . . like the one actor Shalhoub won in 2018
70 Fret (over)
71 Poker buy-in

DOWN

1 Fizzy drinks
2 Our planet
3 Company that makes Frisbees
4 Redundant word in front of "total"
5 Passenger ship in a 1912 calamity
6 Hertz rival
7 Hobbyist's knife brand
8 Cove
9 PC panic button
10 Upbeat
11 Touch down
12 Church recess
13 Someone who is not yet 20
18 Leaning
19 Canine collar dangler
24 Lummoxes
26 WSW's opposite
28 Letter you don't pronounce in "jeopardy" and "leopard"
30 Garden waterer
31 "It's ___ a matter of time"
32 Pursues romantically
33 Swivel around
34 Add to the payroll
35 Without really thinking
36 Mo. for fools and showers
37 Hair removal cream brand
41 Approved
43 To and ___
44 Order to party crashers
45 Annual Westminster event
46 Hawaiian greeting
48 Time of lackluster performance
51 Largest city and former capital of Nigeria
52 Derisive laugh sound
54 Prod
55 Standing upright
56 Where the endings of 17-, 33-, 43- and 63-Across are often found
57 Exam for sophs. or jrs.
58 "Othello" villain
59 In a little while
61 Drink that can cause brain freeze
64 "___ never too late to learn"
65 Abbr. on old vitamin bottles

by Brad Wilber

ACROSS

1 Simba's mate in 23-Down
5 Snoozefest
9 Not fully open
13 First mate?
14 "Runnin'" college team
15 "Call me the greatest!"
16 56-Across, roughly translated
18 Where to have your hair done
19 Song that opens and closes 23-Down and whose title is literally described in this puzzle's center
21 Fully
24 West Coast air hub, for short
25 Bastille Day season
26 "Can't be"
27 "Put a tiger in your tank" gas brand
30 Greek group that's not in Greece
32 Tries to lose some pounds
34 Actress Fanning
36 Seasoning that can lead to high blood pressure
39 Misfortunes
40 Show again
41 One who's looking
42 Only continent larger than Africa
43 Radio band options
44 Repeated "Survivor" setting
45 Globes
47 QB tackle
49 Slip-___ (shoes)
50 Dominate
52 Dug in, in a way
54 Enthusiastic
56 Song from 23-Down
60 Getting long in the tooth
61 23-Down setting
65 Gentrification raises them
66 Spill the beans
67 The "E" in HOMES

68 Best Picture winner based on events of 1979–80
69 College that awarded the first Ph.D. in the U.S.
70 23-Down villain

DOWN

1 One of the Bobbseys, in children's literature
2 Big fuss
3 Martial ___
4 1998 BP purchase
5 Pack animals
6 Suffix with hypn-
7 List quickly, with "off"
8 Valuable Scrabble tiles
9 ___ Sea (almost dried-up body)
10 Director of 23-Down on Broadway
11 Overhead
12 Fleming at the Met
15 Supports
17 Bar mitzvahs and the like
20 Job seeker's success
21 Neighbor of Nepal
22 Tough as ___
23 Disney movie released in June 1994
28 Appear to be
29 Five Norwegian kings
31 Not at the dock, say
33 Russian Revolution target
35 Bean type
37 British singer Lewis with the 2008 #1 album "Spirit"

38 It's worthless
40 Dreaded one?
44 Need for doing toe loops
46 Forehead covering
48 Baby rocker
50 2015 Tony winner Kelli ___
51 Bet
53 Evacuate
55 Long-eared lagomorphs
57 "Do ___ others as . . ."
58 Word after Bay or gray
59 Part of a cash register
62 Tolkien monster
63 Org. behind the Bay of Pigs invasion
64 Lead-in to plop

by David J. Kahn

ACROSS

1 Benchwarmer
6 Shut loudly
10 Calendar units: Abbr.
13 Dried plums
15 Part of a brain or a 59-Down
16 Cry at a fireworks show
17 Beach outing, say
19 Hit CBS forensics series
20 Movie filming locale
21 Merchandise
22 TV studio alert
24 Ice cream drink
25 Engender, as suspicion
26 High point of winter?
29 Sound of ice cream hitting the floor
31 On easy street
35 Raw metals
36 + or − particle
37 Stick in one's __
39 Financially afloat again
44 Adds to the payroll
45 Comics' goals
46 Mother of Calcutta
49 Nota __
50 Mobile app's clientele
51 Sweeping stories
53 Cry at a fireworks show
56 Instagram upload, informally
57 Traffic helicopter, e.g.
60 "Four score and seven years __ . . ."
61 Landlord's due
62 Partner of "signed" and "delivered" in a Stevie Wonder hit
63 Anderson Cooper's channel
64 Utters
65 Wear down

DOWN

1 Coppertone stats, for short
2 Mötley __
3 Peewee
4 Prefix meaning "one"
5 Most widely spoken native language of India, after Hindi
6 Toboggan, e.g.
7 L's meaning, in box scores
8 Aladdin's monkey sidekick
9 Hanukkah display
10 Asian gambling mecca
11 Refuge in the desert
12 Suffix in many English county names
14 Like a thief's loot
18 Like a thief's loot, slangily
23 "Beats me!"
24 Dutch artist known for his "impossible" drawings
25 Gore and Capone, for two
26 "I think," in textspeak
27 Low-__ diet
28 Brainchild
29 Drinks not meant to be savored
30 Phnom __ (capital of Cambodia)
32 Fork prong
33 RuPaul's purview
34 A pop
38 Calendar units: Abbr.
40 Pieholes
41 Savings plan, for short
42 Votes into office
43 Gaelic spirit who wails to foretell a death in the family
46 Rapper Shakur
47 Provide one's digital John Hancock
48 Military info-gathering
49 Recycling receptacle
51 __-weeny (small)
52 Very bad, with "the"
53 Nobel Peace Prize city
54 Ratified, for short
55 Jekyll's bad side
58 Senate assent
59 Place for a stud or a ring

by Erik Agard and Yacob Yonas

ACROSS

1 Science class adjuncts
5 Tyrannical
10 Losing casino roll
14 Double-apostrophe contraction
15 Tough watchdog
16 Old Italian capital
17 Autobiography of a "Star Trek" doctor?
19 Mental flash
20 Afternoon affair
21 Rib
22 Audre Lorde or Lord Byron
23 Kill off a major "Back to the Future" character?
27 Neighbor of Borneo
28 Zero
29 Pal for Pierre
30 Mates for does
33 Birthstone for some Scorpios
37 Typesetter's choice
39 Attach, as a button
41 Languish
42 English class assignment
44 Part of a baker's dozen
46 It might sit on a sill to cool
47 Brand of cooking spray
49 Lament about one's sorry appearance
51 Film star Danny hurriedly leaving the set?
56 Mayberry sot
57 Bemoan
58 Medit. country
59 Something to watch on the telly, with "the"
60 Help film star Steve recover from an action sequence?
65 Marine menace
66 Man in a cast
67 After-Christmas event
68 Bleacher feature
69 Impetuous
70 Give off

DOWN

1 Justin Trudeau's party: Abbr.
2 End of a sweet drink?
3 Niacin and riboflavin
4 Five Nations tribe
5 Lunch meat
6 Org. associated with the Westminster show
7 "__ and the Flash" (2015 Meryl Streep movie)
8 Stone-faced
9 New York's __ Planetarium
10 Bygone street sound
11 No longer plagued by
12 Spinning
13 Like some fertilizer
18 Singer Brooks
23 Jumbo combatants
24 Some "traditional" investments, for short
25 Got along
26 Sch. on the bank of the Charles
27 Unlikely to cause controversy
31 Number of words in the shortest verse in the Bible (John 11:35)
32 Kind of boom
34 Wildly improbable goal
35 Ouzo flavor
36 Scrabble 10-pointers
38 Restaurant with small dishes
40 Like an arm that's been slept on too long
43 Pilot's problem
45 __ Aziz, Iraq War figure
48 Singer Carey
50 Improper application
51 Unpaid factory worker
52 Wombs
53 Family girl
54 New Mexico's state flower
55 Assembles
61 "Bon" word
62 Show sorrow
63 __ Lilly & Co.
64 Stocking material

by Jeff Stillman

ACROSS

1 Talks with a gravelly voice
6 Fastener with a twist
11 Brevity is said to be the soul of it
14 Sir John of London
15 Not get caught by, as a pursuer
16 Patient's insurance option, for short
17 "Affliction" suffered by Fab Four devotees
19 "The Simpsons" storekeeper
20 __ stage left
21 Prefix with -air or -afternoon
22 Big person on the small screen
24 Prince Charles's onetime partner, affectionately
26 Removes from nursing, as a foal
27 "Affliction" suffered by bracketologists
32 Child, legally speaking
35 Villain's retreat
36 Quartet minus one
37 Has left the office
38 Triage locales, for short
39 Enjoy the taste of
40 Move like a butterfly
41 Green stone popular in Chinese craftwork
42 Woods who voiced Cinderella
43 "Affliction" suffered by clothes lovers
46 Track-and-field competitions
47 Insinuates
51 Person with a chrome dome
52 Cow's sound
54 "Gone With the Wind" plantation
55 Atty.'s org.
56 "Affliction" suffered by the winter-weary
59 Big part of a T. rex

60 What diamonds and straight-A students do
61 Gown
62 Commercials
63 Japanese port of 2+ million
64 "Same here"

DOWN

1 One in revolt
2 Amazon Echo persona
3 Reserved in manner
4 Spewing naughty language, as a child
5 Weekly show with a cold open, for short
6 Vehicle that can jackknife
7 Attired
8 Go for elected office
9 Tussle between wiki page modifiers
10 Bobbed and __
11 "Well, I never!"
12 Fill with zeal
13 P.G.A. __
18 Kuwaiti leader
23 Mail addressed to the North Pole
25 Missile aimed at a bull's-eye
28 Off drugs
29 The fourth letter of "circle," but not the first
30 Scrooge
31 Achy
32 Make peeved
33 Capital of Pakistan
34 Peace-and-quiet ordinances
39 Small, medium or large
41 Brooklyn's St. __ College
44 "Quite correct"
45 Wide-eyed
48 Placed money in the bank
49 "Am not!" comeback
50 Ankle bones
51 __ California
52 Stole fur
53 Prime draft status
57 Narrow waterway
58 Agcy. overseeing Rx's

by Ross Trudeau

Note: When this puzzle is done, read the dotted letters line by line from top to bottom to spell a title related to this puzzle's theme.

ACROSS

1 Book of the Bible after John
5 Like some high-end cigars
10 ___ vu
14 Russian rejection
15 Like about 60% of the world's population
16 Daredevil Knievel
17 Org. for the New York Cosmos
18 Alternative to a hedge
19 Answer to "Shall we?"
20 "Come in!"
22 Prez before J.F.K.
23 Bygone car model named for a horse
24 Technique employed in the painting hidden in this puzzle
27 What's far from fair?
29 ___ Fighters (rock band)
30 Counterpart of long.
31 One side of Niagara Falls: Abbr.
34 Had as a customer
36 Dijon darling
38 "Star Trek: T.N.G." character with empathic abilities
39 Bump up in pay
43 Impart
44 $15/hour and others
46 Suffix with elephant-
47 Got ready to be photographed
48 Takes too much, in brief
49 What a Heisman winner might hope to become
52 "Le Comte ___" (Rossini opera)
53 Weaving machine
54 First small bit of progress
56 Artist who created the painting hidden in this puzzle
61 Crime scene clue
62 Rapa ___ (Easter Island)
63 Willem of "The Grand Budapest Hotel"
65 Tower-building game

66 ___ Radio Hour (NPR program)
67 Egg shell?
68 "Awesome!"
69 French religious title: Abbr.
70 Specialty

DOWN

1 Green Gables girl
2 Ink cartridge color
3 Aviators trying out new planes
4 Pope who negotiated with Attila the Hun
5 Half-___ (coffee order)
6 Did, once upon a time
7 Dot on a Hindu woman's forehead
8 Smallish battery
9 Fla.-to-Me. direction
10 Cold cut purveyors
11 With still greater intensity
12 Rocker Joan
13 Plus
21 Falling-out
23 Essential part
25 Koh-i-___ diamond
26 Doily material
27 Elroy's dog on "The Jetsons"
28 Missile detection org.
32 Forty-___ (old prospector)
33 All-in-one undergarment
35 Game cube
37 Chess rating system
40 Minor maladies
41 Counterparts of outs
42 Save for later
45 Dismiss with derision
47 Self-satisfied about
50 Harbor hazard
51 Took in some takeout, say
53 What the French pronounce "Louis" with that the English do not
55 "Well done!"
56 Increased
57 German article
58 Plum pudding ingredient
59 Beyond the horizon
60 Civil wrong
61 Cover of night?
64 Hurricane's center

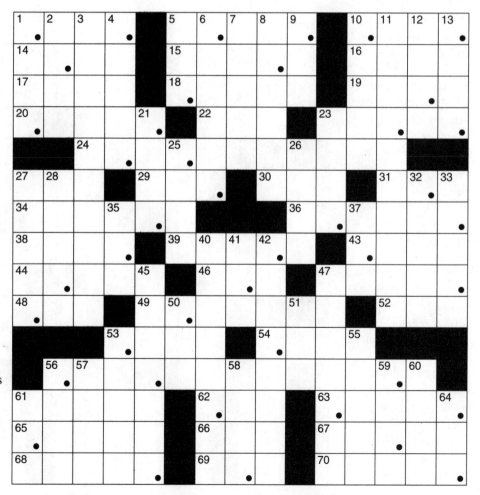

by Alex Eaton-Salners

ACROSS

1 Many flat screens
6 "Red, white and blue" land, for short
11 Zero, in soccer scores
14 Quintet followed by ". . . and sometimes Y"
15 Absolute minimum
16 Rocks sent to a refinery
17 Devil-may-care
19 Piece of lawn
20 Actor Guinness of "Star Wars"
21 Fashion line?
22 Summer romance, perhaps
24 Town crier's cry
28 Diamond great Ripken
31 Gives a red card, in short
32 Lerner's partner on Broadway
33 Carne ___ (burrito filler)
35 Broadband letters
36 Touch
39 Bar request . . . or hint to the letters in the circles
43 German auto sold mainly in Europe
44 Reaction to a body blow
45 Latches (onto)
46 Élan
48 Offering from Hertz or National
50 Message-spewing program
51 Rock drummer whose last name is the same as his band
55 Gift recipient
56 Eggs for fertilization
57 Petri dish medium
61 Hour after midnight
62 Accessing, as a password-restricted website
66 Race, as an engine
67 Pick up the tab for
68 Be of use
69 Slice of time
70 Dark wood
71 Midler of "Beaches"

DOWN

1 ___ funny (genuinely humorous)
2 "You're on!"
3 Goodyear product
4 Give personal assurance (for)
5 Total
6 Belly aches?
7 Run-down
8 Crew blade
9 The Seminoles of the A.C.C.
10 Charge to get cash from a bank, say
11 "Absolutely, positively not!"
12 Humor with a twist
13 Overhang
18 Basketball's O'Neal, informally
23 Permissible
25 Dutch cheese town
26 Disney snow queen
27 Wrestling maneuver
28 G.I. garb, for short
29 "Hurry!," on an order
30 Body of water between France and Switzerland
34 Of the highest quality
35 ___ Jam records
37 Falsetto-voiced Muppet
38 For fear that
40 Wee bit
41 Lunchtime, often
42 Fairy tale villain
47 Gracefully thin
48 Cause for a dental filling
49 Computer science pioneer Turing
51 Love to pieces
52 Recluse
53 Paul who played Crocodile Dundee
54 Easily fooled
58 Flying pest
59 Going ___ (fighting)
60 Part in a movie
63 Space ball
64 Nat ___ Wild (cable channel)
65 Yammer

by Damon Gulczynski

ACROSS

1 Starting players
6 Any classic vinyl record
11 On the ___ (fleeing)
14 Crown for Miss America
15 Satellite signals
16 ___ Jima
17 Actor with the same initials as Michael Rezendes, his role in "Spotlight"
19 Nuke
20 Sloth, for example
21 Have a go at
22 Put in a tandoor
23 ___ Mahal
26 Citrus garnish in a mixed drink
28 Used a riflescope, say
29 For fun
31 See 49-Across
33 Graphic representation of history
35 Fake ID user, often
36 Fruity drinks
37 Image on the back of a dime
39 Cell messenger
41 Serpentine letter
42 Strong string
43 Floating mass in the North Atlantic
45 Eye woe
47 Regularness
49 With 31-Across, actor with the same initials as Alfred Hitchcock, his role in "Hitchcock"
52 Performer with a baton
53 Construction girder
54 Didn't do takeout at a restaurant
56 Altar promise
57 Like lumber
58 Subj. involving telescopes or microscopes
59 Army NCO
61 Grassy field
62 Actor with the same initials as Jake Blues, his role in "The Blues Brothers"
67 Do the wrong thing
68 Fall bloom
69 Set of moral principles
70 Former fast jet, in brief
71 ___ nova (Brazilian music style)
72 "So I was wrong"

DOWN

1 It's stuffed with dough
2 Acapulco aunt
3 Musical sense
4 Temple cabinets
5 ___ status (survey information)
6 Not working
7 Southpaw punches
8 Lack
9 How doodles are generally drawn
10 What that is, in Tijuana
11 Actress with the same initials as Linda Marolla, her role in "Arthur"
12 Come to
13 Relatives of scooters
18 Oral only
22 Establishment that might have a lot of hogs in front
23 "Cheerio!"
24 Parenthetical comment
25 Actor with the same initials as Jefferson Smith, his role in "Mr. Smith Goes To Washington"
27 "You don't have to tell me"
28 Lummox
30 Symbol above the comma on a keyboard
32 Else
34 "___ go bragh!"
38 $100 bill, in slang
40 Took a parabolic path
44 Greek sandwich
46 ___ Kippur
48 Is sociable at a party
49 A wide-body plane has two of them
50 Cavs and Mavs, for example
51 Billionaires' vessels
55 Fork prongs
58 Mediocre
60 Ballerina's skirt
62 Quick punch
63 Bikini top
64 That woman
65 That man
66 Rink surface

by Peter Gordon

ACROSS

1 Al who created Li'l Abner
5 Chatting online, in brief
10 Almost any offer that's too good to be true
14 Doozy
15 "I swear!"
16 Robe in old Rome
17 The "A" of U.A.E.
18 *Basketball position for Magic Johnson or Steph Curry
20 *Level on the military wage scale
22 Player in front of a net
23 What sailors and beachgoers breathe
24 Uncouth person
25 Colorado summer hrs.
26 *Alternative to a brush when coating the side of a house
30 Things coiled on the sides of houses
33 With 44-Across, onetime British slapstick comic
34 Single-stranded genetic molecule
35 ___ and crafts
36 Consumer products giant, for short . . . or a hint to the answers to the eight starred clues
37 Tylenol target
38 "You got it now?"
39 Toyota hybrid
40 North Pole resident
41 *The Beach Boys or Backstreet Boys
43 Amusement
44 See 33-Across
45 Marx's collaborator on "The Communist Manifesto"
49 ___ Field, former home of the Seattle Mariners
52 *Shade akin to olive
54 *Sorority types who go out a lot
56 Eugene O'Neill's "___ Christie"
57 Help with a crime
58 Letter-shaped fastener
59 "Veni, ___, vici"
60 Hellmann's product, informally
61 Daytime or Primetime awards
62 Holler

DOWN

1 Applauds
2 Enveloping glows, old-style
3 ___ del Rey, Calif.
4 *Darts and snooker
5 Somewhat
6 An emoji may suggest it
7 1970s tennis champ Nastase
8 Writer Anaïs
9 Dig into work
10 E. B. White's "___ Little"
11 Unwanted stocking stuffer
12 Prefix with -cultural
13 Prepared, as dinner or a bed
19 Foolish, informally
21 Frees (of)
24 Marching halftime crews
26 Fence in
27 Mom's mom, for short
28 The "U" of I.C.U.
29 Mom's mom
30 Lock securer
31 ___ O's (breakfast cereal)
32 One of 12 in Alcoholics Anonymous
33 Oksana ___, 1994 Olympic skating wonder
36 What may precede Chapter 1 in a novel
37 *Roast accompaniment prepared with drippings
39 $$$$, on Yelp
40 Like choir music
42 Run-down area
43 Lavish meals
46 Counting-off word
47 1980s tennis champ Ivan
48 Creature that leaves a slimy trail
49 What an email filter filters
50 Rhyme scheme for Robert Frost's "Stopping by Woods on a Snowy Evening"
51 Glenn of the Eagles
52 School event with a king and a queen
53 "For Better or for Worse" mom
55 Company that pioneered the U.P.C. bar code

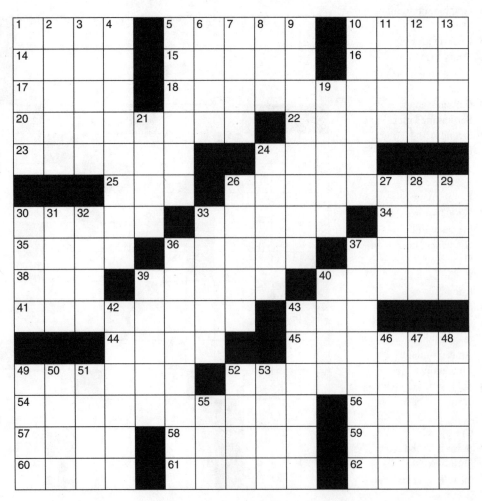

by Ned White

ACROSS

1 So far
6 Jazz style
11 Not an exact amount: Abbr.
14 Note from a 6-Down that might give you jitters
15 Plains tribe
16 To the __ degree
17 Experience, redundantly
19 Opus __
20 Prefix with -tourism
21 Come after
22 "Victory is mine!"
23 Like some telephones and tires
25 Snitch, redundantly
28 Novelist Morrison
29 Dark force, in Chinese philosophy
32 Hoi polloi, with "the"
33 Smidgen
35 "The Highwayman" poet
37 Angsty music genre
38 Moolah, redundantly
41 Automated producer of spam
44 5/8/1945
45 Popeye's creator E. C. __
49 Spaced out mentally
51 Track relentlessly
53 Singer India.__
54 Hack, redundantly
56 F equivalent
58 "Anybody __?"
59 Folgers alternative
62 A/C meas.
63 Word in brackets after a mistake
64 Cottontail, redundantly
67 Get __ on (ace)
68 Can't be found at the office
69 One of 10 in bowling
70 Pro __
71 Self-description after a major lifestyle change
72 Exhorted

DOWN

1 Different sides to observe
2 Ship's galley worker
3 "Give me a simple answer!"
4 911 responder, for short
5 Giggle
6 Head honcho
7 Question to a backstabber
8 Rude person in the bleachers
9 Contraction sung twice in the first verse of "The Star-Spangled Banner"
10 College subj. that covers Freud
11 How train cars are linked
12 Feminist Gloria
13 "Really?"
18 __ 500
22 Hypotheticals
24 The "D" of D.J.
26 "You got that right!"
27 Shocks, in a way
30 How many TV shows are viewed nowadays
31 Wanderer
34 Pandemonium
36 Quickly change one's mind back and forth
39 Video game giant
40 "You got that right!"
41 Goes for, as when bobbing for apples
42 Like laundry being dried outdoors
43 Subject of an I.R.S. consumer warning
46 Potpourri
47 Broadcast slot
48 Said (to be)
50 Shakespearean cry before "What, are you mad?"
52 One of 10 in a ten-speed
55 At this point
57 Problem that has ballooned
60 E pluribus __
61 Memory unit
64 Recycling container
65 Not let go to waste
66 "I'm f-f-freezing!"

by Bruce Haight

ACROSS
1 Cow's newborn
5 Upbeat, as an outlook
9 SWAT team actions
14 Singer India.___
15 Aunt Bee's charge on "The Andy Griffith Show"
16 Disney attraction in Florida
17 Trendy terms
19 Ragú rival
20 Palestinian territory bordering Israel
21 Busybody, from the Yiddish
23 ___ Dhabi, part of the United Arab Emirates
24 Most unspoiled
26 First host of "America's Funniest Home Videos"
28 "Haste makes waste" and similar sayings
30 "Venerable" monk of the Middle Ages
31 "Able ___ I ere I saw Elba"
32 Ship's wastewater
35 State led by Lenin, in brief
36 Magical powder in "Peter Pan"
39 "I do solemnly swear . . .," e.g.
42 Browned bread
43 "Fee, fi, fo, ___"
46 Stick back in the microwave
49 Going from two lanes to one
51 Style of collarless shirt
54 ___ Pieces (candy)
55 Nonkosher meat
56 Say "Nyah, nyah," say
58 Snow queen in "Frozen"
59 To any degree
61 Timesavers . . . or the starts of 17-, 26-, 36- and 51-Across?
64 Scalawag
65 Peace Nobelist Wiesel
66 Length × width, for a rectangle
67 Opening golf shot
68 Pepsi, for one
69 Hang in the balance

DOWN
1 Taxi
2 Peppery salad green
3 Chameleons, e.g.
4 Some Moroccan headwear
5 Aussie marsupial, in brief
6 Grand Ole ___
7 Lesser-played half of a 45
8 Like some straightforward questions
9 Meal
10 Its showers bring May flowers: Abbr.
11 Periods with the largest glaciers
12 Places for pooped pooches
13 Having a heavier build
18 Sushi bar condiment
22 Atlanta-based channel
24 Sound effect on "Batman"
25 Candy bar packaged in twos
27 Touch geographically
29 Open with a letter opener
33 Prefix with -cache
34 Cheese from the Netherlands
36 "Glad that's over!"
37 Addict
38 Word before map or smarts
39 Apple production site
40 Aquarium accessory
41 Biblical group bearing gifts
43 Opening, as after an earthquake
44 Like leftovers
45 British sports cars of old
47 "Crouching Tiger, Hidden Dragon" director
48 ___ Aviv
50 Tablet alternative
52 Trig ratio
53 Mexican artist Frida
57 Hard labor
60 Sentiment on a candy heart
62 Stephen of "The Crying Game"
63 Unhappy

by Ed Sessa

ACROSS

1 Start of an incantation
6 Up to the task
10 Landlocked Asian country
11 DuVernay who directed "Selma"
13 One with a feather duster, maybe
14 'Vette option
15 Speedy Amtrak option
17 Yours, in Tours
18 Grp. that combats smuggling
19 Land made for you and me, in a Woody Guthrie song
21 Demo material for Wile E. Coyote
22 Entertained with a story, say
24 Print media revenue source
26 Copenhageners, e.g.
28 Oasis beast
29 Lawn game banned in 1988
30 In the manner of
32 __ Amidala, "Star Wars" queen
34 "__ quote . . ."
35 Oakland's Oracle, for one
37 Diez minus siete
38 Born
39 Insect feeler
41 The "e" of i.e.
42 The Kennedys or the Bushes, so to speak
44 As a group
46 Country singer __ James Decker
47 Very wee
48 Embarrassing fall
52 Structures illustrated twice in this puzzle through both black squares and letters
58 Male buds
59 Nae Nae or cancan

60 Captain who circumnavigated the globe
61 Flue buildup
62 "Come in!"
63 Influence

DOWN

1 Setting for a classical sacrifice
2 Flinched
3 Adjuncts to some penthouses
4 Nile viper
5 State as fact
6 Org. for docs
7 Military field uniform
8 World's highest-paid athlete in 2019, per Forbes magazine
9 Drops (or adds) a line
11 Got 100 on
12 Et __
15 Iowa college town
16 "Hells Bells" band
19 Bottles that might be marked "XXX" in the comics
20 "Stat!"
23 Not pro
25 Amo, amas, __
27 Sheltered at sea
29 Maker of "No more tears" baby shampoo, for short
30 Pretentious
31 Hathaway of Hollywood
33 Alternative to Chanel No. 5
35 Predate
36 Glassworker, at times
39 "Take me __ "
40 Modify
43 Equally speedy
45 Shenanigans
49 Abba of Israel
50 Fourth-and-long option
51 Subject of a school nurse's inspection
52 Targets of plank exercises
53 Do that might block someone's view, for short
54 Pooh's pal
55 When repeated, calming expression
56 Smallest state in India
57 Wild blue yonder

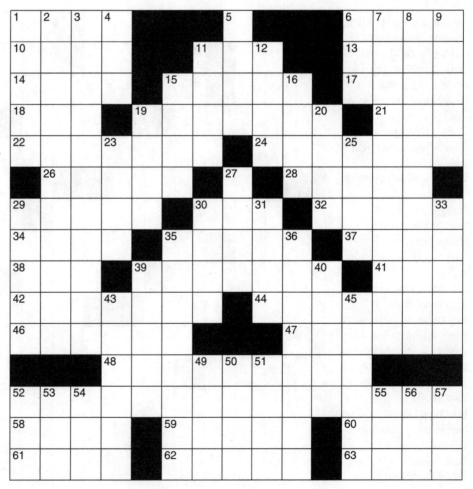

by Ross Trudeau

ACROSS

1 Mushroom part
4 ___ Xing (road sign)
8 Managed to avoid
14 South America's Carnaval city, informally
15 Not doing anything
16 Baltimore bird
17 Psychic ability, in brief
18 Yard event to clear out the attic
20 Manage to avoid
22 Big coffee holder
23 Applaud
24 Louisiana's avian nickname
28 Giant in health insurance
29 Mortal dangers
33 "Phooey!"
35 Commotions
38 Provide with continuing funds
39 Athlete who said "Silence is golden when you can't think of a good answer"
40 Strong-smelling cheese made in England
42 Investment for the golden yrs.
43 Cook's workspace
45 Enroll for another year of duty
46 Work by Wordsworth or Whitman
47 Coughed (up)
49 Ledger entry on the minus side
51 One barely in the water?
56 German carmaker
59 ___ Paulo, Brazil
60 Big name in mattresses
61 Fairy tale question whose answer is spelled out in the starts of 18-, 24-, 40- and 51-Across
65 Fast asleep
66 Mythical beauty who lent her name to a continent
67 Oil producers' grp.
68 "___ to Joy"
69 Singer/songwriter Crow
70 Shipped
71 Gave a meal to

DOWN

1 Slimeball
2 Supermarket section
3 China's is around 1.4 billion
4 Without stopping en route
5 Part of a campus URL
6 "Slippery" tree
7 Co-founder of Rome with Romulus
8 Run off with a boxer, maybe?
9 Gold waiting to be discovered
10 Recognize, as differences
11 Objective for a soccer player
12 Fitzgerald of jazz
13 Profound
19 The "A" of MoMA
21 Conks out
25 Med school subj.
26 Low point
27 Juliet Capulet or Holden Caulfield, agewise
30 Impossible to mess up
31 Set of traditional beliefs
32 Got one's kicks at the pool?
33 Hoarse voice
34 Voice above tenor
36 Grand ___ Opry
37 Prepare for a hard test
40 Search for
41 Coup for a newspaper freelancer
44 Someone dropping by
46 Something that might spring a leak
48 Dreary
50 Cut in half
52 Vote that cancels out a yea
53 Unacceptable actions
54 Musical practice piece
55 Given a PG-13, say
56 Bowls over
57 Thumbs-down response
58 Show gumption
62 Someone not likely to show off intelligence?
63 "Great" hominid
64 Word on a restroom door

by Lynn Lempel

ACROSS

1 Missing school
7 Cousin of a lark
14 Nonsense word repeated in Stephen Foster's "Camptown Races"
15 Literally, "empty orchestra"
16 "Spare me your lame reasons!"
18 Home of Wall St. and Fifth Ave.
19 "Chicago ___" (NBC drama)
20 With 24-Across, food coloring in Twizzlers
21 Compound with a fruity scent
24 See 20-Across
26 Roman emperor who wrote "Meditations"
32 Waiting for a pitch
33 Siesta, e.g.
34 Michael of "Weekend Update" on "S.N.L."
35 Pull an all-nighter
36 Expand
38 Giggle
39 Be laid up in bed
40 Call to a lamb
41 Garden plant also called stonecrop
42 Facial hair for Sam Elliott and Wilford Brimley
46 Equipment hauled by a roadie
47 Course covering axons and dendrites, for short
48 Maple product
50 Chinese zodiac creature for 2019
51 Consumer safety org.
54 1981 hit with the lyric "We can make it if we try" . . . or a possible title for this puzzle
59 So far
60 Getting some shut-eye
61 Composer Bizet
62 Alternatives to Ho Hos

DOWN

1 Mideast's Gulf of ___
2 Squarish
3 Necessity for achieving one's goals?
4 Ending with "umich." or "upenn."
5 Rapper Lil ___ X
6 Topics for book clubs
7 Slated events, in brief
8 Material for Icarus' wings
9 Circle segment
10 Branch of the Olympics?
11 Misplace
12 Gave the go-ahead
13 Anderson who directed "The Grand Budapest Hotel"
17 "Buona ___" (Italian greeting)
22 Rip-off
23 Famed child ruler, informally
24 Compete in Pictionary
25 "You betcha!"
26 Colorful parrot
27 Some heart chambers
28 Card game with suits of four different colors
29 Caffeinated summer drink
30 "You betcha!"
31 Teacher's note that makes one go [gulp]
36 [Oh. My. God!]
37 Piece of siege equipment
38 Get wind of
40 Wander here and there, with "around"
41 Disco ___ ("The Simpsons" character)
43 Any member of the 2019 N.B.A. championship team
44 Meter or liter
45 Mall cop's transport
48 Apartment building V.I.P., in slang
49 Regarding
50 Benches along an aisle
52 "Hamilton" climax
53 Nile biters
54 Put a cork in it!
55 "Star Trek" spinoff series: Abbr.
56 It's groundbreaking
57 Spanish for "bear"
58 Timeworn

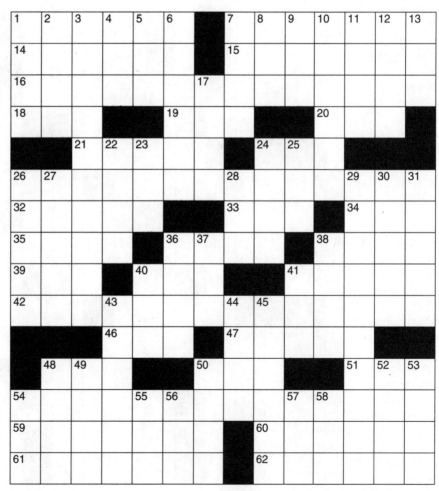

by Kyle Dolan

ACROSS

1 Major uncertainty
6 Canvas for a tattoo
10 Mae who said "I used to be Snow White, but I drifted"
14 "You ___ Beautiful" (Joe Cocker hit)
15 Mexican entree in a shell
16 Large fair, informally
17 Athlete with a mitt
19 Bridle strap
20 Poker stake
21 Bill Clinton's was in the 1990s
22 ___ Haute, Ind.
23 One going for a stroll among urban greenery
26 "Quit wasting time!"
30 Abba of Israel
31 Even a little
32 ___-haw
33 Plumbing woe
37 Official hearing a case
41 Fish that wriggle
42 What's dropped off a cigarette
43 Words of empathy
44 Weights that may be "short" or "long"
46 Tevye's occupation in "Fiddler on the Roof"
48 Herbie Hancock or Chick Corea
52 "Later, amigo!"
53 Employ
54 Bleats
58 William with a state named after him
59 Place where 17-, 23-, 37- and 48-Across might be found
62 Sheltered from the wind
63 Parks in civil rights history
64 Language family of Africa
65 Loch ___ monster
66 "That's enough!"
67 Adventurous journey

DOWN

1 "Ali ___ and the 40 Thieves"
2 Land with an ayatollah
3 Hanukkah "moolah"
4 ___ of Capri
5 Dandyish dresser
6 Van Gogh's "The ___ Night"
7 Boat you might shoot rapids in
8 What a "neat" drink doesn't come with
9 Word paired with "neither"
10 "How fortunate for us!"
11 Apply, as force
12 Former vice president Agnew
13 Printer cartridge contents
18 Meadows
22 Airport screening org.
23 Tug on
24 Turn sharply
25 Skeptic's sarcastic comment
26 Racehorse's starting point
27 Raison d'___
28 Pin the ___ on the donkey
29 Bomb testing areas
32 "Come again?"
34 Semihard Dutch cheese
35 City that's home to the Taj Mahal
36 Sharp-witted
38 "Is it O.K., mom?"
39 Peak near Olympus
40 Leave at the altar
45 Special ___ (military missions)
46 Event that's an "Oops!"
47 "Ah, makes sense"
48 Where Honda and Mazda are headquartered
49 Grammy-winning singer of "Hello"
50 Fan publications, informally
51 Bonkers
54 Lover boy
55 Youngest of the Brontë sisters
56 Things passed in Congress
57 "___ your piehole!"
59 Surgery sites, for short
60 Word after waste and want
61 Cookout, briefly

by Bruce Haight

ACROSS

1 What a coin may go in
5 ___ & Allies (classic board game)
9 Lies lazily in the sun
14 Stun with a gun
15 Brad of "Fight Club"
16 Someone's in the kitchen with her, in an old song
17 Wreck
18 Petty set of procedures
20 Woman who's bid good night in an old song
22 "___, old chap!"
23 "With this ring, I thee ___"
24 Local officials in dioceses
28 Seats in many bars
29 Car
32 Car with a meter
35 Sites of biceps and triceps
36 More cunning
38 & 40 Money required to open a business . . . or a hint to 18-, 24-, 47- and 57-Across
41 Permeates
42 Feature of many an old car
43 Cunning
44 Some beans
45 "Here's how experts handle this"
47 Longest-serving Independent member of Congress in U.S. history
53 Vaccine target
55 Greeting in Guatemala
56 Generate by dubious means
57 Part of a Juliet soliloquy
61 Crème ___ crème
62 Juiced (up)
63 Noted terrier in a 1939 film
64 Scott of an 1857 Supreme Court case
65 Inventor with a coil named after him
66 Lead-in to chat or dragon
67 Time long past

DOWN

1 Unit of bacon
2 Actress Linney of "The Truman Show"
3 Common basket-weaving material
4 Something you'll have to go to court for?
5 Financing letters
6 Midnight, on a grandfather clock
7 Edie Sedgwick and Kendall Jenner, for two
8 Condition of inactivity
9 They're almost always shared by twins, informally
10 Televise
11 Winter play outfits
12 Leafy vegetable that can be green or purple
13 Place to store a lawn mower
19 Fannie ___
21 Locale for a manor
25 Falcon-headed Egyptian god
26 Circumstance's partner
27 Car with a meter
30 Blue-green shade
31 Alternative to Charles de Gaulle
32 Some CBS police dramas
33 Prefix with -sphere
34 Obvious signs of pregnancy
36 Fruity soda brand
37 Selecting, with "for"
39 Ploy
40 Tops of corp. ladders
42 "That'll never happen!"
45 Ones doing loops and barrel rolls
46 Onetime stage name of Sean Combs
48 "The Mary Tyler Moore Show" spinoff
49 ___'easter
50 Month after diciembre
51 Side of many a protractor
52 Garden tool
53 ___ row (some blocks in a college town)
54 Togolese city on the Gulf of Guinea
58 Fish that can be electric
59 Second letter after epsilon
60 "Alley ___!"

by Christina Iverson

ACROSS

1 Group in a play
5 Plasterwork backing
9 Bracelet securer
14 Arthur with a stadium named after him
15 Feeling fluish, in a way
16 "___ me" ("Go along with it")
17 ___ the Man (old baseball nickname)
18 Be overrun (with)
19 "E" on a gas gauge
20 Pre-snap powwow
22 Garden munchkin
24 "How was ___ know?"
25 2012 Best Picture winner set in Iran
27 Kind of toy that moves when you turn a key
31 Semiaquatic salamanders
33 Flowers on trellises
35 Bill in a tip jar
36 Slangy "sweetheart"
37 Horace, as a poet
38 Barrister's headgear
39 Scrub vigorously
41 Manipulate
42 Littlest ones in litters
44 Contagious viral infection
45 Cross ___ with
47 Side-to-side nautical movement
48 Plural "is"
49 First appearance, as of symptoms
50 Toronto N.H.L. team, for short
53 Common ankle injury
55 Biggest bear in "Goldilocks and the Three Bears"
57 "V for Vendetta" actor Stephen
58 Grind, as teeth
60 Withstands
62 Gemstone measure
65 Chopped down
67 3:1 or 4:1, e.g.
68 Superior beef grade
69 They're mined and refined
70 Large, scholarly book
71 "For ___ waves of grain" (line in "America the Beautiful")
72 Water swirl
73 Elderly

DOWN

1 Redeem, as a savings bond
2 Uncommonly perceptive
3 Air-punching pugilist
4 Manage, as a bar
5 "Ciao"
6 Unreturned tennis serve
7 2006 Matt Damon spy film
8 Song sung on Sunday
9 Place with beakers and Bunsen burners
10 Measure of light's brightness
11 Electric guitar accessory
12 Drunkard
13 Jimmy (open)
21 Lecturer's implement with a light at the end
23 Is indebted to
26 Fills, as tile joints
28 Popular yoga pose . . . or a literal hint to the ends of 3-, 7-, 9- and 21-Down
29 The "U" in I.C.U.
30 Cribbage scorekeepers
32 Letter after sigma
34 Nap south of the border
39 Pampering places
40 Bus. concern
43 Persian Gulf country, for short
46 Actress Kendrick
51 What "woof" or "meow" may mean
52 Talked back to with 'tude
54 Best effort, informally
56 Colorful flower with a "face"
59 Pump or oxford
61 Smidgen
62 Helper during taxing times, for short?
63 Triceps location
64 Poke fun at
66 Marry

by Tracy Gray

ACROSS

1 Means of surveillance, for short
5 Co-conspirator with Brutus and Cassius
10 Banter jokingly
14 "I got it! I got it!"
15 What's standard, with "the"
16 ___ breve
17 Litter noises
18 Bottom coat?
20 Slammer
21 Word before and after "à"
22 Had people over for dinner, say
23 Habitat for a walrus
27 "___ seen worse"
28 Actor Dennis or Randy
29 Sports org. that plays in the winter
30 Co-workers of TV's Don Draper
32 Spending jags
34 Locale of the anvil and stirrup
36 Cincinnati sluggers
37 Its motto, translated from Latin, is "If you wish for peace, prepare for war"
40 Fill with cargo
43 A.M.A. members
44 Messed with, with "around"
48 Avoid the clutches of
50 Early nuclear org.
52 Esther of "Good Times"
53 TV show set in Westeros, for short
54 Drill bit alloy
57 Untouched, as an artifact
59 Slack-jawed emotion
60 Good name for a girl born on December 24?
61 1963 Bobby Vinton hit . . . or a hint to both halves of 18-, 23-, 37- and 54-Across
64 Surgeons' subj.
65 Focusing aid
66 Something to believe in
67 Ballet leap
68 Whence the Three Wise Men, with "the"
69 Defeated by a hair
70 Fired

DOWN

1 Pioneering personal computers
2 "Come on, things aren't so bad"
3 Limousine
4 Bygone kind of tape
5 Like the numbers 8, 27 and 64
6 How one's much-loved nephew might be treated
7 Periscope site
8 Low island
9 Leader of Athens?
10 Thriller set around Amity Island
11 Quaint
12 Like LPs and some dresses
13 Coagulates
19 Actress Chaplin of 53-Across
21 YouTube upload
24 Like wedding cakes, typically
25 Posh neighborhood of London or New York
26 Spirit
31 Problem in an old wooden building
33 Guitarist Barrett
35 British rule over India, once
38 Spirited steed
39 Part of a biblical citation
40 Unlike most physicians' handwriting, stereotypically
41 Home of Anne of Green Gables
42 Old Nissan autos
45 Something that may be used before a blessing
46 Put on a pedestal
47 Struck out
49 Outside: Prefix
51 A dependent one might start with "that"
55 Unit of measure with the same Latin origin as "inch"
56 Jacket material
58 Superlative ending with grass or glass
62 Reprimand to a dog
63 Big galoot
64 Best-selling Steely Dan album

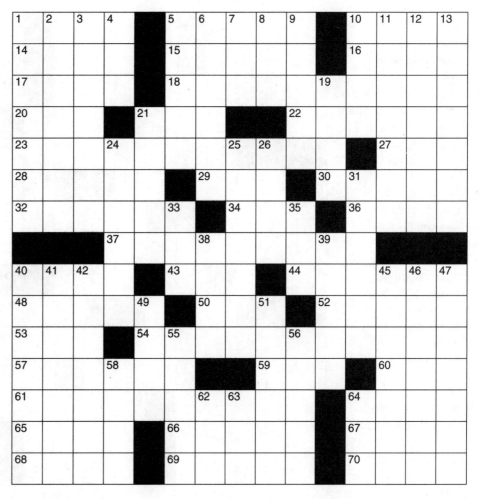

by Jon Olsen

ACROSS

1 Sharp's counterpart, in music
5 "Livin' la Vida ___"
9 Stories with many chapters
14 Like rain forest vegetation
15 "Ars Amatoria" poet
16 Story that lets you off the hook
17 Theatrical honor
19 Mountaineering spike
20 Person to exchange letters with overseas
21 Fortune 500 listings: Abbr.
23 Jane Austen novel
24 "Star Wars" role for Alec Guinness
27 Put into operation
30 They: Fr.
31 Zig or zag
32 Lauder with beauty products
35 Little extra attention, as from a repairer, for short
38 Where education is pursued doggedly?
42 "Mad ___" (Mel Gibson film)
43 "It's a ___ shame"
44 Approximately
45 "You stink!"
46 Sent out, as rays
49 Delivery people?
54 Foundry detritus
55 Environmental prefix
56 Inventor's quest
60 Chicken raised for cooking
62 "Hush, you!"
64 Big-time football venue
65 Honey-based drink
66 Start to deteriorate, as a cord
67 Put back to zero, say
68 A and Z, in the alphabet
69 Chop down

DOWN

1 Theatrical failure
2 Auto maintenance job, informally
3 X ___ xylophone
4 Where stray animals are taken
5 Darkish, as the interior of a restaurant
6 Sperm targets
7 Approximately
8 Supplemental item
9 Weaken
10 "Futurama" figures
11 U.S. base in 28-Down, informally
12 Detonation of 7/16/45
13 Egyptian peninsula
18 Rhyme scheme of Robert Frost's "Stopping by Woods on a Snowy Evening"
22 Irving Berlin's "Blue ___"
25 Teeny-___
26 Certain utility: Abbr.
27 Quark's place
28 Havana's home
29 Image in the "Jurassic Park" logo, informally
33 Biol., for one
34 Guiding principle
35 Legal wrong
36 Misplace
37 Lump of soil
39 Stylized "W" for Microsoft Word, e.g.
40 Wear away
41 Something extremely cool, paradoxically
45 Past
47 Two-wheelers
48 Baghdad's land
49 One of five for composer John Williams
50 Sound loudly, as a trumpet
51 Registers awe
52 "___, All Ye Faithful"
53 Singer/songwriter Leonard
57 Dublin's land
58 Actress Patricia of "Hud"
59 "Bye for now," in a text
61 Singer ___ King Cole
63 Deserving to get gonged

by Jeffrey Wechsler

ACROSS

1 Diana who led the Supremes
5 Masked man's sidekick on old TV
10 Assembled
13 Norwegian city with the Munch Museum
14 "Hey Diddle Diddle" runaway
15 Rich supply of ore
16 Safe for youngsters
18 One of five Greats
19 Ledecky who has been named World Swimmer of the Year five times
20 Bill killer's position
21 Cookout crashers
22 Bit of salt
24 Shankar with a sitar
26 Mum
29 Averts
33 Computer company with a Predator line
34 Soothing lotion ingredient
36 Valuable bar at Fort Knox
37 Actress Arthur with a Tony for "Mame"
38 See 23-Down
40 Kind of testing done at Ancestry.com
41 Rodeo rope
43 Acquires
44 "Turf" half of surf and turf
45 Outside surface
47 Deep-sea fishing nets
49 Yoked pair in a field
50 Profit
51 Flight amenity that costs extra
53 Backbone of a boat
56 Zesty chip dip
60 Savings plans for one's later years, in brief
61 Hit the jackpot
63 Old camera need
64 Idiotic
65 Oklahoma city named for an "Idylls of the King" woman

66 Class for U.S. citizen hopefuls, in brief
67 Disgustingly dirty
68 Pols like Pelosi

DOWN

1 Alternative to rap and R&B
2 Fed. monitor of workplace hazards
3 Narrow cut
4 More substantial
5 Small recipe amt.
6 Founder of Harpo Productions
7 Common lunchtime
8 Drinking spree
9 Ablaze
10 Droplets seen early in the day
11 Tend to some p's and q's, say
12 Golfer's bagful
15 Cause to expand, as bread
17 College V.I.P.
23 With 38-Across, like Romeo and Juliet . . . and like the shaded words?
25 Fervent
26 Expensive dark fur
27 Tool for a Himalayan climber
28 Lowest in importance
29 Baffling question
30 Musical pause
31 Based on major and minor scales
32 H.R.s and R.B.I.s

35 Bitten-into apple, for Apple
38 Apple throwaway
39 "Cómo ___ usted?"
42 Gender discrimination
44 Made do despite difficulties
46 Finishes, as a cartoon
48 Move up
50 Sparkle
51 Desdemona, to Othello
52 Flower named for a goddess
54 Sicilian tourist draw
55 Prohibition and Victorian periods
57 Solitary
58 Svelte
59 Throws into the mix
62 Critically important

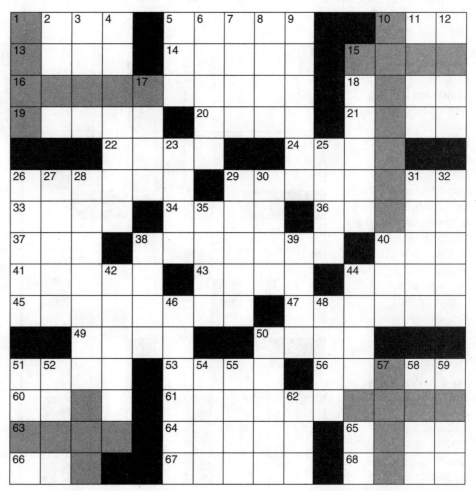

by Lynn Lempel

ACROSS

1 Greek philosopher who was a student of Socrates
6 Disparaging remark
10 Some bake sale groups, for short
14 ___ box (computer prompt)
15 With 52-Down, home of the Leaning Tower
16 French river to the English Channel
17 Parish leader
18 "Yeah, sure"
19 Fill to excess
20 Took in takeout, say
21 *Seesaw
24 What a spin doctor might be called on to take care of
26 Hair stiffener
27 Prepare to be published
28 Coin that's been legal tender since New Year's Day in 2002
30 *Bring forward for display
33 Island near Java
36 Bandmate of McCartney, Lennon and Harrison
38 Tech school on the Hudson, for short
39 Harbinger
40 Falafel sauce
42 Noun-forming suffix
43 Singer DiFranco
44 Birds symbolizing peace
45 Component of natural gas
47 *British hitmaker on Iggy Azalea's "Black Widow"
49 "It's c-c-c-cold!"
50 "Cubist" Rubik
51 Science class, for short
53 Mathematician once pictured on Swiss money
57 *1970 war film about the attack on Pearl Harbor
61 Genesis woman
62 Genesis man
63 Forum garment
64 "The Handmaid's Tale" author Margaret
66 ___ Field (home to the Mets)
67 Stuntman Knievel
68 Freshens, as a stamp pad
69 White Monopoly bills
70 Depend (on)
71 *Clarinetist Shaw . . . or, when said aloud, the only two consonants in the answers to the starred clues

DOWN

1 Michelangelo masterpiece
2 Like sneakers but not slippers
3 PC key
4 *"Sadly, you're right"
5 Fairy tale meanie
6 Desire to harm
7 Defame in print
8 Computer operator
9 *Vermin-hunting dog
10 Stickie
11 *Pasta-serving cafe
12 The "a" of a.m.
13 Palm reader, e.g.
14 Lacking brightness
22 Part of the psyche
23 Febreze target
25 Ivy League school in Philly
29 *Plumbing company whose jingle says "away go troubles down the drain"
30 Suede shade
31 Second word of fairy tales
32 Fork prong
33 Wild pig
34 Prefix with -potent or -present
35 *Say again
36 Pronoun for a ship
37 "___ the season to be jolly"
41 Actress Gardner
42 No ___ traffic
44 Word of warning
46 *Trick-or-___ (kid on Halloween)
48 One of the Three Musketeers
49 Halloween shout
51 Doughnut-shaped roll
52 See 15-Across
54 Téa of "Madam Secretary"
55 Bring to mind
56 Only M.L.B. team that Johnny Bench played for (1967–83)
57 Part of a Chipotle order
58 Chief Norse god
59 Wander
60 ___ avis
65 Jokester

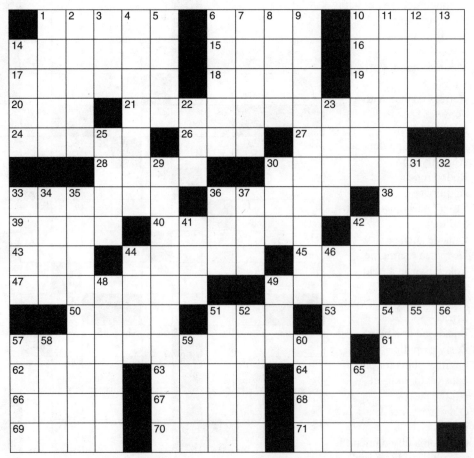

by Peter Gordon

ACROSS

1 School grp. that doesn't include children
4 Amazement
7 "You flatter me!"
13 Museum holdings
14 Disney collectibles
16 Coastal city SE of Roma
17 Souvenir from a concert tour
19 Intense rant
20 Lug
21 Cavalryman under Teddy Roosevelt during the Spanish-American War
23 March parade honoree, colloquially
25 At ___ (stationary)
26 Signal to start
27 Clear (of)
28 Concerns for a dermatologist, informally
32 Revolutionary War battle in Boston
36 Ingredient in jelly beans and M&M's
37 "The Road Not Taken" poet
38 Class for citizens-to-be, in brief
39 Part of a squirrel's stash
41 Prez who established Social Security
42 Leafy course
44 Totals
46 "___ Misérables"
47 It's mostly nitrogen
48 Without ice, at a bar
50 Washington peak named after the second U.S. president
54 Hot order with marshmallows
58 "Ah, gotcha"
59 Late Swedish electronic musician with the 2013 hit "Wake Me Up"
60 Sports item that can be found at the starts of 17-, 21-, 32-, 42- and 54-Across
62 Entertain, as with stories
63 Monogram component: Abbr.
64 Suffix with star- or tsar-
65 Spring celebration
66 Jiffy
67 Santa ___, Calif.

DOWN

1 Network in a park
2 Real pleasure
3 Bought completely
4 German cry
5 More unusual
6 "The Jetsons" son
7 Hush-hush
8 Split ___ (nitpick)
9 Small squirt, as of perfume
10 Relative of a frog
11 Ye ___ Shoppe
12 Waterfront projection
15 Disco ___ (character on "The Simpsons")
18 Semiformal pants
22 Feature on the front of a car
24 Song that can't be sung alone
27 Goes up
29 Worshiped one
30 Host Banks of "America's Next Top Model"
31 Mail
32 Closest of pals, informally
33 Language of Pakistan
34 It's to be expected
35 Regarding this point
39 Home of the Himalayas
40 Rapper with the 2018 #1 album "Invasion of Privacy"
42 Montana's ___ National Park
43 Actress Portman
45 Ski resort vehicle
49 Modern I.R.S. submission option
50 Deimos and Phobos, for Mars
51 Carne ___ (burrito filling)
52 Cantaloupe or honeydew
53 Site of a 1965 civil rights march
54 Part of T.L.C.
55 Iris's place in the eye
56 In a ___ eye
57 Some special FX
61 U.S. consumer watchdog, for short

by Evan Kalish

ACROSS

1 Groups of actors in plays
6 Protective wear for lobster eaters
10 Summa cum ___
15 Outdo
16 Soothing ointment ingredient
17 Neighbor of Hertfordshire
18 Start of a nursery rhyme on a farm
21 Outer part of a crater
22 Feel sorry about
23 Indent key on a keyboard
24 Sport with kicking and boxing, for short
25 Claim without evidence
27 Superlatively kind
29 Bow-tie-wearing cub in Jellystone Park
34 "You're telling me!"
37 Stitch's human pal, in film
38 Singer Minaj
42 Cookie that's 29% cream
43 Pass along
45 ___ fides
46 Clock sound
47 Grow fond of
48 Skyline-obscuring pollution
49 Bring up in a Q. and A.
50 Spanish for "south"
51 Falsehood
53 Palindromic kitchen brand
54 1963 musical that was Dick Van Dyke's film debut
59 What dogs do when they're hungry
61 Former attorney general Holder
62 Photo-sharing app, colloquially
65 Place for driving lessons (the golf kind)
66 The "sun" in sunny-side-up eggs
67 N.B.A. phenom Jayson
68 Didn't venture out for dinner
69 Competitive advantage
70 Put into law
71 Actress Thompson of "Sorry to Bother You"
72 Bucks and does
73 Students sit at them

DOWN

1 Fearsome snake
2 Nin of erotica
3 Bursting at the ___
4 Bathroom fixture
5 Bird that "His eye is on," in a hymn
6 Term of endearment
7 Sick
8 Snaky scarf
9 Result of a religious schism
10 The "L" of L.G.B.T.Q.
11 Volcanic detritus
12 "I'm at your disposal"
13 Judges to be
14 Person living abroad, informally
19 Modern prefix with -correct
20 "Citizen ___"
26 Virtual volume
28 Places infants sleep
30 Having trouble seeing in the morning, perhaps
31 Sound from a piggery
32 Adjective after "Ye" in many a pub's name
33 Suck-up
34 Littlest bit
35 ___ Kringle (Santa Claus)
36 Pork dish of Southern cuisine
39 "How goes it?," in Spanish
40 Fort ___, home of the U.S. Bullion Depository
41 "Othello" villain
43 What's left of a ticket after it's been used
44 Pinot ___
50 One-named queen of Tejano music
52 Made revisions to
55 Some spiritual advisers
56 Gradually disappear, as support
57 Nonsense
58 Nonsensical
59 "Tarnation!"
60 Apt rhyme for "evaluate"
63 Hide, as shirttails, with "in"
64 Quantities: Abbr.

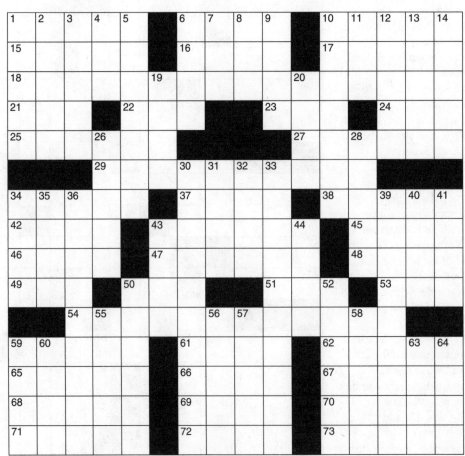

by Erik Agard

ACROSS

1 Head covering similar to a wave cap
6 Hit 2003–07 teen drama on Fox
11 One of the Peróns
14 Fragrance
15 Gardening brand
16 French word on both sides of "à"
17 *Actress McCarthy is wandering*
20 Writer after whom the Edgar Award is named
21 Pal
22 Comfortable with considering
23 History-making events
26 Before a sitting judge
27 Item that may say "his" or "hers"
30 Classic barbecue fare
32 Approx.
33 *Designer McCartney is prepared*
37 Campaign undertaking
38 Helpful
39 ___ Reader (digital digest)
42 *Supermodel Hutton is incredible*
45 Profs' support, for short
47 "What's in a ___?" (line from Juliet)
48 Tennis point just before a win, maybe
49 Hirer's communication
51 Flower parts
54 Contents of hangars
56 Web address ending
57 Yellowfin tuna
60 *Singer Love is erudite*
64 "I'm shocked!"
65 Pin point?
66 ___ Park, N.J.
67 Prefix with -metric or -magnetic
68 Likely to zone out
69 The O.W.L. and N.E.W.T. at Hogwarts

DOWN

1 Clammy
2 Most common commercial name in New York Times crosswords
3 Focus of a casting director
4 Self-reflective question
5 Monthly utility payment
6 "Horned" creatures
7 "48 ___" (1982 film)
8 Subj. of a traveler's text, maybe
9 Home to Xenia and Zanesville, the most populous U.S. cities starting with "X" and "Z"
10 Hiker's aid
11 Still preferable
12 Mountaintop views
13 Put into different classes
18 Direction opposite norte
19 Authorize to
23 Guy
24 One at a new job
25 Places to put potted plants
27 Medicinal amt.
28 Speaker of a Siouan language
29 Competitor of Chase and Citibank
31 Chicken cordon ___
34 Magnetic quality
35 Things florists cut
36 What pounds might be converted to
40 Insurrectionist Turner
41 Ron of "Tarzan"
43 Opposite of "winds up"
44 Sports bar showing on many a Sunday afternoon
45 Head honcho
46 Burning
50 Supersize: Abbr.
52 "___ want a cracker?"
53 "___ you mad?"
55 [Just like *that*]
57 Tolstoy's "___ Karenina"
58 Steering position
59 Pair of promises
61 Pollution watchdog, for short
62 Financial watchdog, for short
63 "Toy Story" dinosaur

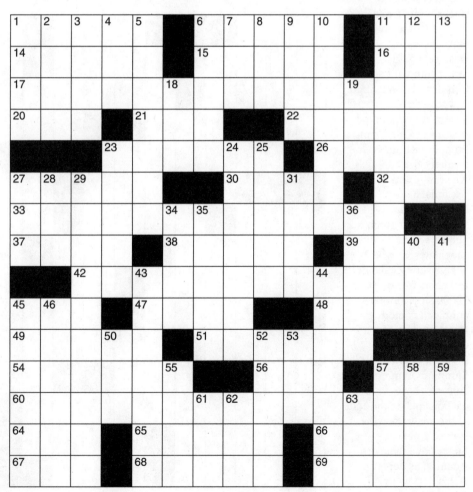

by Daniel Raymon

ACROSS

1 Place to get a mud bath
4 "Got it now!"
7 Airport about 13 miles from the Loop
12 Perfect scores for divers
14 "Good heavens!"
15 Polite palindromic term of address
16 Spice holder
17 *Arthur Carlson portrayer on "WKRP in Cincinnati"
19 Ancient Chinese book of divination
21 Prefix with -angle or -cycle
22 Extremely fun, as a party
23 *Job for a model
26 Website for some custom-designed jewelry
27 Use steel wool on
28 Hacks with an axe
30 Pro-___ (some golf tourneys)
33 Dead set against
34 Street sign with an arrow
37 Country between Togo and Nigeria
39 Sheepskin boot brand
41 Assault or kidnapping
42 Producer Rhimes who created "Grey's Anatomy" and "Scandal"
44 Coupe or sedan
46 National park freebie
47 Showers with flowers and chocolates, maybe
48 Native New Zealander
50 Inflatable transport
52 *2000 stop-motion animated comedy hit
57 Deep anger
58 Colorful pond fish
59 Bust out of jail
60 Summer Olympics contest whose participants do the ends of the answers to the starred clues
64 Sugar bowl invaders
65 Acquire, as debts
66 Helps
67 Traditional wearer of plaid

68 Fitness program popularized in the 1990s
69 Bit of clothing often worn with shorts
70 DeskJet printers and others

DOWN

1 Peel off
2 Popular cobbler fruit
3 Dried chili in Mexican food
4 In the past
5 Belly laugh syllable
6 Toss in
7 Hyatt alternative
8 Mecca pilgrimage
9 *Late-night Cartoon Network programming block
10 Harold who directed "Caddyshack"
11 Opposite of full
13 Comic sketches
14 Goads
18 Company that makes Bug B Gon
20 "Sorry, pal"
24 Member of the largest Rwandan ethnic group
25 A folder is needed for this
26 Still-life vessel
29 Stage comebacks?
30 Muscles strengthened by belly dancing, for short
31 "I'm not impressed"
32 *Winter barrier
35 Org. for physicians
36 "Uh-huh"
38 How some exciting N.B.A. games are won
40 Avocado dip, informally
43 Noted British racecourse
45 Substitutes for coins
49 Ancient Peruvians
50 Hit the ball out of the park
51 Staples Center, for one
53 Component of a drum kit
54 Cowhands' home
55 "Give me five!"
56 Tree houses
58 Corn syrup brand
61 Soaking spot
62 Make up a cover story, say
63 Laudatory poem

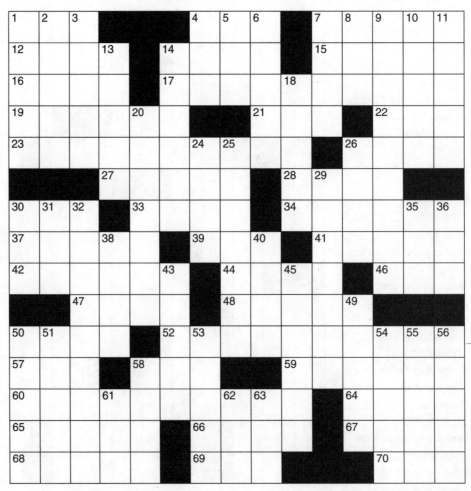

by Zhouqin Burnikel

ACROSS

1 "Sounds exciting," sarcastically
6 First verb in the Lord's Prayer
9 Trim
13 Pages (through)
14 Commercial follower of "-o-"
16 Super-duper
17 Employer of nurse sharks?
19 Name spelled out in a Kinks hit
20 Laudatory lines
21 ___ Claire, Wis.
22 Delicacy in a tiny spoon
24 Fig. in the form XXX-XX-XXXX
25 "It's green and slimy" and "It tastes like the ocean"?
27 Climate agreement city
29 Site of the fall of man
30 Late Saudi journalist Khashoggi
31 "With this ring, I ___ wed"
33 Crushing setback
37 Seal the deal
38 Big scare of a couple of decades ago . . . or a phonetic hint to this puzzle's theme
39 Sign away
40 Own (up)
41 "___ mío!" (Spanish cry)
42 Storied toymakers
43 Deadlocked
45 Less colorful
46 Nerd's goal on a dating app?
51 Yodeler's peak
53 Ciaos at luaus
54 Brouhaha
55 Fruit in some gin
56 Animal relative of a hinny
57 Pointy bill or tail feathers?
60 Dr. ___, film enemy of Austin Powers
61 Bring up . . . or something that might be brought up
62 Unidentified person, in slang
63 Climax in "Hamilton"
64 Dunderhead
65 Having a body mass index over 30, medically

DOWN

1 Actor Edward James ___
2 State of mind
3 Jokey parts of prank calls, often
4 Sci-fi travelers, for short
5 Presidential advisory grp.
6 Times New Roman alternative
7 Accumulated, as expenses
8 "Jeez, I did NOT need to know that!"
9 Fictional sport whose rules are invented during play
10 Sarge's superior
11 Something a bride or groom might acquire
12 Fruit from an orchard
15 Give in (to)
18 Levi's alternatives
23 One of 17 Monopoly properties: Abbr.
25 Traditional wedding wear, for some
26 Really needs a bath, say
28 Complained angrily and loudly
30 What "choosy moms choose," in ads
31 Knot-___ (scout's skill)
32 Necessity for life, chemically speaking
34 Be a hermit, say
35 Supreme leaders
36 Five-time Pro Bowl receiver Welker
39 Diluted
41 Not as bright
44 Itinerary word
45 T.A.'s overseer
46 Having renown
47 Message on a candy heart
48 "Cross my heart!"
49 Pops, to tots
50 Things that might make one cry "Foul!"?
52 Black tea variety
55 Knife
58 Promoter of Teacher Appreciation Week: Abbr.
59 Sellout show inits.

by Christina Iverson and Jeff Chen

ACROSS

1 Sight on a dollar bill
5 Offerings at many coffeehouses
11 Rent
14 Ballet movement
15 Result
16 "For a quart of __ is a dish for a king": Shak.
17 Nyctophobic
19 1990 Sam Raimi superhero film
20 Zoophilist's org.
21 Impermanent fixes
23 1967 thriller for which Audrey Hepburn received an Oscar nomination
26 Surprise winner
27 "A simple yes __ will suffice"
28 Unit in a shopping cart
30 R.M.N. or L.B.J.
31 Battle stat
32 Crowning point
34 Former Mideast alliance, for short
36 Not know something others know
38 Cocktail made with ginger beer
42 Independence in Washington, e.g.: Abbr.
43 A-O.K.
44 Fair-hiring inits.
45 Container in a tasting room
48 National park through which the Virgin River runs
50 Bio lab medium
51 Post-sunset
53 Sweet that lacks milk
56 Uses as partial payment
58 Territory east of Ukraine on a Risk board
59 Little peeve
60 Where Darth Vader gets his strength . . . or what eight answers in this puzzle share
64 Top gun
65 Suck in again, scientifically
66 Didn't doubt a bit
67 Prospector's accessory
68 Many John Wayne films, informally
69 "The Night of the Hunter" screenwriter James

DOWN

1 Eponymous Belgian town
2 Famously nonunionized worker
3 Tel Aviv-to-Cairo carrier
4 Reach quickly, as a conclusion
5 Wheels for four
6 Cash flow tracker, for short
7 Like much freelance work
8 Stinging plant
9 Unoriginal voice
10 N.B.A. All-Star Curry
11 Hedy of old Hollywood
12 Pass
13 Gets ready for a punch, say
18 Critical hosp. area
22 Lose amateur status
23 Baby's first home
24 Grammy winner India.__
25 "Nature's great healer," per Seneca
29 Perfume ingredient
32 Transport to remote areas, briefly
33 Bistro sign word
35 Ended a fast
37 Plain for all to see
38 Erstwhile iPod type
39 Entertaining lavishly
40 Spam, for one
41 Old days
43 Guy in a suit
45 Little shut-eye
46 "I bless the rains down in __" (lyric from a 1983 #1 hit)
47 College of __ Island (CUNY school)
49 Most bone-chilling
50 #49
52 Once more in vogue
54 Checks
55 Planet of 1970s–'80s TV
57 Kind of butter used in cosmetics
61 Train schedule abbr.
62 Poor mark
63 Animal that sounds like you?

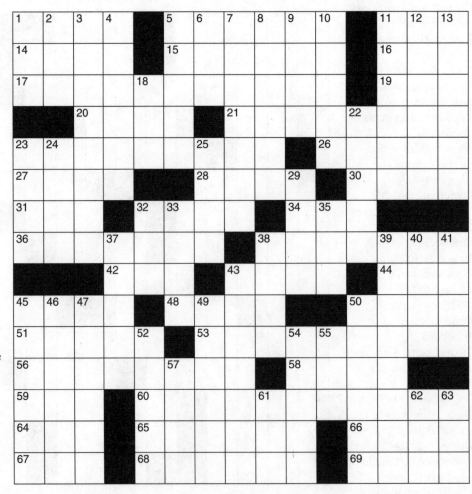

by Ed Sessa

ACROSS

1 Like: Suffix
4 Eponymous character of Disneyland's "Wild Ride"
10 Tangy Greek cheese
14 Usual victim of Bart's prank calls
15 Schwartz who spent Tuesdays with Mitch Albom
16 Robert Bolt's "___ for All Seasons"
17 Early warnings of danger
19 "Miami ___"
20 Economic and legislative capital of Sri Lanka
21 Melancholy
23 Bronze ___
24 English pop diva
26 Radiant display also called the Northern Lights
32 Glee club member
33 "Interstellar" actor Damon
34 Longer forearm bone
35 Biological messenger molecule
36 Extra-small amount, as of lotion
38 "Return from full-screen mode" key
40 "Thy sharp teeth . . ." referent
41 Yardstick part
43 Egypt : pound :: Iran : ___
45 Sacred lamb, from the Latin
47 Now-discontinued Chili's appetizer with a rhyming name
50 Oscar-winning composer Jule
51 Workplace of Jack Bauer on "24," for short
52 "I could go on and on . . ."
55 Tuna alternative
59 Zany anecdote
60 What's an uncommon blood type . . . or a hint to this puzzle's theme
63 Higher-up
64 "Old Man and the Sea" fish

65 Good friend of Stimpy
66 "I'm on your ___!"
67 Flashy one, for short?
68 Tribe of Israel

DOWN

1 Egg-shaped computer, once
2 Darth Vader's son-in-law Han ___
3 Mend
4 Echoic soup slogan
5 Heist figure
6 iPhone alternative, once
7 Southeast Division N.B.A. team, on scoreboards
8 Lack one's usual vitality, maybe
9 Orange sherbet and others

10 "Very Bad Things" and "Swingers" actor Jon
11 Eastern prince
12 Order at Chipotle
13 Freshly
18 Crowd noises
22 "Rah!" at a bullfight
24 Org. for lawyers
25 "Spill the tea!"
26 Soft drink brand
27 Water bill listing
28 One might sleep on it
29 Ranchero's plain
30 Discussion-recapping phrase
31 Suckers or syrups
32 Hollywood-area attraction La ___ Tar Pits
37 End point of a military march

39 Rookie move?
42 Encapsulation
44 Sixteenth president's nickname
46 Outerwear?
48 New York Giants giant Mel
49 Elected congress-woman of 2018, Alexandria ___-Cortez
52 "For Your ___ Only"
53 One alternative to Uber
54 Rep
55 Young otter's home
56 Owl or osprey
57 Unit of the eye containing the iris
58 Dollywood's locale: Abbr.
61 A word from Scrooge
62 Debate stance

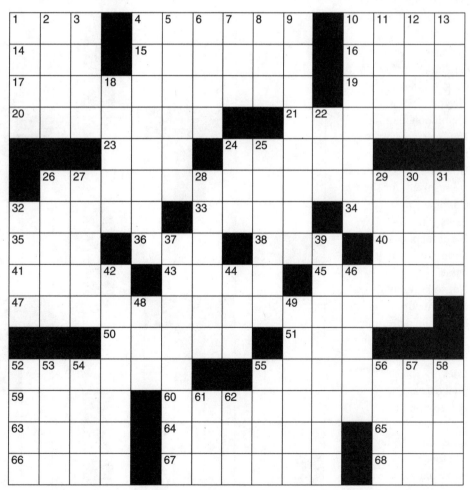

by Amanda Yesnowitz and Joon Pahk

ACROSS

1 I.T. support desk service
7 "Down goes Frazier!" caller
13 Heated house for chicks
14 Like Looney Tunes, theatrically
16 Jane Eyre or Wonder Woman
17 Spicy
18 More than some
19 Characteristic
21 Cook and Curry
22 Spanish boy's name related to the sixth month of the year
24 Baby in a rare birth
26 They leave in the spring
27 Clarifying phrase
28 Harbor sight
29 Letter in the last third of the NATO alphabet
30 Couches
32 Capital of the U.S. for 54 days in 1784
34 Plus
35 Meditation mantras
36 Not interpret correctly
40 Indonesian money
44 How tied N.F.L. games are resolved, for short
45 Common sport fish
47 Pants, slangily
48 Bit of foppish attire
50 Drum kit, by another name
52 Not so brave and determined
53 Brave and determined
54 "You'll never beat my score!"
55 Lock
56 Shakespeare contemporary
58 Comedian Jimmy
60 Longtime "Today" forecaster
61 Amusing incongruities
62 Friendless
63 Make like

DOWN

1 When an opera's musical themes may be established
2 Bit of headwear that often has jewels
3 Cry at night
4 Mince words?
5 Annual winter/spring observance
6 Sets up ahead of time, in jargon
7 What some say God is to them
8 "Leave this to me"
9 Religious group
10 Part of the conjugation of the Latin "esse"
11 Permissive
12 Captive's plea
13 Spicy Indian fritters
15 Textbook unit
20 P.D. alert
23 "For one thing . . ."
24 "Indeed!," colloquially
25 Remove forcefully
26 Go from one place to another
31 Principle
33 Lure
36 Oppressive atmosphere
37 Get with the program?
38 Texas city on the Mexican border
39 Window dressing
40 "Midnight's Children" novelist, 1981
41 First country to establish Christianity as its state religion
42 Sailor vis-à-vis a sail
43 Lathers up
46 Go (for)
49 French port on the Mediterranean
50 Tool with a pointed blade
51 Large beverage dispenser
52 Capital of Albania
57 Drag
59 Stepped

by Alex Eaton-Salners

ACROSS

1 Mary Stuart, for one
5 Taiwan-based computer giant
9 Secretly watched
14 Tea made with milk, sugar and cardamom
15 Rob of "Parks and Recreation"
16 Attacked with a spray
17 Engaged in foul play
20 Burnt __ (old Crayola color)
21 Some batteries
22 One engaged in friendly contention
29 Lith., e.g., once
30 Hands (out)
31 2020, por ejemplo
32 "__ che macchiavi quell'anima" (aria opener)
34 Invalidate
36 "Oh, now they're really going to fight!"
41 Puts up on a gallery wall
42 Colorful spring flower
43 A.B.A. member: Abbr.
44 Stand in a mall
46 HBO competitor
49 Cry "Uncle!"
54 Veg out
55 __ Gay (historic plane)
56 Hold back
62 Elude
63 Gangster
64 Turnabouts, informally
65 Evasive
66 Actor Rogen
67 Crafty website

DOWN

1 Straight downhill ski run
2 Some early "astronauts"
3 Granola treat
4 River of Tuscany
5 Nothing but
6 Corp. manager
7 "Oh, gross!"
8 Do over for radio, say
9 __ campaign
10 Colt 45 brewer
11 Knock off
12 What has a long history in ichthyology?
13 E.P.A.-banned pesticide
18 Slip up
19 Nine-time P.G.A. Tour winner Jay
23 Individual: Prefix
24 Timeout alternative
25 Receptacle for one doing decoupage
26 Smaller than micro-
27 Ample, informally
28 Deeply massage
32 Meringue ingredient
33 "Kidnapped" author's monogram
34 "__ gratia artis"
35 Napoleon's marshal
36 "Take __!"
37 Possesses, biblically
38 __'acte
39 Pageant wear
40 Tennis great Huber
44 Drying oven
45 Coves
46 Like a really good game for a pitcher, say
47 Brawls
48 Stylish and sophisticated
50 Skateboarding jump
51 Forested
52 Full complement of limbs on a squid
53 Exactly as scheduled
56 Lead-in to Man or 12
57 School founded by Thos. Jefferson
58 Make a record of
59 Pronoun that can be spelled with a slash between the first and second letters
60 Wager
61 "Yuck!"

by Mary Lou Guizzo

ACROSS

1 White pizza topping
5 Green bits of ornamentation
11 Masala ___ (hot beverage)
15 Bestower of the Movies for Grownups Awards
16 Keep the beat, in a way
17 Parts of a nuclear reactor
18 Where Miners have majors
19 Type of fluffy wool
20 ___ surgeon
21 Word following sing or play
23 Furrowed feature
25 Wait on
26 Tribal leaders
27 Language that's the source of "gesundheit"
32 Uber alternative?
35 Pint-size
36 ___ Day and the Knights ("Animal House" group)
40 Suits
42 "___ it!" ("Hush!")
43 Place for a bench
44 Ancient name for Ceylon
45 Terse rebukes
46 Invite to the roof, say
47 Like a desk that's a sign of genius, it's said
49 Gobbledygook, metaphorically
50 Flight schedule abbr.
51 The mister, affectionately
56 N.L. East city, on scoreboards
58 Lithuanian, e.g.
60 In the worst way
61 Neighbor of an Arkansawyer
62 It has cork and a bell
63 1950s–'70s football star nicknamed "The Golden Arm"
64 Part of a pot
65 Bra brand
66 Stop waffling

67 Fight protractedly
68 E, F and G, but not H
69 Opposite of the point?
70 Collectors' goals

DOWN

1 Animals, collectively
2 Face-plant, say
3 Ice cream cone, e.g.
4 Breakfast cereal in a green box
5 Routine activity?
6 Beer ___
7 On the ___ (frequently, in slang)
8 Skater Midori
9 Attire
10 "I don't want to hear it"
11 Sounds made by fans
12 Lena of "Cabin in the Sky"
13 Firefighter Red
14 Lands in the sea
22 Hawaiian fish with a palindromic name
24 Ending with pay
28 Squiggle on a musical score
29 Ends up with
30 Sci-fi forest dweller
31 Trees with red berrylike fruit
32 Funnyman Brooks
33 Piece of furniture often covered with crinkly paper
34 Study of rocks
37 What five answers in this puzzle do phonetically, in defiance of their clues?

38 Language of the Canadian Arctic
39 Conciliatory gesture
41 Window frame
43 Trim
48 "Sup, bro!"
49 Yellowstone attraction
50 Work on a tablet
52 Bay Area athlete, for short
53 Kane of "All My Children"
54 Sightings in the Himalayas
55 Oar
57 English city where the Who once recorded a top 5 live album
59 11-Across and others
61 Bumbling bunch

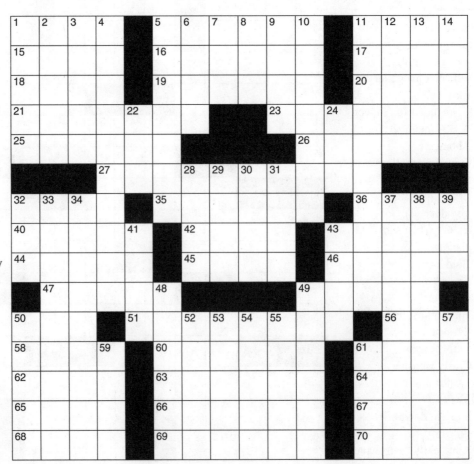

by Erik Agard and Jeff Chen

ACROSS

1 Kind of wine drinker who might remark "I'm getting hints of unripened banana"
5 Tears
9 Tore
14 Biblical shepherd
15 Lovefest, literally
16 Send to cloud nine
17 Like calypso music
19 Atoll material
20 It's a gas
21 Porcelain
23 SS __, onetime flagship of the White Star Line
27 Philly Ivy
29 Actress Meriwether
30 Kind of salad with tomatoes, eggs, olives and anchovies
32 It's often left on the table
34 Second Monopoly avenue
36 "Grody!"
37 Put on
38 Actress Graff of "Mr. Belvedere"
39 Bearded beast
40 Stain
41 Having everything in its proper place
42 Language akin to Thai
43 Spanish queens
44 Hosp. locales
45 Prince of Narnia
47 Art nouveau?
48 Monsieur, across the Pyrenees
50 Criticizes pettily
52 Part of a crystal radio kit
54 Give off
55 Hugo __, longtime Supreme Court justice
57 Result of connecting the circled letters in a certain way, in a punny manner of speaking
62 Woodworker's shaper
63 Halley's comet, to William the Conqueror

64 Poet __ St. Vincent Millay
65 Suit material for Mr. Toad
66 Class
67 Berth place

DOWN

1 Egg pouch
2 Hornets are in it, in brief
3 Anthem contraction
4 Cousins of crepes
5 Stiff and mechanical
6 Promoting peace
7 __ Tour
8 Adjust to match, informally
9 Contents of many an index card
10 Like soliloquy deliverers, typically
11 Moving targets for waves
12 Third Greek vowel
13 Dover's home: Abbr.
18 __ Babies (bygone fad)
22 Ear covering
23 Moby Dick, for one
24 Some casino personnel
25 Launch time
26 Arcade fixtures
28 Horseshoe Falls setting
31 Hosp. locale
33 Radio shortcut
35 Gunpowder alternative, for short
37 Super Mario Galaxy console
39 Terrific time, in slang
40 Spare part, perhaps
42 Rendered pork fat
43 Clothing
45 Altered dishonestly
46 "The nerve!"
49 Nook
51 And the following: Abbr.
53 Those, in Segovia
55 Diner order that often comes with a toothpick
56 Bar code?
58 Pop subgenre
59 Web address ender
60 Santa __ winds
61 Perhaps

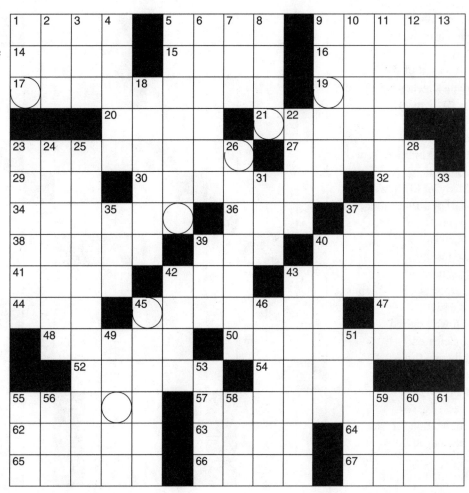

by Alex Eaton-Salners

ACROSS

1 Concerning vision
7 Info for a car service pickup, in brief
10 Drain
13 Estado south of Arizona
14 Glamping site, maybe
16 Madagascar, par exemple
17 It's needed for a push-up, informally
18 So
19 JFK alternative
20 Proudly dresses like Bill Nye or Pee-wee Herman?
23 Like some doors
24 Pivot point
25 Silo filler, for short
27 Bellyache
28 Roughage source
29 What you feel "when the moon hits your eye like a big pizza pie"
30 Layer
31 Mideast diplomat's request, when itching to be challenged?
33 Genesis craft
34 Inc., abroad
35 Premier internet connection?
41 Many an I.R.S. worker
44 Half of a 1960s folk-rock group
45 ___ avis
46 Bogus
47 Fast pace
48 European Union member, to natives
49 Ali who retired undefeated
50 Liberate Louis XIV's palace?
53 Pan Am rival
54 Fries, e.g.
55 Foundation for a home on a bayou
56 Have
57 Boggle the mind
58 Locale for Ernst and Young

59 Vote heard on the floor . . . and at the end of 20-, 31-, 35- and 50-Across?
60 Short albums, for short
61 Some "Toy Story"-themed toys, informally

DOWN

1 Source of material for a feather duster
2 Astronomical rings
3 Start-up worth a billion dollars, in a modern coinage
4 What brakes shouldn't do
5 "Give it ___"
6 Mesmerized
7 It may involve dilation
8 Wind power generator
9 Odysseus' faithful dog
10 Element of some chips
11 Something with an "x" factor?
12 What a shooter may shoot
15 Pull
21 Perniciousness
22 Retiring
26 Soong ___-ling, Madame Chiang Kai-shek
28 Anti-apartheid activist Steve
29 Wine center near Turin
31 Large: Fr.
32 Lead-in for Romeo
33 Wide open
35 Premium network
36 How you might meet someone
37 Land on the Persian Gulf
38 Desiccated
39 Overpopulated, mazy districts
40 Angers
41 "Simmer down!"
42 Something for an artist to have on hand
43 Piles up
46 Like tears
48 Online party request
49 Engine capacity unit
51 Powerful Scrabble tile
52 Second person?: Abbr.
53 Word with garden or party

by Barbara Lin

ACROSS

1 Texting pal, maybe
4 Tank top?
10 Risky thing to go out on
14 QB Manning
15 Lofty ambitions
16 Single's bars?
17 Want an actress from "Soul Food"?
19 The buck stops here
20 Creepazoid's gaze
21 Stripped (of)
22 Hat for a chef
23 Want an actor from "Wonder Woman"?
27 Cobbler's supply
28 Vow to get even?
29 Pennsylvania N.L. team, familiarly
30 Summer hangout
32 Take rudely
36 Want an actress from "Mad Men"?
39 They're often lit
40 Company whose bathroom sinks are named for Swedish bodies of water
41 Female compadre
42 Words of honor
43 Playground rebuttal
44 Want an actor from "Rogue One"?
49 Deck divided into the Major and Minor Arcana
50 Org. seeking clean skies
51 By the dawn's early light?
54 Home of the first man to walk on the moon, the first American to orbit Earth and the first American woman to walk in space
55 Want an actor from "Here Come the Girls"?
58 Just pretend
59 Robotic supervillain in the first "Avengers" sequel

60 Bad marks
61 Colorful neckwear
62 Attempts it
63 Part of a tavern

DOWN

1 Drooping flower feature
2 Sheet of ice
3 Common kind of pen for illustrators
4 Many an animated meme
5 Thinks the world of
6 Stroke on a letter
7 "Leave it to me!"
8 Comedian Wong
9 Ad by MADD, e.g.
10 Something most people don't go into more than once a year
11 Like many dinar spenders
12 Demerit
13 Lie in the sun
18 Car fronts
22 Turkey Day, e.g.: Abbr.
24 Suffix with good and willing
25 Spanish table wine
26 Mixer option
27 "Out, out!"
29 Nightcap go-with, in brief
30 Game of checkers?
31 Danish coins
32 More sticky and viscous
33 Increase the stakes
34 Mythical ship that gave its name to a constellation
35 Words before nose or hair
37 Generic dog name
38 Bread accompanying saag paneer
42 ___-forgotten
43 Addled
44 Happy cowpoke's cry
45 Cable news anchor Hill
46 Quiet corners
47 Univ. units
48 "La Traviata," for one
49 It's monumental
52 Place to veg
53 Medicinal qty.
55 "Who woulda thunk . . . ?"
56 Suffix with crap
57 John Winston ___ Lennon

by Jeremy Newton

ACROSS

1 High-profile pair
8 Means of access
15 Not so obvious
16 Classic Bob Marley song
17 Site of Saguaro National Park
18 It may bring one back to reality
19 Shoot the breeze
20 Insult, slangily
22 Dark period for poets
23 Not written
25 Stinging plant
27 It's often the fish in fish and chips
30 Country bordering Togo
32 "Seize the __!"
33 Chimney output
35 "Don't freak out"
37 Uno tripled
39 Dollar alternative
40 Participate in a common children's game, as illustrated in this puzzle
45 Home of the oldest university in the Americas (founded 1551)
46 Buffoon
47 One of a Disney septet
48 Eclipses, to some
50 GQ or T
52 Like much stand-up comedy
56 Lira : Turkey :: __ : Korea
57 Have high hopes
60 Starchy tuber
61 Practice before a game
62 Crazy popular, as a product
64 Ending to a White House address
65 Root that's roasted and eaten
69 Test the strength of, chemically
71 Rabble-rouse
72 Noted Roosevelt
73 Gift that comes in pieces
74 Classic Bill Withers song

DOWN

1 "Whatever pays the bills"
2 Arrow poison
3 "Star Wars" Jedi, familiarly
4 Competitor of Ruffles
5 Tread slowly
6 St. Petersburg was once named after him
7 Wiped
8 Disappear, as a trail
9 Adams with a camera
10 Snickers
11 Entrepreneur Musk
12 Bowl over
13 Michigan, in Chicago: Abbr.
14 "Get __ Ya-Ya's Out!"
21 Place to find corn dogs and funnel cakes
24 Tripoli native
26 Banks of "America's Next Top Model"
27 Quiet fishing spot
28 "The Grapes of Wrath" figure
29 Work station
31 Book after Ezra: Abbr.
34 Mr. Met, for one
36 "Gangsta's Paradise" rapper
38 Call off
40 Post-blizzard need
41 A long way to go?
42 Part of a church chorus
43 Like some cellars
44 Mob man
49 Spa amenities
51 Sister in a Brothers Grimm tale
53 1998 Olympics host city
54 Positive particle
55 Shout before entering a gunfight
58 Ill will
59 Official of ancient Rome
61 Grows fond of
63 Traditional remedy for a sore throat
65 Chum
66 One may be bronze or golden
67 Oil worker's locale
68 Term of endearment
70 Campaigned

by Emily Carroll

ACROSS

1 Holiday Inn alternative
7 Where you might go through withdrawal?
10 "Kapow!"
14 Left
15 Get major hang time, in snowboarding lingo
17 College in Claremont, Calif.
18 Al who famously drove a white Ford Bronco
19 Brief hookup
21 Fair-hiring inits.
22 No longer in bondage
24 One of the musicians on the 11th day of Christmas
28 Showtime alternative
31 Law partner?
33 "The Scream" and "The Kiss," for two
36 Vein contents
37 American __ (another name for the century plant)
38 Slayer of Tybalt
39 Ardent
40 Hoover, e.g., informally
41 Nonsense line sung by Frank Sinatra in "Strangers in the Night"
43 Infotainment show with an exclamation point in its name
46 Keg necessity
47 Cuts back on
48 What an ID may substitute for?
50 Put away
52 Some garage sale goods . . . or what the answers at 15-, 19-, 33-, 41- and 62-Across have done?
59 Archrivals of the Blue Devils
61 Refrigerator, old-style
62 Verses-vs.-verses competitor

63 Gay who wrote "Frank Sinatra Has a Cold"
64 Healthful leaf vegetable
65 "Straight Outta Compton" group
66 Totally embarrassed

DOWN

1 Tow job, maybe
2 Impulse transmitter
3 Performer without a speaking part
4 Loads
5 They're not just skeptics
6 "Curiosity killed the cat," e.g.
7 Bank no.
8 Ski resort NNE of Santa Fe
9 Daily run, for short?
10 Kvetch
11 Ceded control of
12 Bailed-out insurance giant of 2008
13 Better half, with "the"
16 Mild cigar
20 Hurry, with "it"
23 Mock
24 Something a seismograph detects
25 Honolulu's historic __ Palace
26 Police show, say
27 Just get (by)
29 Deadly African snake
30 Ivy, e.g.
32 Mulligans, e.g.
34 Chicago airport code
35 Death, in Deutschland
39 Legal org.
42 Like some illusions
44 Message written on a car window
45 Blind followers
49 Classic theater
51 "West Side Story" woman
53 Zoomed
54 Racketeer's org.?
55 Poker giveaway
56 Really, informally
57 Symbol of Aphrodite
58 Deleted
59 "Naughty!"
60 Calamares __ romana (seafood dish)

by Ross Trudeau

ACROSS

1 Employer of Detective Lindsay Boxer in a series of James Patterson novels
5 Fragrance since 1932
9 Aviary sound
12 Santa ___, Calif.
13 "Point taken," '60s-style
14 Title partner of Hobbs in a hit 2019 film
15 Reactions to social media posts?
18 Wizard
19 Animation stack
20 "I strongly advise against that"
21 Breeds of hunting dogs?
26 Not legally immune
27 "Head for the hills!"
28 Do a home ec assignment
29 E.N.T. case
30 Depart from a straight line
32 Techie or Trekkie
33 Boxing champs of the 1960s–'70s?
36 Tony Blair, for the U.K.
39 Apothecary's unit
40 "In Old Mexico" or "In Old Santa Fe"
44 It's trained in music school
45 An indispensable ingredient in the elixir of life, per Lao-tzu
46 Domination, in slang
47 Things that scouts earn badges for?
51 Target for holistic healing
52 Stand taken by a speaker?
53 First cellular co. to offer service nationwide
54 Cows' various glands?
58 Paris network
59 Davidson of "S.N.L."
60 Like pipes, again and again
61 Country where the cellphone was developed: Abbr.

62 Port SSE of the Suez Canal
63 Where a batter eventually goes to the plate?

DOWN

1 Partition
2 Fool's gold?
3 Prefix with caution or condition
4 Govt. lawyers
5 Fork foursome
6 Throw into confusion
7 Sequence of 0's and 1's
8 "What a stomach-churning thought!"
9 Takeout option
10 Where a yellow ribbon is tied in a 1973 #1 hit
11 Be attributable (to)

12 Preferred variety of stock
14 Part of a schedule
16 Unit of an estate
17 Heaven on earth
22 Letter-shaped construction piece
23 Airline of 61-Across
24 Part of a weightlifter's routine
25 Parrot's cry
30 Like many antebellum mansions
31 Down-to-earth fig.
32 Jumbo
34 "Here's an ___ . . ."
35 John Wayne Birthplace Museum locale
36 Cry upon opening a hospital bill, maybe

37 Heavens on earth
38 More self-satisfied
41 Portmanteau fruit
42 "Travel" for a bigheaded person
43 Second-grade offering?
45 Bygone monarch
46 Very
48 Very, abroad
49 Whom Italians call "il Sommo Poeta"
50 Expand
54 Ocean State sch.
55 Cruise ship amenity
56 Prefix with lateral or lingual
57 "I suppose that's kinda funny"

by Jake Halperin

ACROSS

1 Vegetable that can get slimy when overcooked
5 Exhausted, with "up"
8 Basketball shots from beyond the arc
14 Frozen treats
16 Locale in the Lord's Prayer
17 Optimistic maxim from Virgil
19 "You __ me one"
20 Chart topper
21 Fanfare
22 Jacob had 12 of them
23 Call to a toreador
24 Genre for Fall Out Boy
27 Reliable things, to Ben Franklin
30 Business index, with "the"
31 Chi-Town or Beantown team
32 Team sharing an arena with the Flyers, informally
33 Means of control
35 Bit of Halloween décor
37 About
38 Mint in a tin
40 Research facility
42 Extra periods, in brief
43 They make loud noises during showers
46 Nurse
47 Lead-in to a Pen used by nurses
48 Old Pontiacs
49 Pasta __ Norma
50 Actress Hagen
51 Car rental add-on
54 Overly optimistic 1910s appellation
59 "Let me try that again . . ."
60 Phrase on an egg carton
61 Pest
62 What each set of circled letters is, relative to the first word in its answer
63 Tumbler turners

DOWN

1 Where Edvard Munch's "The Scream" is displayed
2 Apt radio station to air "Wait Wait . . . Don't Tell Me!" (and it does!)
3 Ramble
4 Hole in one
5 Selects, as a successor
6 Circus
7 Name ender for a lawyer
8 Parents and grandparents, in teen lingo
9 Airtight
10 Scrape
11 "Me" in the Oscar-winning song "You Must Love Me"
12 Moray, e.g.
13 Where an artist works on a sketch, for short?
15 Lorena who was the #1 female golfer for 158 consecutive weeks
18 Atop
22 Affixed, like a patch
24 Puts forth, as effort
25 Paid soldiers, informally
26 Mount near Olympus
27 Throw a party grandly
28 Leaps on the ice
29 Starts to geometric proofs
30 Home to India's Red Fort and Lotus Temple
33 "Shoot!"
34 Indirect, as a glance
36 Fertilizer found in caves
39 Use up
41 Alternative to canned
44 Director Johnson
45 Dahl who wrote "James and the Giant Peach"
49 Not much
51 Stare intensely
52 Hunted animals
53 Entries on 1040s, for short
54 Come out ahead
55 Start of a Latin conjugation
56 Old auto with its founder's monogram
57 Follow relentlessly
58 Pad Thai pan

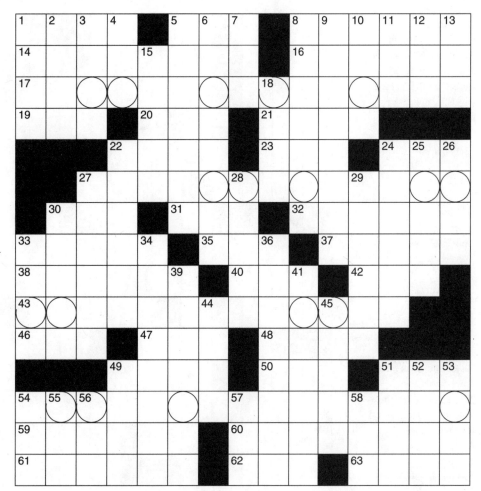

by Rich Proulx

ACROSS

1 Loops in, in a way
4 Marjoram, for one
8 Theater
13 Japanese affirmative
14 Home's edge
15 Relative of a jaguarundi
16 ___ chart
17 Times when teachers go to school but students don't
19 Had
21 Where the lord's work is done?
22 "___, do not think I flatter": Hamlet
23 Vessel for dipping at a dinner table
26 First: Lat.
28 Fair
29 "___ Nacht in Venedig" (operetta)
31 "___ that order!" ("Star Trek" command)
34 Onetime "Truth in engineering" sloganeer
35 "Haven't the foggiest!"
36 Reference that arranges words by concept rather than alphabetically
41 On the house
42 Text-displaying technology for Kindles and Nooks
43 Stows (away)
44 Something found on a neck
45 For the ages
49 Kind of yoga
51 Cousin of a sno-cone
53 Traveler's text message, maybe
55 Swear words
57 Admitted
58 Take a chance . . . or a hint to the letters in the shaded squares
62 Buses and taxis have them nowadays
63 "I Am ___" (2013 best-selling autobiography)
64 Pants, in slang
65 Brooklyn-based sch.
66 Saying
67 Confer, as power
68 People profiled in hagiographies: Abbr.

DOWN

1 Tap
2 Substance applied with a chamois
3 Enlist
4 Classic children's heroine once played in film by Shirley Temple
5 Suffix with Euclid
6 Campers
7 Complaint
8 Many an Arthur C. Clarke work
9 ___ Conference
10 Co-star of 2019's "Marriage Story"
11 Noted painter of scenes of the Napoleonic Wars
12 Place for unique gifts
15 Finished
18 As good as it's going to get?
20 Prefix with tourism
24 Children's author who wrote "There is no one alive who is you-er than you!"
25 Stash
27 German possessive
30 Less deserving of coal in one's stocking
32 ___ Lingus
33 "Woo-hoo!"
34 Pioneer in syllogistic logic
35 Like I Samuel among the books of the Old Testament
36 Some offensive linemen, for short
37 Ruth's was 2.28
38 Locale in Wagner's "Das Rheingold"
39 Singer James
40 Popular Father's Day gifts
44 Kismet
45 Palindromic response to "Madam, I'm Adam"
46 Sources of attar
47 "Go me!"
48 Count
50 "Fooled you!"
52 Dweller on the Bering Sea
53 Humorist Bombeck
54 Super Mario Bros. character with a mushroom head
56 Good resolution provider
59 Video game annoyance
60 Red state
61 Counterpart of sin

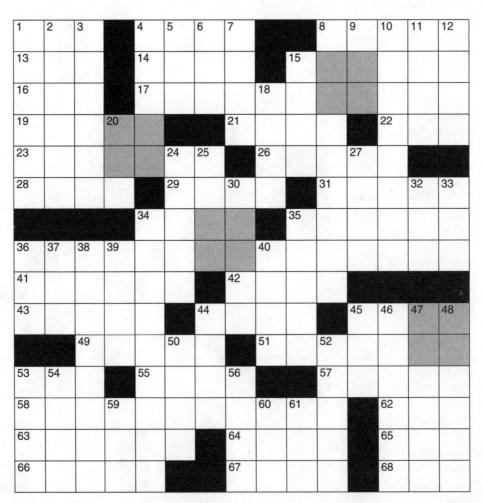

by Amanda Chung and Karl Ni

ACROSS

1 Drop a line?
5 Verb conjugated suis, es, est, etc.
9 Third-place finisher in 1992
14 Language group of southern Africa
15 Neighbor of Cambodia
16 Jelly option
17 Reduces to bits
18 One competing with Uber
20 Iron alloy that includes a bit of tungsten and chromium
22 People in go-karts
23 Mast
24 Picture from a parlor, informally
25 When repeated, a hip-hop dance
26 Add (up)
28 Volunteer for another tour
31 Not yet out of the running
33 Physics 101 subject
35 Tchotchkes
40 Fountain choices
42 Verbal tussle
43 Response to a computer crash
44 Incompetent figure of old slapstick
47 ___ pony
48 Tennis champ Mandlikova
49 Just gets (by)
51 Pony ___
52 T.S.A. requests
55 Grammy category
56 Something of little interest, a homeowner hopes
58 Himalayan language
60 Reject romantically . . . or a hint to the starts of the answers to 18- and 35-Across, phonetically
65 Show interest romantically . . . or a hint to the ends of the answers to 20- and 44-Across, phonetically

67 Lollipop-sucking TV detective
68 Wyatt and Warren of the Old West
69 Suffix with senior
70 Muse of love poetry
71 Something done up in an updo
72 Popular game that needs no equipment
73 Few and far between

DOWN

1 Not get above 60, say
2 Behind bars
3 Like a double black diamond trail
4 Hungarian horseman
5 Fashion magazine with more than 40 international editions
6 Actor Diggs
7 Not just "ha ha"
8 Winter zone in D.C.
9 What a curse might lead to
10 Former attorney general Holder
11 Baltimore N.F.L.'er
12 "Don Giovanni," e.g.
13 Lacking in detail
14 "Just a sec!," in a text
19 Chugged or sipped
21 Go the distance?
24 Popular video-sharing service
26 Project manager's assignment
27 Onetime buffalo-hunting tribe
29 Open, as a purse
30 Part of a church organ
32 Camper's cover
34 Pulp

36 Wedding reception staple
37 Embarrassing thing to have one's hand caught in
38 Member of the cabbage family
39 Kiss amorously
41 Like an overcast night
45 Studio sign
46 ___ walk
50 Harry Potter's Quidditch position
52 Alaska or Hawaii, often
53 ___ flask (thermos)
54 Steeple topper
57 Herbivore's diet
59 24-Down and others
60 Capt.'s inferiors
61 Legislature V.I.P.
62 Tiny, informally
63 It's unavoidable
64 Ring result, for short
66 :15 number

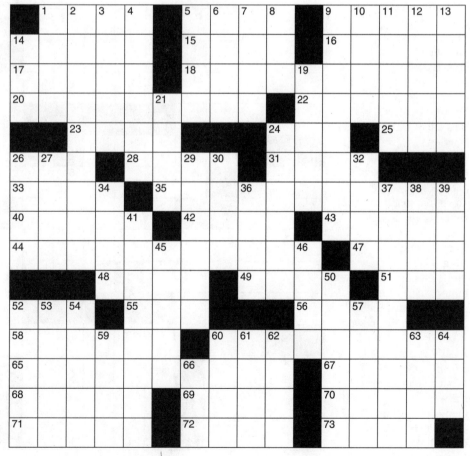

by Alex Eaton-Salners

ACROSS

1 Cantina
4 Two-time Time magazine Person of the Year
9 Say maybe, maybe
13 "The Americans" K.G.B. officer __ Burov
15 Robert Galbraith, to J. K. Rowling
16 Summer cooler
17 Awake during the wee hours, say
18 Gut feeling
19 "That was a close one!"
20 Journalism
23 Showed sudden interest
24 They close at 9 p.m. in New York
27 Smith of punk rock
31 "Excuse me!"
32 Nail site
35 Dismissive response to critics
37 Approximately, informally
38 French greeting
39 Nuke
40 Parking lot event
44 Nation's borders?
45 Basketball Hall-of-Famer Dantley
46 "Sweet and healing medicine of troubles," per Horace
48 Town that inspired "The House of the Seven Gables"
49 Goes (through) laboriously
53 Pirate plunder . . . or a hint to interpreting an appropriate number of squares in this puzzle
59 Adult
61 At dinner and then the cinema, say
62 What a volcano may leave
63 Opposite of drain
64 One may be held by candlelight
65 Hat worn by Charles de Gaulle

66 Go down
67 Chicago's __ Expressway
68 Taste

DOWN

1 Fits
2 __ dog
3 Subleased
4 Where the Ko'olau Range is located
5 Busy day, in retrospect
6 "__ that somethin'?"
7 Speed measure
8 He beat Connors in the Wimbledon final in 1975
9 Oscar-nominated actor with nearly synonymous first and last names
10 Spike Lee film set at a historically black college
11 Notch shape
12 Support for a religious group?
14 Flub
21 Hawaiian food fish
22 Cross
25 Actress Lindsay of "Mean Girls"
26 Is nosy
28 "We can't joke about that yet?"
29 Golfer's obstacle
30 Nation of __
31 Actress Annie of "Young Sheldon"
32 Pockets of the Middle East?
33 Grilled, at a taqueria
34 Eddies
36 Expert
41 Gather dust

42 Hearts or spades
43 Cry of surprise
47 Hit it off
50 People eaters
51 Oprah's "The Color Purple" co-star
52 Word after New York or Las Vegas
54 Spot to lay anchor
55 Blyton who wrote "The Enchanted Wood"
56 Stuffing ingredient
57 For whom Wednesday is named
58 Tricks
59 Sports org. with the New York Guardians and Seattle Dragons
60 Brazil's __ Roosevelt

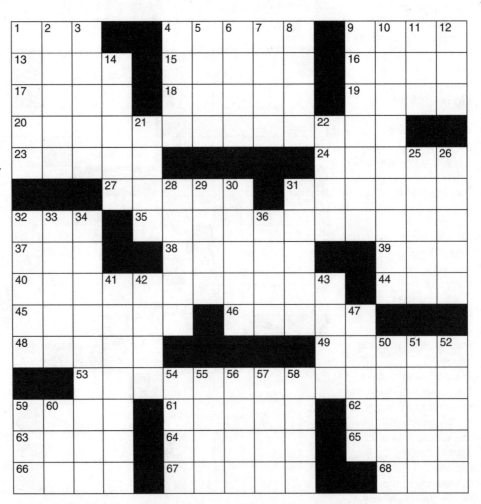

by Joe Deeney

ACROSS

1 Award notably won in each of the "big four" categories by this puzzle's honoree
7 Peeling potatoes as punishment, maybe
11 Krazy __
14 Things used with some frequency?
15 Surf sound
16 Yoko whose work is sometimes described as 17-Across
17 Having no musical key
18 Swear is true
20 "We've Only Just __"
21 Toy brand with plastic figures
22 Maker of the old Dreamcast game console
24 Terse admission
25 2006 #1 Shakira hit
29 Avail oneself of Vail?
32 Actor Morales
33 The Iams logo depicts one
34 Arranged artfully, as fabric
36 Janet of "Psycho"
38 "The __ Squad"
40 Ill-tempered
41 Anise-flavored aperitif
43 Vim
45 Poker giveaway
46 Texting format, for short
47 Art technique that's French for "fools the eye"
50 Some ways off
51 Gait slower than a gallop
52 Butler's "Gladly"
56 __-Japanese War
60 "Check it out . . . I'll wait here"
61 Film with a famous chariot race
62 Squirrel's favorite tree, maybe
63 Gal pal of Dennis the Menace
64 Score early in the game, often
65 Car rental add-on
66 Creatures in Tolkien's Fangorn Forest

67 Hit song by the 1-Across winner whose name is spelled out by the final three letters of 21-, 25-, 47- and 52-Across

DOWN

1 Take hold of
2 Merit
3 "On the internet, nobody knows you're __" (classic New Yorker cartoon caption)
4 –
5 Bellyached
6 Designer letters
7 Test that's all talk
8 Feature of a Manx cat
9 Relative of a cricket
10 Leaders of Canadian provinces
11 Hoda of morning TV
12 Voting nay
13 Easily influenced person
19 Rolled-up grass
21 Old airline with a globe in its logo
23 11 U.S. presidents of the 20th century belonged to it
25 Pitches in
26 "__ to remember . . ."
27 What socks come in
28 Early afternoon hour
29 Binge
30 Actress O'Hara with a Tony for "The King and I"
31 Peaceful pastoral scene
35 Artificial, as some modern pop vocals
37 Chocolaty sundae topping
39 Swimming pool measurement
42 Entices
44 Part of m.p.h.
48 Get situated
49 Ochoa in the World Golf Hall of Fame
50 __ Center (Chicago skyscraper)
52 Eager
53 Soft __ (flattery)
54 Chatters
55 Word after high, heavy or seven
57 Thick hairstyle
58 "Star Trek" role for Takei
59 Airport about 28 miles from Disneyland Paris
61 Short hairstyle

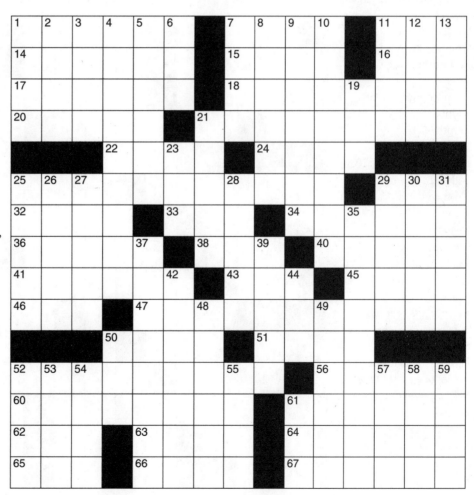

by Francis Heaney

Note: This puzzle has 16 solutions.

ACROSS

1 British brew since 1777
5 Early challenge for Barack and Michelle Obama, for short
9 Streak
12 Usefulness
13 Bill of Rights defender, in brief
14 Dracula accessory
15 Big fly at the ballpark
16 See 14-Down
18 Mantra chants
19 Underground workers
21 "What's the __?"
22 "I, Claudius" role
23 Layers of stone
24 One of the Twelve Apostles
28 Old phone features
30 "__ #1!"
31 Certain rough patches
33 Opposite of masc.
35 Part of Indochina
36 Jargon
37 Palindromic term of address
39 Zenith
40 Bit of baby talk
41 Locale of the 2018, 2020 and 2022 Olympics
42 "You win"
43 Irk
45 Listed
48 Camper driver
50 Joan __, player of Pat Nixon in 1995's "Nixon"
51 Sleeper hits, perhaps
53 A pair
55 See 42-Down
57 Hall-of-Fame hitter Rod
59 Tablet one might take before going to bed?
60 Fearsome part of a Jabberwock
61 Sets straight
62 Crucial
63 A dreadful state, with "the"
64 Leo or Libra

DOWN

1 Sounds that can startle
2 Company division
3 Fruit part that's thrown away
4 The Kaaba in Mecca, e.g.
5 "Ciao!"
6 Quantum mechanics thought experiment in which contradictory states exist simultaneously
7 Bar orders
8 Popcorn container
9 Item in a beach bag
10 Ivy seen along the Schuylkill River
11 "Darn it!"
12 Pronoun that can ask a question
14 With 16-Across, travel internationally
17 Iridescent stones
20 Recent recruits, so to speak
23 Like the boys in "Lord of the Flies"
24 Hole puncher
25 "Swell!"
26 Sag
27 Hi or lo follower
29 "Aladdin" parrot
32 Amazonas and others
33 Go to extremes, foodwise
34 Buildup during vacation
37 Welcome site?
38 Fannie __
40 Hollows
42 With 55-Across, breakup line
44 Puts up
45 Surgery to improve how you look?
46 Go off, but not without a hitch?
47 Big name in cosmetics
49 YouTube data
51 Java neighbor
52 Madras wrap
53 Many a middle schooler
54 Possible reactions to shocks
56 Angel dust
58 Oval thing in the Oval Office

by Andrew Kingsley and John Lieb

ACROSS

1 E-cigarette output
6 Something to shift into or stow
10 Hershey's Kiss covering
14 Best competitive effort
15 Coach Reid of the 2020 Super Bowl-winning Chiefs
16 Garnish for a Corona
17 Dance with a kick
18 Strategy used in basketball and football
20 German appliance brand
22 Maker of tarts and tortes
23 Wis.-to-Ga. direction
26 Cyclops and others
28 Hog's heaven
29 "Sunset Boulevard" actress Gloria
31 Figure in cellphone plans
33 Exclamation of surprise
35 Touch lovingly
39 Dweller along the Bering Sea
40 "That's going to leave a mark!"
42 Big name in little trucks
43 Prank involving yanking underwear
45 "Paper Moon" Oscar winner
47 Major city of west-central Syria
49 Behaves improperly
50 Butter square
53 Turn the dial to a radio station
55 __-crab soup
56 What an acrobat needs to be
58 Buzzards Bay, for one
60 "Water Lilies" painter
62 Birds with effervescent voices
67 Struggling with a decision
68 Fast-swimming shark
69 Outdo . . . or a hint to entering four answers in this puzzle
70 Party goodies
71 TV actor/director Ken
72 Kind of language used by sailors

DOWN

1 Household device with a hose, informally
2 Before now
3 Paella cooker
4 "Srsly?!"
5 20 quires = 1 __
6 Stare at, as another's eyes
7 __ Gay (W.W. II bomber)
8 Either 1 in "1 + 1"
9 Bread with seeded and unseeded varieties
10 Hartz collar target
11 Sounds from a 28-Across
12 "Good to go here!"
13 Skeptical
19 Profile posting, for short
21 "Young Frankenstein" character who asks "What hump?"
23 Extremely muscular, in slang
24 Cut, as lumber
25 "Just be quiet already!"
27 Middle X or O
29 "Major Barbara" playwright
30 Stuffed to the gills
32 Memory triggers, for many
34 All the rage
36 He was raised by Cain
37 Diamond-shaped ray
38 Pizzeria in "Do the Right Thing"
41 Winner of 11 Tonys in 2016
44 Goose : gaggle :: __ : mob
46 One of three on an oyster fork
48 20 Questions category
50 Diplomatic agreements
51 Shining
52 Bejeweled head ornament
54 Long-stemmed mushroom
57 It's breath-taking
59 Numbers for Noah
61 Jimmy Eat World music genre
63 Single-stranded genetic molecule
64 Smoked fish
65 Trail mix bit
66 Use a nanny cam, say

by Tracy Gray

ACROSS

1 Mugged for the camera, maybe
8 Site administrator
15 Preceder of many N.H.L. games
16 "Oh, did you start already?"
17 0%
18 Some male escorts
19 Org. that sticks to its guns
20 List ender, maybe
22 Oscar-nominated actor Clive
23 Exceptional grade
26 Will matter
29 Time in court
31 One-up, say
35 Red choice
37 Gambler's hangout, in brief
39 Noteworthy time period
40 Large guard dogs
41 Aches and pains
43 Jump shot's path
44 Down in the dumps
46 ___ Meyer, principal role on "Veep"
47 Sign on a staff
49 "I agree with both of you!"
51 2009 biopic starring Hilary Swank
53 Apply, as sunscreen
57 Grocery chain with more than 1,900 U.S. stores
59 Chicago airport code
61 That, in Tabasco
62 Like some reputations and kitchen towels
65 Sentence containing all 26 letters
68 Many a limo
69 Major retail outlets
70 Feigns sickness to avoid work
71 Much-traveled thoroughfares

DOWN

1 Much-painted religious figure
2 Villainous conglomerate on "Mr. Robot"
3 Deadly
4 Santa ___
5 Waiter in an airport queue
6 Actress Falco
7 Exam for the college-bound, redundantly
8 Jokester
9 Onetime London-based record label
10 Intolerant sort
11 Lost steam
12 Food cooked in a cornhusk
13 Preparatory school since 1440
14 Hi-___ monitor
21 CBS series with a "Cyber" spinoff
24 Bomber letters
25 Medieval laborers
27 Additionally
28 Dancer's horn
30 Bagel choice
32 Stay behind
33 Surface figure
34 Used to be
35 PC combo key
36 Evil intent
38 Hay-bundling machine
40 Small pouch
42 "Mon ___!" (French exclamation)
45 Penn. neighbor
46 Dog with wrinkly skin
48 Like the sun at sunset
50 Uncle, in Oaxaca
52 Cut into small pieces
54 Catcher with a record 10 World Series rings as a player
55 "Let me repeat . . ."
56 "Enough!," in Mexico . . . or a hint to 11 answers in this puzzle
57 Yours, to Yvette
58 Wyatt Earp, for one
60 "___ Yankees"
62 Cardinals, on scoreboards
63 Cob of corn
64 E.R. or O.R. figures
66 "Planet Money" network
67 Melted ice cream, e.g.

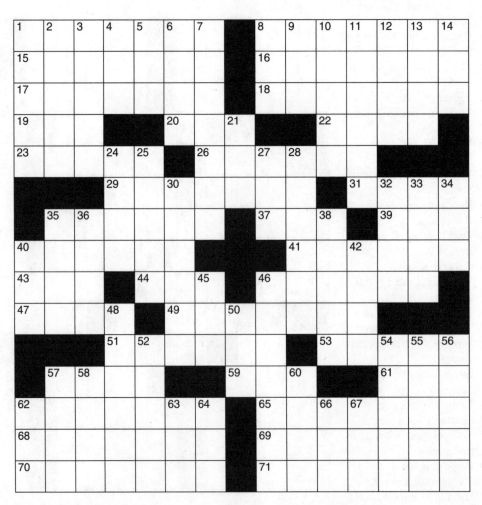

by Zhouqin Burnikel

ACROSS

1 Ingredient in many a sandie cookie
6 Stick in the oven
10 Hooded snake
15 Part of the Dutch Caribbean
16 Voice above tenor
17 Brainstormers' flurry
18 Relent
19 Lead-in to prompter
20 They're on their second decade
21 Singer Ella with the 2018 Grammy-winning R&B hit "Boo'd Up"
22 Hot food?
25 Reason for seasonal shots
26 Biblical garden
28 Bad way to be led
29 Fake I.R.S. call, e.g.
30 Takeback of a car, for short
31 "Georgie ___" (nursery rhyme)
32 Sticky roll
33 Costa ___
35 Word repeatedly sung before "Born is the king of Israel"
36 Torah holders
37 TV gunslinger Wynonna, supposed descendant of Wyatt
39 Plant that yields a potent laxative
40 Hot food?
45 Bo-o-oring
48 Less amiable
49 Jokes
53 It makes a rowboat go
54 "Heavenly" man's name
55 Chinese zodiac animal of 2020
56 Sch. whose newspaper is The Prospector ("Assayer of Student Opinion")
58 Incredible deals
59 Chipper greeting
60 Contrive
62 A fan of
63 Southern terminus of Amtrak's Silver Meteor
64 Words from an emcee
65 Just sit there being mad
66 Word before peace or child
67 One who can never go home again
68 Sunbathes
69 Critics' assignments

DOWN

1 Apt surname for a close-up magician?
2 Literary convenience
3 Hot food?
4 ___ Dhabi
5 Back of one's neck
6 Criticizes venomously
7 High-voltage foe of Spider-Man
8 On the loose
9 Something a sandal shows that a loafer doesn't
10 Ending of four state capitals [Can you name them all?]
11 Reverent poem
12 Hot food?
13 Practiced at the track
14 Make an ass out of u and me, as they say
23 Dog's protestation
24 Requirement for pink hair
27 Credit card-only, say
29 Muscly
34 What MoMA knows best?
36 Actor Mahershala
38 Alternatives to Nikes
39 Jackson 5 dos
41 One with an opening to fill?
42 Mix of red and blue
43 Like leftovers, for now
44 Genius Grant recipients, e.g.
45 Concerned with wealth, possessions and respectability, in modern lingo
46 Gender-neutral neologism added to Merriam-Webster in 2018
47 "That's true about me, right?"
50 Singer Grande
51 Portmanteau coinage for a queer-identified e-sports player, say
52 Alternative to an elevator
57 Knit and ___
59 Bit of help in an escape room
61 "The Raven" poet
63 Prefix with judge or trial

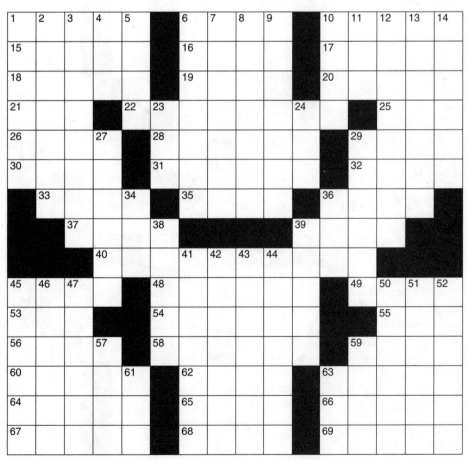

by Erik Agard

ACROSS

1 Card game with melds
8 Divulged
15 Scrubbed
16 Wonder Woman, for one
17 Part 1 of a story attributed to 34-Across
18 Elevate, redundantly
19 Bed of roses?
20 Fortitude
21 Sellout abbr.
22 Institution founded by Benjamin Franklin, in brief
24 Part 2 of the story
26 It adds punch to punch
27 Goes back and forth (with)
29 Nast of publishing
30 Foie __
32 "__ better be good!"
33 Barnyard bleat
34 Author of the concise yet evocative story told in this puzzle
40 Unwelcoming
41 Show of approval
42 Subject of a 1960 expedition by Sir Edmund Hillary
43 Yoga pose
46 Sainted 11th-century pope
48 Feeling of a frosty wind
49 End of the story
51 Montana mining city
53 Mister, abroad
54 One of the only remaining "people's republics"
55 A whole bunch
56 Sneaky critters
58 Like this puzzle's story, in length
61 Dub, say
62 One being dubbed
63 Confirm, as an email address
64 "No making changes now"

DOWN

1 Shortening in a coffee order
2 __ group (hospital classification)
3 Leif Ericson, for one
4 Burning desire?
5 Sullies
6 Let the cat out of the bag
7 Gator's tail?
8 Alternative to a fence
9 Like some smoky Scotch
10 Biometric ID method
11 Article in El Mundo
12 Surmounts
13 Accustomed
14 Oust
20 People found in rows
22 Push
23 Sign of cat love
24 Cat hate
25 "Stardust" composer Carmichael
28 __ party
31 It flows to the harbor of Le Havre
33 The south of France, with "le"
35 1991 sequel to "Gone With the Wind"
36 Part of the DreamWorks logo
37 Struck out on one's own
38 Squabbling
39 Cry of pain
43 Echo, e.g.
44 Unfazed
45 Do loop-the-loops, maybe
46 Not so fast?
47 Popular new holidays gifts of 2001
50 Hit 2008 Pixar film
52 Single
55 Limo window feature
57 Opposite of purity
58 Take to the hills?
59 Kylo __ of "Star Wars"
60 "Dr." with the 2011 hit "I Need a Doctor"

by Ruth Bloomfield Margolin

ACROSS

1 Annual tennis or golf championship
7 "Sign me up!"
11 ___ dispenser
14 Team spirit
15 Detective Wolfe
16 Friend for Philippe
17 Zombies with a sense of humor?
19 Pinch
20 What to do after saying grace
21 Spree
22 Removes, as from a club
24 Had high hopes
27 Gay rights or climate change
29 Grizzlies that don't fall for traps?
33 Writer who went through hell?
36 Rat-___
37 Cheer from the stands
38 Greek god who fought with the mortal Hercules
39 Many a time
41 Prefix with space
42 Small set
43 Surrealist Maar
44 Called off
45 Exam in an interior design class?
49 Singer Luis with the 13× platinum hit "Despacito"
50 Write the book on, so to speak
54 Automaton of folklore
56 Like some spicy food
58 "Snakes ___ Plane" (2006 film)
59 Abbr. before an alias
60 Terrible attempts at peeling corn?
64 Org. that collects 1099s
65 Wonder Woman, for Gal Gadot
66 Mexican dish prepared in a cornhusk
67 "Hmm, I don't think so"
68 Shift and Tab, for two
69 Less fresh

DOWN

1 Called balls and strikes
2 Word before system or panel
3 Deliver a stemwinder
4 Be punished (for)
5 Figure in Santa's workshop
6 Neither feminine nor masculine
7 Lead-in to China
8 Introductory scene in some rom-coms
9 Subj. of the federal tax form 5498
10 "For sure"
11 Like some salmon that's not baked or broiled
12 Give off
13 10001, 10002, etc., informally
18 Ore source
23 Exercise
25 Fifth book of the New Testament
26 Daisy ___ (character who loved Li'l Abner)
28 Astronaut Shepard, first American in space
30 Like almost 0% of tarantula bites
31 Like blue moons
32 Having footwear
33 Harebrained
34 ___ 51
35 "Hey, let me be the first to tell you . . ."
39 Reactions to gut punches
40 Orchard pest
41 Up the ___
43 Nation whose flag is a white cross on a red background
44 Neighbor of F1 and a tilde
46 Outer edge of a golf club
47 Shade akin to turquoise
48 Is
51 One giving directions to a tourist, say
52 Where a pant leg and a sock meet
53 It'll give you a shock
54 Benefit
55 Vegetable that's frequently fried
57 Colors
61 Great distress
62 Lid, so to speak
63 Thurman of "Pulp Fiction"

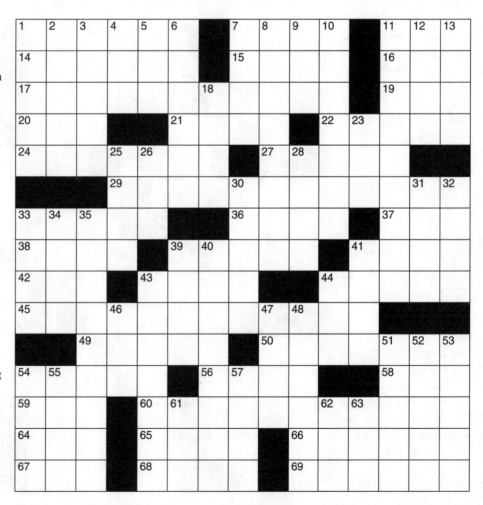

by Ricky Cruz

ACROSS

1 Tends to, as a sprain
5 Popular fitness magazine
10 Ralphie's ammo in 1983's "A Christmas Story"
13 Broadway auntie
14 Pull
15 Scratch maker
16 Where dogs are believed to have been domesticated 10,000+ years ago
17 In __ (irritable)
18 It's bound to be big
19 Protection from piracy
21 Courtroom coverage?
22 Extreme, in a U.S. Forest Service fire danger rating
23 Play area at some fast-food restaurants
25 Authored
29 Prepare for sending on, say
30 Elude
31 Like God's name, in the Lord's Prayer
35 Snitch (on)
36 Keep for later
38 Crumbly salad topper
39 Tangled up
41 B equivalent
42 Old pal
43 Neighborhood bisected by the Pomona Fwy.
44 Twist
47 Cards, on a scoreboard
48 An old gym sock may have one
49 Crest, e.g.
55 Parsley relative
56 U.S. attack helicopter
57 Golfer's choice
58 Horse (around)
59 Strike force?
60 New Orleans side dish
61 Saucer users, in brief
62 Swarms
63 Chop __

DOWN

1 Apple variety
2 Wear after an accident
3 Leader of Qatar
4 Conclude, as a deal
5 Showed obvious interest
6 Like summer in the South
7 On pins and needles
8 Pal of Piglet
9 Place to set a TV remote
10 Hit that goes over the infielders' heads
11 Disney movie with fewer than a thousand words of dialogue
12 "That's awesome!"
15 Jeans that have been summerized
20 Standing on the street
24 "That's funny!," in a text
25 You might see right through it
26 "__ Almighty," 2007 film
27 It's what you would expect
28 "Way to go!," to an antiques buyer
29 Little __ (state nickname)
32 Possible symptom of an allergic reaction
33 List curtailer
34 Just the facts
36 Timesaver . . . as a computer user would see in four answers in this puzzle?
37 12:50
40 Sign of a sellout
41 Course after trig
43 Actor Hawke and others
44 Elude
45 Peabrain
46 Some historic Amelia Earhart flights
47 Longtime senator Thurmond
50 Award started by the Village Voice
51 Things not found in binary code, paradoxically
52 TV streaming device
53 Tales of the past
54 Feb. 14

by Wayne Bergman and Gary Otting

ACROSS

1 Tour de France, e.g.
5 Sonny Corleone, for one
9 Crow
13 Professor in a library, perhaps
14 New Testament epistle
16 Second attempt, informally
17 Laura Dern, in "Little Women"
19 Prelude to a perspective
20 Creepy-crawly, maybe
21 Made tight
23 Actress Thompson of "Selma"
25 Swipe
26 Big name in Dadaism
27 Where R.N.s are always needed
28 Sarah Drew, on "Grey's Anatomy"
31 Shorten the sentence, maybe?
34 Hip designs?
35 Ming-Na Wen, on "Agents of S.H.I.E.L.D."
39 Princess Organa
41 Avowal to a long-distance lover
45 Barbara Billingsley, on "Leave It to Beaver"
49 Santa's helper?
50 QB blunder: Abbr.
51 Half of a centaur
52 One of the Obamas
54 To-go
56 Golf coup
58 Blind as __
59 Chinese appetizers . . . or a punny description of 17-, 28-, 35- and 45-Across
63 Hair on the back of the neck
64 Academic's "and others"
65 Christmas season
66 Crafts' companion
67 Go downhill fast
68 Like quiche

DOWN

1 Engine stat
2 In the style of
3 Gets cozy
4 Watson, Willard and Woodhouse
5 Unconscious condition
6 Dr.'s org.
7 Sequel title ender
8 Prepared to respond
9 Camembert cousin
10 Leftover bit
11 Sticks (to)
12 Positive media coverage
14 Title for M.L.K. Jr.
15 Prepare, as oysters or corn
18 Elizabethan, for one
22 Trigonometry symbols for angles
23 Nervous habit
24 Prefix with system
25 Actress Drescher of "The Nanny"
28 __ ears
29 Canada's smallest prov.
30 Compensates
32 Friend for Françoise
33 Swell
36 Go in headfirst
37 Mother Bethel __ Church (Philadelphia congregation since 1794)
38 Soviet space station
39 Energy snack marketed to women
40 Contest hopeful
42 What might give you that nice warm Christmas feeling?
43 Big name in nail polish
44 International powerhouse in women's soccer
45 Mexican root vegetable popular in salads
46 Relaxed
47 Bursts forth
48 Related to the stars
52 Team head: Abbr.
53 Single-handedly
55 Waze ways: Abbr.
56 Arthurian heroine
57 __ Khan
60 Bit of land in the Seine
61 Component of a relay
62 Crafty

by Laura Taylor Kinnel

ACROSS

1 Amount to make do with
5 Slip up
8 Teleprompter user
14 Late Surrealist Turner
15 Second person
16 Country singer Carly
17 Mercury or Sun, e.g.
19 Volume 1, Number 1 and others
20 Sporty 1980s Pontiac
21 Reprobate
23 Common man's name from Hebrew
24 Some diplomats working in N.Y.C.
26 Mercury or Venus, e.g.
28 ___ Lobos
29 Something to chew on
31 Bronze Age fertility deity
32 ___ Pass (means of foreign travel)
34 Smack
35 Mercury or Earth, e.g.
38 "Yikes!"
40 Invented
41 Liquid absorbed by surrounding soil
44 "Bill ___ Saves the World"
45 Shots fired?
48 Mercury or Mars, e.g.
50 ITV spot
52 Handel's "___ for St. Cecilia's Day"
53 72 things in this puzzle
55 Carson City's lake
56 Lightly burned
58 Mercury or Saturn, e.g.
60 Deep down
61 Vegas casino with the Penn & Teller Theater
62 Kennington cricket ground, with "the"
63 Waged a long campaign against
64 Place for a slop bucket
65 Patches (up)

DOWN

1 Within bounds
2 Current event?
3 They go into battle at the sides of cavalrymen
4 Capture
5 ___ of Providence (image on a dollar bill)
6 Sound in a circus act
7 Buzz
8 Poppy products
9 Upgrade to a box, perhaps
10 Wiimote batteries
11 Only movie for which John Wayne won an Oscar
12 Striped and spotted felines
13 Lives
18 Highest-grossing movie of 1986
22 Not hold back
25 Positive
27 Uncovered
30 Only performer with a speaking part in 1976's "Silent Movie"
32 Slender Japanese mushroom
33 Bit of Wall St. news
35 So to speak
36 Novelist Seton
37 Must
38 Unconscious assimilation
39 Subject of the 2006 biography "Escape!"
42 Submit
43 ___ Age (late 19th century)
45 Parent's admonition
46 NBC Nightly News anchor before Brian Williams
47 Braces
49 Gets in the neighborhood of
51 "Let's go!," in Spanish
54 Hearts, but not minds
57 It's a job
59 Little dog

by Alex Eaton-Salners

ACROSS

1 French Open court material
5 One thing . . . or a twosome
9 Alfred Nobel or Anders Celsius
14 McDonald's arches, e.g.
15 Model/actress Delevingne
16 Ebbed
17 Historic town in Veszprém county, Hungary, noted for its baroque architecture
20 Short line at the top of a column, in typesetting
21 Turn out
22 + or − atom
23 Thigh-baring dress feature
25 Spore-producing plant
27 Soldier clad in gray, for short
30 Bisected
33 Start of Caesar's boast
36 "It's about time!"
38 A Stooge
39 Fits of anger
40 Left tributary of the Vitim River in Irkutsk Oblast, Russia
43 Only ape to orbit the earth (1961)
44 ___ sequitur
45 Colombia's capital
46 Went by taxi or train
47 From Florence or Pisa
49 Like a 1960s–'70s TV "squad"
50 One-size-fits-all garment
52 Opposed to, rurally
54 Piñata smasher
56 Board a moving vehicle
59 Part of a suspension bridge
63 Village between Kruszyna and Jacków in Silesian Voivodeship, Poland (pop. 305)
66 TV newsman Willie
67 Janis's partner in the comics
68 Knoll
69 Retort to "Are too!"
70 One of the Lennons
71 Numbered composition

DOWN

1 End of a hammer
2 Greiner of "Shark Tank"
3 Like Gruyère or Grandpa
4 Idiots
5 R.N.'s workplace
6 What the Lord sometimes does, in a classical expression
7 Land o' leprechauns
8 Sober-minded org.
9 Criticism that might be made behind someone's back
10 Ashen
11 Scotty's domain on the U.S.S. Enterprise
12 Brief how-to
13 Where fruit-picking originated?
18 Wise-looking
19 Gym clothes holder
24 Aim
26 Enjoying the great outdoors . . . indoors
27 Less cooked
28 Prefix with centric
29 Laundry problem for Dracula?
31 Chorus of approval
32 "Hahaha"
34 Unfamiliar with
35 Feels down
37 Where icebergs are found
41 The Rockets, on scoreboards
42 Classic camera brand
48 Cooking oil option
51 Butler of fame
53 Kind of chip
54 Nickname for major-league baseball's Angel Stadium, with "the"
55 "Uh . . . excuse me"
57 Some fund-raising grps.
58 People eater
60 Sonar signal
61 Doozy
62 Serpentine swimmers
64 Letters on a brandy bottle
65 Bridge limit unit

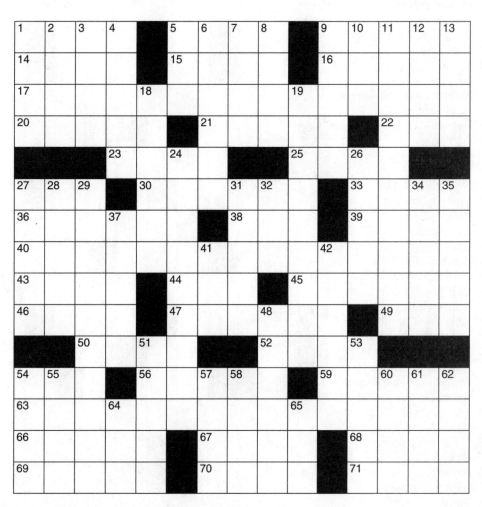

by John Ficarra and Patrick Merrell

ACROSS

1 Graphic in a weather report
4 High-hat
9 Places for to-do lists
14 Potential resource on an asteroid
15 Dessert not for the diet-conscious
16 Things to memorize
17 Social media fad that went viral in 2014
20 Animal also called a zebra giraffe
21 Jack of "Rio Lobo"
22 "OMG, that is soooo funny!"
24 Large-beaked bird found in Africa
28 Only card of its suit in a hand
30 Certain public transports
32 Certain public transport
33 Golfer Aoki
34 Medal for bravery, perhaps
37 Network with the all-time greatest number of Emmys
38 Ado
39 Run a fever, say
40 "There it is!"
41 Say "Yes, I did it"
44 Made, as one's case
45 Philip who wrote "American Pastoral"
46 Up to
47 Poet's contraction
48 Poke around
50 Old PC software
52 Sandwich alternative
54 "Star Wars" droid, informally
57 Fancy-schmancy language . . . or the contents of some special squares in this puzzle
63 Love to death
64 Bloke
65 Chaotic situation, metaphorically
66 Jabber?
67 Analyze, in a way
68 Top of a wizard's staff

DOWN

1 Response when playing innocent
2 Gas brand that's also a musical direction
3 Something not to do before Christmas?
4 Trample
5 Untagged
6 Elf's evil counterpart
7 Whence the phrase "wear one's heart on one's sleeve"
8 Relative of turquoise
9 Tryst locale
10 Part of a diner showcase
11 ___ Wilson, lead singer of Heart
12 M.B.A., e.g.: Abbr.
13 Glasgow-to-Liverpool dir.
18 Cowpoke
19 "Well, ___-di-dah!"
23 Animal often with a "mask" around its eyes
25 Monopoly quartet: Abbr.
26 Christmas, in Italy
27 TV host once with an "Explaining Jokes to Idiots" segment
28 Places where business is picking up?
29 Append
31 Slowpokes
33 Abbr. on a bank statement
34 Manhattan, e.g.: Abbr.
35 Spot on the face, informally
36 Dope
38 Manhattan, for one
42 Ike's W.W. II command: Abbr.
43 What smiles may make
44 Green sauce
47 Winter Olympics powerhouse
49 For
51 Alfalfa's love in "The Little Rascals"
53 Popular Italian car, informally
55 Ricelike pasta
56 Sign of rot
57 A-OK
58 It's a promise
59 Website with the slogan "Understand the news"
60 Afore
61 What 17-Across raised money for, in brief
62 [Poor me!]

by Evan Mahnken

ACROSS

1 Not be heard from anymore
7 Tom who created Jack Ryan
13 Shakespearean fairy king
14 Something to practice percussion on
15 Humorist Ambrose who once defined "alone" as "in bad company"
16 Fans that jeer the home team, informally
17 Quick attack groups
19 Club booklet
20 Blind followers
24 Tennis star Nadal, to fans
27 Like the leftmost stripe on le drapeau français
29 Deli loaf
30 "*There* you are!"
31 Like many TV news interviews
35 Emmy nomination number for which Susan Lucci finally won for playing Erica Kane on "All My Children"
37 Little bit
38 Comic actress Rudolph
39 Went 0 to 60, say
43 Producer of jingle-jangle in the pocket
46 "Good for the earth" prefix
47 Horror film director Aster
48 Grasp
49 Coffee or beer, informally
50 Coke and RC
53 Mom on "Modern Family"
56 Aid for a Thanksgiving chef
61 Reverse course, slangily
64 Wing it?
65 Cry at a revival
66 Kind of sale
67 Clicked the double vertical bar on a YouTube video
68 Precipitates unpleasantly, in a way

DOWN

1 Oodles
2 Dead space?
3 Howl : wolf :: bell : ___
4 Exuberant cry south of the border
5 Title film character who declares "Nobody owes nobody nothing"
6 Show obeisance
7 Gator's cousin
8 Some garage jobs
9 Eschewers of military service
10 "Ask Me Another" airer
11 Scoundrel
12 Fabric measures: Abbr.
14 Real English county on which Thomas Hardy based the fictional Wessex
16 Where you might roll the starts of 17-, 31-, 43- and 56-Across
18 George Orwell's "Animal Farm," e.g.
21 Nook, e.g.
22 One of eight on most spiders
23 Part of an animal farm
24 Was in charge of
25 Fish on a sushi menu
26 Gushing letters
28 On drugs, say
31 Bump on a lid
32 Beaut
33 Driving test obstacle
34 GPS suggestion: Abbr.
36 What may have a ring to it?
40 10/24 celebration of global cooperation
41 Makeup of Elsa's castle in "Frozen"
42 Drag
43 Kind of fly
44 Whiz
45 Pawned
49 Next to
51 Part of some encyclopedias
52 Smooth
54 Certain building beams
55 Get tangled up
57 Had some second thoughts about
58 ___ Modern
59 Division politique
60 Rules and ___
61 One of 21 on a die
62 Actress Thurman
63 Sch. whose newspaper is The Daily Reveille

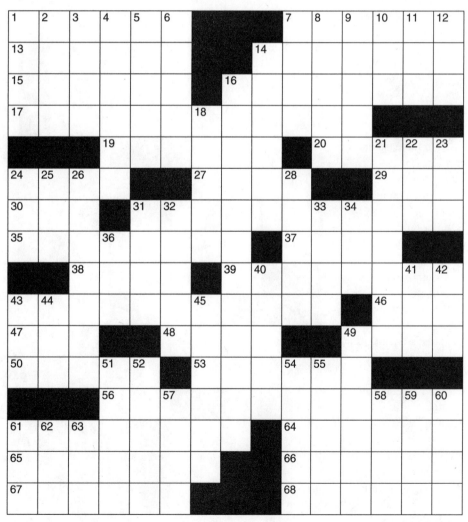

by Sam Buchbinder

ACROSS

1 Cry from a card holder
4 __ Kelly, Democratic governor of Kansas starting in 2019
9 Yoga pose
14 World view?
15 Putin ally in the Mideast
16 "Old Town Road (feat. Billy Ray Cyrus)," for one
17 -able
19 Nickname for an instructor
20 Singer Turner's memoir
21 Alley sight
23 Actress/singer Kravitz
24 Frost formed from fog
25 Big nos.
29 Connecticut collegian
30 Group HQ'd in Ramallah
31 Added some color to
32 Late 1970s
35 Show that Betty White hosted at age 88, informally
36 Op-ed
39 Tear
40 Trick to increase one's efficiency, in modern lingo
43 "That one's on me"
47 Sailor
48 Bond or bind
49 Mil. post, say
51 Soul singer Gray
52 Bit of reproach
53 Updo hairstyle
54 NBC drama that won 15 Emmys
55 Tree that's one of Athena's symbols
58 Method of communication needed to understand 17-, 25-, 36- and 49-Across
61 Target
62 Hybrid fruit
63 __ in Nancy
64 Figures in academia
65 Unlikely Christmas gifts in tropical areas
66 Is written in old Rome?

DOWN

1 Made some calls
2 Sea creatures that move by jet propulsion
3 "When life gives you lemons, make lemonade" outlook
4 Singer __ Del Rey
5 Grateful?
6 Tour letters
7 "Invisible Man" author Ellison
8 Berries, for breakfast cereal, e.g.
9 Intriguing discovery in a cave
10 Date
11 Second-largest private employer in the U.S., after Walmart
12 Cartoonist Hollander
13 Log splitter
18 Prime factor
22 "Up to this point, no"
25 Where to get a polysomnogram
26 __ Crawley, countess on "Downton Abbey"
27 More off-the-wall
28 Nada
30 Talking point
33 It might be shot on a winding seaside road
34 Part of the knee, for short
37 Shere who wrote "Sexual Honesty: By Women for Women"
38 Eschew dinner company
41 Large, noisy insects
42 Route 1 terminus
43 "The Wind in the Willows" character
44 "That's not true!"
45 Daughter of Muhammad
46 One-ups
50 Small hill
51 Big __
54 Gives permission to
56 Camper, e.g.
57 H.S. exam org.
59 Regret
60 Cover some ground

by Alex Eaton-Salners

ACROSS

1 "All Things Considered" airer
4 Sloth, e.g.
7 Wasn't a smooth talker?
13 Singer Grande, to fans
14 "__ soon?"
15 Vanquish
16 Price of a horror film?
18 Expand to 800%
19 Big online site for uploading photos and memes
20 Antique
22 Word accompanying a lightning bolt
23 Spanish direction
24 Spanish royal
25 Balance
28 King in the "Jungle Book" films
30 Be quietly angry
32 "The Good __"
35 Soap opera, e.g.
37 Where It. is found
38 Leave on the cutting room floor
40 This puzzle's theme
42 Word with science or chocolate
43 Like Antarctica among all the continents
45 Historic enemy of the Iroquois
46 Poorly made
48 YouTube statistics
50 Put an edge on
51 Had the reins
52 On
55 Rearward
57 "Take __"
58 Separates into groups that don't communicate
60 "Turandot" composer
63 Shakespeare character who says "I kiss'd thee ere I kill'd thee"
65 They may come with bows and whistles
66 Handle
67 Indisposed
68 Like the word "truthiness," by Stephen Colbert
69 Besmirch
70 Follower of red, pink or black

DOWN

1 Blue-skinned race in "Avatar"
2 Like the two 40-Across in the grid for this answer
3 Telephones
4 Binaural
5 Accelerator bit
6 Infamy
7 Bird of myth
8 DreamWorks's first animated film
9 Like the two 40-Across in the grid for this answer
10 Person pulling the strings?
11 Fish with tiny scales
12 "Dr." who co-founded Death Row Records
15 Wyoming town named for a frontiersman
17 Tonkatsu, in Japanese cuisine
21 Bad look
26 "Black Panther" princess/superhero
27 Cut short
29 Loan-sharking
30 Fry in a shallow pan
31 Common street name in the Northeast
32 Language in which "Thank you very much" is "Diolch yn fawr iawn"
33 Where I-15 meets I-86
34 Like the two 40-Across in the grid for this answer
36 Inverted
39 Like the two 40-Across in the grid for this answer
41 Closest pal
44 Like the two 40-Across in the grid for this answer
47 Military alert system
49 Tiny purchase for a plumber
51 __ Lane
53 Skateboarding maneuver
54 Classic name for a parrot
56 Tucker out
59 Only
60 Chest muscle, for short
61 57-Across, en español
62 Homer's neighbor
64 Big airport inits.

by Bryce Hwang and Rahul Sridhar and Akshay Ravikumar

ACROSS

1 "How to Be an Anti-___" (best-selling book of 2020)
7 Big kahuna
10 Way up to go downhill
14 Totally original
15 Bird that's the source of Kalaya oil
16 Dance sometimes done to klezmer music
17 Play-by-play job?
19 A little cracked
20 Spanish for "weight"
21 Presidential nickname of the 19th century
23 Kansas or Kentucky, politically
26 Cap'n's mate
27 Details, details
29 Certain Miller beers
31 Gear tooth
34 Soaks up a lot of sun
36 Improv comic's forte
38 Chicago-style pizza chain, familiarly
40 Big Ten nickname
42 Architectural style of Nebraska's capitol building, informally
43 Rhetoric for the political base, figuratively
45 Warning sign
47 Word with high or dive
48 "Cómo ___?"
50 Follower of "Too bad," in an expression of mock pity
52 Gomer Pyle's outfit: Abbr.
53 Low humming sounds
56 "Stay calm"
60 Stand-up comedian Bargatze
62 "___ Am Telling You" (song from "Dreamgirls")
63 Traffic go-ahead that should be followed four times in this puzzle
66 Dance done to fiddle music
67 Director Lee
68 No longer under wraps?
69 Lagerfeld of fashion
70 ___ leaf (stew additive)
71 Over a large area

DOWN

1 File type
2 Drunkenness or hypnosis
3 It may be dismissed
4 Some metal castings
5 "Get it?"
6 Onetime United competitor
7 Refuse to pick up the bill?
8 "That's my cue!"
9 Poodles, but not schnoodles or doodles
10 "How strange . . ."
11 Nickname for tap-dancing legend Bill Robinson
12 ___ League
13 Unusual
18 Something waved when a race is won
22 Common mixer
24 P.D. alert
25 Udder end
28 Lord's laborers
30 Warped, as a sense of humor
31 Pancetta or prosciutto
32 "My treat!"
33 Becomes insolvent
35 Inkblot, e.g.
37 Early man?
39 Behaved for a haircut, say
41 Glazier's frame
44 Pack down
46 Long-bodied fish
49 Bug that inspired Poe's "The Gold-Bug"
51 Persistently demanded payment from
54 French river in W.W. I fighting
55 Metaphor for strength
56 Like yin but not yang
57 Suited to serve
58 Simone known as the "High Priestess of Soul"
59 Punk's Pop
61 Water whirl
64 AAA offering
65 Nail polish brand with a Bubble Bath shade

by Ed Sessa

ACROSS

1 Bill-rejecting vote
4 Took a dip?
10 Parent's cure-all, briefly
13 Number on a foam finger
14 Cost of an online banner or pop-up
15 Piece of cake?
16 Kidney or heart
18 Give the go-ahead
19 Guadalajara gal pal
20 ___ mode
21 Joke
22 Seeds on hamburger buns
25 Lollygag
27 Georgia's official vegetable
32 Grenoble gal pal
35 "Little" car in a Ronny & the Daytonas hit
36 Stellar start?
37 Florist's vehicle, typically
38 Suddenly change course
41 Sound of a lightning bolt
42 "Fingers crossed!"
44 Grp. with the hits "Evil Woman" and "Do Ya"
45 Billy or tom
46 Inexpensive table wine
50 Provincial schoolteacher stereotype
51 Short-brimmed hat known as a bunnet in Scotland
55 Org. that launched WaterSense in 2006
57 Co-___ (condo alternatives)
59 Cold hard cash
60 ___ program
61 Specialized lab equipment for drying
64 Fairy tale foe
65 Go by
66 Triage sites, for short
67 Alberto ___ (hair care brand) . . . and a hint to 16-, 27-, 38-, 46- and 61-Across
68 Home security component
69 Setting in "Charlotte's Web"

DOWN

1 Massive pop stars?
2 Genre featured at Tokyo's Comiket convention
3 Folkloric creatures at snowy altitudes
4 A slice of Italy?
5 Brouhaha
6 "I'm beyond frustrated!"
7 Lovesick
8 And others, in Latin
9 "You're welcome," in Spanish
10 ___ torch
11 Top-billed performer
12 Word with war or far
15 Arcade "money"
17 Plant source for tequila
23 Strategic starting piece in a jigsaw puzzle
24 Fill to excess
26 It's more than a pocketful of rye
28 "Two Women" actress Sophia
29 Chichén ___ (Mayan ruins city)
30 Like some interviews
31 "That's a negatory!"
32 Tel ___, Israel
33 Hawaiian for "strong," which, when doubled, means "very strong"
34 Privy to, as a secret
38 Fashion icon Wang
39 Singing animated snowman
40 Thwart
43 Greasy hairstyling product
45 "I totally agree!"
47 Hordes
48 Skewer
49 Powerful tool for compaction
52 Seafarers' sanctuaries
53 Well-caffeinated, perhaps
54 Colorful flower with a "face"
55 Therefore
56 The 18th at Pebble Beach, notably
58 Diagnostic image
60 www.fda.___
62 Emotional highs
63 Grp. that supports American troops

by Tracy Gray

ACROSS

1 Thymus, e.g.
6 Man's name that can follow "v" or "r" to form an English word
10 Blown away
14 Food staple referred to as "the gold of the Incas"
15 PlayStation's creator
16 Prego alternative
17 Direction of some subway trains
18 *"Dude, Where's My Car?"* [1979]
20 What's on the agenda
21 Excessively showy
23 Cheese akin to cheddar
24 *"What's Eating Gilbert Grape"* [2019]
26 Petulant retort
27 Wood strip
28 Snazziness
30 Hill figure, for short
32 Pal of Porthos and Aramis
35 Key of Beethoven's "Eroica"
37 "Qué ___?"
38 *"Who Framed Roger Rabbit"* [1995]
41 C.D. holders, maybe
42 Obsess in front of the mirror
43 Much-abbreviated Latin phrase
44 NPR's ___ Radio Hour
45 Memorization
46 "Swans Reflecting Elephants," e.g.
48 Spur
50 *"How the West Was Won"* [1969, 2010]
54 One of 150 in the Bible
55 Award-winning Streep
57 Hindu avatar
58 *"O Brother, Where Art Thou?"* [1990]

60 Settings for some courts
62 "You said it, sister!"
63 Woody and Buzz's owner in "Toy Story"
64 What was cool for a long time?
65 Supermodel Holliday
66 Top dog
67 One of a noted quintet

DOWN

1 Sanjay of CNN
2 One of about five of blood in the average adult body
3 Out of the ordinary
4 Partner of here
5 "Fiddlesticks!"
6 Children, in legalese
7 Spur

8 Word before child or human
9 Manhattan component
10 Firebug's activity
11 Room for art
12 Results of flattery
13 ___-free
14 Bon mot
19 Thom ___ (shoe brand)
22 Fundamentally
25 Fresh stuff
26 Musical featuring the Jellicle Ball
28 "What ___?"
29 Get a load of this!
31 Have legs, so to speak
32 Beavering away
33 More than a couple
34 Psy-ops, say
36 Scram

37 Breeders' documents
39 "___ reflection . . ."
40 Rug buyer's consideration
45 Film that lost to "Green Book" for Best Picture
47 Café order
49 Valleys
50 Low pocket pair in Texas hold 'em
51 Charged
52 P.R. concern
53 Stun, in a way
54 Cool, '90s-style
55 Like early Elvis records
56 Codas
59 Chocolate ___
61 Elvis's record label

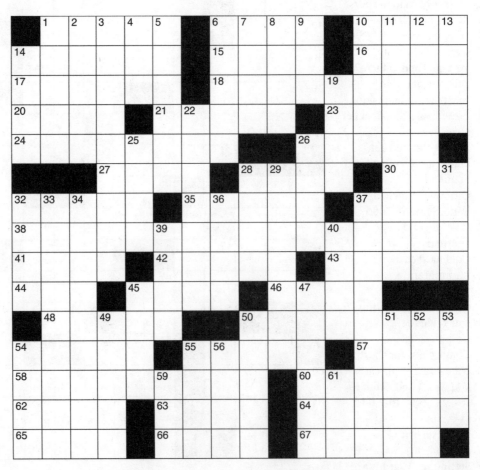

by Andy Kravis, Natan Last and the J.A.S.A. Crossword Class

ACROSS

1 *This is the way the world began, per 51-Across*
8 Track makers
14 Refuge
15 Form a scab, say
16 At an ungodly hour
18 Words before a date
19 Just below C level?
20 OPEC unit: Abbr.
21 Develop wrinkles, say
24 *Literature Nobelist who penned 71-Across*
26 Question from one who's lost
31 Small battery type
32 Away
33 Salon brand with 100% vegan products
35 Throngs
39 Tomorrow's cash flow assessed today
43 Boris Godunov, for one
44 World capital NE of Vientiane
45 ___ lab
46 "Yadda, yadda, yadda"
49 Fictional N.Y.C. locale on children's TV
51 *Physics Nobelist who co-discovered cosmic microwave background radiation, confirming 1-Across*
55 ___-mo
56 Home of the Rosa Parks Museum: Abbr.
57 Fishing net
60 E.P.A. targets since the '70s
64 Classic film series that anticipated the invention of hoverboards
68 Mosey
69 Spots for hoops
70 Conical construction
71 *"This is the way the world ends," per 24-Across*

DOWN

1 What do ewe say?
2 "In that case . . ."
3 Make good progress
4 Chinese dumpling
5 Man's nickname that omits "-old"
6 It's a must
7 [OMG!]
8 "This land," in "This Land Is Your Land"
9 It's west of Yemen
10 "Dig in!"
11 "It was my evil twin!" is not a convincing one
12 ___ octopus, creature so named for its large, earlike fins
13 Like C-O-L-O-U-R or M-E-T-R-E
14 Spot for a soothing scrub
17 All-consonant diner order
22 Reverse, e.g.
23 Rain gutter locale
25 Dalai ___
26 "I ___ bite"
27 Shades
28 James played by Beyoncé in a 2008 biopic
29 Gym shorts material
30 Notions
34 Actress Hathaway
36 Ye ___ Shoppe
37 Supply at a barbecue
38 Airline assignment
40 Head of a country, informally
41 Chuck
42 Container for nitroglycerin, say
47 Dot in "i" or "j"
48 King of music
50 Hairstyle popularized by the Beatles
51 ___ Blue Ribbon
52 Bring joy to
53 Shiny button material
54 Day after 66-Down: Abbr.
58 "That was close!"
59 Two-time Emmy winner Remini
61 27, to 3
62 Family member, in rural dialect
63 French possessive
65 Keystone ___ (character in slapstick comedy)
66 Day before 54-Down: Abbr.
67 Einstein's German birthplace

by Ashish Vengsarkar

ACROSS

1 Seat of Oklahoma's Garfield County
5 Clammy
10 Saddle-making tools
14 One of three at the start of a Pac-Man game
15 Tea party crasher of fiction
16 Person of outstanding importance
17 Ancient pyramid builders
18 Doofus
19 Poet ___ Wheeler Wilcox
20 Ohm, Hertz and Newton
22 87-octane gas
24 Get further mileage from
25 Dunderhead
27 Leave nothing behind?
28 Heartbeat
29 With 38-Across, Emmy-winning HBO drama whose name suggests this puzzle's theme
32 Some remote power sources
33 Baby food
35 Grove
36 Range of sizes, in brief
37 ___Vista, early search engine
38 See 29-Across
39 Text back and forth, say
41 Openly condemn
43 Apple found on Apple Music
44 What Yggdrasil of Norse mythology is
47 Covert Cold War deal
49 Like areas around waterfalls
50 Actress Donovan of "Clueless"
51 ___ Mawr College
53 Sordid
55 Minestrone ingredient
58 Bit of swamp flora
60 The 500s, in the Dewey Decimal System: Abbr.
61 It's bigger than a family
62 Cry of frustration
63 French article
64 Cathedral area

65 Muckraking journalist Jacob
66 "___ es!" (Spanish for "That's it!")
67 50-denomination coin whose reverse side shows the Fatima Masumeh Shrine

DOWN

1 Brand that many people stick with
2 She played Nicole Chapman on "Fame"
3 ". . . know what I'm saying?"
4 ___ list
5 Seriously hurt
6 Germanic language of the 8th–12th centuries
7 Jr.'s son, maybe
8 Nine-time Oscar nominee for Best Director
9 Rodin's thinker?
10 Unalaska inhabitant
11 Who said "Presidents come and go, but the Supreme Court goes on forever"
12 Entertainer once known as the Queen of Las Vegas
13 Wolfs (down)
21 "What is it?"
23 Prime meridian std.
26 West Coast law force, for short
30 Post-op stop
31 Poetic adverb

34 Game show loser's prize
36 Movable aerial platform
37 Nabokov's longest novel
40 Bug
42 Jr. and sr.
43 "In case it's of interest . . ."
45 Uranians, e.g.
46 Drill command
47 Like havarti or Muenster
48 Wield
51 Scouts ___, rebranded name since '19
52 Bring up
54 Super-duper
56 Fervency
57 Yossarian's tentmate in "Catch-22"
59 Sounds of puzzlement
61 Trireme implement

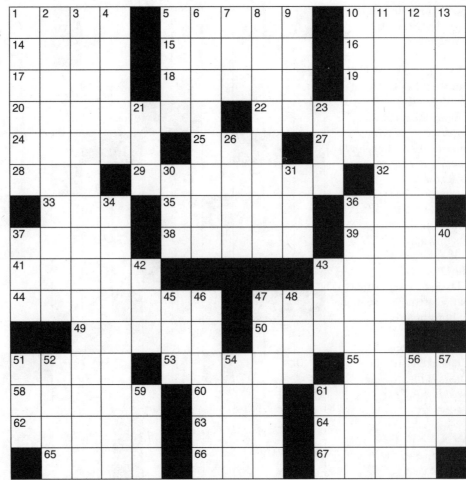

by Trenton Charlson

ACROSS

1 Hairstyle for Billy Preston
5 Pacific nation composed of 250+ islands
10 Fairy tale baddie
14 Brest milk
15 Cold War concern, for short
16 Spot for an ibex
17 Event with minutes that might last hours
20 What choristers may sing in
21 Persistently bothers
22 Shania Twain's "___! I Feel Like a Woman!"
23 Bacillus shape
25 Left after taxes
26 Purchase inspired by a New Year's resolution, often
33 Diamond parts that are rounded
35 Transport from Seattle to Bainbridge Island
36 Kerfuffle
37 Poet Dove
38 Hardly iffy
39 Avocado or olive products
40 Computing pioneer Lovelace
41 Made a peeling?
42 Sound, e.g.
43 Rubella, by another name
46 Suffix with "most," redundantly
47 Item sometimes made with pikake flowers
48 Director DuVernay
51 Surname of father-and-son Latin pop singers
56 Chair wheel
58 Ominous request from a teacher . . . or a hint to the first words (and following letters!) of 17-, 26- and 43-Across
60 Scandinavian name whose masculine equivalent ends in "-var"
61 Get a sense of

62 Show with booths
63 Stash belowdecks
64 ". . . unless I'm wrong"
65 Gorilla expert Fossey

DOWN

1 Song collection
2 Animals of a region
3 Future celebrity
4 Inventor Boykin who helped develop the pacemaker
5 Wunderkind
6 Prominent features on firefighter calendars
7 Played paper against scissors, e.g.
8 Food, in a food fight
9 Tech-obsessed sort, perhaps
10 Largish chamber groups
11 Cheshire cat's signature feature
12 Tirade
13 They run when they're broken
18 Standards
19 Rock powder used as an abrasive
24 Warp
27 Vote of support
28 Hockey game interruption, maybe
29 Like some suites
30 Waves from the curb, say
31 Duty-free?
32 Blog entry
33 Crow
34 Gofer

38 Major pilgrimage destination in Spain
39 Number aptly found in "loner"
41 So last year
42 ___ crest (part of the pelvis)
44 Granny, in the South
45 It's meant to be kept
49 Scooter brand whose name means "wasp"
50 Crime in insurance investigations
51 Goddess sister of Nephthys
52 Courteous chap
53 Kind of block
54 Way off
55 Knock for a loop
57 "Ethan Frome" vehicle
59 Literally, "I"

by Will Nediger

ACROSS

1 Sites for whirlpools
5 Some time __
8 Peppery salad ingredient
13 Pack down
14 It's been called "the art of making a point without making an enemy"
16 Toots one's horn
17 Young woman living in a city, as 58-Across would say
19 Oreos at an ice cream parlor, say
20 __ d'Or (Cannes award)
21 Subject of a squabble between airplane passengers
23 Dedicated work
24 Minnie's promise, as 58-Across would say
28 Bureaucracy
30 "How __ it?"
31 Epitome of simplicity
32 Word with secret or talent
34 Beano competitor
35 When an armistice is signed, as 58-Across would say
40 Hunger (for)
41 Lines of power
42 __ Day (May 1, in Hawaii)
43 G.I. to be worried about
46 Kidding around
50 Looking pretty, as 58-Across would say
53 "Starter" starter
54 Shaky
55 City that's home to the N.C.A.A.'s College World Series
57 Tickets
58 Animated character who's the subject of this puzzle's theme
61 "Madama Butterfly" has four
62 Super Monkey Ball company
63 Small stream
64 Offer from a volunteer
65 Hand pic, maybe
66 Livens (up)

DOWN

1 Daze
2 Marching band event
3 Moseyed along
4 Something you might use a filter for
5 Producer of the Jacksons?
6 __ rights, cause long championed by the Mattachine Society
7 Eightsome
8 Baubles
9 Sporting event in a ring
10 Finally reaches
11 Easy to scare
12 ID theft target
15 Comfy couch accessory
18 Movement associated with crystal healing
22 Curator's deg.
25 Tournament type
26 Counterpart of own
27 "Imperio" or "Crucio" in the Harry Potter books
29 Gentle
33 Service station offering
34 Say all sorts of nice things
35 17-time host of the Academy of Country Music Awards
36 Slow-on-the-uptake cry
37 Major exporter of mineral water
38 Go at a clip
39 Do some farrier's work on
40 Mahershala of "Green Book"
43 Salon foam
44 "Affirmative"
45 "Don't make __!"
47 Drawn
48 Totally useless
49 Twists into deformity
51 When many New Year's parties begin to die down
52 So far
56 Car sticker fig.
57 The Golden Bears of the N.C.A.A., familiarly
59 JFK alternative
60 Sight at a brewpub

by Barbara Lin

ACROSS

1 *Graveyard sight
5 *Emerald or ruby
10 *Ring centerpiece
13 Jet stream direction
14 Word with one or other
15 Man found in America?
17 Deadly snakes
18 "Peanuts" boy
19 Brit's "Nonsense!"
20 Bourbon substitute
21 Delight
22 Tear sheet?
24 Dangerous juggling props
26 Marshy area
27 Country whose flag has two blue stripes and a star: Abbr.
28 Quiets down
29 Tree cover
30 Anthem contraction
31 Nirvana's "Smells Like __ Spirit"
32 Org. seeking alien life
33 __ Murray, two-time Wimbledon champ
34 Historic inn commemorated during Pride Month, as suggested by this puzzle's border answers
37 Political suffix
40 Fillable flatbread
41 Persist
44 Western treaty grp.
45 Section of a wine list
46 H.S. class whose students might cook
48 G.O.P. org.
49 Binary digit
50 Binary question
51 Tokyo's airport
53 Vegetable also called ladies' fingers
54 "There's the __"
55 Discharge
56 Weight on the Isle of Wight
58 Hurtful remark
59 Overcharges, so to speak

60 Skywalker's droid, informally
61 First-year legal student, familiarly
62 *Pennsylvania state symbol
63 *Kind of building seen on "Sesame Street"
64 *Magnetite

DOWN

1 *Online card game with over 100 million players
2 Infield pop-up, say
3 Malign
4 Rehab woe, for short
5 Debutantes, say
6 Elite eight
7 Actress Russo
8 1989 play about Capote
9 Widespread panic
10 Grasps
11 Beach problem
12 Like the words "literally" and "ironic," often
16 *Pit that's spit
21 War of 1812 treaty site
23 Fingerprinting need
25 Where the heart is
26 Ruling on a point of Islamic law
29 Borscht base
32 Mocking
33 Davy Crockett died defending it
35 Start tallying your drink orders, say

36 Literature Nobelist Mario Vargas __
37 *Vital piece
38 Behaved uncontrollably
39 Attribute
42 Spicy Mexican pepper
43 Like many veteran professors
45 Decay
46 This point forward
47 *Quaint street material
50 "See what I mean?," informally
52 Teeny
53 Aware of
57 Defenseman who scored a Stanley Cup-winning "flying goal"
58 Neighbor of Brazil: Abbr.

by Jesse Goldberg

ACROSS

1 Stirs in
4 Signature Obama legislation, briefly
7 It's no free ride
10 British trunk
13 Leavened flatbread
14 High pitch
15 Quite green
17 Furniture also called hassocks
19 Low-cal pub offering
20 Tractor maker
21 Tired and bored
23 Literally, "earth"
24 Member of an ancient Jewish sect
26 Dings on a record
28 Exhaust one's funds for betting
30 Niña companion
34 Catchphrase on "The Simpsons"
37 Gobble (up)
38 "Are you sure about that?"
39 Inits. for a trip
41 ___ pals
42 Word with gender or age
43 Pub offering
45 State with more than half of Mexico's Indigenous language speakers
48 "I can be of service!"
51 Like bad apples and sour grapes?
53 Pound-bound hound, say
54 Seen a lot
55 Fixes, as a hem
57 Peace in Saudi Arabia
61 Top story
64 Currently airing
66 Grown-up pupper
67 Hauls into court
69 Some asylum seekers
71 Come out again
72 Material in some vaccines
73 Rest stops
74 Supply center?
75 Alternative to the euro: Abbr.
76 Pay stub inits.
77 Profession for Elle Woods in "Legally Blonde": Abbr.

DOWN

1 One end of a cell
2 Candlelit dinners for four, say
3 [How boring]
4 In the style of
5 If, and or but: Abbr.
6 Biblical name repeated in a Faulkner title
7 Relatives of glockenspiels
8 Things that are far from basic?
9 Phony internet persona, often
10 Honey
11 React to a gut punch, perhaps
12 TV host Banks
16 Takes effect
18 Kind of health
22 Strengthen one's commitment . . . and a hint to four answers in this puzzle
25 Title on "Downton Abbey"
27 Mini-albums, for short
29 Curry made with hoof meat
31 Pester constantly
32 ___ Paige Johnson, co-creator of TV's "Blue's Clues"
33 Company advertised by a quack?
34 Mythical giant with 100 50-Downs
35 Brewery supply
36 Bit of high jinks
40 Bad fortune
44 Able to practice, in a way
46 Singer Tori
47 Legendary home of Kubla Khan
49 "Peanuts" character with glasses
50 See 34-Down
52 "My bad"
56 Bops or hits, say
58 Sayings attributed to Jesus
59 Spy with questionable loyalty
60 Covered in some green growth
61 Influential D.C. lobby
62 Hotel chain operated by Hilton
63 Alpo competitor
65 Took a turn
68 "Despicable Me" antihero
70 Silly Bandz or Webkinz, once

by Kyra Wilson and Sophia Maymudes

ACROSS

1 Some dash mounts
5 Prepare for the long haul?
10 Juul, e.g.
14 First person?
15 Cropped up
16 Musk of 45-Across
17 Puerto ___
18 Condition better known as anemia
20 Kibitzing passenger
22 With it, in old slang
23 Two-syllable cheer
24 Glistens with shimmering colors
30 Jazz style that influenced the Beat Generation
34 Mauna ___
35 TV addict
37 Baseball stats
39 Disney princess who shares a name with a Shakespeare character
40 The "A" of M.M.A.
41 Blabbing informant
44 Prey of a murder hornet
45 Maker of the Model S and Model 3
46 Best Comeback Athlete, for one
48 Abbreviation that can replace an ellipsis
50 Courtly title
51 Dilettantish know-it-all
59 Hercules on his first labor, or Hemingway on safari
60 Nobel laureate Wiesel
61 Golden calf, e.g.
62 World of Warcraft enthusiast, for one
63 Bone on the pinkie side of the forearm
64 Courtly title
65 Flexible Flyer products
66 Products of Always or Stayfree

DOWN

1 Low-___ diet
2 Sarah McLachlan hit that's 51-Down spelled in reverse

3 Espressos "stained" with a bit of milk
4 Like some salmon and turkey
5 Airplane ticket info
6 Las Vegas resort with a musical name
7 Ilk
8 Like thrift shop wares
9 "Pain and Glory" director Almodóvar
10 Kraft product
11 Soothing succulent
12 Not up to expectations
13 Word after business or bitter
19 Frodo's first cousin (mother's side) and second cousin (father's side)
21 De-tailed detail?

24 Runner-up's rueful report
25 Road trip plan
26 Dial or Tone
27 Nobel Prize winner of 1903 and 1911
28 Modern health risks, for short
29 Their population in New Zealand peaked at 70 million in 1982
31 1968 Jane Fonda sci-fi role
32 Animal that's known to enjoy water slides
33 Asked, as a question
36 Stratagem
38 How presidents swear when taking the oath of office
42 Door fastener
43 See 59-Down

47 Clean, as with a paper towel
49 Drinks down heartily
51 Opera that's 2-Down backward
52 Church cross
53 Overly fussy, informally
54 "I'm just like that," in modern lingo
55 Slender plant
56 Misses the mark
57 Cocktail garnish
58 Oolong and Darjeeling
59 With 43-Down, rapper with the 2021 #1 hit "Montero (Call Me by Your Name)"

by Byron Walden

ACROSS

1 Start of an encrypted web address
6 "Go" follower
10 Hit the ___
14 "Color me surprised!"
16 Everybody: Ger.
17 Leonardo, Michelangelo, Donatello and Raphael?
19 Contractor's fig.
20 ___ Beach, Calif.
21 Following
22 More treasured
24 Counterpart of down: Abbr.
25 Polishing the chandelier in "The Phantom of the Opera" and laundering uniforms in "Hamilton"?
32 Procrastinator's promise
34 Port-___ (French cheese)
35 Like some nail polish shades
36 Day following hump day: Abbr.
37 "The Entertainer," e.g.
38 Trace
39 "___ 2 Proud 2 Beg" (TLC hit)
41 Professor Moriarty's first name
43 Exchange for a tenner
44 Result of a poorly planned invasion of the Body Snatchers?
47 "Let's ___!"
48 Biological cavity
51 Roll-on alternative
54 Tuned in
57 Grp. with wands
58 "I'm tired of all this negative media coverage"?
61 Legendary queen once depicted on Tunisian currency
62 Consumers of audio and visual media only
63 Snail-like
64 Comedian Richter
65 Tessellated creatures in Escher prints

DOWN

1 Brought on
2 "___ days . . ."
3 Equivalent
4 Reason to avert one's eyes, for short
5 Marsh birds
6 X in XXX, maybe
7 Name that derives from the Hebrew word for "earth"
8 First female U.S. attorney general
9 X in XXX, maybe
10 Most expensive spice in the world by weight
11 Frequently
12 Tip-off
13 Model Miranda
15 God depicted wearing ostrich feathers
18 Per
23 Be a political candidate
24 ___ Up, political group formed in response to the AIDS crisis
26 A little over three grains
27 Big name in rental cars
28 One- or two-person vehicles in the Olympics
29 Source of latex
30 Actress Falco
31 Hardens
32 Ending of seven country names
33 River that starts in Pittsburgh
40 Finish some gift-wrapping, say
41 Word before black or Blue
42 Meager
43 "The only way to run away without leaving home," per Twyla Tharp
45 Rudolph on "S.N.L."
46 Carry-on limit, often
49 App's audience
50 En ___
51 Quality control guidelines: Abbr.
52 Hartman who voiced Troy McClure on "The Simpsons"
53 Take two
54 Unknown source, for short
55 Make, as one's way
56 Out of whack
59 It's stranded in a cell
60 Bobbie Gentry's "___ to Billie Joe"

by Sheldon Polonsky

ACROSS

1 Items purportedly burned outside the Miss America Pageant in 1968
5 Prefix that makes a pseudoscience when paired with 44-Down
11 Quatrain rhyme scheme
15 Fancy fabric
16 Embryo's home
17 Barbershop job
18 Tiptop
19 *Jim Sheridan gives Daniel Day-Lewis nothing to work with in this Irish dramedy (1989)*
21 Photographer Goldin
22 Stop up
23 Rapper Megan ___ Stallion
24 Letters seen on some tote bags
25 *Rian Johnson helms this snoozer of a whodunit starring Daniel Craig (2019)*
28 Thorny tree
30 Adorable one
31 It made the peseta passé
34 Have in inventory
35 Handy sorts
37 Fey of "30 Rock"
39 Follower of smart or bad
40 *Elia Kazan bungles this John Steinbeck novel adaptation (1955)*
43 Hit the slopes
45 Tennant of the Pet Shop Boys
46 Foe of Austin Powers
50 Nice dinnerware
52 Tavern offerings
54 Assemble
55 Korean alphabet system
57 *Anne Fletcher misses the mark with this first film in a dance franchise (2006)*
59 1950s White House nickname
60 Word with luck or waiter
63 Nonkosher sandwich
64 Captain's record
65 Led astray . . . or like the films at 19-, 25-, 40- and 57-Across?

68 Muppet with a big orange nose
69 Victorian
70 Make hard to read, in a way
71 Egyptian cross
72 Lip
73 Cleaning tool
74 Online crafts shop

DOWN

1 Item needed for burning, once
2 Indigenous people of Easter Island
3 Pool or fitness center, for a hotel
4 Census info
5 Mountain lions
6 Frustrate
7 "___ out!" (ump's cry)
8 Lit ___

9 Jackman of "X-Men"
10 ___ Jackson, a.k.a. Ice Cube
11 D.O.J. agency
12 Winners of Super Bowl 50
13 "Frida" and "Selena," e.g.
14 Operator of the California Zephyr
20 Gumshoes
22 Big name in tractors
26 For your ___ pleasure
27 Almond extract, e.g.
29 Finished
32 Big guns
33 Unnamed person
36 Job app ID
38 Recipe instruction
41 Gossip, in slang
42 Lose one's cool
43 "Hips Don't Lie" singer, 2006

44 See 5-Across
47 Word that fills both parts of the Shakespeare quote "These ___ delights have ___ ends"
48 Inventor's happy cry
49 Protracted
50 Subjects for Jane Goodall
51 BMW competitor
53 Monk known as the "Father of English History"
56 Baited
58 Respected tribe member
61 Handout from a maître d'
62 Secretly loops in, in a way
66 Private Instagram exchanges, briefly
67 Tater ___
68 Hon

by Finn Vigeland

ACROSS

1 Animal symbol of fertility in ancient Egypt
5 Locale for a salmon ladder
8 Lillian __, the First Lady of American Cinema
12 Top pork producer in the U.S.
13 Twine material
15 __ buco
16 Acronym for some academic grants
17 Syrup source
18 TV host with a "Garage"
19 Grotesque
21 Portable work surface
23 Ailurophiles
25 Accouchement
28 Mary whose short story "The Wisdom of Eve" was the basis for 1950's "All About Eve"
29 Modern pic
33 Publishing IDs
34 "__ Flair Drip" (2018 rap hit)
35 Colorado's __ Park
36 "Me day" destinations
37 Whence the Portuguese creole language Patuá
39 Old man
40 Newly elected California congresswoman of 1987
42 Like wine with cheese, often
44 Chase vehicle, once, in brief?
45 Fox Islands resident
49 Mauna __
50 Places for quills
52 Waves to a hairdresser?
55 Accessories for tablets
56 Historical lead-in to -evna or -evich
60 Cheyenne allies
62 GQ competitor
64 Snapper?
65 Sight from New York City's Riverside Park
66 Flower holder
67 Words to the audience

DOWN

1 With 11-Down, what each of this puzzle's groups of circles represents
2 Side order with curry
3 Was in the red
4 Xbox or PlayStation
5 Group migration
6 Relative of an adder
7 One of las Islas Baleares
8 Finishing touch on the first transcontinental railroad
9 "Gotcha"
10 Info on tax forms
11 See 1-Down
13 Crude content
14 Vault
20 Sticks in the water
22 French for "bent"
24 Guitarist Clapton
25 "Frontal" or "lateral" speaking features
26 White-barked tree
27 Hoops
30 Austere
31 Home with a hole at the top
32 Carne __
37 Drink that might be served with a metal cup
38 Vedic religious text
41 __ Jose
43 "Your point being . . . ?"
46 Regarding
47 Part of a hog farm
48 Trendy ingredient in a healthy smoothie
50 Push forward
51 Features of some leather jackets
52 "Super" orgs.
53 Part of Q.E.D.
54 Sita's love, in Hindu lore
57 Enthusiastic Spanish assent
58 Sports star who split with J.Lo in 2021
59 Actor Auberjonois
61 Synagogue feature
63 Sine __ non

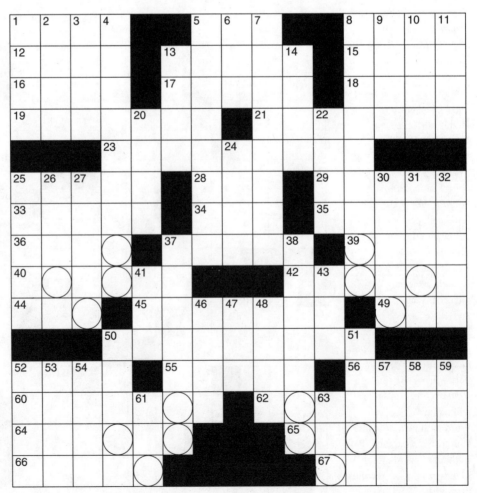

by Blake Slonecker

ACROSS

1 Plays for time, in a way
6 Word repeated by Hamlet before "solid flesh"
9 Hairstyle for Audre Lorde
13 Bozo
14 13th-century Persian mystic who is one of the best-selling poets in the U.S.
16 Cookout side dish
17 Mario Kart contestant
18 The Aggies of the Mountain West Conference
20 "Blech!"
21 Black ___
23 Indigenous
24 Decorative items washed up on the beach
27 Meal accompaniment at a trattoria
28 Flotsam and Jetsam in "The Little Mermaid"
29 Crusty piece of bread
31 Stick up
34 The Lorax's final word
36 ___ Duncan, Obama education secretary
37 Musician Yoko
38 Hollywood's Dwayne Johnson, with "the"
39 Like the blood of a universal donor
41 Tech that enables contactless credit card payments
42 Neither's partner
43 Wedge, e.g.
44 Loquacious
46 Bit of water or snow equipment
47 What a QR code at a restaurant might link to
48 Verdant
49 Digs
51 Most desirable, say, as a ripe peach
55 "Can it!"
57 Where Boxing Day comes *before* Christmas, in brief?
58 Ill
59 Jiffy
61 Underwater ecosystems
63 Cooling succulent
64 It may be taken in protest
65 Start of a saying about staying fit
66 Lairs
67 Is the pope Catholic?
68 Adam who directed "The Big Short"

DOWN

1 Malware, often
2 "Curiosity killed the cat," e.g.
3 Author of "Jurassic Park"
4 Who wrote "To Helen" and "For Annie"
5 Ambles
6 Support structure
7 Not in the closet
8 Muscat's sultanate
9 Actor John or Sean
10 Fleeting romantic interest
11 Give feedback on Yelp, maybe
12 Fall short
15 "Beats me!"
19 It may turn at a station
22 Shift blame to someone else
25 Nerdy sort
26 "Get it together!" . . . or a hint to the highlighted letters
30 'Fore
32 "Roger that, boss!"
33 Corpus
34 Locales for some Grecian art
35 Cozy place
40 Thither
41 Farrier's tool
43 Strike hard, in the Bible
45 Like the same old same old
50 Hiding soldiers in the Trojan horse and such
52 Good things to strike
53 Actress Vergara
54 Quick to snap
55 Lone
56 One providing a ride at a fair, maybe
59 Tricked
60 French word between two names
62 "Exit" key

by Kate Hawkins

ACROSS

1 Michelangelo's only signed work
6 411
10 Like dewy grass
14 Did diddly squat
15 The "you" in the classic song lyric "I'm crossin' you in style some day"
17 Caravan member, perhaps
18 Stick with it
19 In-flight call?
21 Risky
22 "My b!"
23 Cosmetics giant
25 Cat, in Castile
28 "That's ridonculous"
33 Cry in a famous balcony scene
35 ___ Eshkol, third prime minister of Israel
36 Browbeat
37 Aster relative
38 Waste receptacle
39 Timely
41 Blood-typing system
42 Release
44 Hair nets
45 "Someone's going to pay for this!"
48 Warn with a horn
49 Caro who directed 2020's "Mulan"
50 Some remote inserts
52 City near the Temple of Isis
55 Lucy van Pelt's frequent outburst to Charlie Brown . . . or how to fill some squares in this puzzle?
60 One making a scene
62 Woodwind section
63 "The highest result of education," per Helen Keller
64 Oscar winner Berry
65 Picks
66 Without a leader?
67 Take from one medium to another

DOWN

1 Fool
2 Exchanged promises
3 Love to Hug ___ (plush doll)
4 Spots for spots?
5 Supplement
6 Pucklike
7 December number
8 Left behind
9 Slip-___
10 Summer Olympics event
11 With, in France
12 "___ Christianity" (C. S. Lewis book)
13 Quarry
16 Guacamole ingredient
20 Lhasa ___
24 Nickname composed only of Roman numerals
25 Moved up the corporate ladder, say
26 Many subjects of Scheherazade stories
27 Thus far
29 Bush appointee of 2006
30 Marilyn ___, singer with the 5th Dimension
31 "Oh, is that so?"
32 Embark on the Oregon Trail, say
34 Drawing pencil?
38 Indian rice dish
40 "That's better than I expected!"
43 Leader in the civil rights movement, in brief
44 Hunk
46 Since fore-e-ever
47 Praised
51 Pacific greeting
52 For
53 "Cut that out!"
54 Frazier in the Basketball Hall of Fame
56 Historically
57 Pop choice
58 Plantlike growth held up by gas-filled bladders
59 Piece of equipment for a telemarketer
61 Top gear

by Danny Lawson

ACROSS

1 Handwriting style
7 Woodland or wetland
14 E! talk show
16 Similar chemical compounds
17 *Like many old video game soundtracks
19 *Common purchase for a tailgate
20 Getting close, in a guessing game
21 Parts of psyches
23 Tuner that's turned
24 Moves furtively
26 *Sinbad's milieu
30 Singer Stefani
31 "Survivor" setting, often
32 Singer's time to shine
33 Mortgage claim
35 Suggestion made with a wink and a nudge
38 "__ said yes!"
41 *Burger chain named for a father and his sons
43 Minuscule particle
44 Kicked down the road, as an issue
46 Some first responders, in brief
48 Freshly
49 Culmination of a wedding ceremony
51 Resistance units
54 *One of two for the 1990s Chicago Bulls
57 Full of cheer
59 Video hosting service since 2009
60 Like many baby animals
62 Singer's time to shine
63 *Anthem whose French lyrics predate its English lyrics
66 *Former fashion retailer so-named for its 57th Street address in Manhattan
68 "That's two hours I'll never get back!"
69 All together
70 Binge at a buffet, say
71 Fluctuated wildly

DOWN

1 Worries anxiously
2 Science fiction writer Ted with five Hugo awards
3 Came back, as hair
4 (Spoiler alert!) Sole survivor of the Pequod
5 Poker prize
6 "A series of __," infamous analogy for the internet
7 Philip Pullman's "__ Dark Materials"
8 Stage digression
9 Completely confine
10 Stalemate
11 Star of CBS's "Madam Secretary"
12 Circle segment
13 "For shame!"
15 One skewered at a roast?
18 Throw out
22 Bud in the Baseball Hall of Fame
25 Part of a place setting
27 Performance sites
28 Big name in shoes and handbags
29 In a moment
31 Bring up
34 __ al-Adha (Muslim holiday)
36 Citi Field team, on scoreboards
37 "We wanna join!"
38 Altercation
39 "Say what?"
40 Deprive of strength—not, as is commonly believed, to give strength
42 Pioneering computer
45 11- or 12-year-old
47 Draw back (from)
50 Bowl over
52 On a larger scale
53 Credit __ (banking giant)
55 Steer clear of
56 Places for speakers
57 Woman in a 1982 hit who can be reached using the starts of the answers to the starred clues
58 Filled to the brim
61 What might get under your collar?
63 "Well, lookee here!"
64 Cleveland athlete, for short
65 The "A" of D.A.: Abbr.
67 __ pop (genre for Billie Eilish)

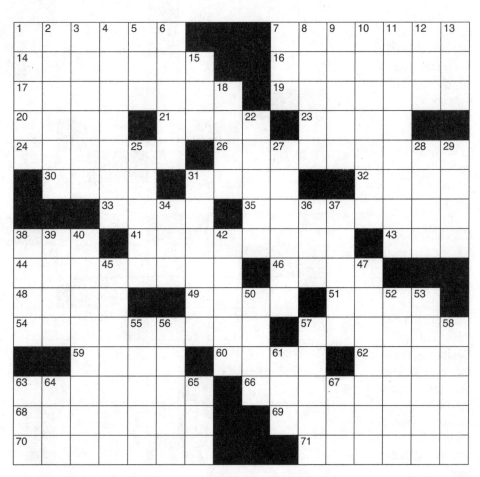

by Christopher Adams and Adam Aaronson

ACROSS

1 Steals and saves, e.g.
6 Feature of a smartwatch, in brief
9 Perniciousness
13 A little snowy, perhaps?
14 Habitat becoming bleached by global warming
16 Crumbly ice cream topping
17 Something that turns light green?
19 Habit
20 "I can't believe I said that"
22 Directory info: Abbr.
25 Skedaddles, cowboy-style
26 Helps with the dishes
27 Doesn't do takeout at a restaurant
29 Polite refusal
30 "Hold it, buster!"
33 Instrument that largely replaced the ophicleide
34 Completely dominate
35 Box score column
39 "This favor doesn't come cheap!"
44 Grow on trees, so to speak
46 C_2H_6
47 Cath lab supply
48 Rhyme for "menorah" in "Hanukkah, Oh Hanukkah"
50 Spring roll?
51 "Really can't count on it, I'm afraid"
54 Capitale of the Lazio region of Italy
55 Overruling of an objection
59 Midwest center of agricultural research
60 Woody in "Toy Story," e.g.
61 Produce safety concern

62 Access to an expense account, perhaps
63 Hunk
64 Curling locales

DOWN

1 Rihanna's first #1 single
2 < —
3 Word with ears or thumbs
4 Squad
5 Luxury hotel chain
6 50s president
7 Is unresolved
8 Come across as
9 Words of befuddlement
10 Stimulate
11 Didn't buy, say
12 They may come to light
15 Casting option
18 It can be stripped or chipped
21 Quarry
22 Lizardlike amphibian
23 Where the Ko'olau range is located
24 Random guess
28 Keep focused
29 Point value commonly assigned to a queen in chess
31 Part of academic regalia
32 "Ick!"
36 Leaning
37 "__ expert . . ."
38 Genesis

40 On the __ (not talking to each other)
41 Tacit
42 She played Sophie in "Sophie's Choice"
43 Amazon, for one
44 In
45 Visibly happy person
47 Bra part
48 Hujambo : Swahili :: __ : English
49 Procter & Gamble brand
52 YouTube journal posting
53 Points of interest
56 South Korean currency
57 Sort
58 First word of the song "Simple Gifts"

by Joe Deeney

ACROSS

1 Triumphant cry
5 Electrical resistance unit
8 ___ Rabbit
12 Mysterious cafeteria offering
13 Sweetheart
15 "Boléro" composer
17 Each
18 Baghdad's ___ City
19 Symbol for 5-Across
20 One who whistles while working
22 Snoozes (like participant #2 in one classic fable)
24 Legally prohibit
26 First name of two Spice Girls
27 Familial nickname
28 Ineffectual
31 Femur or fibula
34 Wonder Woman portrayer Gadot
35 ___ Cooler, "Ghostbusters"-inspired Hi-C flavor
37 ___-Magnon
38 With 71-/72-/73-Across, participant #1's strategy (or the moral of the story)
43 Rhyme with rhythm
44 Living space that may be empty in the summer
45 Overseer of a quadrennial competition: Abbr.
47 "Quiet, you!," quaintly
51 Oaf
53 Org. appropriately found in Elgin Baylor's name
54 Fall behind
56 Word before tube or circle
57 Wagers unwisely (as participant #2 did)
61 Negative vote
62 Grabs skillfully
63 Algorithm part
65 Some TV spots, briefly
68 Prohibition starter
69 Quesadilla alternative
70 One-percenter suffix
71, 72 & 73 See 38-Across

DOWN

1 Water bottle confiscators, for short
2 Tour de France peak
3 Don't knock until you've tried it
4 Response to a verdict
5 Ones providing postpartum care, in brief
6 Pressure, in slang
7 Palindromic term of address
8 Warner ___ (film company)
9 Incarnation of Vishnu in a Sanskrit epic
10 "That may be the case, but . . ."
11 Win back
14 Nerd on '90s TV
16 Fall back into one's old ways
21 Express road
23 She plotted to kill Clytemnestra
24 Really liked
25 Those: Sp.
29 Shoulder blade
30 Amtrak stop: Abbr.
32 Mischief-maker
33 Feathery wrap
36 A little strange
39 Boston Bruins icon
40 Soak (up)
41 Ancient Greek festival honoring the god of wine
42 Farm connector
46 Subway component
47 How Timothy Leary spent some time
48 Premium TV streaming service until 2020
49 Fiji alternative
50 Beer in a red, white and blue can
52 Comparable (with)
55 Imply
58 Painter Schiele
59 Fast former fliers, for short
60 ___ support
64 "The Fall of the House of Usher" writer
66 Parabolic path
67 Understand

by Peter A. Collins

ACROSS

1 Slip
7 Sections of online dating profiles
11 Baseball, e.g.
14 Wrap up
15 "Hamilton" won one in 2015
16 Very beginning?
17 Fashionable
18 "Look what we have here!"
20 Some change
21 Coffee liqueur originally from Jamaica
22 Symbol of strength
23 St. __, neighborhood in north London
27 Creature whose eyesight has four to five times the acuity of humans
28 Nashville-to-Louisville dir.
29 Jules who lent his name to an article of attire
31 Some women's donations
33 Standing
34 Slipped
36 Like tom yum soup
39 It can be two-way . . . with a hint to four squares in this puzzle
41 Puts on top of
42 "Antiques Roadshow" determination
44 It's always getting into hot water
46 Eroded, with "away"
47 Thor, for one
49 Dazzle
52 Funny Poundstone
54 Libel or slander
55 "__ Father . . ."
56 2001 Broadway hit with an exclamation mark in its name
58 Conductor Georg
60 Frenzied
62 Something to meditate on
63 Big speedway sponsor
64 "Buona __"
65 Intertwine
66 Sound a biker doesn't want to hear
67 Basket made from behind the arc
68 Progressive people?

DOWN

1 Guiding light
2 Like some museum exhibits
3 Not amplified, in a way
4 Windfall
5 One who has spent years at sea
6 Onetime record label with a poetic name
7 Salaam, e.g.
8 "Su-u-u-ure"
9 More slick, in a way
10 Rich, but not born that way
11 Oppressive boss
12 Feeling "Whew, that was close!"
13 Composer Bartók
19 Wit
24 "Warm"
25 Set down on paper, as music
26 Beethoven, to Haydn
30 Cheese that's often grated
32 Things that may be classified
33 Collect dust
35 Piano performance in an old music hall
36 One of the "Big Four" domestic carriers, once
37 Short shorts
38 Town tour guides
40 Upper: Ger.
43 Certain flag position
45 Specialty of Franz Schubert
48 More egocentric
49 Figure in a horror film
50 Best in a film audition, say
51 Sets down on paper
53 Strike caller
56 Not catch
57 Ending with some large numbers
59 Look lecherously
61 Low island
62 A word in passing?

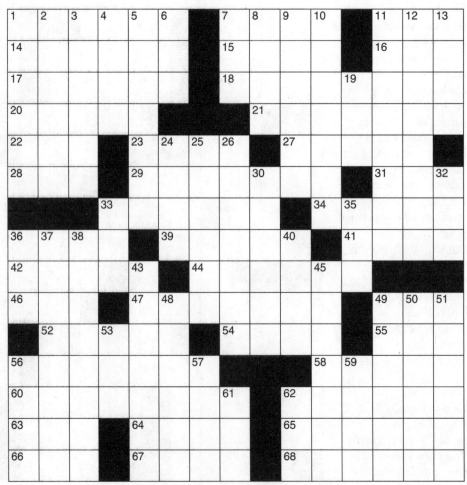

by John Lampkin

ACROSS

1 Gets rid of, so to speak
5 Parties with glowsticks
10 Old-fashioned taste?
13 Menu at un café
15 Amazon's biz
16 Subj. for some aspiring bilinguals
17 Clamoring for "The Bonfire of the Vanities"?
19 They can help you get out of a rut, for short
20 Business plan
21 One of 20 on the Titanic
23 TV alien played by Robin Williams
24 Selling someone on "The Importance of Being Earnest"?
26 Group with lodges
28 Exam with logic questions, for short
29 "Any other place besides here?"
34 Genesis creator
37 Curse
38 Kindle, e.g. . . . or a hint to this puzzle's theme?
41 Hair color of about 2% of the world's population
42 Not fooled by
44 They're a bit of a stretch
46 Some jeans features
49 Humorist Bombeck
50 Spot to store "A Confederacy of Dunces"?
54 ___ Zor-El, real name of Supergirl
58 Battle with clearly defined sides
59 "Now wait just a second!"
61 With 14-Down, what "Fin" might mean
62 Positive review of a Nancy Drew mystery?
64 "Jingle Bells" contraction
65 Architect born in Guangzhou
66 A dance or a dip
67 Narc (on)
68 Six of the first 10 elements on the periodic table
69 Units of poetry

DOWN

1 Philosopher with a "razor"
2 Crime drama set in the Midwest
3 Fast-food fixture
4 Rascal
5 Counterpart of "FF"
6 Bikini, e.g.
7 Sound
8 Towering figure of architecture?
9 Is out
10 Creatures that have the densest fur of any mammal (up to 1 million hairs per square inch)
11 Hayes with three Grammys and an Oscar
12 "Lady Lazarus" poet Sylvia
14 See 61-Across
18 Onetime popular blog that covered Manhattan gossip
22 Predisposition
25 R&B's ___ Brothers
27 Big name in jeans
29 "___ goes there?"
30 Lay figure?
31 People person, perhaps
32 Portuguese title with a tilde
33 Cusps
35 "My word!"
36 Often-skipped parts of podcasts
39 Coarse
40 Dashboard abbr.
43 "Essential" things
45 Gold insignia of the armed forces
47 Babe or Wilbur, in film
48 Conceptual framework
50 Aristotle, to Alexander the Great
51 Tony nominee Milo
52 A host
53 Host
55 Singer of the titular song in 2012's "Skyfall"
56 Clear one's plate, in a way
57 Bothered terribly
60 Gives the thumbs-up
63 "___ Last Bow" (Sherlock Holmes story)

by Amanda Rafkin and Ross Trudeau

ACROSS

1 "Delish!"
5 "___ Sexy" (1991 dance hit)
10 Single at a bar, perhaps
13 Brown powder
15 Brown powder
16 Costa ___
17 Popular pops
18 Point a finger at
19 Fan fave
20 Kennel sound
21 Southern newspaper that William Faulkner once contributed to, with "The"
24 Prefix with beat or futurism
26 Toy dog from Tibet
27 Sport with Native American origins
30 Melodramatist
31 Kind of saxophone
32 Rapper for whom Harvard's Hip-Hop Fellowship is named
34 Get cozy
39 Cultivars known for their yellow flesh
43 "Excuse me"
44 Do some patching, say
45 Book after Joel
46 Compadre
48 Quantity that's tied to one's carbon footprint
51 Second way of viewing things, figuratively
56 Appear
57 What a solver might growl after catching on to this puzzle's theme?
59 Genre for the Mighty Mighty Bosstones
62 Mine find
63 Mother-of-pearl
64 Motorola smartphone
66 Flubs it
67 Not using profanity, as a comedian
68 "___ is easily deceived, because it is quick to hope": Aristotle
69 Central concept of philosopher Zhuangzi's teachings
70 Repeatedly comments (on)
71 The first one in The New York Times appeared in 1970

DOWN

1 Southwest desert plant
2 Dock
3 Metric of grossness
4 Classic comedy figure who sported a bowl cut
5 Certain warhead transport, in brief
6 Phoenix and Washington, e.g.
7 Low culture, disparagingly
8 Brass band sound
9 Showily deferential
10 Neaten
11 Clickable things
12 Prefix with -lithic
14 Lone Star State athlete
16 Certifier of music sales, for short
22 Apple devices run on it
23 "Along ___ spider . . ."
25 Palm part
27 Easy two-pointer
28 ___-Seltzer
29 Not Ready for Prime Time Players show, for short
33 Where a zipper gets caught?
35 Put on
36 Popular hot-and-sour Thai dish
37 Some summer babies
38 To be: Lat.
40 Headgear for many an extreme athlete
41 Using intuition
42 Have
47 Syllables said with fingers in one's ears
49 Night sch. class
50 Thin, as a voice
51 Small screech, for example
52 Actress Birch
53 Green power option, informally
54 A scallop has up to 200 of these
55 Not so cold
58 Second place at a math competition?
60 Symbol of highness
61 Focus problem, for short
65 Joey of children's fiction

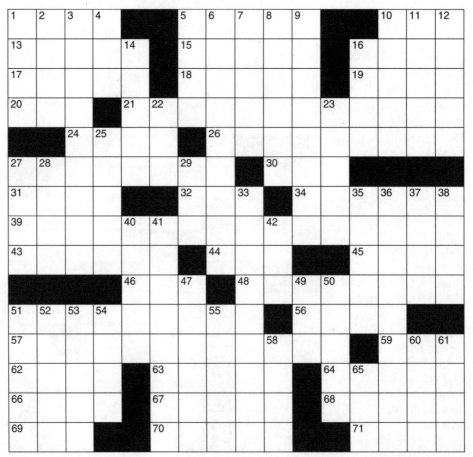

by Max Carpenter

ACROSS

1 All-time leading scorer for the Lakers, familiarly
5 Modern-day horse-and-buggy users
10 Bird with a reduplicative name
14 Old pro
17 Raucous music style similar to boogie-woogie
18 Big Dance org.
19 Action after a bad golf drive
20 "Don't make me eat that!"
21 Bolivian capital
25 Got an A+ on
26 State in Tornado Alley: Abbr.
27 Overhead cost of manufacturing?
28 Drunkard
29 ___ du jour (bistro special)
31 '50s campaign button name
32 Fanciful ideas
35 Become rusted
37 Seminal punk band, with "the"
39 Potato ___ (appetizer)
40 Nap sack?
41 Well-kept
42 Lowest-ranking G.I.
43 Island WNW of Molokai
45 Wall St. credential
46 Who said "The only difference between me and the Surrealists is that I am a Surrealist"
48 Spaces (out)
49 Globe
50 Studied (up on)
51 ___ Reader
53 The titular Nelsons of a classic sitcom
60 Dish with tomatoes and mozzarella
61 Animal whose name consists of the postal codes of two states it passes in its migration
62 British meat pie
63 Nest protest

DOWN

1 Cold War inits.
2 Hybrid citrus fruits
3 Native American canoe material
4 Columnist Klein
5 ___-American
6 "That's not impressing me"
7 Response to "Who wants some?"
8 "Law & Order" spinoff, for short
9 Bucks and bulls
10 Blue state?
11 Speechify
12 Partner of confused
13 This clue number minus deux
15 Passions
16 Large unit of resistance
20 Like some insensitive remarks, for short
22 Encompassed by
23 Give a pointer?
24 Info on a dating profile
28 Bundle up
30 Super-hoppy craft brew
33 Make easier to recite, as the Great Lakes via HOMES
34 Vodka cocktail with cranberry and grapefruit juice
36 Available to watch, in a way
37 Speckled coat
38 Wild guess
40 Bit of sweet talk
44 Take by force
46 Construction vehicle, informally
47 ___ Day, Down Under holiday
50 U2 frontman
52 It costs about twice as much if it's round
54 European peak
55 Actress Vardalos
56 Some N.F.L. linemen: Abbr.
57 It can be tipped . . . or collect tips
58 Whichever
59 Restaurant water choice

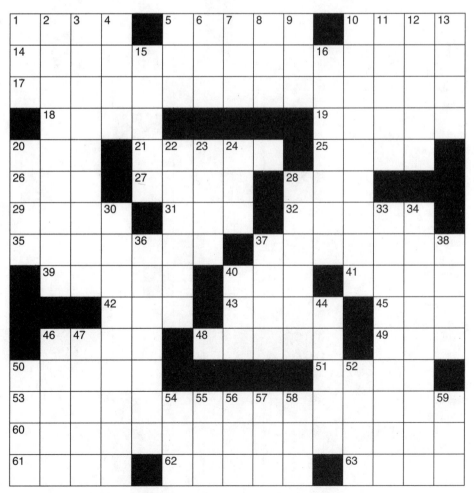

by Alex Vratsanos

ACROSS

1 Bad singer?
4 Start (with)
8 Thingy
14 "I kissed thee ___ I kill'd thee": "Othello"
15 T, as in tests
16 Cause to boil
17 Ones sporting man buns and ironic T-shirts, say
19 Early 1900s kitchen appliance
20 Closest living relatives of whales
22 Land of plenty?
23 Strikebreakers
24 It may get pushed back on the weekend
28 Aggressive campaign
32 Pelvic joints
34 Finely ground quartz
35 They enforce discipline among legislators
40 Gusto
41 "Where'd you get that ___?"
42 Locations of some dives
44 Like park ranger's pants, often
46 ___ Ziff, Marge's ex-boyfriend on "The Simpsons"
47 Kind of gland
49 Three sheets to the wind
54 Bob of "Full House"
56 Common bit of golf attire
57 Inseparable . . . or like three pairs of answers in this puzzle?
62 Quiet
63 Little dipper?
64 Can't stand
65 Maker of Brownie Brick Road ice cream
66 4 × 4
67 Meetings for two
68 Muscle targeted by military presses, in brief
69 ___ school

DOWN

1 Get back into shape
2 Come up
3 Lukewarm
4 ___ the Autopilot, inflatable balloon character in "Airplane!"
5 Dicing onions, mincing garlic, etc.
6 Symbol that Mac users get by pressing Option + Shift + 2
7 Contents of birdhouses
8 Home to Planck, Einstein and Heisenberg when they won their Nobel Prizes
9 Nightmare personified
10 Petite, for one
11 TV journalist Pressman with a Peabody and 11 Emmys
12 Freudian topics
13 State since 1845: Abbr.
18 Dust-up
21 Admits
25 Noticeably unfriendly
26 Does a groundskeeper's job
27 Exhibited relief, in a way
29 Smart ___
30 Dorm room feature
31 Tel. number add-ons
33 It can be heavier in the summer
35 Rodentlike relative of a rabbit
36 Condition that fidget tools can help with, for short
37 Bring up
38 Not stay neutral
39 Compete in a Summer Olympics event
43 Stephen of "The Crying Game"
45 Most asinine
48 Deal sealers
50 Particular, for short
51 Run-of-the-mill
52 Upper echelon
53 Took performance-enhancing drugs
55 Caught on audio
57 Taunt
58 Like some high-fiber cereal
59 Changing fortune, metaphorically
60 Texter's farewell
61 Biblical verb with "thou"
62 E.P.A.-banned pesticide

by John Guzzetta

ACROSS

1 Buds that are very close
5 "For those who think young" sloganeer, once
10 Drainage collector
14 Cookie that has been deemed kosher since 1997
15 Walled city of Spain
16 Sports event in which athletes try to avoid being touched
17 Porky's significant other
19 Gillette razor handle
20 Make wise through experience
21 See 53-Across
23 Exceedingly
26 Letters at a bar
27 Signal that a reply is coming in a messaging app
30 Accept responsibility for
31 Terrific
34 Diatribe trigger
35 Official proceedings
37 Attempt to block
38 Original __
39 Make art like 53-/21-Across (as suggested by this puzzle's circled letters?)
41 Suffix with quartz
42 Pat who wrote "The Prince of Tides" and "The Great Santini"
44 Male hedgehog
45 Homer's neighbor on "The Simpsons"
46 Source of some rings
47 Industry that encourages strikes?
48 Modest reply to a compliment
49 Biol. or chem.
50 Oklahoma's state tree
53 With 21-Across, artist known to 39-Across pigments back and forth onto canvases
56 Melodic passage
60 Removal from danger, informally
61 __ station, Central London railway terminal

64 Long ride?
65 Suffered a wipeout
66 Leaning to the right: Abbr.
67 Org. for Lt. Columbo
68 Jetés, e.g.
69 One leaning to the right

DOWN

1 Conks
2 Unoccupied
3 Cheese in a spanakopita
4 Boozehounds
5 Noted colonial pamphleteer
6 Señora Perón
7 Small hard seed
8 Moccasin, e.g.
9 False friend in Shakespeare
10 Babe in the Arctic
11 Somewhat
12 Chicago exchange, in brief
13 Like times that are the most expensive
18 Veterans Day mo.
22 Daffy Duck, notably
24 Indian flatbread
25 Low-ranking sailor
27 What you need some wiggle room to do?
28 Betelgeuse's constellation
29 Where you might find love away from home?
32 Fragrant compound
33 Like an oboe's sound
35 Dreamboat of a guy
36 Weep
37 Greeting in Rio
40 "Be __" (motto for Wikipedia contributors)

43 Pacific food fish
47 Highly decorated
48 "That's cool, daddy-o!"
51 Taunts so as to get a reaction
52 Samovar
53 Come together
54 Running shoe brand
55 Gem that's a woman's name
57 Palindromic guy's name
58 Succeed and then some
59 "Recycle __" (sign on a bin)
62 Narc's org.
63 Tango flourish

by Alex Rosen and Brad Wilber

ACROSS

1 Founding member of the U.N. Security Council
5 Station
9 Fly (by)
13 Native Rwandan
14 Follower of "catch" or "latch"
15 Misanthrope of Victorian literature
16 Tesla, e.g.
17 Pop star Halliwell of the Spice Girls
18 Made an impression?
19 Land____
22 ____more and more
23 Vouch for
24 Chinese artist and political activist Ai
27 Let
31 It fits in a lock
32 Big Four bank, for short
35 Accented approval
36 God depicted in a figure called an "amoretto"
38 Where bursitis may appear
39 "Asleep"
40 I___, for one
43 NATO alphabet letter in "NATO"
45 Deputies
48 Test format . . . or a hint to understanding three of this puzzle's clues
53 Thurman of "Gattaca"
54 Soap opera, e.g.
55 Point of a dancer who's en pointe
56 Turf
57 Hurricane-level winds, on the Beaufort scale
58 Barely manage, with "out"
59 U.S. Navy O-1: Abbr.
60 Like hair at salons
61 "Make yourself comfortable"

DOWN

1 Stumbling syllables
2 Wouldn't settle, say
3 Word with bacon or rumble
4 Chafes
5 Some bouncers use them
6 Garment that typically has snaps
7 Valuable violins, for short
8 Items in a travel kit
9 School attended by Warren Buffett
10 Plugs
11 Gist
12 What the verb ending "-ise" isn't spelled with
20 Red Rose
21 Prefix with penultimate
24 Grief
25 Aid in balance
26 Civil War ships
28 Important info for concertgoers
29 Bow-making choice
30 Haaland who became secretary of the interior in 2021
33 Alternative to L.L.C.
34 Matcha, e.g.
37 Indicator of approval
39 With 44-Down, only playwright to have a New York City theater named after him while still alive
41 Spots to keep watch?
42 On hold
43 Practicable
44 See 39-Down
46 Mushroom eaten with udon
47 Olympics event whose participants shoot for the gold
49 Pond dweller that can regenerate its eyes
50 Unlikely trick taker
51 One of a Roman septet
52 Roof part

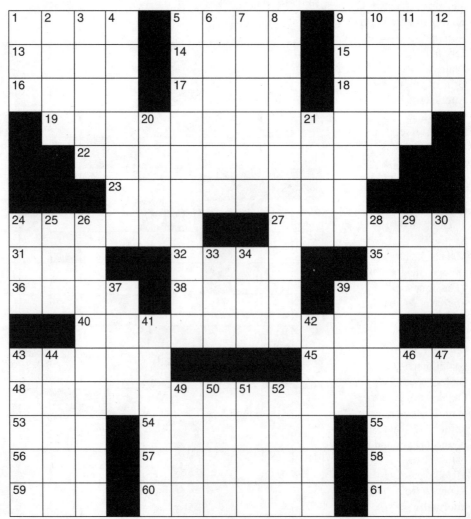

by Trenton Charlson

ACROSS

1 ___ alphabet
5 Dream big
11 ___-Signal
14 Mystery writer?
15 Place to hide in hide-and-seek
16 Donkey Kong, for one
17 Classic song that starts "I was working in the lab late one night" [2003, 1970]
19 Hwy.
20 Viking beverage
21 Popular New Orleans dessert
23 Start of the Depression [1987, 2004]
27 ___ vera
28 Bequeaths
29 Works of Picasso y Goya
30 Gotham inits.
31 Small wind instrument
32 Gamblers' calculations
33 Line at the top or bottom of a website [1997, 2019]
36 Help up a slope
38 Popular depilatory
39 Busy body?
42 It was cool in the '90s
43 Search blindly
45 Strives (to)
46 Commuter's headache [1998, 2000]
49 1986 #1 hit for Patti LaBelle and Michael McDonald
50 Throne material on "Game of Thrones"
51 Lovelace of early computing
52 Editing device suggested by 17-, 23-, 33- and 46-Across?
57 Crossed
58 Michelle Obama or Jill Biden, informally
59 Request accompanying puppy dog eyes, maybe
60 ___ Lankan
61 Mac-versus-PC and others
62 Lead-in to sax

DOWN

1 "Full Metal Jacket" setting, in brief
2 Surprise for a statistician
3 "Funky Cold Medina" rapper
4 In the bargain bin, say
5 Tennis feat
6 Nikon D3500, e.g.
7 Certain lap dog, informally
8 Allende who wrote "City of the Beasts"
9 Goes back to square one
10 Moral code
11 Alma mater for Martha Stewart and Joan Rivers
12 Hurdles for many honor students, in brief
13 Something most babies do at around six months
18 The Rams scored none of these in the '19 Super Bowl, and the Chiefs none in '21
22 Ex-seniors
23 Sickly-looking
24 Mattress size
25 Big break
26 58-Across between Lou and Bess
31 Supporting
32 ___ Lady of Guadalupe
33 Often-frazzled comics character
34 Rank below adm.
35 Seating section
36 What the N.B.A.'s SuperSonics became in 2008
37 Type of rice
39 Like some glasses
40 Highly respected
41 Help button
42 Some celebrity sporting events
43 Rampage
44 Dwindle
45 Birthplace of Homo sapiens
47 So-called "Godfather of the Teamsters"
48 Be bedridden, say
53 Big Apple subway inits.
54 Opposite of norte
55 Email addenda, for short
56 Vegas hotel and casino that is the longtime host of the World Series of Poker

by Brandon Koppy

ACROSS

1 Big, in adspeak
5 Game show shout-out
10 "Miss ___ Regrets," jazz standard performed by Ethel Waters and Ella Fitzgerald
14 Draft picks
15 Grammy category
16 Sport shooting variety
17 After the top half of a 7-Down, sophisticated lady
19 Total War game company
20 His murder elicited the first wail of mourning, in Islamic accounts
21 Lead-in to care
23 Icy remark?
24 When the Lyrid meteor shower typically peaks
26 Bucolic call
27 Sport shooting variety
29 King of cubs
30 Before the bottom half of a 7-Down, tipple and then some
32 That, en España
33 Carrie in "Sex and the City"
34 Flash point?
36 Savage
40 Stopped producing new leads, as an investigation
44 Apt rhyme for "lumberjacks"
45 After the top half of a 42-Down, circles around the block?
48 Leave out
49 Silly
50 "Live well" sloganeer
51 You can see right through it
52 MC ___ of N.W.A
53 Talk up
55 Where you might search for a lead?
56 Stained, in a way
58 Before the bottom half of a 42-Down, keeps arguing after something has been decided
62 Prerelease, in Silicon Valley
63 Japanese automaker
64 Isle known as "The Gathering Place"
65 Funk
66 Throat malady, for short
67 Graph component

DOWN

1 Portrait seen on renminbi bank notes
2 Pole worker
3 "Cool it, lovebirds"
4 Rubbish receptacle
5 Cry of pain . . . or laughter
6 Major talking point on CNBC, maybe
7 Hybrid creature of myth
8 City sieged by Joan of Arc
9 Anti-D.U.I. org.
10 "Fourth periods" in hockey, for short
11 A host of answers?
12 "Seconded"
13 Rival of Athens
18 Sushi bar choice
22 Follower of Christmas or Easter
24 Son in "Tess of the D'Urbervilles"
25 ___ Pizza (punny trattoria name)
26 It may be wireless
28 Green smoothie ingredient
30 Liquid-Plumr alternative
31 Some tribal leaders on "Game of Thrones"
33 Playwright Bertolt
35 Bucolic beasts
37 Certain protective parent, colloquially
38 Graph component
39 "Sounds like a plan"
41 Late-night interviewee, e.g.
42 Hybrid creature of myth
43 "Lord of the Rings" baddie
45 Gummy candy brand
46 Kicked things off
47 Connect with
48 Hard one to teach, in a saying
51 Inits. in a.m. TV
54 They might be tied using a taiko musubi ("drum knot")
55 "Time ___!"
57 Maneuverable, in nautical lingo
59 Philosopher Mo-___
60 Sushi bar choice
61 Letdown at a fireworks show

by Adam Wagner

ACROSS

1 Prefix with day or night
4 "You can't possibly mean me?!"
7 __ Khan (Muslim title)
8 "Malternative" beverage
15 It's mostly nitrogen on Earth, but carbon dioxide on Mars
16 Preschooler, say
17 With 8-Down, light blue Monopoly property
18 Jan. honoree
19 Zoned out
22 Kareem Abdul-Jabbar's alma mater
23 "Mamma __!"
24 Footnote abbr.
25 Dude
28 iPad Pro, for one
31 With 48-Down, promotional phrase on some product packages
32 1996 double-platinum Beck album
33 Regulator mechanism, for short
34 Utter hell, say?
35 N.B.A. great with five championship rings as a player and three as a head coach
37 Fix, as loose laces
38 Seemed confused, maybe
46 One told to "Go get 'em!"
47 Provider of a canyon trail ride
49 Appeared poker-faced
55 Whittle (down)
56 Brand with the record for a single car driven the most miles (3+ million and counting)
57 It's $550 for 17-Across/ 8-Down with a hotel on it

58 Directive before "awake" or "woke"
59 "Adorkable" one, maybe
60 20,310 ft., for Denali

DOWN

1 Taiwan Strait's __ Islands
2 "Roger that"
3 Result of a damaged hard drive
4 One whose porridge was too cold for Goldilocks
5 Pennsylvania petroleum center, once
6 Peeved
8 See 17-Across: Abbr.
9 Paved the way
10 1981's "Gorky Park" or 2012's "Gone Girl"
11 Luxury hotel chain
12 "Stuffed" food item at a pub
13 Musician Yoko
14 N.B.A. scoring stat: Abbr.
20 Name of 11 pharaohs
21 Support column
26 Muppet with a unibrow
27 Effect created by a guitar pedal, informally
29 Magazine highlighting Clio winners
30 It's been known to chase Wild Turkeys
36 Letter before theta

38 Pair of cymbals in a drum kit
39 Ancient marketplace
40 Loser to Truman in 1948
41 "__ you for real?"
42 Certain Wall Street takeover, in brief
43 Highly unconventional
44 Large bay window
45 Danish coin
46 Bakers' amts.
48 See 31-Across
50 Blu-ray forerunner
51 Partner of then
52 World Cup cheer
53 "Killing __" (Sandra Oh series)
54 Swarm

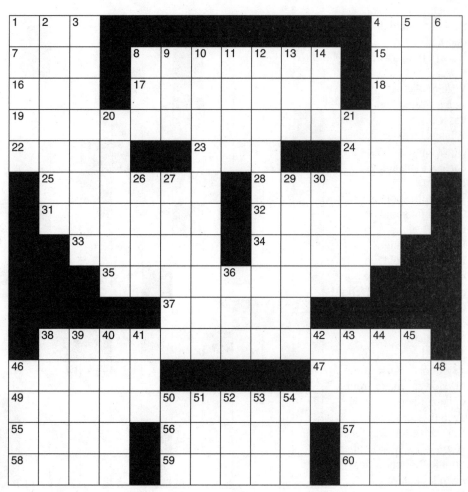

by Joe DiPietro

ACROSS

1 Alternative to a Ding Dong
5 It's found near a trap
9 Sped
14 To be remembered for all time
15 Shade akin to turquoise
16 Sister publication of Jet magazine
17 Actor Laurie of "House"
18 *Sensitive part of the elbow
20 *Oft-wished-upon sighting
22 When doubled, "Good one"
23 Heart chart, for short
24 Part of A.B.S.: Abbr.
25 Common typo for an exclamation point
27 Sprout
30 Serving with dal makhani
32 Hazard in maritime travel
34 With 51-Across, something to "read"
36 Passed out
40 What each asterisked clue's answer does, to correct a misnomer?
43 In the main?
44 Word with sport or spirit
45 One might stand on a table
46 French greeting
48 It was once sold medically under the commercial name Delysid
50 Great time, informally
51 See 34-Across
54 Dynamism
55 Not well
57 *Symbol of Australia
63 *Headwear made from jipijapa fibers
64 Tech review site
66 Repetitive musical form
67 Actress/TV host Palmer
68 Standout in one's field
69 Faun lookalike
70 Freshness
71 Drill, for instance

DOWN

1 Sound of a snicker
2 "Mr. Holland's __," 1995 film for which Richard Dreyfuss received a Best Actor nomination
3 Grate pains?
4 Golf great Lorena
5 Preposterous
6 Lead-in to -vocal
7 Sally __ (English teacake)
8 Beside the point
9 Obama's Secret Service code name
10 Help wanteds?
11 Computer processor parts
12 Figure in international relations
13 Some textile specialists
19 Org. with gym memberships
21 Globe
25 One in a pod
26 "Good stuff!"
28 Sch. with a campus in Narragansett
29 " " "
31 Author Gaiman
33 Kind of market
35 José __ (frozen foods brand)
37 Superficially
38 Home to the oldest continuously functioning university in the Americas (since 1551)
39 Spice qtys.
41 First name in Surrealism
42 Tour de France units: Abbr.
47 Stretch of the red carpet?
49 Leave inconspicuously, with "out"
51 Michelle who was FIFA's Female Player of the Century
52 Warmer in the winter
53 Needle
56 Lawful
58 "__ Bird" (2017 film)
59 Titaness of myth
60 Store near Rockefeller Center, familiarly
61 Sporty vehicles
62 Some summer deliveries
65 Channel with the slogan "Boom."

by Jake Halperin

ACROSS

1 Breaded and topped with tomato sauce and mozzarella, for short
5 "Holy mackerel!"
9 Instrument played by indie rock's Sufjan Stevens
13 Black-and-white item in a sleeve
14 V.I.P. on base
15 Winter bugs
16 With 26-Across, game that uses a blindfold
18 Part of the food pyramid
19 Gardening tool
20 Fruit in the William Carlos Williams poem "This Is Just to Say"
22 Edward Snowden's former employer, in brief
23 Black History Mo.
26 See 16-Across
29 "Why?"
31 Puts up
32 Bird that had no natural predators until humans arrived
33 Tick (off)
35 Babe Zaharias was the first woman to compete on its tour, in brief
36 Item exchanged in a so-called "yankee swap"
41 John Lewis was born here: Abbr.
42 Org. that oversees O.T.C.s
43 Campaign expense
45 Get situated
48 Pacify
50 Frequent reveler, or a hint to 16-/26- and 36-Across
53 Hit the slopes
54 "___ be my pleasure"
55 Lots
56 Hearty laugh
58 Tidy
60 Cartoonist suggested by this puzzle's theme
65 Brand in the ice cream aisle
66 Aches (for)
67 Words after a gasp

68 Its underside might be covered in gum
69 The first cloned mammals
70 Yarn

DOWN

1 Dad
2 "Midsommar" director Aster
3 ___ faire (historical re-enactment event, for short)
4 Fly-by-night type?
5 Fuel up, in a way
6 Visual in an annual report
7 Nimble
8 Hornswoggle
9 Toggle option
10 Artist's starting place
11 Get-go
12 Guest ___, what The New York Times calls op-eds
14 What an asterisk might suggest
17 Centaur's foot
21 Transform
23 Repeated string in a chain letter subject line
24 Website with articles like "10 Surprising Ways to Use Mayonnaise Around Your Home"
25 Things best kept under one's hat?
27 Data structure with a root node
28 Undo
30 Half of a half-bathroom
34 Tiny toymaker
37 Tucker who had her first hit in 1972 and won her first Grammys in 2020
38 Cheese used in Babybels
39 Fruits whose seeds can act as a substitute for black peppercorns
40 Something to do
44 Latin gods
45 Shared one's views
46 For all ages, as a video game
47 Tell
49 Also
51 At all, in dialect
52 Combined
57 Pretzel, basically
59 Shaming syllable
61 Drug dosages: Abbr.
62 Light bulb moment sound
63 Show with the recurring character Target Lady, in brief
64 "Piggy"

by Alina Abidi

ACROSS

1 Vaping device, informally
5 ___ Roy, patriarch on HBO's "Succession"
10 Successfully solicit, with "up"
14 Arizona city near the California border
15 Where Dalmatia is
16 NPR's ___ Totenberg
17 Stand-in for the unnamed
18 Monopoly cards
19 Buffalo Bill's surname
20 Walked
22 End
24 It has a cedar tree on its flag: Abbr.
25 World's highest-paid actor in 2021, familiarly
27 2007 Nobel Peace Prize winner
29 Brand of taco kits and sauces
30 Mobile homes of a sort
32 Castle defenses
33 Bargain bin abbr.
35 N.Y.C. nabe near N.Y.U.
36 Life preserver? . . . or a hint to six squares in this puzzle
39 ___ Romeo
42 Starting lineup
43 Dispirit, with "out"
46 Heraldic symbol
49 Noted Venetian bridge
51 Separate seed from
52 Be perfectly sized
53 The "e" of "i.e."
54 Home to the golden pavilion known as Kinkaku-ji
57 Planted
58 ___ Jones, former Alabama senator
60 Best ever, in sports slang
62 Org. known for counting backward
64 "Yeah . . . I don't think so"
65 Fresh blood
66 Mobile home?
67 Actress Amanda
68 Works hard, old-style
69 Some creatures in the ocean's "midnight zone"

DOWN

1 ___ of Ra, symbolic depiction in Egyptian art
2 Dog-eat-dog
3 Turkish inns
4 In large numbers
5 Flat-screen option, for short
6 Rival of Hoover
7 Facial feature named for an animal
8 Operatic daughter of the king Amonasro
9 World capital on the island of New Providence
10 Blues org.?
11 1970 John Wayne film
12 Sworn
13 "It's possible"
21 Prairie stray
23 Chicago conveyances
25 Waits on an album release?
26 Late media columnist David
28 Cohort before millennials, for short
30 Begins to get exciting, with "up"
31 It's not a good look
34 Chew (out)
36 Spot of espresso?
37 Italian home to the Basilica of St. Nicholas
38 Excludes
39 Misbehaved
40 Repulsive
41 Magazine with an annual Investor's Guide
43 Extraneous computer programs that slow down a system
44 Part of a place setting
45 Rapper Kool ___ Dee
47 Pose
48 Beat
50 Immediately
52 Economics Nobelist Robert
55 Where I-70 meets I-71
56 Polo on TV
59 Snookered
61 National Book Award winner for "Them," 1970
63 They're used in a crunch

by Oliver Roeder

ACROSS

1 Packs of alpacas
6 Abbr. in a library catalog
10 Partner of willing
14 Kind of daisy
15 Material for toy darts
16 Like business in the off-season
17 *"Please continue your generous support of the church"*
19 Prepare, as prosciutto
20 Give off
21 Brand with a paw print in its logo
22 Follows, as advice
23 Undesirable bunkmate
25 Frigid temps
27 *"This device makes prepping cherries a breeze"*
31 Tweak
34 Made explicit, in a way
35 Grow long in the tooth
36 Historical record
37 Snake along the Nile
38 Discover unexpectedly
40 Passing remark?
41 Singer Mai with the 2018 hit "Boo'd Up"
43 Least polite
44 *"Students should report to the gym for a special presentation"*
47 Sailor's "Stop!"
48 For dogs, they're often in the shape of bones
51 Japanese noodles
53 Snap back?
55 Boor
57 It shows a lot of plays, but no musicals
58 *"This medicine will reduce your temperature in no time"*
60 Glen or dale
61 Timeline spans
62 Beautifully blue
63 Exceeded the legal limit

64 Philosopher known for his paradoxes
65 Word that comes from the Lakota for "dwelling"

DOWN

1 Smartphone button
2 End-of-semester hurdles
3 Pine secretion
4 Gilead in "The Handmaid's Tale," for one
5 What floats your boat?
6 To a certain extent
7 Appear
8 Support on the shoulder
9 Pro Bowler's org.
10 Initial part of a roller coaster ride
11 It leans to the left
12 Tennyson, for one
13 Dolly and her fellow clones, e.g.
18 Imam's quality
22 Recruit selectively
24 Colonial sharpshooter
26 Prefix with dermis
28 Writing assignment
29 Big personalities
30 Cancel ___ (tenant rights movement)
31 ___ Harris, sister and campaign chair of Kamala
32 There are two in "101 Dalmatians"
33 Spit in a tube, say
37 Mentally sound
39 See through rose-colored glasses
42 Scale abbr.
43 Dressage competitor
45 Made uniform
46 Words from one doing a demonstration
49 Rolled out of bed
50 Bolivian capital
51 Goes "vroom vroom"
52 "Stat!"
54 First czar of Russia
56 For whom the bell tolls
58 Hat similar to a tarboosh
59 Have down ___

by Adam Vincent

130 MEDIUM

ACROSS

1 Pink alcoholic drink, for short
6 Spree
9 "Not a chance!"
15 Music rights org.
16 Absorbed, as a loss
17 Where to turn for self-knowledge
18 Important map information
19 Measure of conductance
20 Bikes without pedaling
21 It comes first in China, but second in the U.S.
23 Important part of a taxi
24 Suffix with infant
25 Need for making pochoir prints
27 Raid shelfmate
31 2019 World Series champs
33 Coach
34 "Uh-oh. Better get __" (auto repair slogan)
35 Poker declaration
37 Together, in music
39 Indefinite ordinal
40 One way to run . . . or a hint to four geographical intersections found in this grid
44 O'er and o'er
46 Real first name of Spider-Man villain Doctor Octopus
47 Pangs
50 V.I.P.s
52 Cover story
55 Neat and orderly
56 Datum
57 English channel, familiarly
59 Animal house
60 Statue of Ganesha, e.g.
62 Found an occasion
64 Wiggle room
67 Apposite
68 Media exec Robert
69 Small storage unit
70 Part of STEM: Abbr.
71 Naming, informally

72 First airline to complete a round-the-world flight
73 L.A. winter hrs.
74 Meshlike

DOWN

1 First space probe to enter Saturn's orbit
2 Kissing-related
3 Strategy that stokes fear
4 Bad start?
5 Warms up the crowd, in a way
6 Signal-blocking device
7 To whom the Greeks dedicated the Parthenon
8 Bygone Chevrolet division
9 Actor Williamson who played Merlin in "Excalibur"

10 __ about
11 Title character in a classic John Cleese comedy
12 Functioned as
13 "A jealous mistress," per Emerson
14 Sari measure: Abbr.
22 Validate, with "to"
23 One studying the Vedas
26 "Bye now!"
28 "Capisce?," in '70s slang
29 Bat Appreciation Month, appropriately: Abbr.
30 Japanese dance/drama
32 Dear fellow
34 Drug in "Breaking Bad"
36 Pipe buildup
38 Loose
41 Lesley of "60 Minutes"
42 Suitable-sounding name for a kid on Santa's naughty list?

43 Elem. school basics
44 Bungler
45 Where some keys are found: Abbr.
48 U, V, W or Y, but not X
49 Jargony rationale for a business merger
51 Blot
53 Predecessors of Lenovos
54 "Amscray!"
57 Grab by pinching, as an ice cube
58 Hippie happening
61 Per __
63 Current event
64 Swab
65 Carrier to Japan
66 Rapper MC __
67 Shakespeare's "poor venomous fool"

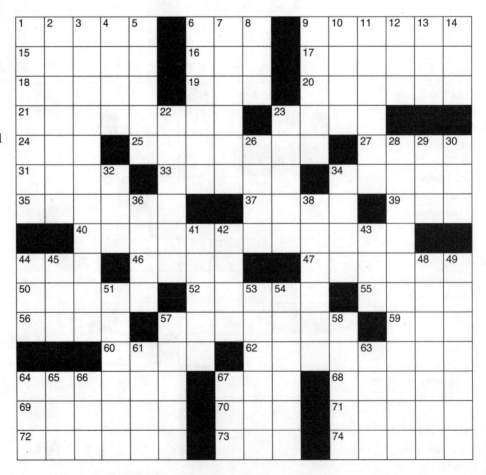

by Ashish Vengsarkar

ACROSS

1 Fire proof?
4 Midsection section, informally
7 Bad break
14 Pop singer known for performing in a face-obscuring wig
15 Sch. whose campus contains Washington Square Park
16 Core
17 "Lookout" signal, in brief
18 "Come now, it'll be OK"
20 Carmichael who composed "Heart and Soul"
22 Letter after pi
23 Wallet items
24 Body feature for roughly 90% of people
25 McKellen who played Gandalf
26 Online help page, for short
28 Young newt
29 Health class subj.
30 Slip past
33 Anybody home?
35 That, in Spanish
36 Farm cry
37 Put numbers on the board
38 "Wowza!"
39 Nickname for the Miami Dolphins, with "the"
40 Certain recyclable
41 U.K. honour
42 __ Stardust, alter ego of David Bowie
43 Rose Granger-Weasley, to Harry Potter
44 Word on either side of "à"
45 Rose of rock
46 Bench with a back
47 Main ingredient in the Japanese dish tamagoyaki
48 Requirements
51 Easy __
53 Onetime Russian space station
54 "My take is . . ."
55 1948 western starring Bob Hope as "Painless" Potter

58 Sign
59 Budget carrier from 1993 to 2014
60 Message often written in large letters
61 Suffix with Gator
62 Actress Angela of "How Stella Got Her Groove Back"
63 Weed
64 The "S" of iOS: Abbr.

DOWN

1 Japan's largest beer brand
2 Nurse, as a beer
3 They can rate up to 350,000 on the Scoville scale
4 "Nevertheless . . . look at our current situation"
5 Party invite inits.
6 Grass-roots group focused on addressing climate change
7 Difficult to understand
8 G.I. entertainers
9 The Spartans of the N.C.A.A.
10 Letters on the "3" button
11 Performer known as the "King of Latin Pop"
12 Performed very well on
13 "I'm game"
19 Exclamation upon seeing this puzzle
21 Priceless keepsakes?

26 Mo. during which the N.B.A. All-Star Game is usually played
27 Good as new
31 "Shoot!"
32 Website with much custom-designed jewelry
33 Channel owned by Disney
34 Dark purple fruit
42 Most out there
49 Hunky-dory
50 Comedian Wanda
51 Open __ (plan to pay later)
52 Like the majority of Iraqis and Bahrainis
56 Pull-up muscle, for short
57 Soft murmur

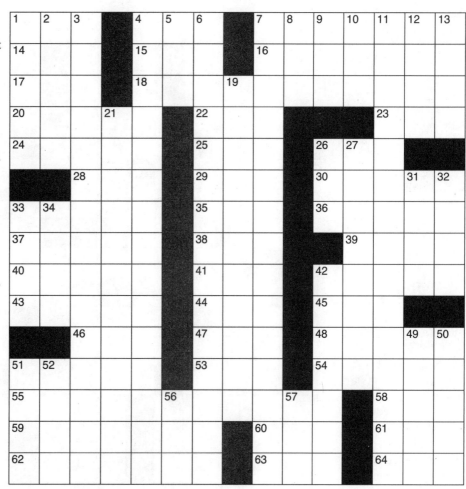

by Sean Yamada-Hunter

ACROSS

1 Part of V.A.T.
6 Curious
9 Taste
15 Aerial view provider
16 "I was stuck in traffic," maybe
17 Titania's spouse, in Shakespeare
18 Fencer's cry
20 Like "h" among "h," "i" and "j"
21 Link between two names
22 Sean of "Stranger Things"
24 Scene in Edward Hopper's "Nighthawks"
25 Wishy-washy R.S.V.P.
27 Style of diamond with a flat base
29 ___ dog
30 Apple on Apple Music
31 Tesla had one in 2010, for short
32 K–12 subj.
33 Like someone receiving baseless accusations, maybe?
35 Generates dubiously, with "up"
37 Spot for a dinner plate
40 Takes (down)
41 Actor Rhames
42 Sign of a hit
45 Gen ___
46 Rapper featured on Flo Rida's "Low"
49 Long Island home of Brookhaven National Laboratory
51 Roadside restaurant sign
53 Roger on the high seas
54 Giant on both the Nikkei and N.Y.S.E. indexes
55 N.B.A. great with a doctorate in education
57 Screening grp.
58 "Alice in Wonderland" cry
60 On and on . . . or how to read 18-, 27-, 37- and 51-Across to understand this puzzle's theme?
63 Fix, in a way
64 Expert

65 Spouts
66 Completely cover
67 Ottawa N.H.L.er, to fans
68 Discussion group

DOWN

1 Wood-shaping tool
2 "Pigs will sooner fly!"
3 Rumble in the Jungle promoter
4 Get involved
5 Org. with strict schedules?
6 Parents and grandparents, in slang, with "the"
7 Slimming aid
8 Co-star of 2019's "Joker"
9 Scatter
10 Bear
11 Something that nearly one million Americans practice regularly

12 Union agreements?
13 Not beat
14 French lead-in to "chat"
19 Snitch
23 Prefix with binary
25 Contents of a certain shelf
26 Hilton alternative
28 Astronomer Carl
30 Key ring item
34 Throw it away
36 He can help you after a crash
37 Spreadsheet command
38 Prints, perhaps
39 Low point: Abbr.
40 First name on "Star Trek: The Next Generation"
42 Harold who sought the Republican presidential nomination nine times over 48 years

43 "I"
44 It appears twice in the Fibonacci sequence
45 Buckingham Palace figures
47 Expert
48 Trojan War hero
50 Where lab coats get cleaned?
51 Be a kvetch
52 Gives zero stars, say
53 ___ ears
56 Mideast locale of Sira Fortress
59 Lead-in to long
61 Rafael Nadal's home country, in the Olympics
62 Designer inits.

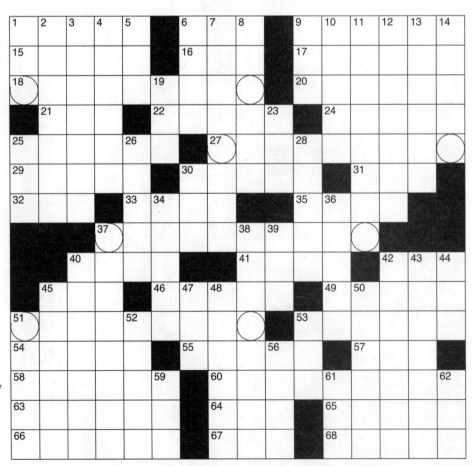

by David W. Tuffs

ACROSS

1 Chinese provincial capital more than two miles above sea level
6 Japanese national sport
10 Red felt hat with a tassel
13 TV's "Marvelous Mrs."
14 ___ glass (translucent ornamental material)
15 The "A" of 38-Across
16 "Hurry up!" to a batter?
18 Sticky stuff
19 Unit commonly following "40," "60," "75" and "100"
20 Add to the kitty
21 Roman who said "After I'm dead I'd rather people ask why I have no monument than why I have one"
22 Play ___ with (make trouble for)
24 "Hurry up!" to a dancer?
27 Lobbed weapon
30 "Put your pencils down!"
31 Semi
32 Singer Ora
34 Wish granters
38 Hoppy brew
39 Person giving someone a ring
41 Med. scan
42 Green cars
44 Vulcan mind ___
45 Take home the gold
46 Angers
48 Tiny purchase at a haberdashery
50 "Hurry up!" to a zombie?
54 "What ___ care?"
55 Bengay target
56 Cowardly ___
58 R&B great Redding
61 Word that rhymes with its exact opposite
62 "Hurry up!" to an omelet chef?
65 Common piercing site
66 Chills and fever
67 Small piano
68 Important messenger
69 Daddy-o
70 Dangles

DOWN

1 Actress Condor of "To All the Boys I've Loved Before"
2 "Hurry up!" to a nitrous oxide user?
3 Actor Kutcher
4 "Get it?"
5 Actor Alan
6 ___ Sudan (U.N. member since 2011)
7 Buoyant
8 Bad beginning?
9 Exclamation with an accent
10 Ruinous, as some flaws
11 Send to heaven
12 Experience of space flight, informally
13 Cut (down)
17 Beginnings
21 French city where William the Conqueror is buried
23 First lady before Hillary
25 Rwanda's capital
26 Corrected
27 Toughness
28 Yellow, as a banana
29 Pump option
33 Device that usually has a touchscreen, for short
35 "Hurry up!" to a server?
36 "Spamalot" writer Idle
37 What some ships and hearts do
40 Power source for the first Green Lantern
43 Thumbs-up icon meaning
47 Clog with sediment
49 Gave shelter to
50 Crust, mantle or inner core, for the earth
51 Body resting in bed?
52 "Gone With the Wind" name
53 Nasty habits
57 Poet Ogden
59 Chemical suffixes
60 Rank above cpl.
62 "Mind the ___" (London tube sign)
63 Swollen head
64 Figurehead?

by Lee Taylor

ACROSS

1 Covered up
5 Robinson of TV's "I Think You Should Leave"
8 Charity bowling event, e.g.
13 Home to Waianuenue Falls
14 0, for 0°
15 Conspicuously unfamiliar party guest, informally
16 One-__ punch (kung fu technique)
17 Frequent rock soloist
19 Liberal leader?
20 Words before "Yes, I cried, yes I cried" in "Return of the Mack"
21 "When has that ever been true?"
23 Amusement, online
24 Trash collector
25 __ theory
28 Filter feeder's fodder
30 "In that case, move on!"
33 Table salt is made of them
34 Some natural history museum exhibits, for short
35 Brand image
36 Create a diversion from a damaging issue, in politics
38 Podcaster Marc
39 Names
40 Senegal-to-Togo dir.
41 Actress Chaplin
42 Show of hands?
47 Collection of 10 directives written by Vladimir Lenin
50 Animal whose name sounds like you?
51 Place to get a cold brew
52 "Bearing gifts we traverse __" ("We Three Kings" lyric)
53 Mohawk Valley city
54 "Now __ even"
55 Took off

56 2020 Christopher Nolan sci-fi thriller
57 Yearbook grp.
58 Licks, say

DOWN

1 Pants material
2 Pants material
3 Role for Malcolm-Jamal Warner on "The People v. O. J. Simpson"
4 "Gah!"
5 Keep busy
6 On the whole
7 Site for a movie poster?
8 Commonsensical
9 Actor John of Broadway's "Carousel"
10 Unfooled by
11 Congressman Kinzinger
12 "Gimme, gimme, gimme!"
14 Casino game that's 100% luck
18 Beings made from smokeless fire, in the Quran
20 Elided pronoun
22 British composer Gustav
25 Warehouse cost
26 Brand whose last letter is in the shape of its product
27 Saturday morning character
28 Christchurch resident
29 Spot for a hairpin
30 They're not the main event
31 Artist in the avant-garde Fluxus movement

32 Actress Glazer
34 Old automaker with the models Firedome, Fireflite and Firesweep
37 W.W. II fighter plane
38 May celebrants
41 __ citato (in the work quoted: Lat.)
42 Enchantress in Greek myth
43 Fisher with a stownet
44 FAQ checkers
45 "Gimme, gimme, gimme!"
46 Longtime mint brand that doesn't contain any mint
47 Appear alongside
48 Sneaky __
49 Line from a bit?
52 [So adorable!]

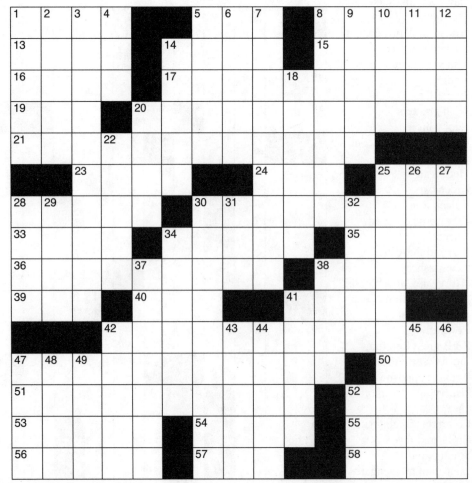

by Brendan Emmett Quigley and Paolo Pasco

ACROSS

1 Rush order
10 Capital on the Gulf of Guinea
15 Bet involving score totals
16 Sight at low tide
17 Mental or fiscal tightness
18 Just under way, so to speak
19 "90 Day Fiancé" channel
20 TV lingo for using established hits to prop up weaker shows
22 Govt. plant inspector
24 The Greek philosopher Empedocles leapt into its flames, in legend
25 Annual celebration during which sweeping is taboo
27 Car model whose name becomes an N.B.A. superstar when its middle letter is removed
29 Move, informally
30 Needing a jolt
33 Iranian port near the Iraq border
35 Out of whimsy
36 In the works
37 Waifs
38 Latin American spread
39 First two words of Shelley's "Ozymandias"
40 Falling hard?
42 Bivouac sight
43 Term terminus
44 Roves (about)
48 Someone who has it all
51 Favorite
52 Favorite novelist of Twihards
53 As you like it
55 Sty sound
56 Completely routs
57 Try to get down
58 Got in a lather, say

DOWN

1 Admit
2 Cricket fields, e.g.
3 Swag for sale
4 Sounds of hesitation
5 Give notice
6 Access to a country club, in brief?
7 "Better off not knowing"
8 Hockey players who face off in a face-off
9 Superman's dog
10 Havens
11 "Parasite" co-star ___ Woo-shik
12 Considered a participant
13 Chaparral or savanna
14 Calculus prerequisite: Abbr.
21 1914 Freud essay that introduced the concept of "ego ideal"
23 Mostly online writing genre
26 Kingdom whose capital is Nuku'alofa
28 Effervescence
29 Tartare topper
30 "___ is the beginning of wisdom . . . not the end": Spock
31 Shortly
32 "Right back atcha"
34 Hippie confab
36 Ancient siege weapon for launching stones
38 Florida city with a large Cuban American population (70+%)
41 Electron attractors
43 Malt liquor bottle, in slang
45 Where some high schoolers get DNA tests?
46 Burrow (into)
47 Marengo, for Napoleon
49 "Jobs vs. Gates: The Hippie and the ___" (2015 TV movie)
50 Hip-hop subgenre
52 Slush pile contents: Abbr.
54 Greeting in Rio

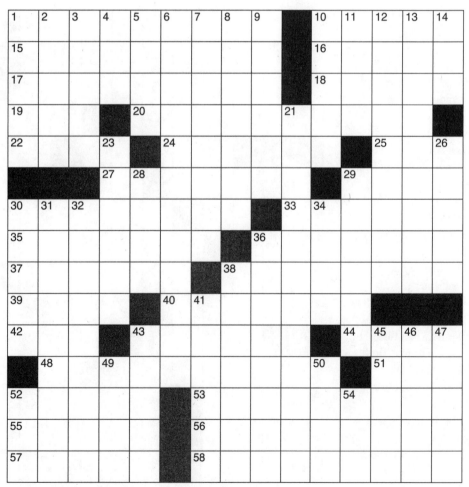

by Byron Walden

ACROSS

1 Hack job
11 Lean
15 News alert of old
16 Choose from the restaurant menu
17 Hybrid citrus fruit native to China
18 The toe of a geographical "boot"
19 Bad reasoning
20 Piece of the action
22 "We'll handle this one"
24 Literally, "disciple"
25 Gamete producer
28 AAA service
30 Gives a hand
33 Clodhopper
34 Unexplained by science, say
36 LAX approximation
37 Meeting after a meeting
38 Paris-to-Zurich dir.
39 What fuel economy standards might address
41 Cry of relief
42 Get ready to drive
43 Anago, on a Japanese menu
44 Cat With __ of Joy (emoji)
45 Some Christmas purchases
47 Platform for a performer
49 Nickname for Chicago's Cloud Gate sculpture
52 Words when throwing caution to the wind
56 Rain or shine
57 What comes after the fall
59 Fibrous part of a potato
60 Feeling of otherness
61 Absolute delight
62 Backgrounds in theater

DOWN

1 __ bra
2 Skater's leap
3 "G2G"
4 Colored rings
5 Intruded, with "in"
6 On again
7 Performing tasks according to encoded instructions, as a computer file
8 Dispenser in many a vestibule
9 Edit out, as from a photo
10 Name associated with boxers
11 Upset of the century, say
12 __ the 25-Down, founder of the kingdom of Hawaii
13 Emmy and Golden Globe-nominated actress __ Rachel Wood
14 Passed
21 Finished with
23 More contrite
25 See 12-Down
26 Navel type
27 Travel authority?
29 Pending acceptance, in a way
31 __ tag
32 Heaps
34 Matar, in Indian cuisine
35 Marshal under Napoleon
37 Cellist Jacqueline
40 Cavil
41 Jewelry creator Elsa who helped define the Tiffany brand
44 Earths, in sci-fi
46 Perceived to be
48 "A-a-a-and __!"
49 Common sitcom rating
50 No-goodnik
51 River personified by the god Hapi
53 Kristen of "S.N.L."
54 Comment after a cue
55 Top marks
58 Small grouse

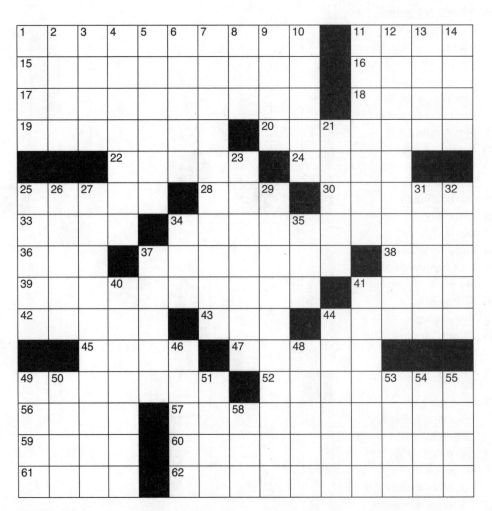

by Adrian Kabigting

ACROSS

1 Cause for alarm?
8 Lake ___, where the Chari River empties
12 Compete for speed, say
13 Cheery refrain
14 Eyeroll-inducing response to "How did you do that?"
15 Work on some issues together?
16 Stuck a fork in, say
17 Buddhism's founder
18 Kind of vest
19 #1 on Rolling Stone's "100 Greatest TV Shows of All Time" list, with "The"
20 Old-fashioned endings?
21 Fashion designer ___ Saab
22 Ball with a yellow stripe
23 Meets and eats, perhaps
26 Publisher of "The 1619 Project," for short
27 "None for me, thanks"
29 Stephen of BBC's "The Honourable Woman"
32 Things auditors watch for
34 Top
36 One-named singer with the 1968 hit "Abraham, Martin and John"
37 Composer Zimmer
39 She was Time magazine's 2019 Person of the Year
41 Composed
43 Acts like a nudnik to
44 Parts of a platform
45 Smartphone screen displays
46 Home of the only world capital to border two other countries
47 Turns up
48 Where to see Print
49 Take a ___
50 Corkscrews, e.g.

DOWN

1 Cut (in)
2 Liable to be lost, in a way
3 Yak, yak, yak
4 Join the table
5 Oktoberfest buy
6 Word with rain or rock
7 Letter accompanying a personal statement, informally
8 Ariadne, e.g.
9 Knew someone, so to speak
10 Split payment
11 Quantitative analyst's fodder
12 Take a ___
13 Go all over
15 House style with shingle exteriors and flat-front facades
17 Happening
19 Title sort of person in 2008's Best Picture
21 Panaceas
24 Computer programs used in 3-D animation
25 Euphoria
28 What may be corrected on a trans person's birth certificate
29 Group to which Don Rickles joked he "never received an official membership card"
30 Order
31 "Tell a joke or something . . . I'm so bored"
33 One who puts down a few chips?
35 Course selection
38 Oktoberfest buys
40 Puts down a few chips, maybe
41 That's a wrap!
42 Hirsute figure in the Bible
44 Piece of intimate wear
46 United Airlines hub, for short

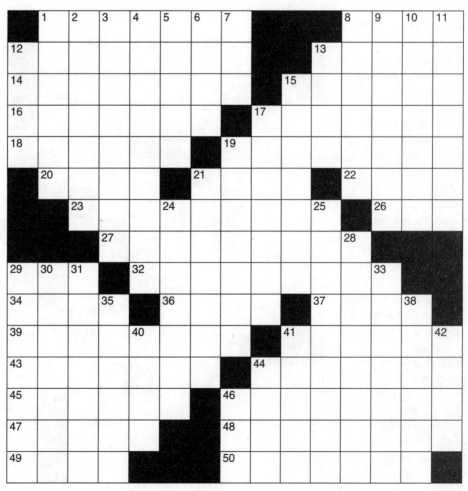

by Sid Sivakumar

ACROSS

1 Group whose name means "the people of the waters that are never still"
9 To boot
13 2014 animated film whose protagonist, aptly, is a construction worker, with "The"
14 It sticks out in a dance studio
15 Jam-packed
16 Imperial title derived from "caesar"
17 Quinceañeras, e.g.
18 Social protest lecture series
20 Possible response to "Who took the last cookie?"
21 Pentagon bigwig
23 Twice-hyphenated ID
24 Musicians are often on it
25 Instruments for Annapurna Devi and Anoushka Shankar
28 Comedian Notaro
29 Criticize, with "on"
30 Brand whose logo includes a schoolboy with a ball for a head
31 Largest U.S. union
32 Ground shaking stuff?
34 Composes (oneself)
36 Ancient gathering place
37 Locale for bowed heads
38 Aspirational hashtag
39 Breaks off
41 S_c_ _d (time in time)
42 Showers with sparkles
47 __ smarts
50 Reciprocally
51 Monkey head mushroom, by another name
53 Mountaintop home
54 Muscle car acronym
55 Cheese whose name is a semordnilap
56 One celebrating Grounation Day, which commemorates a visit by 8-Down

57 Go against
58 All up in another's business
59 What may be considered worse when done well

DOWN

1 Mix of many different cultures
2 Stared at
3 Red __
4 Succinct "I think"
5 Animal associated with the Egyptian goddess Hathor
6 Online image
7 Crane of "Frasier"
8 Ethiopian emperor revered by 56-Acrosses
9 To boot
10 Its destruction marked a turning point in World War I
11 Actor Sebastian __
12 Between you and me
13 Surrounded and attacked, with "to"
15 Typist's help to avoid repetitive strain injury
19 Team whose song "The Super Bowl Shuffle" earned a Grammy nomination
21 Big game
22 Throw __
24 Short-crust pastry fillings
26 Wind on the water?
27 Cheek
30 Texter's segue
33 Sharper image co.?
34 Some works by Petrarch
35 Caution on a silica gel packet
37 Lady, but not the Tramp
40 Ones who are sent packing?
41 Confuse wasabi with guacamole, say
43 Perfect vis-à-vis good, in an aphorism
44 Portmanteau for a messenger bag
45 Water filter brand
46 Tiptoe, maybe
47 Took a dive
48 Tucker
49 Part of the mouth
52 Hurly-burly

by Matthew Stock

ACROSS

1 Qt. and gal.
5 Letting in a little light, perhaps
9 Org. at the center of modern "name, image and likeness" legislation
13 Surname on a 2010 "True Grit" poster
14 Home of a massive flock
17 "Oh, our sides are hurting!"
18 In great demand
19 Makeup kit for a summer look
21 No neophyte
22 Left with nothing
23 Subject of the 2018 best-selling account "On Desperate Ground"
26 __ fly
27 2010 Atlantic hurricane that was the largest up to that time
28 Close one
29 Poetic contraction
30 What a ganzfeld experiment tests for
31 Homoerotic viewing
33 "That's quite enough!"
36 Actress Claire of "The Crown"
37 "Ni __" (Mandarin greeting)
38 Metaphor for a 100-degree day
39 "__, like morality, consists of drawing the line somewhere": G. K. Chesterton
40 Upgrade for a train passenger
42 Deadlock
45 Have a drink, old-style
46 Really risked it
49 Start of many a party
50 Join (up)
52 Common dorm accommodation
53 Post hoc, __ propter hoc (logical fallacy)

54 Cause of lightheadedness?
55 Sister brand of Guess? and Calvin Klein
56 File type

DOWN

1 Patella neighbor, in brief
2 Some parenting websites
3 Tragic downfall?
4 Buttinsky
5 E-commerce alternative to Square or Stripe
6 Grand __
7 Bio lab supply
8 Beat poet?
9 Genre popularized by Limp Bizkit and Korn
10 Star journalist?
11 Not quite right
12 Riz __, Emmy winner for 2016's "The Night Of"
15 Squeeze
16 Holds the door for, say
20 150-year-old org. that filed for bankruptcy in 2021
21 Merle Haggard tune "__ From Muskogee"
24 Custom
25 Leading character
29 Force behind many disinformation campaigns
31 Started fuming
32 Stroke, perhaps
33 What might be next to cue cards
34 Humans, in sci-fi slang
35 About
36 Stereotypical kegger attendee
38 Traveler around the world
39 Like some sleeping problems
40 Aid in breaching castle walls
41 Kind of change
42 "Wouldn't that be nice"
43 Anime genre featuring giant robots
44 Made the case against?
47 "All right, we get it!"
48 Strip lighting
51 Mess of hair

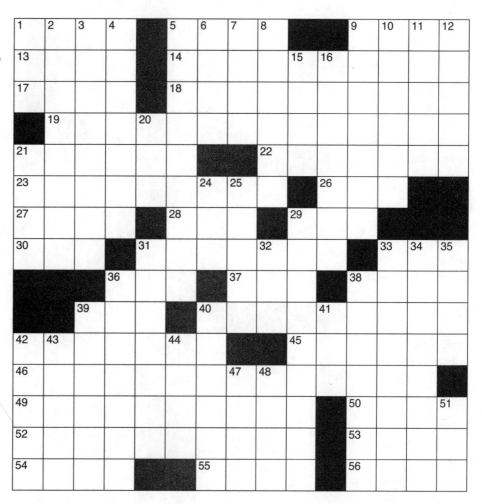

by Ryan McCarty

ACROSS

1 What's not to like?
10 Big ink purveyor
15 The singer Björk, for one
16 Lustrous shell compound
17 Black hairstyle with square-shaped sections
18 Yet to be processed
19 Cabinet department with a buffalo on its emblem
20 Place for fast growth
21 Valuable carriers
23 Green symbol on Rotten Tomatoes
27 Sliding __
28 Ran off (with)
30 "__ Possible" (2000s animated series)
31 Give kudos to
35 Quadrennial bonus
37 Daily in Paris
39 Some pubgoers
40 Little drawing?
42 Bearer of the earth in Iroquois creation stories
43 Choice cut
45 Scanner feature
46 "Well, there's a surprise!"
51 Pulling down
52 Paid athletes with day jobs
57 Well lit?
58 Aircraft with low drag
59 Not requiring much attention, say
60 Help on wheels
61 Sibilant sobriquet for "Summertime" singer Sarah Vaughan
62 Hit from behind

DOWN

1 Nickname in Israeli politics
2 Milton Friedman's subj.
3 It might end in an emoji
4 River through Bohemia
5 Like many a documentary film
6 [Live!]
7 Lesson for an advanced language learner
8 Component of many sandstone features in the Southwest
9 Hospital drama sets, in brief
10 What genes do, biologically
11 Medicare Advantage, by another name
12 Apparatus with a harness and flippers
13 Get to eat
14 List for a survivalist
20 Skateboarder's wear
22 Skateboarder's apparatus
23 Successfully convince
24 "No contest," for one
25 Important calculation for a weightlifter
26 Galaxy array
29 "I'm __ myself here, but . . ."
31 Dance around?
32 Snacks for some beetles
33 Waiting for an assignment, maybe
34 It's not a good look
36 Festive season
38 More than a few
41 Find satisfaction, slangily
43 Sunday best
44 Grp. of Pelicans
46 Some prayer leaders
47 Sicilian word that roughly translates as "swagger"
48 Actor Claude of "B.J. and the Bear"
49 Copter cousins
50 Affaire de coeur
53 Not just live in the present
54 £ : pound sterling :: R : __
55 __-over
56 Pip
58 __ Mediterráneo

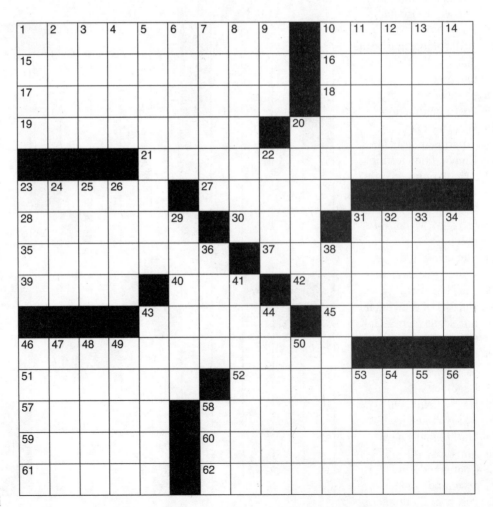

by Stella Zawistowski

ACROSS

1 Industrial V.I.P.
6 Flower that's also the name of a "Downton Abbey" character
14 Developing, after "in"
15 "Mahatma," in translation
17 International telephone prefix for Russia
18 Greek goddess of memory
19 Imperial title
21 Abbr. in a birth announcement
22 Turkish honorific
23 Legal conclusion?
24 Chickens (out)
27 Big family
28 Like favorite films, typically
30 Like Seth, among the offspring of Adam and Eve
31 Like dry mud on a dog's paws
32 "Gotcha"
33 Site of the impact of the asteroid that killed the dinosaurs 66 million years ago
37 Long lunches?
38 Some avian homes
39 At __ (befuddled)
40 Shipping option for books
44 It's full of fiber
45 Capybara, for one
46 Raleigh-to-Richmond dir.
47 Boosts
48 "Look what I found!"
49 Kind of typeface or Pepperidge Farm cookie
51 Sport with a "capture the flag" variety
55 Wanderer
56 Food dyes, e.g.
57 Drop, in a way
58 Turned vertically
59 Handy device for making gazpacho

DOWN

1 Street musician
2 Loose
3 Run through
4 Rock group
5 Campaign catchphrase of 1988
6 Grand opening?
7 Sports agent Tellem
8 Pulled (in)
9 There are 70 in a Shakespearean sonnet
10 Some muscle cars
11 W.W. II spy grp.
12 Stalwart
13 It may be in your jeans
16 Tragic lover of myth
20 Rowdydow
25 Poet Silverstein
26 Drew in
27 Rhetorical inversion device seen in "Champagne for my real friends, and real pain for my sham friends"
29 Confront
30 Like the red panda, blue whale and black rhino
32 Interim
33 Mexican dish named after a small boat
34 Rooftop landing sites
35 1960s–'70s detective series set in San Francisco
36 Presage
40 County that's split in two by the Grand Canyon
41 Low on energy
42 Enter by force
43 Word finishing ring or band
45 Newswoman Roberts
48 Palindromic number in Italian
50 __ me tangere (Latin warning)
52 Quibble
53 Spy novelist Deighton
54 Drug known by its German initials

by Adam Simon Levine

ACROSS

1 Barrel of fun?
4 Like Marcia, among the "Brady Bunch" daughters
10 No longer following
14 Diminutive suffix in Spanish
15 Cry at sea
16 Jay-Z's "___ the Next One"
17 Fictional home with a secret basement
19 "___: Hawaii" (TV spinoff)
20 Whom Sarah had in her early 90s
21 Super group
23 Part of FWIW
25 Part of Q.E.D.
26 Pacific evergreen with orange-red bark
30 ___ Lynch, first African American woman to serve as U.S. attorney general
34 Put away
35 Range of consideration, metaphorically
37 Activity with a rake
39 Good name for a wrestler?
40 Badger
41 Some corporate holdings, for short?
43 Open ___
44 Hydration locations
46 Some formal promises
48 Open ___
49 Its products often come with Allen keys
51 Where uniforms are worn with sweaters?
53 Environmentally friendly way to travel
56 Soviet fighter jets
57 Locale below 17-Across, as suggested by three images in this puzzle's grid
59 Keeps informed, in a way
62 ___ urbis conditae
63 Cartoon character who says "Come over here, you skwewy wabbit!"
64 Cover-up in old Rome
65 Completely, after "in"
66 Does some crime scene work
67 Sample collector, maybe

DOWN

1 This will never fly
2 Headwinds can push them back, in brief
3 His "La Maja Desnuda" was never publicly shown in his lifetime
4 Members of a certain college
5 Flight
6 It's self-replicating
7 First name of the poet whose "candle burns at both ends"
8 Past the approval stage, in construction slang
9 They don't put up with any bull
10 Enduring
11 Years back
12 Not remain completely asleep
13 Caber ___ (Scottish athletic event)
18 Depilatory brand
22 Snitch (on)
24 Hitch or glitch
26 Econ subfield
27 Sunlit spaces
28 Like the loser's locker room after a stunning upset
29 Driver around a lot?
31 An eagle is the most common one in the U.S.
32 Its players never want to be at the top
33 Foolery
36 Written designs that are also readable when flipped or rotated
38 Cry to a baby
42 Jaime ___ a.k.a. the Bionic Woman
45 Some hospital supplies
47 College dept.
50 Made a move
52 Inits. that often precede "+"
53 "Now!"
54 "This can't be happening . . ."
55 Org. with a list of Supreme Court cases on its website
58 Old pro
60 "Star Wars" staple, for short
61 Fool

by Jim Horne and Jeff Chen

ACROSS

1 Bagel choices
8 Info on a medicine bottle
14 How a first date is experienced
16 ___ d'état
17 Penalty for a polluter
18 Biased
19 Sprout
20 Pearl Harbor hero for whom a future U.S. aircraft carrier is scheduled to be named
22 Student in College Station, Tex.
24 Some bags in boxes
25 New Deal program, for short
26 Judge
27 Props for some plays?
29 "The Godfather" actor
30 Accords, e.g.
32 Date you might not put on the calendar
33 Ate the last cookie, say
36 Goes bad
37 Intensify
38 Big name in Deco
39 What's the big deal?
40 Subjects of the 2018 book "Seeds of Science," for short
44 At least one
45 Item of prison contraband
46 Was serious about
47 Like mysterious matters, often . . . or hotels
51 Dr.'s order
52 Cigarette that's assembled by hand, informally
53 Cost-effective
55 Filers of amicus briefs, often
56 Place to get a cab
57 Feel it the next day
58 Goes gently to the bottom

DOWN

1 "Great news!"
2 Bring to a boil
3 Heavy hitter
4 Floor support
5 Café du ___ (landmark shop in New Orleans's French Quarter)
6 Within: Prefix
7 Leave a mark
8 Most Best Picture winners
9 Refueling spot
10 Window part
11 Invariably
12 Lapped, e.g.
13 One in the running
15 Canned lines?
21 Blows a gasket
23 "Uh-huh"
27 Like the years of most presidential inaugurations
28 Quick fix
29 [awkward]
31 Pair seen three times in "All's Well That Ends Well"
32 Lao-___
33 Lawn game seen regularly on ESPN beginning in 2017
34 Screams over
35 Mini-albums, for short
36 Alaskan king, e.g.
39 Posers are forever saying it
41 The hare, but not the tortoise
42 One way to serve chili
43 Nowheresville, with "the"
45 Lift user
46 Painter with a famous garden
48 Muse of history
49 TV series with Agt. Leroy Jethro Gibbs
50 Something you might watch with your parents
54 Leftover morsel

by Wendy L. Brandes

ACROSS

1 Epiphanies
11 Spoke to a judge, say
15 Classic Warhol subject
16 Lead-in to -stat
17 Like hitting a million-dollar jackpot
18 Grps. receiving Our Children magazine
19 Classic O'Keeffe subject
20 Get into
22 Fox's ___ Choice Awards
23 Pub container
25 The "F" in F = ma
27 Object
30 Musician on the cover of Rolling Stone, often
34 Martial arts actor Steven
35 Obtain a sum via special relativity?
36 Some like it dirty
37 Model/TV personality Chrissy who wrote the cookbook series "Cravings"
38 One who objects to screw caps, say
39 Shocked
40 Cry heard at a shoe auction?
41 Per diem, e.g.
43 Shortening used in many recipes
47 Reason for a colonial "party"
48 Mendeleev who created the periodic table
50 Timely query
51 "I'm ba-a-ack!"
54 Anti-D.W.I. org.
55 Be in direct competition
56 Insult, slangily
57 Epiphanies

DOWN

1 Not straight
2 Bud
3 More than enough
4 California county that's home to Muir Woods
5 Great Plains tribe
6 Packs
7 Spanish pronoun
8 Head, in slang
9 New Orleans university
10 Iota
11 Homemade headwear for kids
12 "Time to eat!"
13 Ballpark figs.
14 ___ Equis
21 Like many fancy parties
23 Moderate pace
24 ___ tear (sports injury)
25 Place to roast marshmallows
26 Norse war god
28 Prefix with technology
29 A bit too articulate, perhaps
30 Eponym for an Italian ice chain
31 25-Across on Earth, in brief
32 "Superfood" commonly used as a smoothie bowl topping
33 Frat party stunts
34 All there
36 Like bell peppers, on the Scoville scale
38 Earned
40 Classic gag gift at a bachelorette party
42 Negro League legend Satchel
43 Portmanteau for a certain hybrid feline
44 Washington, but not Jefferson
45 Previous
46 Right triangle ratios
47 Like the ancestry of 37-Across
48 Challenger ___ (lowest known point in the earth's oceans)
49 Bud
50 Nuclear bomb, e.g., for short
52 Business card abbr.
53 Jersey greeting

by Yacob Yonas

ACROSS

1 Travel item
5 Battle cry
11 Pop group?
14 Smart __
15 Its national animal is the beaver
16 Sustainability indicator
17 Painter whose cataract surgery allowed him to see and paint in ultraviolet
19 Knee part, for short
20 __ Richmond, former head of the Congressional Black Caucus and senior adviser to Joe Biden
21 Order in the court
23 Certain exotic pets
25 Dishevel
26 Baseball team whose mascot is Screech the eagle, familiarly
27 Sinking fastballs
32 Ron who played Tarzan
33 Start of a count
34 Conductor's cry
35 Popular podcast genre
36 Advanced degree
39 Equal opportunity
40 Local legends
41 Dance move
42 Egglike
44 Sticky candy?
49 "Bam!" chef
50 "That's gotta hurt"
51 Where you might get the ball rolling
53 Arm muscle, slangily
54 Place
55 The Grim, in the Harry Potter books
56 Fig. often written with X's
57 Shapes of some dog treats
58 Soft or hard finish

DOWN

1 Big shot?
2 More than discouraged
3 Part of a Navy officer's rotation
4 Luxury vehicles since 1986
5 Ephemeral palaces
6 __-o'-shanter
7 Hoity-toity type
8 Die out
9 Some stand concessions
10 Velocity, e.g.
11 __ film
12 Purpose of a pass
13 Shapes
18 Hullabaloo
22 Repair
24 Strauss's "Also __ Zarathustra"
28 Scales up?
29 Much-covered New Orleans standard based on Mardi Gras chants
30 Relays, e.g.
31 Ripped
33 Arc-shaped musical notation
34 Disney redhead
35 Bit of auto design inspired by the jet age
36 Easygoing
37 One may be personal
38 Spartan, e.g.
39 Blows away
40 Keep one's head down
41 Units of land, with or without the first letter
43 [I can't believe what I just read]
45 Okonkwo's people in "Things Fall Apart"
46 Left on board, say
47 Boo-boo
48 "Help!," for example
52 It's all over the papers

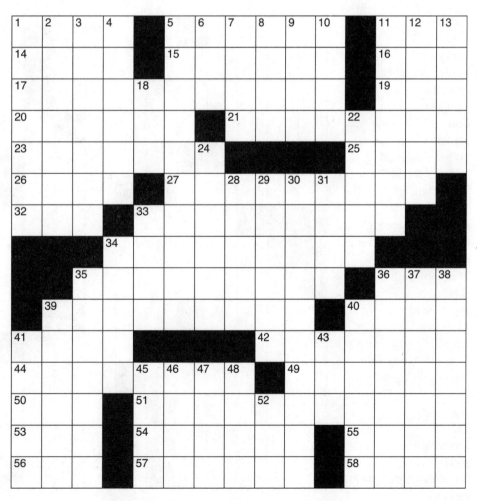

by August Lee-Kovach

ACROSS

1 Enthusiastic assent
5 Certain service
9 Packs (down)
14 Important leadership skill
16 Classic neo-grotesque typeface
17 "Losing some illusions . . . perhaps to acquire others," per Virginia Woolf
18 Gloomy and drab
19 Cause of an early lead, maybe
20 Like a spitball
21 Darth Vader's childhood nickname
22 Author who wrote "The heaventree of stars hung with humid nightblue fruit"
24 Sticky stuff
25 Hardly mainstream
28 Pluto, e.g.
29 Sudden sensation
30 Cutesy "I beg your pardon?"
34 "What a shocker"
35 "Heaven forbid!"
36 Singer Mitchell
37 Shapiro of NPR
38 John B. Goodenough is the oldest person ever to get one (at age 97)
42 Travel guess, for short
43 Joyous song
46 "Ambient 1: Music for Airports" musician
47 Candy cooked until it reaches the hard-crack stage
50 Approach
53 Tell all
54 Strutting one's stuff
55 Kind of moment worth recording
56 Xenomorphs, e.g.

57 Cart contents
58 What air is not for an anaerobe
59 Looked at suspiciously

DOWN

1 Throw on the couch
2 Angel said to have visited Joseph Smith
3 Like shunga woodblock prints
4 What breaks as it first comes out
5 "The Pinkprint" rapper
6 Belligerent, slangily
7 "Put a sock in it!"
8 500 letters?
9 "I did it!"
10 Like Mars
11 Psychological trick
12 It's just the beginning of the story
13 Sneaky sort
15 Model (for)
20 Composer Anton who used the 12-tone technique
23 Main component in the Chinese street food jianbing
26 Children's classic originally written in German
27 Nov. 11 honoree
29 Sauce whose name derives from "pound" in Italian

31 Double curve
32 Crowdsourced Q&A site
33 The Promised Land
34 Honest-to-goodness
35 Fall apart
36 Zippy resort rental
39 Joint application?
40 Tempt
41 Took inventory?
44 Home with a view
45 Unembellished, as the truth
48 Bit of deception
49 Lodge group
51 Loud bugling, e.g.
52 Concerning
54 Appearing ill or exhausted, say

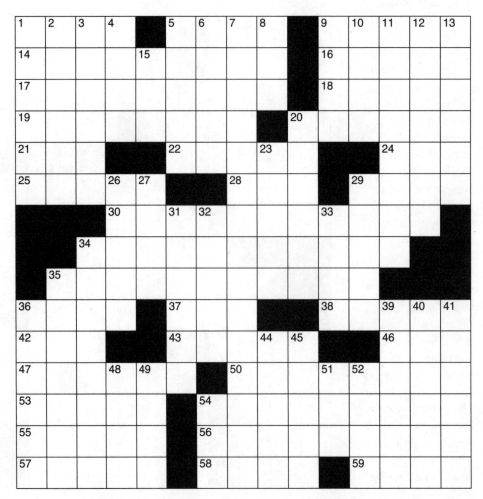

by Ashton Anderson

ACROSS

1 It's said to have been born on Orange Street, in Kingston, Jamaica
4 Big to-do
8 Bright night lights
13 Popular baby shower gift
15 "Sorry if you were offended," e.g.
17 Pop music nickname
18 Catchphrase for Olivia Pope on "Scandal"
19 Usher
21 People also known as the Cat Nation
22 Wolf's home?
23 "I could a tale unfold ___ lightest word / Would harrow up thy soul . . .": "Hamlet"
24 Run one's eyes over
25 Water gait?
26 Call near the end of a card game
27 Squalor
29 Regional dog variety
30 Big award in French cinema
32 Very bottom
33 "No hard feelings?"
35 Better part of 1999?
37 L.G.B.T.Q.I.A. follower
41 Certain swinger
42 Street in a James Baldwin title
43 Co. bigwig
44 Say the same thing as
45 Metalworker's union
46 Unlikely to give a strong reaction
48 For choice
49 Spill
50 Photographer's staff
51 "Wait, wait, don't tell me!"
54 Its anthem is "Terre de nos aïeux"
55 Having trouble making a call
56 Did some P.R. work on
57 Undesirable bedmates?
58 Common Christmas tree decoration
59 Realize

DOWN

1 Blow it
2 Eighth incarnation of Vishnu
3 Sit on a windowsill, say
4 Huff
5 Babysitter's charge
6 Check for bugs
7 Showing uncritical enthusiasm
8 Zip
9 Discontinued
10 One prone to blowing off steam
11 Like some nonbinary people
12 State capital near Bondi Beach
14 Life lines?
16 Royal ___
20 Zebra
24 Steady partner?
25 Supply in a golf bag
28 Date sacred to Jupiter
29 Converge (on)
31 National fruit of the Philippines
32 Court infraction
34 Showy blossom in the iris family, for short
35 "Zing!"
36 Quickly
38 Treats that come in plastic tubes
39 Fail to follow along
40 Still going
41 "That's uncalled for!"
42 Beauties
45 Victor Hugo's Cosette, e.g.
47 Tiny carps
49 Opposing forces
50 Part of UX
52 Utmost degree?
53 Erstwhile camera and satellite maker for NASA

by Caitlin Reid and Erik Agard

ACROSS

1 Abundant
6 "__ and Basie!" (1963 jazz album)
10 Calendar heading named for a Norse deity: Abbr.
13 "Everything's going to be fine"
14 Bucolic spots
15 Artist colony in a desert
16 Digital color presentation?
18 Vegetable also called "ladies' fingers"
19 Seriously
20 Colon or semicolon, in an emoticon
21 "Men in Black" antagonists
22 Long run?
23 Bonny ones
25 __ Explorer
26 Something that may be packed
28 Heckerling who directed "Look Who's Talking" and "Clueless"
29 Courtroom conclusion
32 Comment after an amazing statement
33 What might be found between X and Z?
34 Small amphibian
35 Subj. for class cut-ups?
36 Direction of many a lavatory on a plane
37 One-fourth of KISS
39 Olympic skater Midori
40 __ Chang, Harry Potter's first love interest
43 1982 Disney film with a 2010 sequel
44 Kitty food?
47 It covers a lot of ground
48 "Walk"
49 Endor native
50 Spirits of Greece
51 Like a tapestry
52 __ Sarnoff, Warner Bros. C.E.O. beginning in 2019
53 Participated in a pistol duel
54 They're full of opinions

DOWN

1 Helicopter traffic reporter on "The Simpsons"
2 Intended
3 Bends at the Bolshoi
4 [I forgot the words . . .]
5 Local alternative
6 Actress Pompeo of "Grey's Anatomy"
7 Adornments sometimes made with kukui nuts
8 Hold up
9 Vapers don't get it
10 Tries chai, say
11 Quartet in Revelation
12 Nation conspicuously missing from the Wilson-proposed League of Nations, in brief
15 Santa's sleighful
17 How you might count to five
20 Dining with one's child?
23 Countertop or flooring materials
24 Children's author/illustrator Hoff
25 Problem for a king
26 Cry made while swinging a baton
27 "Put a tiger in your tank" sloganeer
29 Roman army leader
30 Cellphone plan concern
31 Card game in which jacks are the top four trumps
32 Got out of Dodge, say
33 Some kitchen appliances
38 Tennessee governor who became president
39 "Say no more"
40 Herb often used in preparing potatoes and omelets
41 Upped
42 Is on first
44 Really come down
45 Move, maybe ominously
46 Take to another dimension?
47 Lead-in to cow or lion
48 Uranus, e.g.

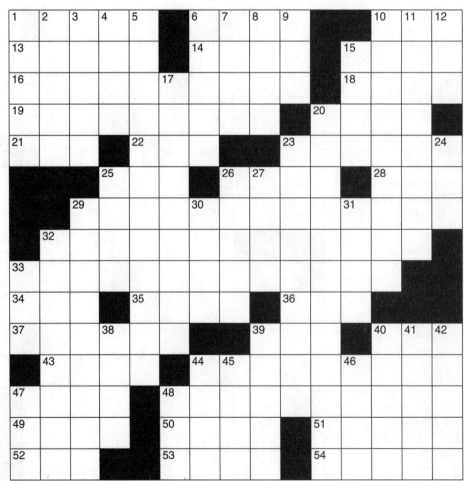

by Robyn Weintraub

ACROSS

1 Questions of surprise?
8 Certain native of the Mideast
15 Like cranks
16 Indian spice mixes
17 Duraflame product
18 Cause of a decrease in the cost of gasoline
19 Contents of some wells
20 Literally, "one who is sent off"
22 ___ Chinmoy, onetime Indian spiritual leader
23 Pass it on!
25 Law school subject
26 What's mixed with bismuth, lead and cadmium to make cerrosafe
27 A host of, in brief
29 "Stronger With ___ Tear," 2009 hit album for Mary J. Blige
30 Fail badly
31 Words of acceptance
33 "Is this such a good idea?"
35 Request from a host
37 Where I-25 meets I-40: Abbr.
38 Pippi Longstocking feature
41 Things on the heads of some outlaws
45 Controvert
46 Dix minus un
48 Pass through D.C.?
49 ___ and ran
50 L.A. jazz venue where Thelonious Monk recorded a live album, with "the"
52 Get
53 Duds at an awards ceremony, maybe
54 They've got to hand it to you
56 ___-tip (beef cut)
57 Quickly and soon
59 Headliner
61 "Oh, that's good!"
62 Sunblock blocks it
63 Manor house attendant
64 Some charges for animal lovers

DOWN

1 Standard Disney fare
2 River with the second-largest discharge volume in the New World, after the Amazon
3 BBQ specialty
4 "Por ___?"
5 First sch. to win 100 N.C.A.A. titles
6 [knock on wood]
7 Baby-to-be
8 Face of the internet?
9 Online marketing giant with a primate in its logo
10 Some vacation getaways
11 Low-quality paper
12 Likely M.V.P. candidate
13 Bullish
14 Cry of ineptitude
21 Popular baitfish
24 Potential topic to discuss in science class?
28 Meat
30 Strenuous
32 Rabbit ears
34 "Wot's dat over ___?"
36 Hybrid Thanksgiving dessert
38 Flower in the nightshade family
39 Rounded, say
40 Quiet period
42 Charge for some truckers
43 Drawing of the body without its skin, from the French
44 One of the Lesser Antilles
45 Kind of pool
47 Go from E to F
50 Challenge for a language learner
51 Musical equivalent of two whole notes
55 What halophobia is the fear of
58 Baby
60 "What's the ___?"

by Sam Ezersky

ACROSS

1 Discontinued rhyming ice cream treat
10 They may be loaded or covered
15 What there will be if you cross the wrong person
16 If you ask her to make you a sandwich, she'll say "OK, you're a sandwich"
17 Boob tube?
18 Foolish in an endearing way
19 Summer setting in the Windy City
20 Ten C-notes
21 Bachelorette party accessories
22 One in the Jenner family
24 One might begin "It was a dark and stormy night . . ."
26 High rollers' rollers
28 Some world leaders
29 Way to go: Abbr.
30 Absolved
32 French word that sounds like a letter of the alphabet
33 Ask "Why should I?," say
34 Vote by __
36 Org. involving course work
38 Dept. store stock
41 Neighbor of Caps Lock
43 N.B.A. team coached in the '70s by Bill Russell
47 Sea eagle
48 [More worms, mama!]
50 Easy-peasy
51 Nickelodeon's longest-running game show
54 Hairstyle for 2-Down
55 Tight (with)
56 Certain blood vessel, to a physician
58 __ Burgundy, Will Ferrell persona
59 Shield adorned with Medusa's head
60 Ginormous
62 Static, e.g.
63 "That sounds 'bout right"
64 Twisted look
65 Lewis Carroll character who asks "Does your watch tell you what year it is?"

DOWN

1 Response between a smile and a belly laugh
2 Woodstock headliner
3 Bygone
4 The Browns, on scoreboards
5 Oaxacan "other"
6 Burgs
7 Individually
8 I Spy or Backseat Bingo
9 Spanish "Hey!"
10 Fierce
11 Most desirable, as guests
12 Ulta competitor
13 Whizzes
14 Accepts a ring, perhaps
21 Ice cream shop supplies
23 River in Picardy
25 Yemeni money
27 Facial spot
31 Gave faithfully, in a way
33 __ Stark, role for which Sophie Turner was Emmy-nominated
35 Put down
37 __ step further
38 Traffic dividers
39 Talk long and boringly
40 Wearable blanket
42 Virtuosa's display
44 Short person's group photo position, ideally
45 Go barhopping, say
46 Name on many a sports jersey
48 Dealmaking pro
49 Taking a heavy science course load, perhaps
52 Capital near the old Oregon Trail
53 Eldest son of Cain
57 "Puppy Love" singer, 1960
60 He/__ pronouns
61 Caught

by Aimee Lucido

ACROSS

1 Words on some flashcards, informally
6 Stuff
10 "___ are . . ."
14 Academia, it's said
16 TV host who was the subject of the documentary "You Laugh but It's True"
17 One paid to be in an audience
18 Pot price
19 Its larva is eaten as a delicacy in the Mexican dish escamoles
20 Suffix with carboxyl
21 Loved, on social media
23 Found through searching
25 "Olympus ___ Fallen" (2013 film)
27 Quiet (down)
28 Defeated, in a way
30 Source of cheap caviar
32 What Real Madrid and F.C. Barcelona play in
33 Clerical garment
34 Many take notes using one
35 Milk purchase: Abbr.
36 "___ love is better than high birth to me": Shak.
37 Lacking focus
39 Low-lying areas?
41 City name on both the East and West Coast
42 Elwes of "The Princess Bride"
43 Letters that further extend letters
44 You can't leave home with it
47 One who likes to dish?
48 Ohio congressman Ryan
49 Corn's place
52 Princess ___ Martell on "Game of Thrones"
53 Mystery prize
56 Refrigerate
57 Locale for athletic competition
58 A long, long time
59 Something that may be broken in a kitchen
60 Reveal

DOWN

1 Checked item for some travelers
2 ___-ready
3 Outer layer
4 Linocuts and such
5 Without a doubt
6 Grammatical mistake
7 ___ Together (punny name for a hardware store)
8 Snickers piece?
9 Didn't do the right thing
10 Hot
11 "I might be out late. See you in the morning"
12 Occasions for hiring a sitter
13 Get rid of
15 "Alas!"
22 Commercial success
23 One of 768 in a 35-Across: Abbr.
24 Overseas rate: Abbr.
25 Commotion
26 Walking
29 Count against?
30 Screening sites
31 One whose work is always cropping up?
32 Loser to "The Shape of Water" for Best Picture
35 Some slumber party activity
38 Caulks, e.g.
39 A.I. on Discovery One
40 Go (for)
42 Vigorous exercise
45 Substantial
46 Titular Menotti opera character
47 Singer Peniston with the 1991 top 5 hit "Finally"
49 Opposite of relaxed
50 Thereabouts
51 ___ Prairie, suburb of Minneapolis
54 It's hair-raising
55 Wretchedness

by Michael Hawkins

ACROSS

1 Result of a rise, perhaps
8 Other half
14 One of the Balearic Islands
15 Dessert order at a Mexican restaurant
16 Quirky sort
17 Life-form led by Optimus Prime in the "Transformers" movies
18 Monthly expense
19 Ballpark figure
21 __ Lonely Boys, group with the 2004 hit "Heaven"
23 Button for enlarging an image
24 Mark of perfection
25 Expose
28 Really, really
31 Gender-__
34 T-Bird alternative
36 Cabbage alternative?
37 "This isn't a trick question"
40 "__ c'est Paris" (French soccer club slogan)
41 Vibe
42 Airs during the holidays
43 Jimmy of high-end footwear
45 Made it through
47 Pro in D.C.
49 Exaggerated
50 "The Bachelorette" network
53 Deli lunch options
57 Sound after a sip
59 Midcruise milieu
60 Where Bill and Hillary first met
62 In
63 Budgeting class?
64 Automotive amenity that offers an annual Santa Tracker
65 Stingrays, often

DOWN

1 Emissions concern
2 Like some pools
3 "Thus . . ."
4 What something bacillary is shaped like
5 Word with wonder or designer
6 Protest movement launched in 2011, familiarly
7 Peace slogan
8 Barricaded
9 To __ mildly
10 Cry from a balcony
11 Big adventure through the concrete jungle
12 Emissions concern
13 Ciudad del __, Paraguay's largest city after Asunción
15 Sound investment in the 1980s?
20 Follower of Jesus Christ?
22 Paper cut, e.g.
26 Troubles
27 __ power
29 Sovereign land, so to speak
30 Excuses
31 It has a $100 billion line of credit with the Treasury Dept.
32 Cousin of a firth
33 Ones calling the strikes?
35 Zwölf minus elf
38 Chill
39 "__ problem"
44 Acorn, by another name
46 Fine wool source
48 Cybertruck maker
51 Mowgli's teacher in "The Jungle Book"
52 Belt wearer, perhaps
53 Lead-in to -graphic
54 Keeping current with
55 Graduation class
56 This is taking fore-e-ever
58 Many start with "I": Abbr.
61 Sinus doc

by Joseph Greenbaum

ACROSS

1 Trash
5 Kind of rock
9 Toni Morrison title character who lives in the Bottom
13 Lower-cost option at a supermarket, usually
15 Fresh
16 Furry creature that Wallace becomes during the full moon, in a "Wallace & Gromit" film
17 Bio subject
18 "___ changed"
19 Feature of the inner planets
20 Thread count?
21 Facebook allows for more than 50
23 Reciprocal of a siemens
24 Sharon Olds's "___ to Dirt"
25 Hush puppies alternative
27 Restaurant starter, informally
30 Prominent attire for Jr. Pac-Man
35 Assumes
36 Grande and others
37 Actress Susan
38 Order at a lodge
39 It's sold by the yard
40 Good things to have for a private party
41 What a trip!
45 Alliterative partner of 45-Down
48 Proceeds smoothly
50 Creature whose male incubates the eggs, during which it won't eat, drink or defecate for 50+ days
51 Trails
52 New York City setting of the "Eloise" books
54 It may be bonded
55 "Much obliged!"
56 Whom to call "maman"
57 Guard, perhaps
58 Current

DOWN

1 Martin or Harvey
2 Actress with an Academy Award for 1960's "Two Women"
3 Amount to
4 Maker of the world's first diesel-powered passenger car
5 Photographer Diane
6 Pickup line?
7 Still alive, so to speak
8 Noted organochloride, in brief
9 Boston exurb
10 Bell Labs development of the 1970s
11 Took off
12 Floors
13 Amount from a flask, maybe
14 Amounts from a distillery, maybe
20 Program replaced by "CBS This Morning"
22 Olympics rule-breaker
23 Like Tony-winning plays
25 Brightens, with "up"
26 ASCAP and A.S.P.C.A.: Abbr.
27 Lead-in to date
28 Walk on water?
29 Disposable shoe liners
30 What cognitive behavioral therapy might treat, in brief
31 Grade
32 "Capisce?"
33 Sure thing
34 Home of the two deepest canyons in the Americas (each 11,500+ feet)
40 Response at the door
41 Gave off, in a way
42 ___ Hall
43 Change in writing
44 'Tis the season to be jolly
45 Kind of rock
46 Behind
47 2008 animated film with the tagline "He's got a monster of a problem"
48 Barents Sea sight
49 Quad part
52 Stone
53 "Absolument!"

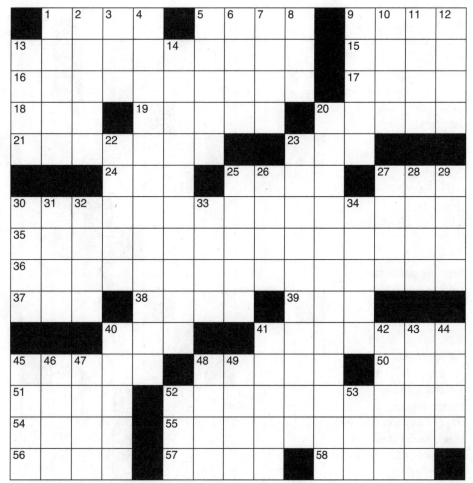

by Brooke Husic and Will Nediger

154 HARD

ACROSS

1 San Francisco or Fire Island
9 Lift one's spirits?
15 Brutish boss
16 Unnatural
17 Orthodontist's recommendation
18 Lengthy Twitter post, often
19 Not take for granted
20 Units equivalent to ⅙ of an inch
22 Hosp. diagnostic
23 Throw or shoot
25 Imitation
26 Primed (for)
30 Serving with shawarma
31 Shrimp in a shell, maybe
32 Interminably
34 Tusked beast
37 Movie series set inside a simulated reality, with "The"
38 Home to Mayan ruins like Caracol and Lamanai
39 Many a bill's name in Congress
41 Spare clothes?
42 Young stud
43 Troubadour
45 Actress Amanda
46 Cherry-pick
47 Subscripts on Scrabble tiles
49 C, for one
50 International cricket matches
51 Neat and clean
56 Heartburn reliever
58 Focus of the 2009 Lilly Ledbetter act
60 Dot-com whose name is stylized with two converging arrows
61 Prepare on short notice
62 Greek locale once described as "the island of overmastering passions"
63 Hunter of fish

DOWN

1 Hiker's handful
2 Swear
3 "Monsters, Inc." character who loves snow cones
4 Jason with the 2008 hit "I'm Yours"
5 Architect Saarinen
6 Fan gathering, informally
7 Entered quietly
8 Purposeless
9 "Imagine a case in which . . ."
10 Soft shoes, informally
11 Zero reaction?
12 Hotel hummer
13 Covering for a cold one
14 Bauer of leisure apparel
21 Arcade game feature
24 Miniaturist's supply
25 Accompanier of a black eye
26 2018 film for which Alfonso Cuarón won Best Director
27 Off the mark
28 Copper containers?
29 Commit to a course
31 Long way to go
33 By ___ of (due to)
35 Countenance
36 Heroic exploit
40 Ones who'll manage somehow?
41 Succinct, if nothing else
44 Changes
46 Leviticus calls it "unclean" and not fit for consumption
47 Puzzles
48 Be found not guilty, shockingly
50 Rumpus
52 Civil rights activist Baker
53 Video file format
54 Name of six popes, including one in the 20th century
55 Info described on a Tinder profile
57 Where to fill a flask with alcohol
59 2026 FIFA World Cup co-host

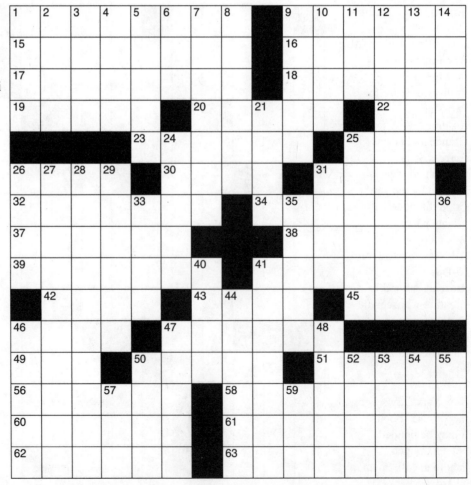

by Patrick John Duggan

ACROSS

1 Maker of the Karma quadcopter drone
6 East Timor's capital
10 Call to a mate
14 Like white-eyes and wheatears
15 River that's a letter off from 20-Across
16 Default result, maybe
17 Chilling
18 Capital whose name means "smoky bay," referencing the steam from its hot springs
20 Sea that's a letter off from 15-Across
21 Hockey star Patrick
22 ___-friendly (ecolabel)
23 Netflix series that caused a 2017 surge in Eggo sales
26 Stadium refrain
27 Palme d'Or field
28 Groups with lots of issues to talk through
31 Not-so-big shot
34 Needing to be charged
35 Donnie ___, title role for Jake Gyllenhaal
36 "Slick"
37 Monitor of a tap
38 Activity with a drawing of names
40 Car music player button
41 Epitome
42 Something good eaters "join"
47 Passages in a long story?
48 ___ Parker (handbag retailer)
49 Suddenly show (up)
51 "Ah, yes, of course . . ."
53 Director Sam
54 Lead-in to medicine
55 Savory sauce made with chocolate
56 Most likely, in a text
57 Home of the Sultan Qaboos Grand Mosque
58 Got rid of
59 Collection of brains

DOWN

1 Mother (and wife!) of Uranus
2 Stay out for too long?
3 Notorious online hub for illegal file sharing, with "The"
4 Reading, for instance
5 With 39-Down, "Wait!"
6 "Anyone who has ever worn a ___ spells it '___,'" per a 2018 New York Times article
7 Nobel-winning daughter of Marie and Pierre Curie
8 What bakers might do their level best to make?
9 Sort
10 "Prego" preceder
11 County that's home to Plymouth, England
12 Mocking, maybe
13 Joins
19 Heads
21 Heavily engaged (in)
24 ___-country
25 Chalamet of 2021's "Dune"
26 9-to-5, e.g.
29 You might take the bait from one
30 Foul up
31 Eponym of Israel's largest airport
32 Scented products that cause underwater "explosions"
33 "Don't wait!"
36 You might have a file for this
38 Word with talking or horse
39 See 5-Down
40 Shade of pink
42 Casual pants material
43 2019 Super Bowl loser, for short
44 Lead role in "The Vampire Diaries"
45 First person to appear simultaneously on the American and British covers of Vogue (Oct. 2021)
46 Played out
50 Site of a famous tilt in European history
52 Sport with a big pay-per-view audience, in brief
53 Spinning inits.

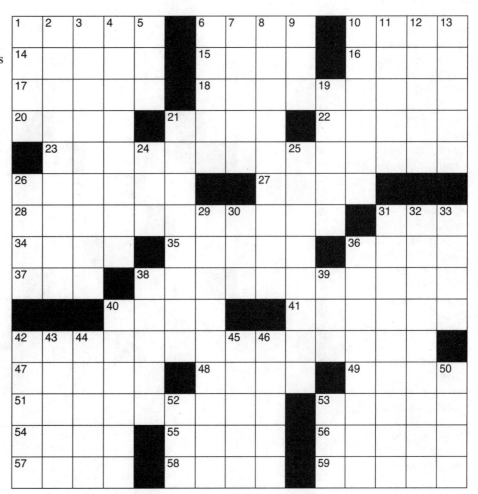

by Adam Aaronson

ACROSS

1 Phrase popularized by Long John Silver of "Treasure Island"
16 It's "on a dark desert highway," in song
17 Ways in which different cultures interact
18 Le Dakota du Sud or le Dakota du Nord
19 Like some traditions
20 Listens, old-style
21 Have that *wow* factor
22 Name ending for Mari- or Rosa-
23 Things people often claim to have read when they haven't
24 Typesetting unit
27 Funky stuff
29 N.B.A. M.V.P. of 2015 and '16, familiarly
31 "I don't do ___. I am ___": Salvador Dalí
32 Eponymous instrument inventor Adolphe
35 Smaller than usual, endearingly
37 "What do you call cheese that isn't yours? Nacho cheese!," e.g.
39 Periods that aren't usually added, for short?
40 "Live in ___" (clothing slogan)
42 Water colors
43 Japanese camera
44 Protagonist of "The O.C."
45 What may be thrown down for a duel
47 Popular video game series with cars, for short
49 Nickname that drops "An-"
52 Show petulance, in a way
53 Former-Yankee-turned-broadcaster, to fans
54 Clean, as decks
55 "Don't sweat the naysayers"
58 Opening statement of an appeal?
59 Digs near a flower bed, say

DOWN

1 Black ___
2 "Too ___ Handle" (Netflix reality show)
3 "We've all been there"
4 Let it all out
5 Hebrew name meaning "my God"
6 Pioneering brand of caffeine-free soft drink
7 Combine
8 Longest-serving U.S. first lady, informally
9 One might be open for business
10 "___ tree falls . . ."
11 Big time for long-distance calling
12 Prickly shrubs
13 Vast, poetically
14 Places for curlers
15 Be wise to
23 Apparel often worn with sandals
25 Computer addresses, for short
26 Green stew
28 Outfit
29 NorCal airport
30 Syllable of disapproval
31 "Whip It" rock band
32 It travels at Mach 1
33 Black sorority with 300,000+ members, in brief
34 Marks, as a survey box
36 The Cowardly Lion's counterpart in Kansas
38 Presidential monogram of the early 1800s
41 The cool kids, e.g.
43 "That really isn't necessary"
44 Original "S.N.L." cast member
45 Home to Lake Volta, the largest artificial reservoir in the world
46 Volume measure
48 Island nation near Fiji
50 Betray, in a way
51 Critic who said "Art is the closest we can come to understanding how a stranger really feels"
52 Daniel Webster or Henry Clay
53 Sheik's peer?
54 Part of a fancy bedding set
56 ___ Juan
57 Like the mizzenmast

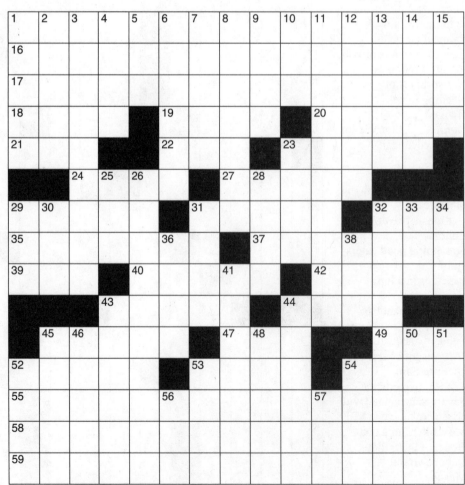

by John Hawksley

ACROSS

1 Sassy
6 Drink with a shot balanced on chopsticks over a beer
14 Meredith's half sister on "Grey's Anatomy"
15 Pack man
17 Certain record
18 Gracious words when accepting an honor
19 Eroded
20 Exhibition that might attract eye rolls, for short
21 Went quickly
22 Third-most-popular baby girls' name in 2020, after Olivia and Emma
23 Serengeti grazer
25 Make out
26 Joint winner of Time's Person of the Year for 2020
30 "Incorrect!"
31 "Intolerable Cruelty" director, 2003
32 Org. associated with the note series G-E-C
35 Author who referred to his works as a "legendarium"
37 More vexing
39 Word before now
40 Scoop often used in Indian cuisine
42 Ship on which Darwin collected material for "On the Origin of Species"
43 Encouraging words
45 "Mmm hmm . . ."
48 Ingredients for pastry cream
49 Gumshoe
50 Term of address for a noble
53 Mass Appeal Records co-founder
54 Sheltered place
55 French phrase in many bistro names
57 Daughter of Elrond in "The Lord of the Rings"

58 Fearless
59 Like the flame between exes, sometimes
60 Century of note
61 Examinations

DOWN

1 Played in the wind, say
2 Fixer-upper
3 Above and beyond, with "the"
4 Part of an equine bloodline
5 Song word sung twice before "goodbye"
6 Opened up during an examination
7 The first one printed in America was in 1639
8 Metric speed meas.
9 ___ Olmert, former Israeli P.M.
10 Foe of the Fighting Tigers
11 Multicolor hair effects
12 Fountain fare
13 Censor
16 Whirl
20 The highest form of flattery?
23 Pacific Ocean phenomenon
24 Lemon ___
27 Query
28 Running gear named after running animals
29 Legends, often
32 Ones late to work?
33 "Seriously!"
34 Symbols on the flags of Algeria and Azerbaijan

36 Kind of blue
38 Kit ___ Club ("Cabaret" locale)
41 Genre for "The Dark Knight," appropriately
43 Medieval servant
44 Secretive things?
45 One-named model and philanthropist
46 Storage units prone to explosion
47 Lift a lot
51 Tennis star of the 2000s, familiarly
52 It covers a lot of ground
54 Native of central Canada
56 Word in some South American city names
57 Refined oil product?

by Mary Lou Guizzo and Jeff Chen

ACROSS

1 Small headache
5 Onetime chain that offered Free Battery Club memberships
15 10-Down highlight
16 Best-selling heavy metal band named for a torture device
17 Big ol' mouth
18 Brushing, e.g.
19 TV character who said "I am so smart! I am so smart! S-M-R-T!"
21 Old worker with pads
22 Big ol' mouth
23 Pine product
25 It's flat on a snapback
26 Coin-__
27 8 vis-à-vis 2
29 Aimee __ McPherson, evangelist behind America's first megachurch
34 Vulnerable newcomers, in slang
37 Field
38 Duo in an ellipse
39 Intoxicate
41 They might be gathered by the pound
42 Bio subj.
43 Labor union offering, perhaps
45 More than dangerous
48 Part
49 Banned Books Week org.
50 __ Yaga (folklore villain)
52 Release
54 Its structure was evidenced by Photo 51, an X-ray captured in 1952
57 Several Russian czars
59 Cocktail tidbit
61 Going from 99 to 100, say
64 Archer of note

65 In hot pursuit
66 See 60-Down
67 Experts in English?
68 Sharp, in a way

DOWN

1 Trail
2 Like a butterfingers
3 Bucky in the comic strip "Get Fuzzy," e.g.
4 Patches up, in a way
5 Clear
6 Foe of Wonder Woman
7 "Stay in touch!"
8 Place underground
9 Subjects of a certain sultanate
10 Strauss work with the "Dance of the Seven Veils"
11 Flashin' Fruit Punch brand
12 #1 dad?
13 Michael who played George Michael Bluth on TV
14 Was aware
20 Like angel investors and devil's food cake
24 Not sensitive (to)
26 Viscera
28 Queen's subjects
30 Not natural
31 The art of politics?
32 Entitled sort
33 Desire of a quick study?
35 Emperor's order in "Star Wars"

36 Fatty tuna in Japanese cuisine
40 Register
44 Stay good
46 Goes along with
47 Extravagant
51 Where to get money in Milano
53 Bit of a character
54 Go down
55 You shouldn't do this
56 What you might unthinkingly be on
58 Gone down
60 With 66-Across, "Good thinking!"
62 Senators' org.
63 Three for a trey: Abbr.

by Kate Hawkins

ACROSS

1 Act the cynic, maybe
6 Embarks on a newly righteous path
13 Felt off
14 "This is no laughing matter!"
16 Operative
18 Realizes
19 Where Jesse Owens ran college track, in brief
20 Kitchen extension?
21 Soirée invitee
22 Big gun, you might say
24 Brilliant display
25 Small boat of East Asia
27 Draft letters
29 Spot early on?
30 Gardening practice that minimizes the need for water
34 The book of numbers
36 Low member of a marine ecosystem
38 Symbol on an ancient sarcophagus
41 People credited with discovering mechanoluminescence, using quartz crystals to generate light
42 More like mud
44 Savage
46 Something out standing in its field
49 Head of Hogwarts?
50 Bit of hunting gear, for short
51 Today preceder
52 It started smoking again in 2021
53 "You can come out now"
58 Those tending to the fallen warriors called einherjar, in myth
59 Collage application
60 Dangerous place for a leak
61 Put up

DOWN

1 Hot spots
2 Channel owned by HBO
3 Prompting nostalgia, say
4 Schedule listings
5 Who famously offered this speaking advice: "Be sincere, be brief, be seated," in brief
6 Variety offering
7 Sri Lanka-to-Singapore dir.
8 ___ curiam (by the court)
9 Reconstruction, e.g.
10 Man's name that's an African country if you change the last letter
11 Maneuver in dancing or football
12 He wrote "Appear weak when you are strong, and strong when you are weak"
14 Anjou alternative
15 Rather inclined
17 It welcomes change
22 Rescue
23 England's Middleton, younger sister of Kate
24 The world's most-visited city (20+ million travelers annually)
26 5-Down, e.g., in brief
28 Self-playing instruments
31 Deals
32 Tool with an eye
33 Jazz great Stan
35 One might determine fertility
37 Newborn
38 Where "Lost" could be found
39 Foe of Popeye
40 Emmy-winning actress Adlon
43 Didn't just tee-hee
45 Hits hard
47 One in a one-on-one session
48 Unchanged
52 Vivacity
54 Castor ___ (old cartoon character)
55 Lennox of R&B
56 Vice principle
57 Book reviewer?

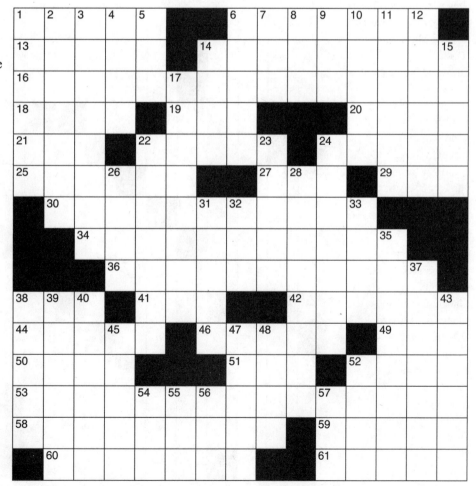

by Trenton Charlson

ACROSS
1 This and that
5 God of fertility, agriculture and the afterlife
11 "Big Love" network
14 Cassowary kin
15 Doing something wrong
17 Objectives
18 Fresh burst of energy
19 Five-star
21 Class structures?
22 Makeup palette assortment
23 Coruscates
25 Less likely to happen
27 You might seek forgiveness for this
28 Scans, say
29 New parents' purchases to block off staircases
34 Actress Mara of "Pose"
35 Empanadas and patatas bravas
36 "Happy to help!"
37 Nice position to be in?
39 Kind of cup
40 Just gets (by)
41 Go to bat for
42 San ___, seat of California's Marin County
45 Not expired
46 Everything one could possibly offer, with "the"
47 Mariah Carey and Madonna, for two
50 "Later, dude!"
53 ___ oil, extract obtained from the Amazon rainforest
54 Reverent
55 Pirate's activity
56 "Five Guys Named ___" (1992 Broadway musical)
57 Back-combed
58 Oh, to be in France!

DOWN
1 Challenge while sitting
2 Answer to the old riddle "What's round on the ends and high in the middle?"
3 Play with fire
4 Blanks
5 Out-of-office procedure?
6 72 answers and 34 black squares, for this puzzle
7 Hankering
8 Quintana ___, Mexican state that's home to Cancún
9 Spot for the night
10 Covering some ground?
11 Vertical dimension of a flag
12 Bops
13 "___ are . . ."
16 Longtime newswoman Ifill
20 Gender-neutral possessive
23 Holder of emergency supplies
24 Giant in chip manufacturing
25 Gets to
26 Many a Guinness Book record
27 Shade akin to royal blue
29 6-0 set, in tennis slang
30 "Whatever!"
31 Pet that's mostly black with a white chest
32 Ellie Kemper's role on "The Office"
33 ___ money
35 Kid
38 Firmly fixed
39 Offerer of fresh cuts
41 Made last night, say
42 Its participants are in for a wild ride
43 Pop up
44 Completely bomb
45 Fuzzy
46 Not cool—not cool at all!
47 Some Twitter postings
48 Brand that offers "Leg Mask" products
49 One of nine for a traditional Baha'i temple
51 Pro
52 Org. at Grand Central Terminal

by Claire Rimkus

ACROSS

1 [Perfection!]
10 Face to scale
15 Some exercise wear
16 Artist __ de Toulouse-Lautrec
17 What the name "Renée" means
18 List of pointers
19 Pull (out)
20 Overdrawn account?
21 Actress MacDowell
22 Classical music tradition from Hindustan
24 "Dear future me . . ."
27 Nest egg yield
29 He's been called the "Father of Science Fiction"
30 Pastoral sound
31 Quarters
33 Bit of mayo?
34 Scuttled
35 Taps
37 With some side-eye
39 Some transcript omissions
40 Strips
42 Home to the three highest capital cities in the world
43 March alternative
44 Big inits. in admissions
45 Alternatives to toilet paper
48 "Can we chat real quick?"
52 Nose-crinkling
53 They rate very high on the Scoville scale
55 "I got you"
57 Food truck output
58 Fictional Harvard Law student played by Reese Witherspoon
59 Favored, with "with"
60 Artful
61 Like many apartment rentals
62 Bash

DOWN

1 Connection point not seen much anymore
2 Establishment where indoor smoking is permitted
3 Beyond the pale
4 Deadly household appliance, according to Korean urban legend
5 Sterilize, in a way
6 First female dean of Harvard Law
7 Straight
8 Wasn't generous
9 Digits on a paper card, for short
10 Trousers named for an Asian country
11 Gives, as credence
12 They don't have a major-label contract
13 Like many jobs in the gig economy
14 Make whole
21 Book with scales
23 Rock group whose name came from letters found on a sewing machine
25 __ Sports Bureau (official 32-Down keepers)
26 Mountebanks
28 Stay quiet
32 See 25-Down
34 Minimalist style
36 Polite form of address, abroad
38 Blades used in "Kill Bill"
41 Masked warning?
43 Notre Dame setting
44 Follower of an "I'm late" text, in brief
45 They might be loaded with singles
46 Poker declaration
47 Deadpan
49 Like Falstaff
50 Take the edge off?
51 One might fly close to the sun
53 Printmaker?
54 "No Ordinary Love" singer
56 Pastoral sound

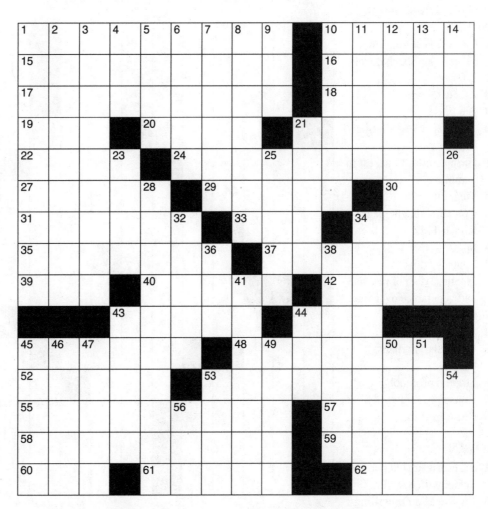

by Nam Jin Yoon

ACROSS

1 Ensemble purchase that includes sheets and pillowcases
10 Cheek-related
15 Heading for
16 Set apart
17 Skew conservative
18 "__ boogie!"
19 Meat
20 Period at the beginning of the Stone Age
22 Value
24 Wilson on the Hollywood Walk of Fame
25 Back on board
26 1968 Peace Nobelist Cassin
27 Garments that sound like you'd exercise in them
30 "Let's __!"
31 California setting of several Steinbeck novels
32 I, for one
34 At a discount
38 Big brass
40 __ fever, a.k.a. allergic rhinitis
41 Have a natural interest in gambling?
44 Wear out
45 Company that helped launch TMZ
46 Spot
47 Spots for dips
48 Japanese dish of raw fish and vegetables over rice
51 Kind of limit
52 Was peripatetic
53 Untrained, perhaps
57 Up
58 Ignored protocol
59 House of __
60 Beat reporting?

DOWN

1 __ esprit (gifted person)
2 Suffix with acetyl
3 Involve as an unwilling participant
4 Charge, in a way
5 Many a frontline worker
6 Words after keep or going
7 Importune
8 Albert Camus or Isaac Asimov, religiously
9 What over 40 million U.S. adults do annually
10 They're known for their holiday gifts
11 2019 rap hit whose title follows the lyric "How much money you got?"
12 Mandrake the Magician's sidekick
13 Modern protest movement
14 Jerks, say
21 Rightful praise
22 School for the college-bound, informally
23 Bench warmer?
24 Rush while racing?
27 Springs
28 Ones using a x-walk
29 One side of a coll. football "Holy War" rivalry
31 Vintner Claude
33 Intl. Rescue Committee, e.g.
35 Largest college sorority by enrollment (380,000+ members)
36 Noble title
37 Goes green, say?
39 Golden Ball winner in 2019's Women's World Cup
41 Of holy rites
42 Christmas cheer?
43 Twist in a story
44 Lethargy
47 Neil __, drummer/ lyricist for the rock band Rush
49 Inbox category
50 Puts on
51 Level
54 Subj. of supercoiling
55 Same old, same old
56 "Let's __ . . ."

by Joe DiPietro

ACROSS

1 Producer of inflation
4 Ranking no.
7 Confront, in slang
13 Some origin stories
16 "Rumors are carried by __, spread by fools and accepted by idiots" (old saying)
17 Moles are found in it
18 1991 platinum debut album by a female singer
19 Fantastic voyage
20 Collaborative resource
22 React to a baby, maybe
23 Promulgate
25 Food often served with plastic grass
27 Onetime Mughal capital
29 Dirt farm?
32 Ran
33 Army __
34 Befuddled
36 Ushered
38 Medalla material
39 "Ain't gonna happen"
40 Country rocker Steve
41 Small-batch publication
43 It's often framed
44 Treatment for jet lag
46 One of the Scooby-Doo gang
47 Elder brother of Moses
48 Like talk, they say
50 Pentagon inits.
52 "It would __ . . ."
54 Elizabeth of cosmetics
56 Question that introduces doubt
58 Something a judge might show
61 "It's nothing," in Spanish
62 Where some unsolicited advice comes from
63 Course challenge
64 Black __
65 "Cool, dude!"

DOWN

1 Prone
2 Where the Noah's Ark story is thought to have occurred, today
3 Essential work
4 One might be educated
5 Unsettle
6 Subject of David Remnick's "King of the World"
7 "All Eyez on Me" rapper
8 It's thought to ward off bad energy
9 H
10 One making good points in the classroom?
11 Something no two people can be
12 __ buco
14 17-Across offering
15 Spotted
21 Kind of muscle contraction
24 Tender union?
26 Cousins of crew cuts
27 Fit
28 Twinkle
30 San Rafael's county
31 Director Sergio
35 Struck dumb
37 One face of the moon
42 Bolster
45 Identifier seen in the "Six Feet Under" title sequence
49 Actress Alexander of "Get Out"
50 2010's __-Frank Act
51 Name for a Dalmatian, perhaps
53 Card games are played in it
55 Grp. with much-discussed amateurism rules
57 Spanish seasoning
59 Have
60 Paycheck abbr.

by Hal Moore

ACROSS

1 Popular Korean rice dish
9 Facial expression
15 Bach's "Christmas __"
16 Offline activity?
17 Towered over
18 Sugar in one's coffee, e.g.
19 Ancient land that included parts of modern Iraq and Turkey
20 Place to buy overpriced drinks
21 Keane who drew "The Family Circus"
22 Do some light cardio
23 Ink
24 Quarters feed into them
27 Kind of salami
29 His debut album was 1987's "Rhyme Pays"
30 Tears
35 "Ahhh!"
37 "Wow, wow, wow!"
38 It's made by coagulating soy milk
39 Mammal with four toes on the front feet and three on the back
40 Pleasantly flavorful
41 Financing figs.
45 C'est un article défini
46 Certain judge's ruling
47 Portmanteau for a dumpster-diving anti-consumerist eater
49 One might be offensive
53 Just peachy
54 Deliberately damage
55 Possible cause of fatigue
56 Mean figures
57 People people
58 Milky Way and others

DOWN

1 Bubble tea
2 Ticks off
3 Amp knob
4 Minute
5 Northern New Jersey county
6 Oven setting
7 Sophia Loren title role of 1953
8 He once wrote "I became insane, with long intervals of horrible sanity"
9 Fifth-century invaders
10 "That's my cue!"
11 Challenge in an alley
12 Dutch-speaking Caribbean island
13 Insinuated
14 Wisconsin governor Tony
20 The original Frankenstein wasn't one, despite popular belief
22 Competes in the Aquabike World Championship
24 Jedi foe
25 Second
26 Fast finish?
27 Shook one's defender, in sports lingo
28 "__ You Experienced" (Jimi Hendrix album)
30 It's all downhill from here
31 Passing financial concern?
32 Per
33 First name in U.N. diplomacy
34 Draw counterpart
36 Follower of F.D.R.
40 Madame, across the Pyrenees
41 It has a duck float in the Macy's Thanksgiving Day Parade
42 Inclined
43 Have a ball
44 Directive to talk
46 Some smears
48 A little too slick
49 It's hot stuff!
50 Noted gift givers
51 He won a posthumous Pulitzer Prize in 1958
52 Adjective-to-noun suffix
54 Slump

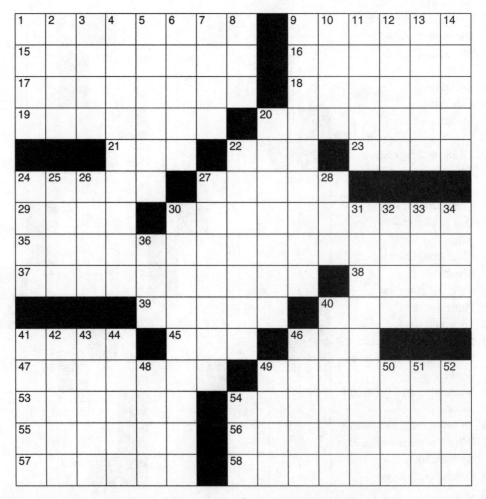

by Evans Clinchy

ACROSS

1 Two things in Broadway's "Dear Evan Hansen"
5 Goes off
10 Puts on
14 Wonderful review
15 ___ Stadium, longtime home of college football's Hula Bowl
16 Spree
17 Scratch-off success
19 Princess ___, main role in Pixar's "A Bug's Life"
20 "Didn't expect that to happen!"
21 Treats often topped with caviar
22 The point of writing?
23 Modern-day put-down popularized by a 2019 TikTok video
25 Flavor similar to fennel
26 Vintage eight-track purchases, maybe
27 Stress specialist?
28 "Britain's first family of harmony," per Brian Wilson
29 With 51-Across, package recipient's cry
30 Terrible review
31 Kind of exam with an "Auditing and Attestation" section
34 "Hey man, listen up . . ."
35 Speak loudly and harshly
36 What's at home on the range?
39 Pieces together?
40 Doesn't delete
41 Sires
42 Heavens
43 Kids might make a stand for this
45 Top-___
46 Something promoted on the front of a magazine
48 Challenge for a free soloist
49 Unit of firewood
50 Main ingredient in the Japanese dish tekkadon
51 See 29-Across
52 Visibly shows embarrassment
53 Opposite of ginormous

DOWN

1 Actress Nicole ___ Parker
2 "Let's stop. Is this really necessary?"
3 "Dallas" or "Atlanta"
4 Info for a group of performers
5 Industrial dept.
6 Resort locale east of Snowbird
7 Lead-in to a grave pronouncement
8 "Not so fast!"
9 Eastern honorific
10 Buffaloed
11 Complete a sentence, say
12 Not-so-common extension
13 One way to the top
18 What may come as a relief?
21 Basic framework
22 Champagne ___, one of Drake's nicknames
24 Funeral fixtures
26 Firsts in flight
28 Wade in the Baseball Hall of Fame
30 Colin Kaepernick was one, familiarly
31 Hollered
32 Crop circles, e.g.
33 Pro group?
34 Separate
35 Alternative to a Lamborghini
36 Furnish with feathers, as an arrow
37 Go out of business?
38 "Capeesh?"
39 Biden and Harris, once: Abbr.
41 Nowhere near engaged
44 English adjective that becomes a French noun when an accent is added
46 Print examiner, for short
47 "___, me!"

by David Distenfeld

ACROSS

1 Retreated
9 Drop
13 Artificial intelligence system modeled on the human brain
15 Something that gets passed around a lot
16 Golfers Ernie Els and Retief Goosen, for two
18 So much
19 All the king's men?
20 Simple and glib
21 School with the slogan "Ex scientia tridens," familiarly
22 Ancient symbols of life
23 Velcro alternative
25 Democratic leader?
26 Recipe direction
27 Strong, dark quaff
28 The British royal family has one called the Cambridge Lover's Knot
30 Some abbey attire
31 Up
32 "I wasn't going to say anything, but since you brought it up . . ."
36 Crew
37 Many a confession on a theater stage
38 Throws, informally
39 "I'm game"
40 Last __
44 __ Miguel Island, largest of the Azores
45 Currency units in Peru
47 Puccini opera . . . or the first five letters of the maestro who conducted its La Scala premiere
48 What Twix bars are sold in
50 Companion of the droid BB-8, in the "Star Wars" universe
51 Ear hair?
52 Calculus calculation
53 Gained some courage
55 What Shøp on "The Simpsons" is a parody of
56 Agronomic analyses
57 A cold wave can produce one
58 Yule log?

DOWN

1 Sequencing locale
2 Polish
3 Triumphant shout
4 "Black Boy" memoirist Richard
5 Gets the batter out, say
6 "__ poor Romeo!": Shak.
7 Wolf's home
8 Monitor
9 Besides Brunei, the only current sovereign sultanate
10 Creation date, file size and location, for an iPhone photo
11 "That doesn't bother me anymore"
12 Like an F.B.I. director's term
14 Fast fashion?
17 Office address abbr.
23 Ones making insulting offers
24 Part of many university names
27 Flamboyant prop
29 "Black" follower
30 "The gymnasium of the mind," per Blaise Pascal
32 Question that cannot be answered if its answer is "no"
33 Two-wheeler at a charging station
34 "__ away!"
35 Cardinal points?: Abbr.
36 Alternative to litmus paper
40 It's the truth!
41 Noted basilica town
42 Things picked up on a trail
43 Most likely to burn, maybe
46 Kind of chart, informally
47 Decorum
49 Underground band
51 One end of the Mohs scale
54 GameCube successor

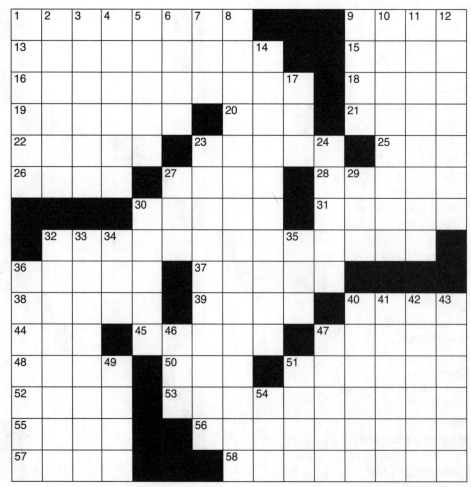

by Evan Kalish

HARD 167

ACROSS

1 Things you might snap on, nowadays
10 Something suddenly fashionable
12 Welcome sign of spring
14 Bases of support
15 Writer whose initials, when doubled, become another answer in this puzzle
17 Charge
18 Fly far, far away?
19 More familiar name for hydrated magnesium silicate
20 Sam who directed "A Simple Plan"
24 Ball __
25 Body opening?
26 Stuff
28 Subject of some MK-Ultra experiments
29 "Let's pray it never comes to that"
31 Sarcastic response to an attempt at intimidation
33 Java has a rare species of one
34 "What __?"
36 Members of filmdom's Breakfast Club
37 The oldest known one was found carved into a mammoth tusk (~25,000 B.C.)
40 Battery type
42 They're filled with dough
43 Aquaman portrayer
45 Side (with)
46 Listing in the Fortune 100
49 W.N.B.A. M.V.P. in 2015 and 2019
50 Jumper, e.g.

DOWN

1 Relating to sound
2 One cycle per second
3 1979 Donna Summer hit . . . or where it was heard
4 Model and body positivity activist Holliday
5 Pained expression
6 Help lift something, maybe?
7 Checkout choice
8 Some spreads
9 Lug
10 Bad way to be disguised
11 "Bad Lieutenant" star
12 Dulcé __, correspondent for "The Daily Show" beginning in 2017
13 Classic "I messed up" gift
14 Souvlaki go-with
16 Be behind bars?
21 Switch letters
22 Some news on Wall St.
23 Linguist Okrand who created Klingon
26 21 popes
27 Japanese beer
29 Lose it completely
30 One straying from the norm
31 "No way!," spelled out in a text
32 Refuse
33 Pass on
35 Places to get waxed
36 Reins in
37 Spongelike delicacy
38 Enough
39 Cannonball targets
41 Units equal to 10 micronewtons
43 Manner
44 Father of many children with Aphrodite
47 Ohio pro athlete, informally
48 Kick in

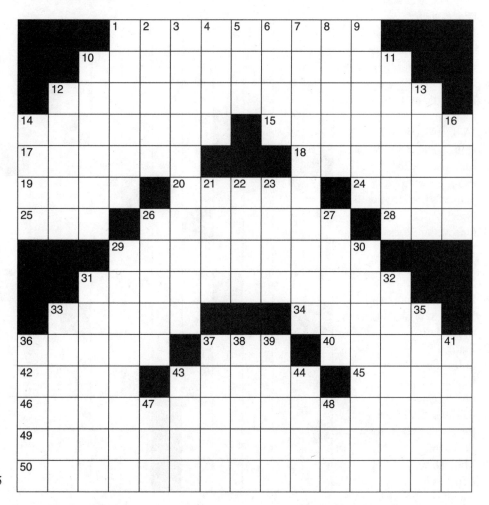

by Johan Vass

ACROSS

1 Colorful custardy confection
10 Sudden inspirations
15 Waltz onomatopoeia
16 Love
17 Classic diner orders
18 Apply, as ointment
19 Kitchen brand whose name is an ambigram
20 Pit-___
21 More might come before it
22 Its employees might get under your skin
24 Thing with rings
25 Legal action
28 Some Disney-inspired Halloween costumes
30 "___ me!" (request to a fridge-goer)
31 Like blue and green ski trails, vis-à-vis black diamonds
33 Pep
36 Looks the other way
39 Modern ___
40 "A ___ place is in the House, and in the Senate" (bumper sticker)
41 Actress Kendrick
42 Sharon's predecessor as Israeli P.M.
43 One of the Blues Brothers
45 One of the Coen brothers
48 Relative by marriage
50 Where to do as others do, it's said
52 Stain
53 Sprinkling
56 Canon competitor
57 Street featured in Fellini's "La Dolce Vita" (that's also 50-Across)
59 Still sticky
60 Make thin
61 Crushes it
62 Couple in the back of a car

DOWN

1 Snap
2 Component of three of the five French "mother sauces"
3 "That's . . . never gonna happen"
4 "Double" or "triple" drink
5 Actress Taylor of TV's "Bones"
6 Agatha Christie novel named after Death's mount in Revelation
7 Make ___ for
8 Danger for desert hikers
9 Ending with four or six, but not five
10 Teri of "Mr. Mom"
11 Does laundry or pays bills, in modern lingo
12 Clearheaded
13 Novel content
14 Tell
21 Couldn't let go of
22 Group portrayed in "Slacker" and "Reality Bites," familiarly
23 Straighten
25 Proficient
26 ___ review
27 One quadrillion: Prefix
29 Trio of horrors?
32 Target
33 Rosso o bianco
34 Driver's license fig.
35 Ren Faire concession
37 United competitor, once
38 "Heavens!"
42 Squarish
44 Not yet manifest
45 Spurns
46 Longtime "Inside the N.B.A." commentator
47 Writer Jong
49 South America's Río de la ___
51 Eponym of the World Series M.V.P. award
53 "Have no ___ of perfection—you'll never reach it": Dalí
54 Suffix with towel
55 Melancholiac's list
57 Dictionary abbr.
58 Rapa ___ (Easter Island)

by Meghan Morris

ACROSS

1 First person?
7 Backups
13 First name in daytime talk
14 Red Guard's attire
15 Like "To be or not to be"
16 Baking aisle mascot
17 Smart device feature
19 Ice Breakers alternative
20 Aftermath
21 Engagement calendar info: Abbr.
25 "That's *so* not the case!"
26 Fodor's listing
27 Assembly at a camporee, perhaps
28 Anti-trafficking org.
29 Comic strip with the 1998 collection "I Am Woman, Hear Me Snore"
30 Skylar of the "Pitch Perfect" films
31 Start of many a Google search
32 Line just before a comma
34 "Anything to ___?"
35 Brand with an iComfort line
37 Leporine creatures
38 Bags one might have when tired?
39 Tanks and such
40 Botched
41 "Got it"
42 Intersections requiring a turn
43 Singing duet?
44 Bartolomé de las ___, social reformer during Spain's colonial era
45 Coin featuring Lady Liberty and a bald eagle
48 Part of a forecast without clouds
51 Colonnade sight
53 Pirates, in old slang
54 Rumpled, say
55 "Yeah, sure"
56 Like some fruits and tennis players

DOWN

1 Setting of the Robert Graves memoir "Good-bye to All That," in brief
2 Mopey teen's lament
3 "Can't eat another bite"
4 "I don't want to hear any excuses!"
5 Some major productions
6 Oil-___
7 Press "K" while on YouTube
8 Jordan is found on one, notably
9 Yoga retreat locales
10 Central point
11 Lead-in to diversity
12 Home for a farrow
14 Pastry that gets pulled apart
16 Where scenes on Tatooine were filmed for "Star Wars"
18 They're full of twists and turns
19 Feverishly tries to open
22 Cookout dish
23 Big outdoor June event
24 Length of a president's veto window
26 Adolphe who invented a musical instrument
27 Costco rival, familiarly
29 Titan
33 Still in the box, say
36 Beyond what's needed
41 Phone line?
43 Goes on
44 Singer with the 1962 album "Sentimentally Yours"
46 Aces have low ones, for short
47 Major production
48 "___: Vegas"
49 One of a piano trio
50 ___ oxygénée (hydrogen peroxide: Fr.)
52 Like diamonds

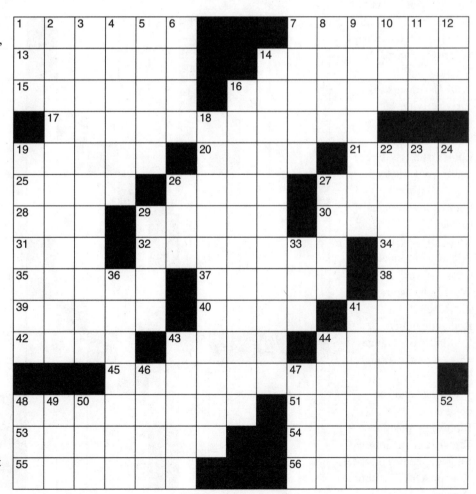

by Peter Wentz

ACROSS

1 Something you may want to clear up
5 Othello, for one
9 Loses sheen, perhaps
14 One of the Aesir
15 Uncovered
16 ID seen at the post office
17 Nobel winner Morrison
18 Dressing room encouragement
20 "Stop trying to help!"
22 A counting job?
23 Own up (to)
24 Purpose
25 Eva Perón was one: Abbr.
26 You can bet on it!
28 Simple matter of probability
33 Numbers not meant to be shared
34 Speedy sci-fi technology
35 Secretly unionize?
36 Drop the ball
37 With 11-Down, kids' party activity
38 "Peter Pan" princess
40 Lashes makeup
41 Look that might freeze you in your tracks
42 Martini option
43 Subj. of international treaties
44 Bon ___ (high society: Fr.)
45 Friendly introduction?
47 Cause of weakness
51 What Babe aspires to be in "Babe"
53 Romantic bunch
55 ___ Mountains, range crossed on the Trans-Siberian railway
56 What "he" and "do" don't do
57 Biblical preposition
58 Terpsichore or Calliope
59 Strategic bodies of water
60 "Out of Africa" author Dinesen
61 Little drones

DOWN

1 Story that goes over your head?
2 One constantly craving kisses?
3 "It was not my intention to make anyone upset," often
4 CNN's Burnett
5 Scavenger hunt cry
6 Little sucker
7 Substance
8 Towering figure in "The Two Towers"
9 "Wake up, sleepyhead!"
10 Kake ___ (Japanese dish)
11 See 37-Across
12 Biblical pronoun
13 ___ vide (culinary technique)
19 Substitute for legal tender
21 Ports, e.g.
25 Pathetic
27 Metaphorical knowledge
28 Eric who wrote "The Very Hungry Caterpillar"
29 Accomplice in "Romeo and Juliet"
30 Broadway show where everyone knows the ending?
31 Country named for a now-banned trade
32 They can be felt
33 Org. for Carl Sagan
34 "That's odd . . ."
39 Rapper/producer who won the 2018 Pulitzer for Music
42 Gets by
44 Letter in the Greek spelling of Athens
46 Looks like a jerk
47 Driver in "House of Gucci"
48 Canceled
49 Book after II Chronicles
50 Runners' event
51 Figs. assigned randomly since 2011
52 Animal also known as a catamount
54 Air France confirmation

by Robyn Weintraub

ACROSS

1 Number pattern named after a 17th-century French mathematician
16 Teddies and such
17 Exhausted beyond belief
18 Certain acct. info
19 Diatribes
20 Longtime distributor of James Bond movies
21 Immersed in
23 Business __
24 Lot
25 Maipo Valley exports
27 Pings, maybe
28 __ Gervasi, director of 2012's "Hitchcock"
29 Union IDs, for a performer
31 Basic analysis?
32 Market debuts, in brief
33 Mini-__ (small retailer)
34 One way to manage expectations
37 Eschew Uber, say
41 More steadfast
42 "For once maybe someone will call me '__,' without adding, 'You're making a scene'": Homer Simpson
43 __ Player, first Black woman to become president of a four-year college
44 Taking off
45 Setting for "La Bohème"
47 Calm
48 Hominid
49 Some stylish suits
51 Measure of volume
52 Do some modeling
55 "Life is short. __" (Jacques Torres quip)
56 Captain's phrase

DOWN

1 Two-person log cutters
2 Loss of smell
3 Biblical punishment
4 Loc. __
5 Marcello, Rodolfo, Colline and Schaunard, dans "La Bohème"
6 Turpentine-yielding conifer
7 Certain anti-inflammatory medicines
8 Hymns of thanksgiving
9 Yelp reviewers, say
10 Shuffles and such
11 Rental units: Abbr.
12 "Don't reckon so"
13 Reaction to a really bad pun
14 Stretches
15 Lean protein
22 Tenths, in statistics
24 Increased likelihood of extreme scenarios, in statistics
26 Taste
28 Mammal in the Soricidae family
30 Spreadsheet specification
31 Golf Hall-of-Famer Se Ri __
33 Only M.L.B. team never to have played in a World Series
34 National geographic books?
35 "Again . . ."
36 Small knapsack
37 Diatribes
38 Certain sports instructor
39 Whatever's left
40 Works that may require leaps of imagination?
42 Savory Indian pastry
45 Uninspired, as writing
46 Like the most recent Pope Paul among all popes named Paul
49 Seasoned
50 Jewelry store?
53 Canine protection org.?
54 Russian fighter jet

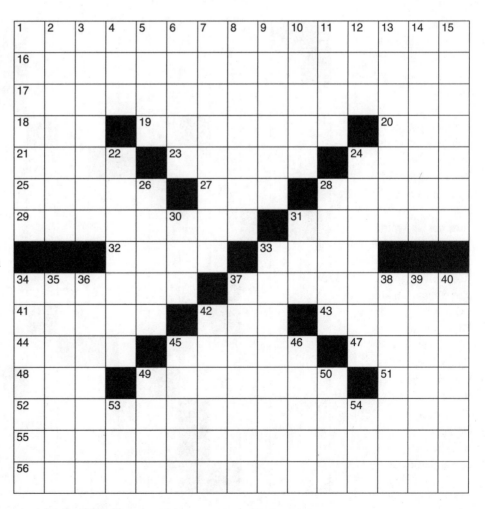

by Freddie Cheng

ACROSS

1 One playing second fiddle, perhaps
9 St. Louis clock setting, briefly
12 Move a cursor across
13 Burn
14 Where to try out some gunpowder?
15 Italian verse form
16 "Cars 2" competitor ___ Bonn
17 ___ Academy, organization for self-paced education online
18 Kicked butt
19 They can be friendly while patronizing
21 Not allowed to go back, say
23 Author of "What I Know for Sure," familiarly
24 Place of rest away from everything
26 ___ Jones
27 What purple prose and technical jargon have in common
29 Donations for life?
30 Modern source of juice
34 Summer sip suffix
35 Build-your-own IHOP order
36 "Coolio!"
37 Responds to an alarm, in a way
38 They outrank viscounts
42 Dandy accessories
44 Stir-fry recipe step
45 "Cool it!"
46 Abbr. near zero
49 Doing
50 Assents asea
51 Sith superpower
53 Stronghold
54 "This better not get out"
55 When repeated, an expression of disapproval
56 Playing God?

DOWN

1 Headwear for many a barbershop quartet singer
2 Google Docs feature
3 Org. whose initials are found in "unsafe," ironically
4 Hotels have ones in front
5 One who's light-headed?
6 Footwear brand
7 Osaka and others
8 Bit of work
9 Hybrid fair fare
10 2013 Macklemore/Ryan Lewis hit with the lyric "And I can't change, even if I tried"
11 Conflict that may involve sanctions
12 Got together
13 Heart
14 DoorDash designation
18 Shifted in a theater, say
20 Once-ler's opponent in a Dr. Seuss book
22 When repeated, call to someone going to bed
24 Go gaga for
25 Choice in a cabin
28 "Please ___" (printed request)
30 World of ___
31 It's a challenge
32 "Warning!"
33 Study
39 Skill event that might follow barrel racing
40 Bath water unit
41 Blackthorn
43 Like the universe
44 Fail to be
47 Accumulation
48 "___ Enchanted" (2004 romantic comedy)
51 . . . : Abbr.
52 Miroir image?

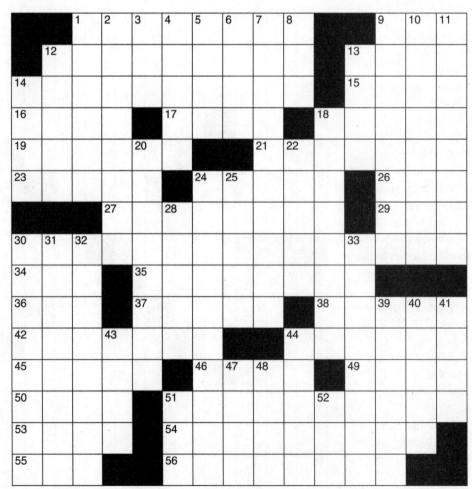

by Matthew Stock and Sid Sivakumar

ACROSS

1 Squarely
9 Not straight up
15 Old World bird with distinctive ear tufts
16 Baby's barnyard bovine
17 Sympathetic response to dissent
18 A-to-Z
19 Crashing an online meeting
21 One might be loaded
22 Creatures whose newborns have striped bodies
23 Prattles
24 Watch here!
26 All __
27 Boxy delivery vehicles of old
29 London's __ Square
31 Make slicker, maybe
32 Wined and dined, say
35 Spiritual object
37 Wiped out
39 W.W. I, W.W. II, etc.
41 What rotates throughout the office?
46 Gold units: Abbr.
48 Any of the Seven Dwarfs
49 Something you might raise a flap about
50 __ tide
51 Kind of drive
52 Locale 60 miles south of the California/Oregon border
55 Creator of the first pumped-up athletic shoe
57 Catchphrase of Winnie-the-Pooh
58 Popular typeface similar to Bauhaus
59 "To be honest with you . . ."
60 Out of it
61 Date format on digital forms

DOWN

1 Gets stuck, as an engine
2 Youngest-ever QB to be named Super Bowl M.V.P. (2020)
3 Grow too old for
4 Simoleons
5 Spot for a bus stop, in Bristol
6 Get into a pose, perhaps
7 What God is, per an Ariana Grande hit
8 Cold weather layer
9 Eye-opening declaration?
10 One jotting down a few notes?
11 Area for development
12 Like apples and oranges
13 Safe
14 Some brief updates
20 Locale for a castaway
25 Stick around school
27 2010s fansite craze whose members joined Hogwarts houses
28 Start of many a criticism
30 "Ho" preceder
33 Main ingredient in hitsumabushi
34 Mirabile __ (wonderful to say: Lat.)
36 Takes advantage of a situation, so to speak
38 How things typically are
40 Majestic
41 Blue-nosed sorts?
42 Get smart
43 Like many apps with faulty features
44 Country song
45 "Things aren't looking so great"
47 Dalmatian mascot of the National Fire Protection Association
50 Well-suited?
53 Response akin to "So what?"
54 Word after foot or before hands
56 2021 Super Bowl champ

by Sam Ezersky

ACROSS

1 Boost
6 Many a fund-raising event
10 New York, Chicago and Los Angeles, in brief
14 Be a big-time troublemaker
16 Star quality
17 Swarmed by mosquitoes, say
18 "Hello, mate!"
19 Tan writing books
20 Kid in expensive shoes?
21 Duck, duck, goose, e.g.
22 Routine parts
23 Pair
25 Heard the confession of and absolved, old-style
28 Pastry appropriate for a camping trip?
31 Word with surplus or secret
32 One with lots of pull?
33 Like some designs on Etsy
34 One-star, say
35 "Dido's Lament," for one
36 Has a 4.0 average
38 Big name in cosmetics
39 Food brand whose last letter is its company's stock symbol
40 Bulb units
41 Having long, thin limbs
42 Puts one over on
43 Extremely excited, in modern lingo
45 Happening
47 __ Twist (best-selling children's book character)
50 Display of choppers
51 What an old car might be sold for
53 "All right, cool"
54 Song title following the lyric "Scuzza me, but you see, back in old Napoli . . ."
55 "M*A*S*H" co-star
56 Legendary print maker
57 "Jeez!"

DOWN

1 Field
2 Respectful term of address
3 __ party
4 Wield
5 Sitting with one's hand under one's chin, perhaps
6 Outbursts of laughter
7 Keen
8 Hippie accessories
9 Person of extraordinary skill
10 Amulets
11 "Sister Outsider" essayist/poet
12 One being asked for donations, often
13 Makes known
15 It's high in France
21 Speak sharply
22 Antismuggling device
24 R-rated, perhaps
25 Forest males
26 Corp. trainer
27 Means of domestic pest control
28 Cold and miserable
29 Video game franchise based on a sci-fi film franchise
30 Helps finish a nursing program?
32 Grouse
34 It's a waste
37 The Beatles' "__ She Sweet"
38 Comics-based film character played by Rosemary Harris, Sally Field and Marisa Tomei
40 Informs at a later stage, with "in"
42 Relative of a raccoon
43 "Let's weekend!"
44 __ Minor
46 Campus group
47 Over
48 Counterpart of truth
49 Tavern menu heading
51 Dump
52 Onetime member of the record industry's Big Four

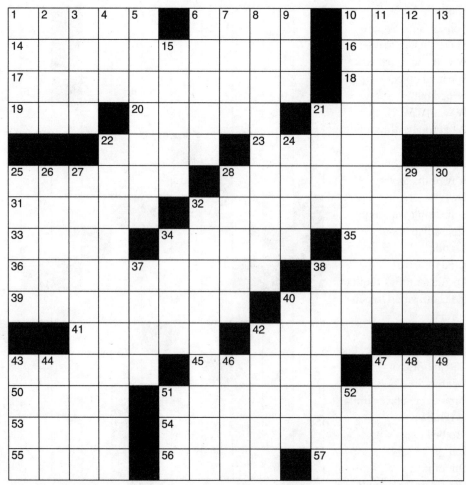

by Kyle Dolan

ACROSS

1 Underlying
6 Foggy
12 Thanksgiving and Pride both have one
13 Person who lives on discarded food
15 Dark-magic device with which to achieve immortality, in Harry Potter
16 "Desperate Housewives" co-star
18 Boo-boo
19 Well done, in Italy
20 Makeup of some canopies
21 Coarse flour
22 Gentle giant on "Game of Thrones"
23 Heartless
24 Over and done with
25 Actress Phillipa of Broadway's "Hamilton"
26 Lacto-___ vegetarian
27 Bordeaux et Bourgogne, par exemple
28 Icy drink
32 Cognitive contortions
35 Words read with feeling
36 Relieve
37 Abraham Lincoln, for one: Abbr.
38 Enero o febrero, por ejemplo
39 Speed of sound
40 Smallish branch
41 Scissors Palace, Anita Haircut or Do or Dye (all real places!)
44 Hose problem
45 Man of the cloth
46 Familiar soap opera device
48 Scorches
49 Creates

50 An unrivaled champion, in slang
51 [More details below]
52 Comical character in "A Midsummer Night's Dream"
53 Brought (in)
54 Secretly watch

DOWN

1 Home to the largest football stadium in Europe
2 Like eyebrows
3 Mumbai wraps
4 Together, musically
5 Justinian law
6 Solvent
7 Like some "Monty Python" humor

8 Depression
9 Danish tourist attraction with multiple play areas
10 Result of a compliment, typically
11 Ventured
12 Kind of coffee made with a flask and a filter
14 Young hombre
15 Hair-straightening tool
17 Atmospheric prefix
19 Like a breakup gone bad
21 Animal skin ailment
24 Tablets
25 / or \
27 One with a big heart?
28 Chips, e.g.
29 Gorilla with a job to do
30 Kind of sandwich

31 Exercise with Zener cards
33 Chalamet of "Dune"
34 Fated
39 Shot an airball, say
40 Serenaded
41 Screen rating, in brief?
42 Regrettably
43 Schlump
44 Kunta ___ ("Roots" role)
45 One of the seven gifts of the Holy Spirit, in Catholicism
47 Warm covering
48 Factory
50 Venue for many TV reruns

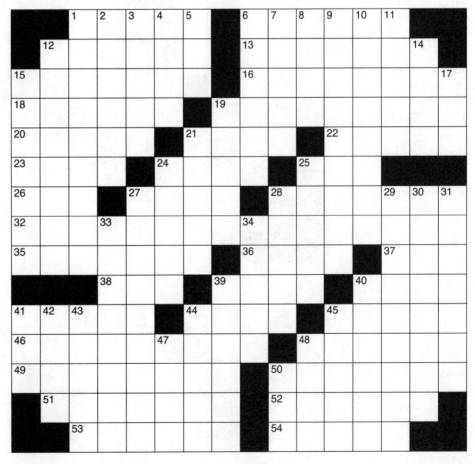

by Daniel Okulitch

ACROSS

1 Solicit, in slang
6 About
10 Chinese dynasty in which the terra-cotta army was built
13 Not appropriate
14 __ shark
15 Year, in Brazil
16 "North and South" writer John
17 Source of a big scoop
18 Key next to Q
19 Egyptian sun deity
20 Begotten
21 Word before doble or Robles
22 Actor who received an Emmy nomination for playing Dr. Anthony Fauci on "S.N.L."
24 Like bogeymen
26 Egg container
27 "Let's see here . . ."
28 "Whew, that's hot!"
29 Occasion for kids to stay up late
32 Extreme athletes with parachutes
34 Space force?
36 Less clear
39 Were present?
40 Poppycock
42 Grow on trees, so to speak
43 Cheesy sandwiches for snackers
45 Structure with many layers?
46 Sentences
48 Drink with a polar bear mascot
49 Cartesian conclusion
50 Member of G. W. Bush's cabinet, familiarly
51 Insinuated
52 Had

53 Kid's cut, perhaps
54 Express lane tally
55 Some trip on it
56 Not taken by
57 __ Islands (autonomous part of Denmark)

DOWN

1 Some head coverings
2 Caught
3 Alternative to "walk" or "go by bus"
4 Flip
5 Spread makeup: Abbr.
6 Moving images, apparently
7 Badgered at length
8 Like many a lemon, eventually
9 Stadium cry
10 Like Al Jazeera
11 "Be right there!"
12 Chopped liver, so to speak
17 Student of the classics, say
20 Regained one's composure
21 Some of the Dead Sea Scrolls
23 Introduce gradually
25 Actor Emilio
28 Director of the "Evil Dead" franchise
30 Add some flair to

31 Snub-nosed dog
33 Less forgiving
35 Words before un beso
36 It may involve a mask
37 Some subs
38 Met with someone online, maybe
41 Literally, "fly," in Setswana
43 Event with clowns
44 Endemic flora and fauna
47 "Will do!"
50 Crib sound
51 Animated snippet

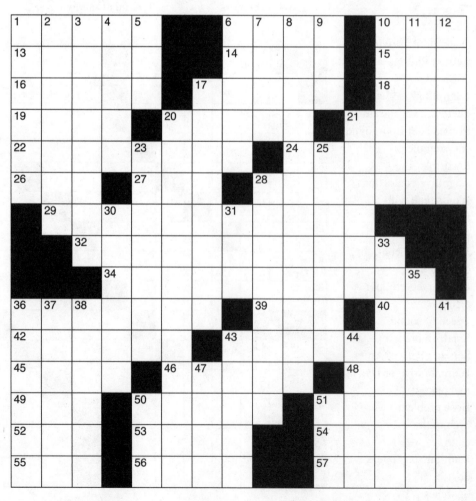

by Jem Burch

ACROSS

1 Showed derision, in a way
5 Food chain inits.
8 Greeting that means "presence of breath"
13 Cantata number
14 Winners' circles?
17 Vuvuzela, for one
18 What a cheater might throw
19 Catchy communication, for short?
20 Ticks off
21 Bolted
22 Parking around back
24 Shucks
26 Growth from stagnation
27 Something for nothing
30 Something that not a single person can go in?
33 Outburst before a maniacal laugh
34 One known for making House calls
35 "A likely story"
36 Lead-in to boost
40 Direction at sea
41 Compounds containing molecular variants
43 Bygone Japanese coin
44 Parody
47 Style of music whose name is derived from scat
48 "We've all been there"
51 Access point
52 Court feat of 2003 and 2015
53 New York city
54 Lose __
55 Get on
56 Site for shopping small

DOWN

1 Habitat for the addax antelope, which can go a year without drinking
2 Power forward
3 It's subject to inflation in the auto industry
4 Shoe hue
5 Qaanaaq dwelling
6 Leave home
7 Actor Ruck of HBO's "Succession"
8 Upper Midwest town with the world's tallest concrete gnome
9 Opened
10 Funny, but not "ha-ha" funny
11 Area of recession
12 Ciudad official
15 Subj. of Rachel Carson's "Silent Spring"
16 Pick up
20 Opposite of scruffy
23 Gambling venues with a portmanteau name
24 Certain landing pad
25 Element of heavy metal
27 __ artist (film professional)
28 "That's how we __"
29 Nonhuman host of a talk show on HBO Max
31 Kid-lit authors Margret and H. A.
32 Storybook bear
33 Chichén Itzá's carvings, e.g.
34 They're just getting started
35 They may be worn with cholis
37 Second incarnation
38 Curlers' equipment
39 Cousin of a kite
41 Aid in getting home
42 "So I was wrong, big deal!"
44 Underground line
45 Local borders?
46 "The Lion King" role
49 Name-dropping word
50 Bio material
51 The kid in 2010's "The Karate Kid"

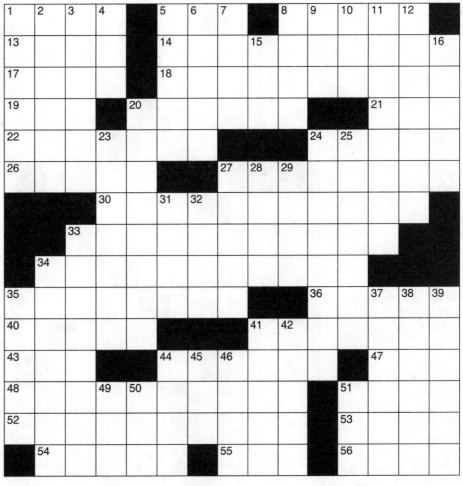

by Andrew Ries and Caitlin Reid

ACROSS

1 Letters between two names
4 Deliberately gives bad information
10 Like the start of an Ironman race
14 Ben & Jerry's sundae with an estimated 14,000 calories
16 "Yeah . . . never gonna happen"
17 Bowie song that begins with the lyric "It's a God-awful small affair to the girl with the mousy hair"
18 Nonprofit with the tagline "No More Victims"
19 Quarters
20 Company at the heart of an early 2000s scandal
22 Driving stabilizer
23 Issue with image quality, informally?
25 Essence of the Hippocratic oath
27 Naval agreement?
29 Traces
30 Fiscal arm of the executive branch, in brief
33 Henchman
34 Easy __
36 Uses one's brain
38 Nickname of 6' 9" N.F.L. great Ed Jones
39 Food brand since 1922 with a Chinese character in its logo
40 "Horse, Pipe and Red Flower" painter (1920)
41 Relative of Inc.
42 Winter Olympics equipment
43 Most smelly
45 Stop working for good?
47 Squares, e.g.
51 Acapulco gold
52 "Jeepers!"
54 Corroded
55 Stain
57 1987 sci-fi comedy spoof
59 Ireland's best-selling solo artist

60 Potentially destructive marine growth
61 Ones in charge: Abbr.
62 Apt
63 San Francisco's __ Valley

DOWN

1 Where a high school yearbook club may meet, informally
2 Actress Knightley
3 Spoke spaniel?
4 Casual, casually
5 Pensione relative
6 Lemony Snicket antagonist named after a Salinger orphan
7 Placeholder
8 Little rascal
9 Director Welles
10 Sigma, in math
11 "I can't afford NOT to buy it!"
12 Not stress so much?
13 Online hookup
15 Comic partner of Stiller
21 Altogether pretty good
24 Indiana's state flower
26 Comedian Kevin
28 A call for help
30 The Magic, on scoreboards
31 Kind of cup
32 "America's Missing: Broadcast Emergency Response" vis-à-vis Amber Alert, e.g.
34 Less gracious when losing, say

35 Pampering, in brief
37 Hebrew letter on a dreidel
38 That's the point!
40 Figure that determines an air passenger's status
43 __ effect
44 Wreck
45 Clan symbol
46 H-1B and B-1, for two
48 Head, in slang
49 "The Bare Necessities" bear
50 Part of a classic breakup line
53 Bamboozle
56 Popeye's anchor, e.g., for short
58 Not-so-common studio apartment shape

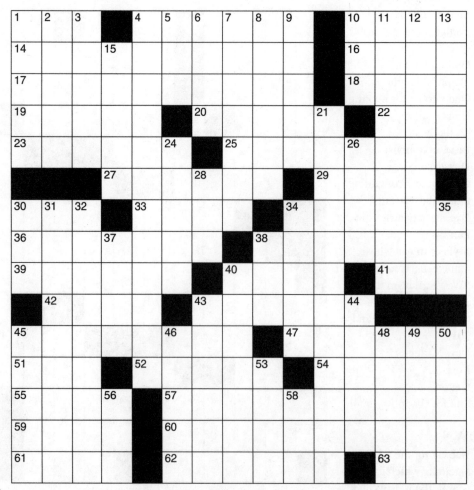

by Joseph Greenbaum

ACROSS

1 Birdie of Broadway's "Bye Bye Birdie"
7 Maize patties
13 Throw on the floor
15 Poet who wrote "Love is so short, forgetting is so long"
16 Korean rice dish often served in a hot stone bowl
18 Silent partner?
19 Replete (with)
20 Like the villainous Max Shreck, at the end of "Batman Returns"
22 Like typical projects in Popular Mechanics magazine, in brief
23 Palindromic periodical title
24 Crime show extras, for short
25 Memory measure
26 Word with bass or bed
27 Humble
28 ___ noires (bugbears)
29 Certain pie filling
31 Archetypal bossypants
32 Result of selling out
33 Part of a quote
34 Tears
35 It's a racket
38 Horne of music
39 Disbands
40 Live on water, say
41 Part of a play group?
42 Sayings attributed to Jesus
43 "I can row a boat. ___?" (groaner joke)
44 Dome
46 Sugar substitute?
48 Russian writer and dissident Limonov
49 There's no doubt about it
50 Gets tight
51 "Ruff ___ Anthem," 1998 hit single for DMX

DOWN

1 Old-time messages
2 Colorful bird in the blackbird family
3 Crab ___
4 Subject of an end-of-year office memo, maybe
5 Horde
6 Talk over?
7 Home to the highest active volcano in the world
8 Kind of grass
9 Period
10 Sighting in a classic Looney Tunes cartoon
11 Appointed by the court
12 Accept a proposal
14 Marijuana, some say
17 The right one can produce a smile
21 Bronze producers
24 ___ Vecchio
25 Eponym of a lifetime achievement award in fashion since 1984
27 Holiday pancake
28 Majors, say
29 Kufrin of "The Bachelor" and "The Bachelorette"
30 Disgusting buildups
31 One way to put on a coat
32 Like early uncensored Hollywood films
33 Hollywood precursor?
35 River that flows through or beside 10 countries
36 Compound with a chemical "twin"
37 Nonproliferation treaty subjects, in brief
39 Gets tight (with)
40 Staged
42 Bygone Vatican money
43 Booker of the Senate
45 Oomph
47 "___ Mutual Friend" (Dickens's last completed novel)

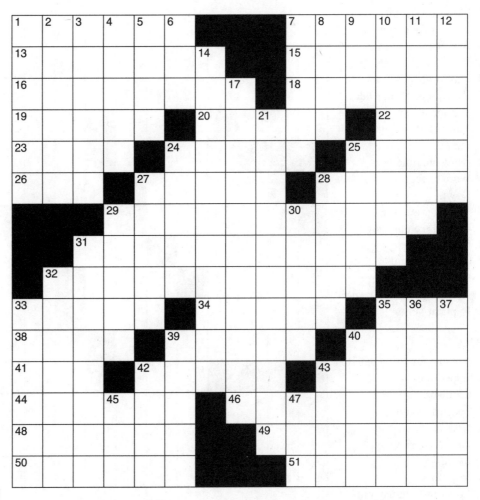

by Kameron Austin Collins

ACROSS

1 Words to a skeptic
16 What friendly opponents may do
17 Subject of the so-called "surgeon's photograph" of 1934
18 Squad leader?
19 Cinemax competitor
20 Judicial ratings grp.
21 Terra's Greek counterpart
22 British territory in the Atlantic
27 Pioneering automaker
28 Handmade signs?
29 "En __!"
30 Language spoken along the Mekong
31 Account
32 Collectible print, in brief
33 Morale booster
34 Certain list recipient
35 Bailiwick
36 Big __
37 Philosopher Diderot
38 High point of the Old Testament, for short
40 Blues Hall-of-Famer James
41 [How horrible!]
42 Word of regret
43 Down
44 Mo. for watching the Perseid meteor shower
45 Fade away
48 Gives an earful
54 Rhetorical question lamenting a lack of respect
55 Implicatively

DOWN

1 Notable founding of 1701
2 Impediments to teamwork
3 Tolkien creatures
4 "Yuck!"
5 Gradually slowing, in music
6 Inventory
7 Lover of Italian opera
8 Field stats

9 Food named for a world capital (but pronounced differently)
10 1962 pop hit with a rhyming title
11 Some unauthorized drawings
12 Justice Dept. bigwigs
13 N.Y.C.'s first subway line
14 Buttonless garment
15 Singer with a 2018 Grammy for Best R&B Album
21 __ Richter, contemporary artist whose painting "Abstraktes Bild (599)" sold at auction for a record-setting $46.3 million dollars

23 The X-Men, for example
24 Muse for Galileo
25 Muscles strengthened by push-ups, informally
26 Offshore
27 Flat-bottomed riverboat
28 Flash
29 Circumference
32 Hasty getaways
33 Become harder to bear
34 Give oneself something to aim for
36 "Just try to be calm . . ."
37 Reynolds's co-star in 1981's "The Cannonball Run"
39 Carol opener

42 Exclamation of exasperation
45 Exclamation of disappointment
46 Big name in frozen confections
47 Some terminal info, for short
48 Piece of BBQ
49 Amarillo-to-Dallas dir.
50 Creature without ears that uses vibrations to "hear"
51 Company that introduced Saran Wrap
52 Tolkien creature
53 Onetime cable giant acquired by AT&T in 1999

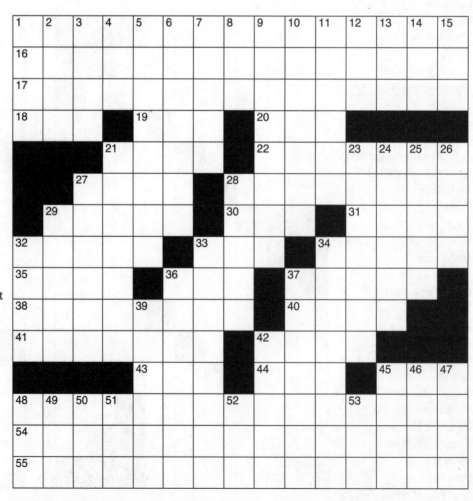

by Trenton Charlson

ACROSS

1 Fast food order
6 Balderdash
14 Making of an impression?
15 1962 #1 hit for the Crystals featuring a biker on the record sleeve
17 Rock genre
18 Bit of census data
19 Slips
20 ___ hulu manu (feathery adornment)
21 Actor James of "The Blacklist"
22 People with a language of the same name
23 Steamed source of stimulation
25 Famille member
26 Voting rights activist who founded Fair Fight Action
30 Russian dumplings
31 Facility
32 Some undergrad degs.
35 Where an athlete might dunk
37 Miser
39 Org. tracking metadata
40 A sculpture of a three-legged one is considered lucky in feng shui
42 ___ James, the so-called "King of the Slide Guitar"
43 "You have to look at the bigger picture"
45 Group whose logo is a mirror ambigram
48 N.B.A. great Baylor
49 Goddess: Lat.
50 Cavort
53 Central square, perhaps
54 Though commonly known as vegetables, botanically they are fruit
55 Wicca symbol
57 Two-time Grammy winner Bryson
58 Condiment made with peanuts
59 Conversation starter
60 Dodge S.U.V.s
61 Pal of Kent and Lane

DOWN

1 Figure skating move based on the arabesque in ballet
2 Theatrically exaggerated behavior
3 Population calculation scope
4 Cuup products
5 Olive ___
6 Comic relief role in "Tarzan"
7 1970 music documentary that won an Oscar for Best Original Score
8 Hard wood
9 Goes for the gold?
10 What comes before the fall?
11 Features of many season premieres
12 Stomach
13 "Great" man
16 Zither relative
20 Flatter effusively
23 Italian for "tied together"
24 Modern and Classical periods
27 Parent of a cygnet
28 Antithesis of a hedonist
29 Noted spelling expert
32 Focus of literary agents
33 Obliging
34 "Later!"
36 Not fancy in the least
38 Ashram sounds
41 Fast-food chain with the slogan "UnFreshing Believable"
43 Three-beat gait
44 Annual event with Ski Slopestyle and Skateboard Vert
45 Starters, for short
46 It's found at the bottom of the food pyramid
47 Language family of Swahili or Zulu
51 ___ Milà, landmark building in Barcelona
52 2011 Pulitzer winner Jennifer
54 Spa offering
56 Word after throw or scatter
57 Aromatic noodle soup

by Mary Lou Guizzo

ACROSS

1 Offers a fist, in a way
5 Speak like Clint Eastwood
9 Irritated
14 Fort ___ (Peace Bridge terminus)
15 Middle range
16 Can't get enough of
17 Mental goof
19 Sophia of "Two Women"
20 Deep-fried Japanese pork cutlet
21 They come in waffle and sugar varieties
22 Faint theatrically
23 General on a menu
25 A.T.M. maker
27 ___Kosh B'gosh
30 Recruits
33 Hamilton and Burr, for two
36 Pool class
37 Steamy period pieces
38 Pans
39 Common way to communicate at Gallaudet University, in brief
40 Equinox mo.
41 Latest gossip, in modern lingo
43 Restraint
48 Not *quite* a failure
51 It's bald on its face
54 Green features
55 It's hardly Châteauneuf-du-Pape
56 Dana Elaine ___, a.k.a. Queen Latifah
57 Torpid
58 Cared for, as some injuries
59 Belgian Expressionist James
60 What might have ___
61 "Any ___?"

DOWN

1 Credit card charges, essentially
2 Keyboard symbol
3 Soft
4 Japanese watch brand
5 Host
6 Lead-in to some regrets
7 Walk around like you own the place
8 Dope
9 Beyoncé song with the line "I got my angel now"
10 Thick noodle
11 Field that involves blood, sweat and tears?
12 Some works by Goya
13 Deep desire
18 Small-scale study, for short
21 Some pinball machines, e.g.
24 Tibetan ethnic group
26 I.C.U. figures
28 Most of the alphabet, in Washington, D.C.
29 Something drawn by an invisible horse outside Disney's Haunted Mansion
31 Was revolting?
32 Mideast ruler
33 Corrupting sorts
34 "Affirmative"
35 Popular gear retailer
36 Nagged and nagged and nagged
37 First K-pop group to perform at the Grammys
42 Terminal type
44 Buzz Aldrin's given name
45 Children's character who asks herself "And what is the use of a book without pictures or conversations?"
46 Tendon
47 Obeys
49 One side of a classic late-night feud
50 Red states, once, in brief
52 Toll unit, at times
53 Sharp
54 It might turn up a plot
55 Diner's neckwear

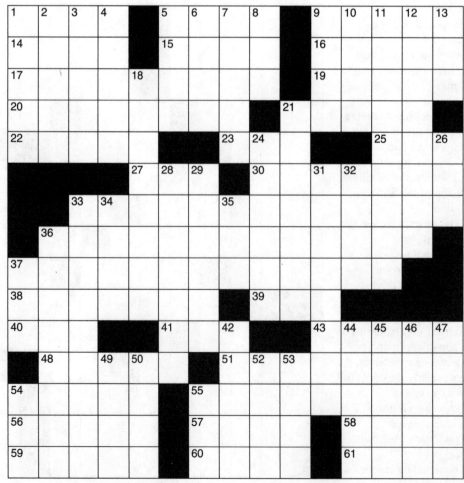

by Aimee Lucido

ACROSS

1 "Botheration!"
7 Makes a point
13 That's a wrap
15 Web browser with a majority market share
16 Let drop, say
18 Like twill and faille
19 Rap's Lil __ Vert
20 "Told ya!"
22 Balconette or racerback
23 Be in limbo
25 First national fraternity to officially welcome transgender members (2014), informally
26 Close-knit group
27 Pined away?
29 Coffee store
30 Plugs away
31 Dog that smells a lot
34 Group of commuters?
35 Issue ultimatums, e.g.
36 Commissions
37 Diesel often found in a muscle car
38 Wait on
42 Beauty brand
43 Get across
45 Earth
46 Musical lead-in to "So Fine" or "So Shy"
47 "Hmm, let's think where this leads us"
49 Exercise
50 Roots
52 Callous to an extreme
54 Start of a snap count
55 Gorgon's lock
56 Uptight
57 Takes for a while, in a way

DOWN

1 Unceremonious
2 Band with the lyrics "When I was younger, I used to go and tip cows for fun, yeah / Actually, I didn't do that 'cause I didn't want the cow to be sad"
3 Ditch
4 Be with a group?
5 Language in which "thank you" is "khàawp khun"
6 Shows moodiness
7 Substitute for real money
8 I.O.U.
9 Earth, poetically
10 Bamboozle big-time
11 May birthstone
12 Common body types
14 Smarter than smart
17 They graduate quickly
21 Flipped
24 Michael E. __, pioneer in coronary bypass surgery
26 Transcript list
28 Lead-ins to some prank calls
30 They catch flies
32 Earth
33 Snookums
34 First foreign-language film to win Best Picture
35 Endurance test in gym
36 Cry on Christmas
39 Ways
40 Clear Eyes rival
41 Puts in a seat
43 Actress/screenwriter Taylor
44 Make a long-distance call?
47 One of two for a Valkyrie's horse
48 Bug
51 Mr. High-and-Mighty?
53 Many a beauty therapist's employer

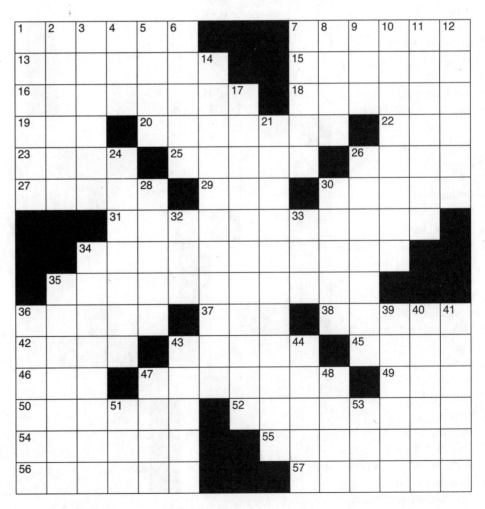

by Billy Bratton

ACROSS

1 Brightness measures
4 One sense
9 Home of Mount Aconcagua
14 Not agree in a dispute, say
15 Lashes
16 One leader of the Army of the Potomac
17 ___ school
18 Breezing through
19 Whomped but good
20 "Your mileage may vary"
23 Developed into
24 Win over
25 Counterpart to projections, in accounting
27 Alternative to a blind, in poker
28 Question of faux indignation
29 Homegrown
31 Quid pro quo
35 They often appear by thumbnails
37 Network connections
38 Quash
39 "Who ___?"
40 Proficient in
42 Carp variety
43 Took off on
45 Hawaiian, e.g.
47 Go around and around
50 Got in a lather
51 Comment to someone who talks too much
55 1980s sitcom title role for Jane Curtin
56 Pennsylvania Avenue V.I.P.
57 Pulled off
59 Put off
60 Dugout, e.g.
61 Qualifier in a text
62 Some military choppers
63 Step up, perhaps
64 Post-Manhattan Project org.

DOWN

1 Movement
2 One represented by a blue-and-white flag with four fleurs-de-lis
3 It's tempting
4 Actor Crothers
5 Chief inspiration for the Mannerist style of art
6 Kazan of film
7 Navel-gazer's discovery, maybe
8 Streaming impediments
9 Come (to)
10 Spot for a daily assembly?
11 Exile of 1302
12 Dropsy, clinically
13 No-yeast feast
21 Symbol for torque in mechanics
22 Certain something
23 Classic 1942 film based on a book subtitled "A Life in the Woods"
26 Wasn't overturned
27 Big name in cosmetics
30 Union pledge
32 Much-visited website run by a nonprofit foundation
33 It's usually in short supply for new parents
34 Practiced sedulously
36 Western wildflower named for its distinctive shape
41 Kind of leg
44 They get what's coming to them
46 Francis ___, "Love Story" composer
47 Strip that's been mowed
48 Rice dish
49 "Huh!"
52 Special bars for shoppers
53 Punt, e.g.
54 Italian place whose name comes from a Greek word meaning "I burn"
58 Marty's pal in "Back to the Future"

by Damon Gulczynski

ACROSS

1 Symbol of the National Audubon Society
6 Auto download?
10 Includes surreptitiously, in a way
14 Pianist/composer Schumann
15 Do amazingly, in slang
16 Biblical mother of Levi and Judah
17 Sun spot?
19 Spanish pronoun
20 Rent out
21 Eggs Benedict recipe word
22 Annoyed, in slang
23 Not much
25 "Naughty you!"
26 Christian Bale and Val Kilmer, for two
27 Close relatives of ours
29 Nonstarter
30 Wunderkind
31 Irrefutable statement
34 Openly discussing one's kinks, say
35 End of a waiting list?
36 Auto import
37 Use a shuttle, say
38 Nonsensical song syllables
42 Magazine that's marketed to marketers
44 Pro with stereotypically messy handwriting
45 Philosopher Watts
46 OK, in a way
47 Accumulate
49 Big oaf
50 Fall for it
51 Revelations
53 "Couldn't agree more!"
54 Peacockish
55 Late comedian Bob
56 Driven group
57 Celebrity chef Burrell
58 Microscopic

DOWN

1 Green research site
2 Stick on
3 Boho-chic furniture material
4 ". . . __ I again behold my Romeo!": Juliet
5 Cover up in a shower
6 Book with an eagle on its cover
7 Word with tie or belt
8 Pricing word
9 City on the New York/ Connecticut border
10 Cry like a kid
11 Person you're in with
12 West Coast school where Einstein once taught
13 N.F.L. kicker Graham who played for 14 teams
18 As you might say
22 TV witch
24 Chief magistrates in Italian history
26 Cutesy term of affection
28 Part of the foxtrot
29 Long
32 Winter D.C. clock setting
33 Part of the palate
34 It makes waves
35 Was in prison
36 Moroccan quarter
39 Charge
40 Name that's an anagram of UNREAL
41 On edge
43 Fix, as text
44 Scheduled to land, say
47 Running mate of 2012
48 Noodge
51 Actress Noblezada of Broadway's "Hadestown"
52 When doubled, a 2010s dance craze

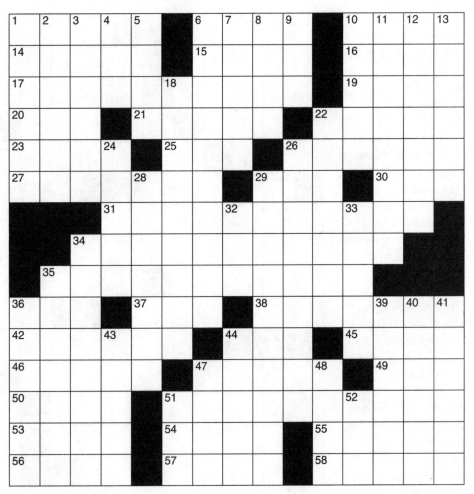

by Ori Brian

ACROSS

1 Better suited
6 Genre for "Jersey Shore" and "The Real World"
14 Brand owned by Campbell's
15 Respect
16 "Little" one of rhyme
17 Cold brew alternative
18 Spots where you might count sheep
19 ___ Carter, protagonist in 2018's "The Hate U Give"
20 It's all work and no play
21 Letter opener?
22 Preserves, as flavor
24 One of two in a 747
26 Tactic of radical environmentalism
31 Emmy-winning title role for Rachel Brosnahan
34 Iraqi port city
35 Needed help
37 Food fungus, in Fulham
38 1950s #1 hit with the repeated lyric "Bring me a dream"
39 Like Trump's presidency
41 Point ___ Peninsula, WNW of San Francisco
42 Tweaks further
45 Shepherded
47 El color del mar
51 Like those celebrated with an annual Day of Visibility on March 31
52 ___ car (Amtrak train component)
53 Give up
55 Woman's nickname that sounds like its first and third letters
56 Shady, as a street
57 A red one is concerning
58 Low numbers?
59 Burns out

DOWN

1 Waldorf salad ingredient
2 Captain Marvel portrayer
3 Basis for a case
4 Things oologists study
5 Civil rights activist Wilkins
6 What might get stuck in a window
7 Promises too much
8 ___ Daniels, main role on "The Wire"
9 Surfer's destination, in brief
10 Behind
11 Catch ___
12 Half of "Guys and Dolls"
13 Leave quickly, with "out"
15 Actress Wilson
19 Question asked while pointing a finger
22 Run down, in a way
23 Lack of objections, in a phrase
25 Roe source
27 Behind
28 "I'm too busy right now"
29 Kitchen flare-up
30 Pull in
31 Note
32 Like some feuds and foods on a stove
33 Attention
36 Defects
40 Get the services of, as a lawyer
43 Pitted fruit
44 Like many TV broadcasts since the 1990s
46 Specs
47 Secondary social media accounts, informally
48 Novelist ___ Neale Hurston
49 Put into service
50 Dregs
52 "Going Back to ___" (hip-hop classic)
54 Popular women's health app
55 Kit ___ bar

by David Distenfeld

ACROSS

1 Much of Iceland's greenery
5 "I don't believe you"
12 Fictional device in which to convey secret information
14 Needle exchange?
15 "Calvin and Hobbes" character described as "a six-year-old who shaves"
16 Imperturbable
17 "Duck Soup," for one
18 They may be dealt or folded
20 "Uh-huh"
22 Green lands
23 "Doing OK for myself"
25 Georgetown athlete
27 Org. created in the wake of "Silent Spring"
28 Kind of scrum
29 Unlikely to tip
31 Rat out
33 Steamed masa dishes
37 Surname in a Virginia Woolf title
39 Tesla, for one
40 Counsel council, in brief
41 Pertinent
43 Letters on a pass
44 Imitation
46 Like a dewlap
47 Fix
48 Vibes
50 Time constant symbol
51 Spanish term of endearment
52 Attempt to play peacemaker
54 Scooched over
57 Robe for a sumo wrestler
58 Wrap order?
59 Fretted
60 Common bake-off challenge
61 Additive once extracted from kelp

DOWN

1 Expression ending with a rising voice
2 Low dice roll
3 Halter?
4 "Same"
5 Play mind games with
6 Costa, to a botanist
7 Chancellor Scholz of Germany
8 Easily bought
9 Course option
10 Contracting sheet
11 ___ Teng, singer dubbed "Asia's eternal queen of pop"
12 Very best
13 It's booked before getting caught
14 "Not a chance"
15 Incapacitate
19 Sparkling alternative
21 Rule to take exception to
24 "The Jungle Book" character
26 Allow
29 Answer rudely
30 Traditional filling for momo (Nepalese dumplings)
32 Takes responsibility for
34 Many a Pablo Neruda work
35 Word shortcuts
36 Leaches
37 Reversible patterned fabrics
38 Something to meditate on?
42 Animal that climbs cactuses to eat their flowers
45 Word often seen in comic book lettering
47 "Hairspray" co-creator Shaiman
49 Kind of wave
51 Bother
53 Green light
55 Inits. for East Germany
56 Ryan of "You've Got Mail"

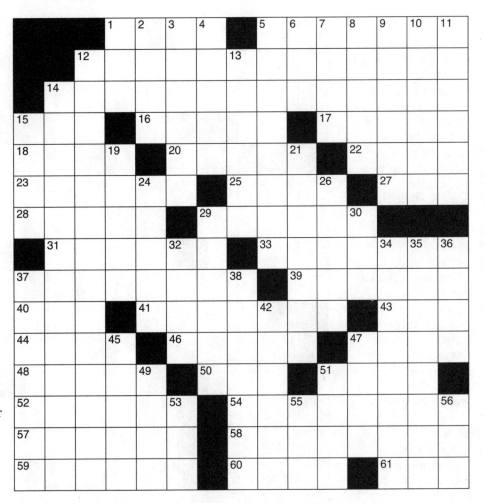

by Nam Jin Yoon

ACROSS

1 Parent company of Stroh's and Schlitz
6 Acronym on a pay stub
10 Many Kellogg School grads
14 "Sorry, can't stay"
16 Lake bordering four states
17 It's a blank
18 Key __
19 "The Simpsons" grandfather
20 Name of a family that took in an extraterrestrial
21 Some tributes
22 Kvetcher's list
24 Like a screwdriver
27 Noncommittal committal
31 Dolly-esque, say
32 Gave a "ta-da" moment
35 He's no scoundrel
36 Company whose corporate logo is known as "the Fuji"
38 Points on a math test
39 Approved
41 Freak out
42 Website space-savers
45 Largest digit in a set
46 What noise cancelers may cancel
47 Scourge of the 2020s, colloquially
48 Propose (to)
50 Smattering
53 Get in the __
54 Characters at checkout
57 Pumpkin, e.g.
58 Opportunity to rack up extra points, perhaps
59 Features of stringed instruments
60 Major affront
61 World-weary sort?

DOWN

1 Moussaka go-with
2 "Grand, ungodly, god-like" man of fiction
3 Term of endearment
4 Show on which Mariska Hargitay stars as Olivia Benson, informally
5 No. to call
6 Common setting for a Grimm tale
7 Land south of the Caspian Sea
8 Tough __
9 Actress de Armas
10 Kitchen gadget also known as a Parisienne scoop
11 Short-term financing option
12 Rocker Mann
13 Goes with
15 Cho's predecessor in the "Star Trek" franchise
22 Multiweek quadrennial event
23 Marine __
25 Shankar with a Lifetime Achievement Grammy
26 Agreement between mates
27 Tha __ Pound (hip-hop duo)
28 Permanently
29 It rarely includes chains
30 Muse of love poetry
33 Color whose name comes from the French for "unbleached"
34 Becomes less sharp
36 Pedigree alternative
37 Ecosystem that comes and goes
40 Word often contracted in contractions
41 Org. with a Morning Rounds daily briefing
43 Finish
44 Some etiquette rules
45 Singer with the alter ego Ziggy Stardust
47 "Regrets," perhaps
49 1960s–'70s Soviet space program
50 Unfair?
51 __ Turnblad, John Travolta role in "Hairspray"
52 Joins a union
54 James Corden's network
55 Org. targeted by Moms Demand Action
56 Military crashing site

by Robyn Weintraub

ACROSS

1 Paid off
7 Pinky swear, e.g.
11 Pause in the middle of a line of poetry
12 Creature also known as a greenfly
14 Substitute for coffee
17 Baptisms by fire
18 Palmed, say
19 Prefix with consciousness
20 Last word of the first sentence of Kafka's "The Metamorphosis"
21 Pick
22 "Don't Look Up" star, in tabloids
23 Parts of baseballs and mines
24 Country with two official languages—Guaraní and Spanish
26 Move from side to side, as a ship
27 2000 Sisqó hit with a rhyming title
29 1924 tale of derring-do
30 New Jersey's "unofficial rock theme of our State's youth"
31 Something picked up by a silent butler
34 Minions
35 Basic technique in skateboarding
37 Nitwit, to a Brit
38 "What do you want me to do about it?"
39 Be plucky?
40 Hollywood, with "the"
41 Astronaut Jemison
42 Didn't cause trouble
43 "Golly!"
46 It might work on a block
47 They might work on a block
48 Floor
49 Europe's oldest capital

DOWN

1 Lumbering tool
2 Turn in
3 Musician who helped save Carnegie Hall from demolition
4 Put up
5 Muffs
6 "Against the ___" (Thomas Pynchon novel)
7 On equal footing, in Latin
8 Mirrored
9 Tea, in Mandarin
10 Result of a poor audio connection, perhaps
11 Part of the body first successfully transplanted in 1905
13 Exponential ___ (function in physics)
14 Like many street-level apartments
15 Juice boxes?
16 Rumpus
21 Danced to the music of Carlos Acuña, say
22 "We / Jazz ___" (line in Gwendolyn Brooks's "We Real Cool")
24 Popular dishes in Québécois cuisine
25 Went round and round in circles
28 Record holder for the most M.L.B. All-Star selections
29 Spell
30 Attire at some academies
31 Exams for British 18-year-olds
32 Jewelry store tools
33 Minds
34 Mentally worn out
36 Mount with facility
37 Vegan sandwich, for short
39 Enforcement mechanisms, metaphorically
41 Where to pick sides?
42 Handful, say
44 Overly rehearsed
45 Occupation of Leo Bloom in "The Producers," for short

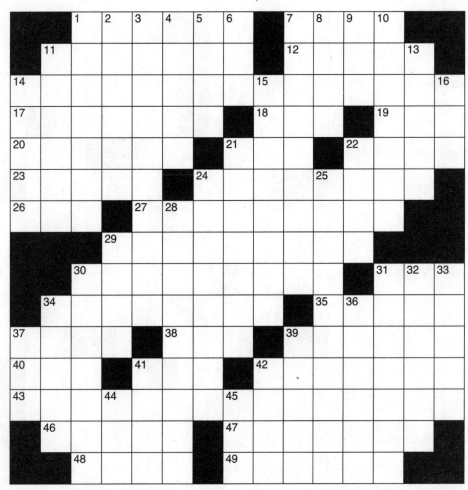

by Natan Last

ACROSS

1 Longtime cosmetics brand
5 Dematerialize
14 De segunda __ (secondhand: Sp.)
15 Surest shot
16 Things stuck with toothpicks
17 "Don't rush!"
18 Like the more interesting twin, some would say
19 Power __
20 Allied (with)
21 Many a Tumblr share
23 Lead-in to -logical
25 Articulated
26 It might come with a spoon straw
28 Attractively bold self-assurance, casually
32 __ Bryant, 20th-century singer/civil rights activist
34 Do most of the work for, as a team
36 Long __
37 Not exactly a priority
40 __-pitch
41 Island that's part of Maui County
42 Word with rock or hard
43 Set of eight for most spiders
45 Bring (out)
46 Soul seller
47 Pants: Ger.
49 Program
52 Courts of sorts
55 "Future Nostalgia" singer Dua __
58 Sum preceder
59 Acknowledgment that another person is at least partly right
61 "Twilight," for one
62 March participants, maybe
63 Thick noodle
64 "Not literally"
65 Cross products

DOWN

1 Ale category
2 Key for a trumpet
3 Stretching to see just a teensy bit better, perhaps
4 Pretty darn good
5 Winter homes, for some
6 Clear indication?
7 Basics to build with
8 The musical "Come From Away" has one
9 What a rebellious teenager may be going through
10 Spots for grills
11 "The Walking Dead" role
12 Height
13 Oregon college whose mascot is a griffin
15 Undercard listing
22 Symbol of strength
24 Garden variety?
26 "Tell me about it!"
27 Ingredient in some mole
29 Exchange words
30 Let develop, in a way
31 Sensational, as certain details
32 Filipino national hero __ Rizal
33 Singular
35 Eliciting an "Ick!"
38 They may emit as many as 200 beeps per second
39 Elevates
44 Indigenous religion of Japan
48 Music/comedy duo Garfunkel and __
49 __ doute (definitely: Fr.)
50 Encourage, maybe too much
51 Sounds that might accompany foot-dragging
52 Short courses?
53 Spanish wine region named for an animal
54 Laughfest
56 Store with a three-syllable name in four letters
57 Gym membership, maybe
60 Shortening in a recipe

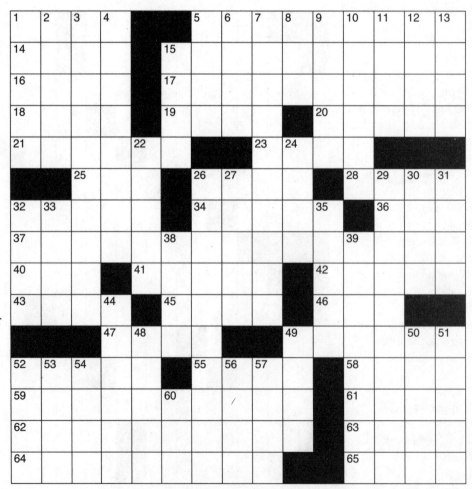

by Claire Rimkus and Brooke Husic

ACROSS

1 It means "father of" in Arabic
4 Catty remark?
7 Rated PG-13 or R, say
12 Sylphlike
14 Fit out
15 "Amaaazing!"
16 Is a witness
17 Comedian John who is said to resemble a love child of Harry Potter and Owl from "Winnie-the-Pooh"
18 Ottawa leader
19 Stun gun
20 Like part of a dress affected by static cling, say
22 Hootenanny
24 Word with gag and ground
25 Headwear for the big game?
27 Levy of "Schitt's Creek"
28 Isn't open about oneself
30 Drink cooler
33 Stereotypical Silicon Valley types
35 Act huffy?
37 Came out of the blue?
39 Launched weapons
41 Unwanted autocorrections
43 Bonny young lady
44 Influenza
45 Some Buddhist mandalas, e.g.
46 [More details below]
47 Acknowledgment of a poor performance
48 Schoolmaster for the classroom, e.g.
49 Italy's longest river
50 Spec for a script
51 Atlanta-based network

DOWN

1 Parcel
2 Place to study cultures
3 They're issued by the Bureau of Consular Affairs
4 Suit cut between "classic" and "slim"
5 House of Saud title
6 Like some blankets and bars
7 Along with the anteater, one of two animals in the order Pilosa
8 Less hurried
9 "Pfft, this one doesn't work"
10 Count ___
11 Currency whose name means, literally, "round"
13 More than a couple
14 Skin-toned cosmetic
16 Silent film star known as the "Man of a Thousand Faces"
18 Disciplinarians, at times
20 Something often seen with trunks
21 Fold
23 British pop star with more "Ed Sullivan Show" appearances than the Beatles
26 It gets bald over time
29 Going down the drain, in a way
30 Inits. at a bar
31 Place to get a wax
32 Summit goal
34 Back
36 Occupied
38 Can opener
40 Cattle-grazing tract
42 Looks like
44 Good name for a biologist?
45 Collect dust
46 ___ Taylor-Johnson, director of "Fifty Shades of Grey"

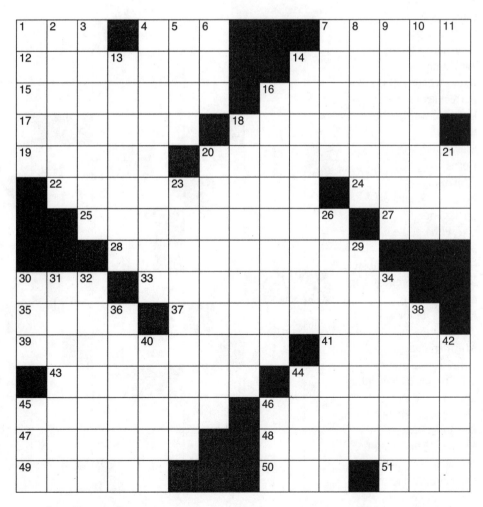

by Ryan McCarty

ACROSS

1 Break down fully
8 They might help with the dishes
15 Adage attributed to Virgil's "Eclogue X"
17 Not be completely open with everyone, to put it mildly
18 Letters seen on N.F.L. scoreboards between 1995 and 2015
19 Unless, to a lawyer
20 Kids' rhyme starter
21 "__ sight"
23 "Fiddlesticks!"
26 4.92892 mL
27 Where to see license plates that say "Greatest Snow on Earth"
28 Encrusts
30 Gray, in a way
31 Alternative to an autocamp
33 Exam where 100 is not a perfect score
35 Dreaded words from a teacher
36 Stew over, say
37 Loses
41 Crown topper
43 Prepares to take off
44 Sacked out
47 Car with open-source patents
49 Org. that was the subject of a 2021 Supreme Court antitrust ruling
50 Maude's widower on "The Simpsons"
51 Minimal change
52 Palindromic title
54 Traditional 20th wedding anniversary gift
56 Goddess of fertility
58 Chill
60 Mantra in the face of criticism
64 Conceitedly dogmatic
65 Cause for concern
66 What father knows best?

DOWN

1 Pandora releases
2 Like some confrontations
3 Judge
4 __ school
5 Defeatist's wail
6 Group of signs
7 Nephew of Cain and Abel
8 Difficulty
9 Member of the order Anguilliformes
10 Something to believe in
11 Man is one
12 Puts on a coat
13 Mischief-prone
14 Somnolent
16 "I just need to know this one thing . . ."
22 Like many crossword puzzles (though not this one)
24 Spin, as old yarn?
25 Deploy
27 Speakers' hesitations
29 Aces, of a sort
30 Within reach
32 Canadian band with the 1999 top 10 hit "Steal My Sunshine"
34 Boomer that went bust, in brief
38 Really dig
39 The sun's is approximately 865,370 miles
40 Govt. org. since 1946
42 Cleared one's cookies?
44 Something that's thrown out while using it
45 Act one's age
46 Minced words, say
48 Key of Beethoven's "Für Elise"
51 Winter air
53 The crane pose, for one
55 Squishy material
57 Short cut
59 What some dropouts go on to get, in brief
61 Rest area
62 __ economy
63 Baleful?

by Evans Clinchy

ACROSS

1 Wave one's arms?
9 Maker of some replacement heads
14 Lose focus, in a way
15 Sight from Maui's west shore
16 Classic song with the line "Give him a lonely heart like Pagliacci / And lots of wavy hair like Liberace"
17 "The same"
18 Fan belt?
19 Headache
20 Load off
21 Not totes
23 Mire
24 Repeated voice role for Steve Carell
25 Lacking zip?
27 "Duke" for Marmaduke
28 Item on a library shelf
29 Sarcastic "Oh, like you thought of that yourself"
32 "Who's with me?"
34 Horizontal group hug session
35 Code with tags
36 Like some telephone nos.
37 What "chicken" and "egg" are examples of
41 Philanthropist Broad
42 Polaroid's SX-70 camera, for one: Abbr.
43 Traffic marker
44 Ragtag
46 Best-selling sports video game franchise
49 Bank in London, for example: Abbr.
50 West Point grad, informally
51 Animal that can grow up to 3,000 teeth in its lifetime
53 Child's play
54 "I've heard enough"
55 Ones making the rounds?
56 Final act

DOWN

1 Home to Museum Island
2 Begrudge
3 Tube letters
4 Ne plus ultra
5 Bro
6 Watson and others
7 Something found under a mattress
8 Female salmon
9 Hoary
10 Inveigh (against)
11 Sophocles heroine
12 "Peace, bro"
13 Algae, at times
14 Draw on, in a way
20 Goes back to the beginning
22 Alpine folk dress
23 Supercapacitor unit
26 With gusto
27 Washington nickname
28 Of the moment
30 Outcast
31 Setting for Melville's "The Encantadas"
32 Live a little
33 Words on a ticket
34 Place where students can find solutions
38 Charles ___, artist whose bust of M.L.K. Jr. was the first image of an African American displayed at the White House
39 The end of Wikipedia?
40 Ostinato provider in Ravel's "Boléro"
42 Oozes
45 "Not so!"
46 Imperfection
47 Slavic form of Elijah
48 Member of the world's happiest people, per repeated World Happiness Reports
51 Something of your neighbor's not to covet, per the Ten Commandments
52 Te-___ (Mexican cigar brand)

by Ashton Anderson and James Mulhern

Note: This puzzle has four different solutions. When you're done, read the circled letters from top to bottom to find another one.

ACROSS

1 You might bid on it
5 First man, in Maori mythology
9 Lead to
14 Plant
15 Encumbrance
16 It makes il mondo go 'round
17 Bathroom cabinet item
19 More than flirt with
20 Vegas machine with the best odds?
21 A head
22 "American __" (Neil Gaiman novel that won the Hugo and Nebula)
23 Japanese electronics brand
24 Brain freeze cause
27 Product often advertising 99.99% effectiveness
31 "Headliner" of the first Warner Bros. short to win an Oscar
32 __ Ren of "The Force Awakens"
33 Big 12 sch.
36 Makes a small, plaintive sound
37 K.C.-to-Detroit direction
38 Ad Council output, for short
39 Grp. that advertised in "The Book of Mormon" playbills, surprisingly
40 Command after mistakenly pressing Ctrl+Z
42 Spicy kind of seasoning
44 It might help clear things up
47 Nocturnal marsupial
49 Event with Easter eggs
50 Runs
51 Behind
52 Where the cucumbers are not for eating
55 Play matchmaker for
57 Sound filler
59 Upper atmosphere
60 Little rascal
61 Damage
62 Authority
63 Federation formed in 1922, for short
64 Like many college film projects

DOWN

1 __ Raducanu, 2021 U.S. Open winner
2 Kick hard
3 Who might be asked for a donation, in brief
4 "__ again . . ."
5 Illegally parked car, maybe
6 How some pet food is sold
7 Potent marijuana
8 Suffix with bull or bear
9 Cry of contempt
10 Citizenship test taker, perhaps
11 Get put away
12 Eat at
13 It may be perfect for writing
18 Job at a bank, say
23 Some sources of vitamin C
24 Ocular affliction
25 Wee
26 Emmy winner Aduba
27 Code inits.
28 How you might feel looking at the Northern Lights
29 Fit for a big write-up, say
30 "Right?!"
34 Closing activity
35 __ interface
37 Biblical land near the kingdoms of Judah and Moab
38 Scotch flavorer
40 E.R. staffers
41 Brown. follower
42 Mess
43 Get more 45-Down
45 See 43-Down
46 Gets ready, as a cue stick
47 Fertile spots
48 Masterwork completed in 1499
51 Snack brand owned by PepsiCo
52 Holiday cookie shape
53 Sassy
54 Drove
56 Whiz
57 Nickname that's an alphabet trio
58 "I've got it!"

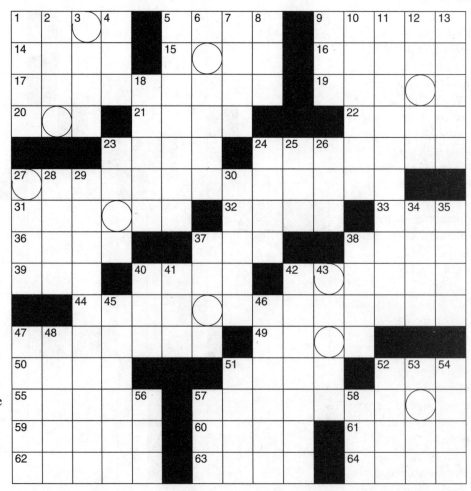

by Evan Mahnken

ACROSS

1 Office held five times by Julius Caesar
7 Not physically, say
15 Program commemorated on the back of the Eisenhower dollar coin
16 Do some wedding planning
17 Withdraw
18 Preposterous
19 Word with club or queen
20 Stuff, but not junk
21 Where "the cheese stands alone," in a classic song
22 They're tops to Scots
23 Lug
25 Faulty: Prefix
26 Grow up
27 Color not generated by light
29 Very nearly resemble
31 Livened (up)
35 Picked up
36 Sushi chef's tasting menu
37 Literally, "substitute"
38 Midwife's focus in the third stage of labor
39 Dazzling skill
41 2019 World Series winner, in brief
42 Org. with clubs, in two senses
45 "Anything!"
46 Veronica __, author of the "Divergent" trilogy
47 Orange candleflower, for example
49 "Mastering the Art of French Cooking," for one
50 Expert with picks
51 "Whatever you say . . ."
53 __ chai (Indian beverage)
54 Short hooking pitch
55 Eventually
56 Herbalists' panaceas
57 Muscle connectors

DOWN

1 Setting for drinks and deals
2 Met someone?
3 Policy around the publicity-shy, say
4 In-verse functions?
5 It runs up the arm
6 Offering for a developer
7 Capital of ancient Persia
8 In an elegant way
9 Canny
10 Campaign fund-raising letters
11 "That __ love thee, Caesar, O, 'tis true": Shak.
12 Tore
13 Where 23-Down was coined
14 Flushes, e.g., in poker
20 Gloucester catch
23 The art of appearing effortlessly nonchalant
24 Institution roughly two millennia old
27 Submitted
28 It started in 1964 as Blue Ribbon Sports
30 Allure
32 Salvo from Old Ironsides
33 Acts of will?
34 Sci-fi effects that are beyond stunning
36 Source of some nostalgia
38 Many human anatomy students
40 Unlikely to pontificate, say
42 Some ribbons and shells
43 Congee, e.g.
44 Coming in waves, in a way
46 Up now
48 Barrier against burrowers
50 Digital job, in brief
52 Match
53 1–12: Abbr.

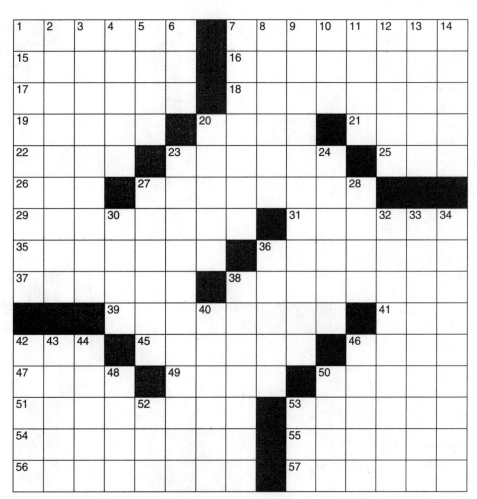

by Kyle Dolan

ACROSS

1 Setting for "A Few Good Men," informally
6 Hang (around with)
9 Frustrated outburst
12 Nubian Museum locale
13 "Gotcha," in a groovier era
15 Start to a logical conclusion
16 That's the spirit!
17 Revealed all
19 Tiny seeds of green fruits, technically
21 Expert problem solver
22 Sign of fall
25 Like refrigerators at night, sometimes
26 Key element of opera seria
27 Subjects of Monet paintings "in Venice" and "at Lavacourt"
30 SeaWorld roller coaster ride
32 __ bar
33 "Shameless" airer, for short
36 This isn't what it looks like!
39 Jenny, for one
40 Really, really fancy
41 In and of itself
42 Boost someone's signal, in a way
44 In and of itself?
45 Go back to see again, maybe
48 Hardly worth mentioning
50 Biggest stars
53 A bunch of crock?
54 Raw footage?
56 Off the chain, say
59 Ammonia has one
60 __ brilliant (diamond cut)
61 Musical based on a comic strip

62 Mint
63 Letters on some foundations
64 Grand

DOWN

1 __ order
2 Ending with freak or fool
3 Safety net?
4 GranTurismo maker
5 At the ready
6 Insta post
7 Levine of pop music
8 Pacific Coast capital
9 Love of lucre
10 5.5-point type size
11 Refined

14 "Puh-lease!"
15 Actress Tracee __ Ross
18 Woos with words
20 Nuclear unit nickname
22 Where lavalava skirts are worn
23 Shooting game
24 Wanted one
28 Easily had
29 Pique
31 Gives some stress
33 Fatal attraction?
34 Popular leafy perennial
35 Former center of Los Angeles
37 Like Los Angeles's Griffith Observatory

38 Increment on a scale
42 Stage support
43 Number 1, with "the"
45 Was fueled by
46 Escape
47 Black __
49 Toddler's eruption
51 Makes purr, maybe
52 Speak sharply
55 2003 film in which the title character exclaims "Son of a nutcracker!"
57 Mononymous singer of "Alive," 2015
58 Sushi fish that's not served raw

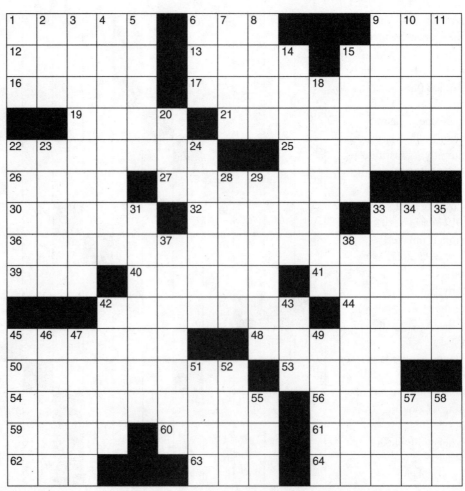

by Caitlin Reid

ACROSS

1 "Wish I could live like that . . ."
11 Some radio announcements, in brief
15 First winning presidential ticket to alternate vowels and consonants
16 Schmooze
17 Where the entirety of the "Lord of the Rings" trilogy was filmed
18 Folderol
19 Common Italian verb ending
20 Brewery supply
21 Amoeba feature
23 Michael of "Superbad"
25 Shake hands, perhaps
26 Many jingles
30 People of Burundi
31 Huffing and puffing, e.g.
33 Spread out at a party
34 Free
37 Bishop's group
39 Some fridges
40 Deadlines?
42 It might be captured on a safari
44 Who famously said "I really didn't say everything I said"
46 Some seaside gatherings
50 "In the end . . ."
52 Rear guard?
53 Drink that comes with a wide straw
54 Chinese __, food also called nagaimo
57 Approval inits.
58 Like much of Sudan
59 One with news to share, often
62 Musical Case
63 Counter request
64 Sharp
65 People might have personal ones for what they do

DOWN

1 R&B artist with the 3× platinum 1995 debut album "Miss Thang"
2 Went for a ride, in a way
3 Carpenters, at times
4 Website with a "Got a Tip?" page
5 Boxing champ Max
6 Site for a snipe
7 It turns red in Exodus
8 B.C. neighbor: Abbr.
9 Gathering that occurs once per decade
10 Call everything off
11 Caused a ruckus
12 Poor cell connection?
13 What you find kitsch in
14 Sources of some tips
22 Line on a map: Abbr.
24 Land on the Med.
25 Alternative to a Gallup survey
27 "Utter your gravity __ a gossip's bowl": "Romeo and Juliet"
28 Tennis great with the most consecutive weeks ranked #1 in the world (377)
29 Devices used to sterilize medical equipment
32 Racket
34 Take the money and run, say
35 Rule that's often broken
36 Kawasaki offering
38 Cold War inits.
41 Walk all over
43 Put down
45 Word with fair or film
47 Garment of the Middle East
48 Like Meg among the March sisters
49 Close calls
51 CVS Health acquisition of 2018
54 Subject of numerous hoaxes
55 Tablet collection
56 Grow out of something, say
60 Doctor's orders, for short
61 Mens __

by Sam Buchbinder

ACROSS

1 Means of supervision?
9 Co-winner of the 1994 Nobel Peace Prize
15 Kisses and hugs
16 "I can __"
17 What can strike up a tune?
19 Tiny bit of concern
20 Saint associated with the Russian alphabet
21 __ jure (by the law itself: Lat.)
24 Discover fortuitously
26 Rail construction
29 "Buzz off!"
30 Florida city in the middle of "horse country"
31 Soft shade
32 Pioneer in instant messaging
33 Fire (up)
34 Watch from the shadows, say
35 Industrial support
37 Easy mark
39 As it happens
40 Critical
41 Silent __
42 Small grouse
43 Refreshers
44 Unlike filibusters
47 Shelter from a storm, perhaps
48 Negotiation site that led to the 1994 Nobel Peace Prize
49 Appropriate
50 Draft teammates?
51 Mythological lyrist
53 Fictional narrator whose first name is a fruit
55 Epitome
61 Wireless network necessity
62 Toon with a brother named Castor
63 Oxford pad, e.g.
64 Locale in SW France

DOWN

1 Beyond steamy
2 Boy's name that means "king"
3 Rose by another name?
4 "Anybody there?!"
5 Fair
6 Accompaniment for a bottle of rum
7 Beautiful and rare
8 Chaz, to Cher
9 __ Game, annual event on the second Saturday of December
10 Raise
11 Everything considered
12 Occasion for Druids to gather at Stonehenge
13 Absorbed
14 Winter festival
18 Grandes __, part of France's higher education system
21 Reiterated refusal
22 Admissions to a counselor
23 Network of nerves in the abdomen
25 Rarer than rare
27 Keep on keeping on
28 Stop for a bit
36 Employ for lack of better options
37 Place to pick up litter?
38 Comeback that sounds like a "Star Wars" character
45 Without incident
46 Alchemist's offering
47 Flimflammers
52 His brother was no keeper
54 One end of the narthex
55 Prefix with -assic
56 Countless lifetimes
57 Keystone figure
58 Who wrote "All that we see or seem / Is but a dream within a dream"
59 Pipe cleaner
60 High rails

by Trenton Charlson

ACROSS

1 Like much White House press
8 Stick with
14 Social elites
16 Susan who wrote "The Orchid Thief"
17 Line of Pokémon
19 Actor James of "The Fresh Prince of Bel-Air"
20 ___ Who Code (nonprofit)
21 Forerunner of rocksteady
22 Bad thing to miss
23 Native Costa Ricans, informally
24 Something that might be raised in a fight
25 Amount to
26 Locales for the Jets and the Sharks
27 Like wicker chairs
28 Daisy Dukes, e.g.
30 Draft status?
31 Excessive coverage, perhaps
32 Mounted
33 Daylight saving time adjustment: Abbr.
34 You might have one on the side
37 Roaster
38 Sound of the West Coast
39 What stamens are, in botany
40 Word with change or color
41 Unmasked, say
42 Swears at
43 Travel around the world
46 Stuck in the Middle Ages?
47 Summer cooler
48 Early Macedonian capital
49 Divinity

DOWN

1 Famed Portuguese explorer
2 Good luck with that!
3 "Oh, get outta here!"
4 Lead-in to physical
5 Suspension of a sort
6 Onetime trade org.
7 Sue
8 Target alternative
9 "De dónde ___ ?" (Spanish 101 query)
10 ___ borer (beetle)
11 Russian Revolution figures
12 Silent counterparts, once
13 Where cruise passengers end up
15 Propensity for pilfering
18 Practice that yields mixed results?
23 New York county near Pennsylvania
24 Big name in crackers
26 1998 Robert De Niro crime thriller
27 The heart of Paris
28 Try to win, in a way
29 Author/screenwriter Ben
30 "Drink marvelously" sloganeer
31 Trailer
32 Look up, in a way
34 Something a 38-Down likes to eat
35 Current weather concern?
36 Tried-and-true
38 An adult one can spend up to 16 hours a day eating
39 Footslog
41 Contests in which the competitors are eliminated one by one
42 Pulitzer winner Maureen
44 Syringe amts.
45 Soft-spoken words

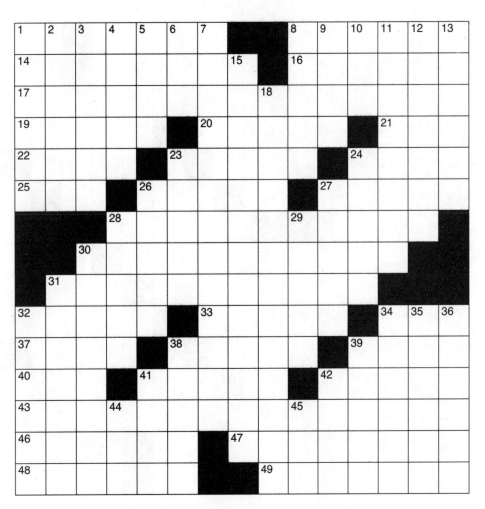

by Hemant Mehta

ACROSS

1 Cheap trick, perhaps
9 Apply pressure to
15 "Stupid me!"
16 Recherché
17 Food, water, a place to live, etc.
19 Decreases?
20 Who wrote "The poetry of earth is never dead"
21 Drawing method
22 "__ I do!" (informal assent)
23 Rivals of the 1980s "Showtime" Lakers, to fans
24 Part of a pool
25 Regulation followers, for short
26 Cuts (down)
27 "Wassup, my dude"
28 Intended
29 Winter slopes activity
30 One born in the wrong generation, maybe
33 Expands
34 Works with 17 units
35 Like speeders, often
36 Features of some glasses
37 Wade in the Baseball Hall of Fame
38 Manhattan campus around Washington Sq. Park
41 Where to set une couronne
42 Name spelled with six dashes and six dots
43 Air
44 Where Wonder Woman first worked: Abbr.
45 Words of agreement
46 "Gotcha"
47 Soak up the sun, say
50 What I might be in a lab?
51 Multiheaded dog guarding the gates of the underworld, in myth
52 Features of some accents
53 James Baldwin, e.g.

DOWN

1 What an aphrodisiac boosts
2 Eastern lodging
3 North Atlantic island group
4 Tweak
5 Sweeties
6 Modern "art"
7 Young male chicken
8 Prepared to propose, perhaps
9 Holds up
10 Greek counterpart of Discordia
11 See 18-Down
12 "Perfect!"
13 Dealing directly (with)
14 They're saved for a rainy day
18 High school alternatives to the 11-Down
23 After Kipling, the youngest-ever Literature Nobelist (1957, 44 years)
24 Turn
26 Reverential
27 Historically Germanic observances
28 Offer to help
29 Shade
30 "You're such a tease!"
31 It ends after midnight in New York, with "The"
32 Pepsi Max, e.g.
33 Spots for archaeologists
35 As an exception
37 Word with shop, shot or shape
38 Sushi variety
39 2013 #1 album from Kanye West
40 Civil disturbance
42 Biblical figure with a large staff
43 Walk in a leisurely way
45 Track, say
46 "__: Duets" (2007 country album)
48 Main component of britannium
49 Invoice info: Abbr.

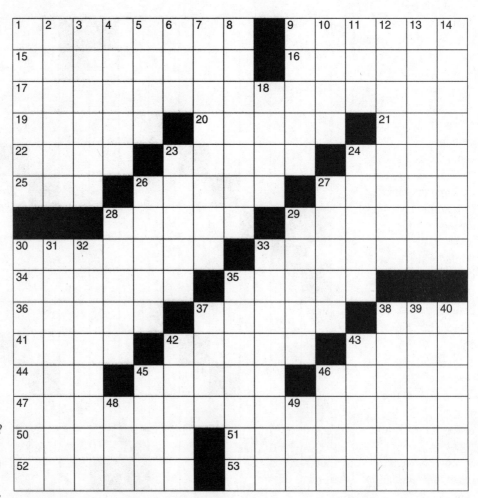

by Daniel Sheremeta

1

H	O	M	E	■	E	B	B	S	■	C	U	B	E	S
U	N	I	T	■	T	R	O	N	■	A	S	A	N	A
M	E	R	C	U	R	I	A	L	■	M	E	R	C	I
O	R	A	■	G	A	G	S	■	V	E	N	I	A	L
R	O	N	A	L	D	■	T	O	O	■	E	S	S	O
M	U	D	P	I	E	S	■	P	L	A	T	T	E	R
E	S	A	U	■	C	I	T	G	O	■	A	D	S	■
■	■	M	A	R	T	I	A	L	■	■	■	■	■	■
I	M	P	■	P	R	I	S	M	■	Y	E	L	P	■
W	O	R	S	H	I	P	■	A	P	P	A	R	E	L
O	N	I	T	■	E	T	S	■	L	A	K	O	T	A
J	O	V	I	A	L	■	P	O	O	R	■	S	S	N
I	M	A	L	L	■	S	A	T	U	R	N	I	N	E
M	E	T	E	S	■	E	C	I	G	■	B	O	O	T
A	R	E	S	O	■	T	E	S	H	■	A	N	T	S

2

R	A	S	T	A	■	E	D	G	A	R	■	A	R	C
A	L	T	O	S	■	T	I	A	R	A	■	C	A	R
F	L	A	T	S	T	A	N	L	E	Y	■	T	K	O
■	S	T	E	N	O	■	■	E	N	E	M	I	E	S
I	T	E	M	■	G	E	E	N	A	D	A	V	I	S
F	A	L	S	E	■	A	L	A	■	■	N	E	N	E
S	R	A	■	D	I	R	E	■	G	I	S	■	■	■
■	■	W	I	N	O	N	A	R	Y	D	E	R	■	■
■	D	A	N	■	N	O	M	E	■	O	W	E	■	■
E	A	S	Y	■	K	O	I	■	A	C	M	E	S	■
S	M	A	L	L	W	O	R	L	D	■	R	A	T	S
C	O	U	L	E	E	S	■	E	D	E	N	S	■	■
R	E	D	■	A	T	H	L	E	T	I	C	C	U	P
O	B	I	■	D	R	E	S	S	■	T	H	E	I	R
W	A	S	■	S	Y	R	U	P	■	Z	E	S	T	Y

3

G	R	A	B	■	A	C	A	D	S	■	T	E	S	T	Y
L	E	N	A	■	S	O	B	E	R	■	A	L	T	A	R
O	M	I	T	■	P	U	F	F	I	N	B	O	O	K	S
S	A	M	O	A	■	G	A	I	■	A	L	I	C	E	■
S	K	U	N	K	C	A	B	B	A	G	E	■	K	O	D
Y	E	S	■	B	A	R	■	■	A	S	T	R	I	D	E
■	■	A	A	S	■	A	S	H	■	■	A	N	D	Y	■
■	Z	E	B	R	A	C	R	O	S	S	I	N	G	S	■
B	A	L	E	■	■	A	M	Y	■	T	N	T	■	■	■
O	N	E	L	U	M	P	■	R	Y	E	■	M	B	A	■
A	I	M	■	P	A	N	D	A	E	X	P	R	E	S	S
■	N	E	A	T	H	■	I	L	L	■	T	A	X	I	S
P	E	N	G	U	I	N	S	U	I	T	■	B	I	D	E
O	S	T	E	R	■	A	C	M	E	S	■	A	C	E	S
E	S	S	E	N	■	P	O	S	S	E	■	T	O	S	S

4

A	T	O	P	■	S	P	A	■	P	A	G	E	D
R	I	P	O	S	T	E	S	■	O	R	O	N	O
T	R	I	P	T	Y	C	H	■	S	I	F	T	S
S	E	E	P	Y	■	S	O	C	I	A	L	■	■
■	■	E	L	S	■	R	O	T	■	Y	I	P	■
■	M	R	R	I	P	L	E	Y	■	D	A	M	A
A	Y	E	■	Z	A	G	■	A	O	K	A	Y	■
G	R	A	V	E	Y	A	R	D	S	H	I	F	T
A	I	D	E	D	■	M	A	P	■	T	A	O	■
P	A	S	T	■	S	U	N	R	I	P	E	N	■
E	D	A	■	U	R	N	■	E	R	L	■	■	■
■	L	E	N	A	P	E	■	A	U	S	S	I	■
B	R	O	A	D	■	E	G	O	T	R	I	P	S
O	F	U	S	E	■	G	I	V	E	A	R	I	P
O	D	D	E	R	■	S	S	A	■	L	E	N	S

5

T	H	R	O	B	■	S	T	O	P	■	B	O	W	L
A	M	I	N	O	■	H	A	H	A	■	U	V	E	A
T	O	O	T	S	I	E	P	O	P	■	R	E	A	M
■	■	■	H	O	M	E	S	■	E	T	E	R	N	E
G	A	T	E	M	A	N	■	A	R	E	A	■	■	■
A	R	I	D	■	C	A	P	N	C	R	U	N	C	H
S	M	E	L	T	■	R	O	U	E	■	A	L	I	■
B	A	S	■	A	C	C	E	N	T	S	■	P	A	P
A	N	O	■	K	A	Y	E	■	A	B	A	S	H	■
G	I	N	G	E	R	S	N	A	P	■	A	L	S	O
■	■	R	I	O	T	■	R	O	A	D	M	A	P	■
I	N	S	I	T	U	■	R	E	N	T	S	■	■	■
C	O	N	N	■	S	O	U	N	D	B	I	T	E	S
E	P	I	C	■	E	D	N	A	■	A	D	O	R	E
S	E	T	H	■	L	E	G	S	■	T	E	N	E	T

6

U	N	P	A	I	D	■	S	P	A	■	U	G	L	I	S
P	O	O	R	M	E	■	C	A	L	■	P	O	I	N	T
D	U	K	E	O	F	K	E	N	T	■	E	E	N	S	Y
A	G	E	S	■	Y	I	N	■	E	O	N	S	■	■	■
T	A	R	O	T	■	S	T	A	R	K	N	A	K	E	D
E	T	S	■	A	H	S	■	V	E	E	■	H	A	L	O
■	■	I	C	E	■	S	A	G	E	■	E	T	A	L	■
F	O	U	N	T	A	I	N	S	O	F	W	A	Y	N	E
A	T	T	A	■	T	N	U	T	■	F	E	D	■	■	■
W	R	E	N	■	M	A	C	■	B	E	E	■	P	A	S
N	O	S	Y	P	A	R	K	E	R	■	P	S	A	L	M
■	■	C	O	P	A	■	R	A	T	■	A	S	E	A	■
B	R	E	A	D	■	B	A	N	N	E	R	Y	E	A	R
L	A	S	S	I	■	I	D	S	■	C	O	H	O	S	T
T	Y	P	E	A	■	C	O	T	■	H	O	I	S	T	S

7

```
W A D E · W N B A · S C R A P
O P E L · H O E R · U H U R A
K E E L S O V E R · C A N T S
· S T I C K A F O R K I N I T
· · S O N · W E E · Y E S · ·
A L I · P E L E · B R O · · ·
G A G M E W I T H A S P O O N
O G L E · · A A A · E B A Y ·
G O U N D E R T H E K N I F E
· · S O U · S A D E · S S T ·
A T E · N R A · · I N T · · ·
C O M E T O T H E T A B L E ·
E N O L A · P U T O N A I R S
R A J A S · A L O U · L E G O
B L I N K · R U N T · L U S T
```

8

```
A S T R O · S E X Y · A W A Y
S T R A W · W A K E · T O L D
H O U S E P E T E S · A M O S
E A C H · H A I · Y A R E N ·
S T E · F O R T H E W I N E S
· · T A B · A S L · S T A · ·
B A B Y S I T E S · S E L I G
O N E K · A O R T A · A I M E
O G R E S · B E A R C U B E S
T I N · U T E · N I X · · · ·
H O O V E R D A M E S · M G M
· G U I D O · H I S · J U R E
A R L O · G U E S S N O T E S
B A L L · G N A T · S H E B A
A M I S · S O D S · A N D E S
```

9

```
W E B B · G O N G · A B E T S
H A R I · R H E A · N O V A K
E C I G · I B E T · I T A L Y
T H E C O L O R O F M O N E Y
· · H O L Y · L A X · · · · ·
M A K E M E · P A U L · S P A
A D R E P · S E L F · B A R R
T H E S H A P E O F W A T E R
R O M E · D I V E · H B O G O
I C E · F I N E · H E Y N O W
· · A L E · B U L B · · · · ·
T H E S O U N D O F M U S I C
W I D O W · O R F F · G Y R O
O V I N E · R I F E · G N A W
D E T E R · I P O D · Y E N S
```

10

```
A R C S · · S A G E T · C P A
P O L O S · A F L A C · L O U
P O U L T R Y F A R M · E U R
· M E A R A · A R T · N A N A
· · R A Z Z I E A W A R D S
L O L · P O O R · G A G A ·
A P E D · R O S S · R A S P S
V A M O O S E · O P E N M I C
S L O T H · Y M C A · O U T A
· · N E H I · E A R P · D A B
B O W L I N G A L L E Y · ·
A B E L · G U N · O N E A L
L E D · W E S T E R N A S I A
M S G · M A T T E · E S T E R
S E E · D R O O L · T O N E
```

11

```
W O K E · E L B A · C H A S M
O H N O · R A I N · L O C K E
W I E N E R D O G · E A T I T
S O W · S O L · S A R I · ·
· · S C R E E N E R D V D S
· H A S H · T O V · S E E N
D I N N E R D A T E · P L O
O D D · R O W · I R A · L A W
L E I · B A N N E R D A Y S
E M T S · I D O · G U Y S ·
D E S I G N E R D R U G · ·
· G M O S · E V E · B A G
C R O O N · I N N E R N E R D
B O O N E · P A I R · A L I A
S E D E R · A T M S · S T A Y
```

12

```
V O W E D · A B C S · T U B
C R O C U S · R O L E · E R E
R E M A K E · F R I E D E G G
· A R E N T · N O M I N E E
C A N D I D A T E · S A I N T
H E I S T · S H O E · L E T S
I R S · O A T Y · R H O · ·
C O M P U T E R P R O G R A M
· · E T A · O U S T · E R A
S W A T · D R I P · H O T E L
U H U R A · E D I T O R I A L
N O N A M E S · L A T I N ·
G O T T A R U N · G H O U L S
O P I · S I L T · S O L E I L
D I E · S E T H · T E S T Y
```

13

```
GASPS . AWE . BALKS
ASTRO . DOG . EVENT
SCOOBYDOO . RECUR
EONS . ATE . FINITE
STEP . MORNINGDEW
. TEAS . INGE .
ACORN . SINE . RSVP
MOO . NOCANDO . TAR
POLO . MANY . ABATE
. USER . BRIT .
POSTAGEDUE . MEAT
AMELIA . INN . ORZO
BATIN . PASDEDEUX
SHUNT . ONE . CAPRI
TAPES . PAR . OLSEN
```

14

```
ANKLE . PAPA . AAHS
BRIAN . APOP . UTAH
SAMPLESALE . RAVI
. SARTRE . PERON
. SECRETSERVICE
ABIDE . NEO .
BOX . SIMPLESIMON
CZAR . CAPER . RARE
SOMEDAYSOON . SEX
. DOH . ILOST
SUDDENLYSUSAN .
CHEER . TEENSY
RUIN . SYLVIASYMS
URGE . ERLE . NOELS
BAND . ASSN . SNAKE
```

15

```
LACES . FRY . PABST
SLATE . LIE . ALOHA
DIRTCHEAP . SAFES
. PUTOUT . ATMFEE
TAO . GRASSROOTS
ELOPES . ICY .
APLUS . MAGI . SWAT
THEPLOTTHICKENS
SARA . TIES . PINTA
. PHD . BUSTER
BUSHLEAGUE . RDS
ONTOUR . LAREDO .
ODIUM . JUNGLEGYM
SENSE . IED . KAUAI
TREES . FYI . SLEPT
```

16

```
POOF . POPBY . BAS
JONI . ATRIA . PIPE
SHELLSHOCK . AREA
. EASED . MIDST
PROCTOR . PEELOUT
CARLIN . HURT . NIL
STEEN . SARI . NATE
. GROUNDSCREW .
AMOK . FATE . AGILE
PAN . TOGO . AZARIA
PITBOSS . SLOWEST
ENRON . AUDRA .
AMAL . COMPOSTBIN
RAID . ADIEU . TIVO
SNL . PEERS . STEW
```

17

```
CAL . SCORES . ABIT
ALA . ISRAEL . TROY
BAT . SPARROWHAWK
AMIE . ALE . ALGAE
LONDONBRIDGE .
. LIU . MUSTERS
SCOTCH . ZAC . EXIT
TOV . HIJACKS . TSA
EKES . JUG . SURREY
PERUSAL . MIA .
. RUBYSLIPPERS
ASHEN . PAN . EXEC
BLACKFRIDAY . THE
LAVA . RECENT . RAN
EVEN . OPENED . ABE
```

18

```
CTRL . ACTIN . LATS
OREO . TOADY . ALEE
DUSTJACKET . GOIN
. ETTU . KEA . FUNGO
USA . TRAILBLAZER
PER . SAT . AARONS
SLED . ROE . DID
. FASHIONPOLICE
. TUT . DAM . ARMS
TRAUMA . YES . EEO
HOLDINGTANK . ART
EDGED . RUB . EATS
NEON . FOLLOWSUIT
BURT . BUSEY . IRON
APES . IPASS . SENT
```

19

```
B E S O . A L I C E . W H E W
L A I N . V E N O M . H O L E
A S T A . I V A N A . E R I E
H Y B R I D E N G I N E S . .
S A Y O K . R E A L I Z E S .
. . . L E T . . . T E M P E
. K A L A H A R I D E S E R T
F E N . . A L I K E . A A A
G E N D E R I D E N T I T Y .
S L I E R . . . Y U M . . .
. S E S S I O N S . N A V A L
. H I T C H I N G A R I D E
A J A R . B Y C A R . E M M A
D A L E . M O O R E . T E E N
O W L S . S U L K Y . S O N S
```

20

```
D A I S . I S P O S E . T M C
E D N A . B E A R O N . Y A Y
J U D Y G A R L A N D . P V C
A L A . U R B A N . P E E L
. T H I N . S U G A R C A N E
A H O K . . E R O S . . .
R O U E S . S A M M Y . A W E
L O S A N G E L E S A N G E L
O D E . O A T E N . L O A N S
. . E R M A . . . E R T E
M O V I E S T A R . A L P S .
S H I N . E N E M Y . L O X
N Y G . O T A N N E N B A U M
B O O . Y E S I A M . A T T A
C U R . S T E E L E . H E H S
```

21

```
Q A N D A . A T T I C . H O N
T H I R D . L A I D A S I D E
I M T O O O L D F O R T H I S
P E R U . L E A F . P E O N S
. D O G T A G . L O L . .
. . H A V E N O O O M P H .
M A T T E . I M P L O R E D
E R R . R A N G E . . E M O
W A I T H E R E . E G Y P T
. B O O O F F S T A G E .
. . E R S . E U G E N E
S H A R I . S I N N . W I N G
I T S A Z O O O U T T H E R E
S T E G O S A U R . H I T O N
I P A . N U R S E . O Z O N E
```

22

```
L A P E L . T A L C . S T A R
O B A M A . O L G A . O H I O
F I N I S . M O B S . R E N O
T T T T T T T T T T T T T T T
. . . S A O . F L U S H .
E A R W O R M . L I T . I D A
G R A I N . P A N . A N O N
G G G G G G G G G G G G G G G
O U I S . I R A . A R I E L
S E N . U N A . E N M A S S E
. . G A S S Y . B A E . .
B B B B B B B B B B B B B B B
L O U D . U L E E . A E I O U
A C L U . R U S T . L A N D S
H A L L . G E T S . L U G E S
```

23

```
C A S C A . A M Y . B L I P
T R E A T . W E E . P R A D O
R E A L M . M T A . R O V E S
. A L L F L A S H N O C A S H
. . M E I N . . I F C . .
S A T E E N . N O T F O R M E
I C H . D O O R . E L I A S
T H A T C A N T B E R I G H T
B O N Z O . U R S A . I R E
Y O G A P O S E . T R A D E R
. . T O O . . R U E D . .
J A Z Z U P T H E P L A C E .
I Q U I T . O O H . I G A V E
L U C K S . M B A . E I D E R
T I K I . B O B . F O S S E
```

24

```
Z I N G . T A U . Z A P S
A C R E . G O T H S . E X I T
G U A C . I N O U T . S E X Y
. K E V I N H A R T .
M O R O S E . G A Y B A R
I M O . P A N P I P E . R U E
N E W T . H O O H A . W I N S
A G A R . O T T E R . H A T E
J A N E D O E . A T F I R S T
. B E T S . R Y A N .
. M A L E . W E B B
D I V E R S E . H I N D L E G
A L E . X E D . A D O . O A R
V A R Y I N G . D A V I N C I
I N T E N S E . A H E A D O F
D O S A G E S . T O R M E N T
```

25

B	A	T		M	A	P	S		S	C	A	M
A	T	A	D		A	R	A	L		T	O	I	L	E
R	I	M	E		G	I	L	A		S	P	O	T	S
E	D	I	S	O	N		O	P	R	A	H
D	E	L	I	V	E	R		S	E	R	I	F
	R	A	T	E	R		A	S	S	E	T
D	E	K	E		S	P	O	O	L		T	R	A	P
A	V	E		U	S	C		A	R	E
S	E	G	A		S	T	E	E	D		S	L	O	P
	R	E	C	A	P		N	A	I	V	E
	L	A	G	E	R		N	A	M	E	T	A	G
	D	E	C	A	L		L	A	M	I	N	A
S	E	T	I	N		D	U	A	L		S	N	A	P
S	P	R	A	T		A	B	L	E		O	G	R	E
S	T	U	N		R	E	E	D		E	T	S

26

C	A	M		M	A	G		A	D	H	E	R	E	S
O	R	E		A	G	E		L	E	A	D	E	R	S
N	R	A		G	A	N	G	E	S	R	I	V	E	R
T	E	N	N	I	S	R	A	C	K	E	T
R	A	T	E		S	E	P		E	A	S	E
A	R	T	E	M	I	S		M	I	D	D	L	E	C
	S	O	D	A		H	I	R	E		L	E	O
	A	S	I	R	E	C	A	L	L
Z	I	P		O	N	Y	X		T	A	C	K
A	L	D	E	N	T	E		G	R	A	P	H	I	C
P	L	A	Y		R	A	E		E	I	N	E
	E	A	S	T	E	R	I	S	L	A	N	D
D	O	L	L	A	R	S	I	G	N	S		N	E	A
R	O	B	E	R	T	A		L	E	T		T	A	R
S	H	O	T	P	A	R		E	R	S		I	R	S

27

A	N	T	E		T	B	S		T	R	I	B	E	S
D	E	A	L		I	O	U		R	A	C	E	M	E
D	U	P	E		C	O	M	M	U	N	I	Q	U	E
	R	I	C	O		N	A	I	L		C	U	L	T
T	O	O	T	H	D	E	C	A	Y		L	E	A	H
I	N	C	O	M	E			G	E	S	T	E
T	S	A	R		R	E	V	I	S	E		T	E	D
	S	O	B	R	I	Q	U	E	T
A	N	G		D	Y	N	A	S	T		V	A	T	S
G	O	O	N	S		R	O	S	T	R	A
E	S	S	O		M	U	R	R	A	Y	T	H	E	K
G	I	S	T		O	S	A	Y		S	U	E	S
A	R	E	Y	O	U	O	K	A	Y		D	I	T	S
P	E	T	E	R	S		E	N	E		I	S	L	E
S	E	T	T	E	E		S	S	W		O	M	E	N

28

A	V	E	R	T		B	I	L	L		I	L	K	S
P	I	X	A	R		I	S	E	E		N	E	O	N
P	O	P	S	I	N	G	L	E	S		S	A	R	A
S	L	O	P		A	A	A		N	E	V	E	R
	G	I	M	M	E	A	B	R	E	A	K
B	A	N	A	L	L	Y		L	S	A	T
A	L	I	C	E		A	M	I		C	H	U	G
C	O	N	T	E	M	P	T	O	F	C	O	U	R	T
K	E	E	N		O	I	L		L	I	N	G	O
	A	M	O	S		S	P	O	N	G	E	S
W	H	A	T	A	R	A	C	K	E	T
H	A	M	U	P		A	I	D		O	H	M	Y
I	B	A	R		F	A	L	L	I	N	L	O	V	E
N	I	N	A		I	T	L	L		A	D	O	P	T
E	T	A	L		B	E	S	S		P	E	P	S	I

29

E	C	H	O		T	W	I	X		F	I	O	N	A
T	H	A	R		H	I	K	E		A	L	V	I	N
H	O	M	E	O	W	N	E	R		C	L	E	A	T
A	L	S	O	R	A	N		S	M	E	A	R
N	E	T		C	R	O	C		U	P	S	H	O	T
O	R	E	S		T	W	O	O	F	A	K	I	N	D
L	A	R	A	S		R	O	T	I		T	E	S
	T	A	T	T	O	O	I	N	K
I	C	K		S	W	A	N		T	O	O	T	H
T	H	I	S	S	I	D	E	U	P		A	C	R	O
T	I	N	T	I	N		T	S	A	R		O	I	L
	G	O	N	E	R		E	S	I	G	N	E	D
O	N	T	O	E		P	E	T	S	O	U	N	D	S
D	R	U	G	S		G	R	A	B		S	O	T	O
D	A	T	E	S		S	E	X	Y		T	R	O	N

30

P	A	T	C	H		O	L	A	F		A	C	M	E
S	N	O	R	E		N	A	N	O		G	A	E	A
A	D	A	I	R		A	S	T	U	D	E	N	T	S
L	O	S	T		I	C	H	I	R	O		Y	E	T
M	R	T		T	M	I		S	P	O	O	L
S	R	I		R	O	D	I	N	O		A	U	R	A
	A	N	D	Y		S	E	A	L	Y
	G	E	T	C	R	A	C	K	I	N	G
	C	O	C	O	A		L	E	I	F
T	O	G	O		S	E	C	A	D	A		L	A	D
S	H	A	R	E		D	O	C		L	I	E
K	I	M		K	I	M	C	H	I		K	E	N	T
T	O	B	L	E	R	O	N	E		L	A	T	T	E
S	A	L	E		A	M	E	R		E	N	T	E	R
K	N	E	E		N	A	T	E		D	E	E	D	S

31

A	L	O	H	A		S	E	R	F		S	M	O	G
C	O	N	E	S		I	D	E	A		P	A	P	I
C	H	E	A	P	T	R	I	C	K		L	Y	E	S
R	A	N	D		R	E	E	S	E		A	I	N	T
A	N	D	S	O	O	N		D	I	S	C			
			L	A	Y		S	Z	E	C	H	U	A	N
G	O	T	A	T		C	H	E	E	K		T	M	I
U	T	E	P		G	R	O	U	P		L	I	O	N
A	T	E		Q	U	I	T	S		W	O	N	K	A
C	O	N	S	U	L	T	S		F	A	N			
		V	I	A	L		R	O	Y	G	B	I	V	
L	O	O	M		I	M	E	A	N		J	U	D	E
I	A	G	O		B	O	D	Y	D	O	U	B	L	E
S	T	U	N		L	O	G	O		U	M	B	E	R
T	H	E	E		E	D	E	N		I	P	A	D	S

32

S	E	A		P	E	S	T	L	E		W	I	S	P
A	P	T		A	R	A	R	A	T		A	N	N	A
T	I	T		T	E	X	A	S	R	A	N	G	E	R
I	D	A	H	O		W	H	E	W		E	E	K	
R	E	G	I	O	N	A	L		C	R	A	Z	E	
E	M	I	T	T	E	D		A	D	M	I	R	E	R
S	I	R		T	R	A	D	E	O	N				
	C	L	O	T	H	E	S	H	A	N	G	E	R	
			P	R	E	P	P	E	D		D	I	N	
A	F	F	A	I	R	S		R	E	S	T	I	V	E
D	E	A	L	S		M	E	R	C	U	T	I	O	
A	R	K		H	O	B	O		A	X	M	E	N	
P	R	E	T	A	M	A	N	G	E	R		E	R	A
T	E	R	I		A	Y	E	A	Y	E		N	A	T
S	T	Y	X		R	H	Y	M	E	S		U	S	E

33

J	A	D	E		C	F	O	S		C	R	E	P	E
A	L	E	S		R	A	M	P		L	O	W	E	R
M	O	N	T		A	N	N	O	T	A	T	O	R	S
B	U	Y	A	P	I	G	I	N	A	P	O	K	E	
			D	A	S		G	U	S	T				
	E	X	O	T	I	C	P	E	T		I	N	C	H
I	T	T		O	N	T	O		G	L	O	R	Y	
T	H	I	S	I	S	S	P	I	N	A	L	T	A	P
Z	I	N	C	S		O	D	O	R		O	N	E	
A	C	A	I		S	U	N	S	T	R	O	K	E	
		E	L	A	N		A	E	R					
	F	I	N	I	S	H	I	N	G	T	O	U	C	H
B	R	O	C	A	S	A	R	E	A		M	O	R	E
T	O	W	E	R		N	O	R	I		E	M	I	R
U	M	A	S	S		D	C	O	N		O	O	P	S

34

L	A	P		S	H	A	R	D	S		M	A	N	E
A	C	E		A	U	L	A	I	T		E	K	E	S
D	H	L	A	W	R	E	N	C	E		T	I	C	S
S	E	T	S		D	E	V	I	A	N	C	E		
			H	O	M	E	R	S	I	M	P	S	O	N
C	A	M	E	L	O	T		A	S	H				
O	L	E		E	R	U	P	T		O	P	E	D	
D	I	A	M	O	N	D	J	I	M	B	R	A	D	Y
E	T	T	A		E	S	T	E	E		A	G	E	
		M	O	I		E	N	S	U	R	E	D		
B	A	T	M	A	S	T	E	R	S	O	N			
A	V	I	A	T	O	R	S		U	S	E	D		
S	E	E	M		M	I	T	T	R	O	M	N	E	Y
T	R	O	I		E	N	A	M	O	R		A	R	K
E	T	N	A		R	I	S	I	N	G		P	O	E

35

L	I	S	T	S		D	E	B	T		M	A	C	R	O
A	T	E	U	P		A	R	E	A		A	L	G	E	R
T	H	E	M	E	A	N	I	N	G	O	F	L	I	F	E
K	A	Y		C	I	T	E		B	I	O				
E	C	O	C	I	D	E		S	P	L	A	Y	I	N	G
	A	U	R	A	S		C	O	L	A		S	T	E	M
	L	O	L		T	O	N	E	D		C	O	O		
	J	A	C	K	I	E	R	O	B	I	N	S	O	N	
T	O	T		T	H	E	M	E		E	A	U			
W	H	E	T		C	E	R	A		V	A	U	L	T	
O	N	R	U	S	H	E	S		B	I	R	D	D	O	G
	S	H	E		S	E	A	M		N	O	E			
P	R	E	S	I	D	E	N	T	C	L	I	N	T	O	N
A	I	S	L	E		B	E	A	K		S	A	B	L	E
D	O	P	E	S		B	O	N	Y		S	H	E	D	S

36

A	G	A	P	E		P	A	C	T	S		C	A	N
R	E	L	A	X		O	L	L	I	E		L	I	E
D	E	B	T	C	E	I	L	I	N	G		A	D	O
O	N	E	H	O	P		N	E	W	S	M	E	N	
R	A	E		P	A	T	T	I		A	U	S		
			H	A	C	K	Y	S	A	C	K			
R	O	L	F		T	A	R		A	S	S	U	R	E
O	T	O	E		H	I	T	I	T		E	C	I	G
T	O	W	N	I	E		A	R	E		D	E	B	S
C	H	E	C	K	M	A	R	K						
	R	E	N		C	E	S	A	R		S	P	A	
G	O	D	S	E	N	T		P	I	S	T	I	L	
A	G	E		W	E	S	T	E	R	N	W	A	L	L
T	E	C		I	N	U	R	N		S	A	M	O	A
E	E	K		T	E	P	I	D		E	M	P	T	Y

37

T	E	S	L	A	■	A	T	I	T	■	T	A	G	S
G	R	I	E	G	■	C	E	D	E	■	D	R	O	P
I	G	N	O	R	E	T	H	A	T	■	P	E	T	E
F	O	G	■	E	R	I	E	■	■	D	A	N	T	E
■	■	L	E	A	V	E	S	U	N	S	A	I	D	■
M	A	L	A	I	S	E	■	I	R	A	S	■	■	■
I	C	E	I	N	■	■	U	G	G	■	■	U	A	E
C	H	A	N	G	E	S	T	H	E	W	O	R	L	D
E	E	K	■	■	D	Y	E	■	■	E	A	S	E	D
■	■	■	G	A	I	N	■	F	A	N	T	A	S	Y
A	R	M	Y	R	E	C	R	U	I	T	S	■	■	■
W	H	O	M	E	■	■	A	T	M	S	■	M	A	O
M	O	O	R	■	B	O	N	U	S	T	R	A	C	K
A	N	N	A	■	O	D	O	R	■	A	B	L	E	R
N	E	S	T	■	G	E	N	E	■	G	I	L	D	A

38

J	I	M	■	H	O	B	O	S	■	■	S	T	A	B
A	R	E	■	B	E	A	U	T	■	■	A	U	D	I
C	O	R	P	O	R	A	T	E	W	O	R	L	D	■
K	N	E	E	■	■	■	O	N	O	■	B	E	E	■
■	■	■	W	O	R	D	F	O	R	W	O	R	D	■
L	E	T	S	D	I	E	■	■	N	A	B	■	■	■
E	C	O	■	O	O	M	P	H	■	L	O	F	T	■
T	O	R	O	N	T	O	R	A	P	T	O	R	S	■
O	N	C	D	■	S	N	O	R	E	■	S	E	A	■
■	■	H	O	G	■	S	P	A	T	T	E	R	■	■
H	O	R	R	O	R	S	T	O	R	Y	■	■	■	■
E	V	E	■	B	O	A	■	■	P	S	S	T	■	■
M	U	L	T	I	P	L	E	C	H	O	I	C	E	■
A	L	A	S	■	E	E	R	I	E	■	T	A	R	■
N	E	Y	O	■	S	M	E	A	R	■	H	M	M	■

39

A	R	D	E	N	■	P	M	S	■	S	T	R	U	T
L	E	A	V	E	■	R	A	E	■	H	E	A	T	H
B	U	M	A	R	O	U	N	D	■	A	L	T	E	R
U	S	N	■	D	U	N	G	E	O	N	■	E	R	E
M	E	R	E	■	R	E	A	R	W	I	N	D	O	W
■	■	I	A	M	S	■	■	E	A	U	■	■	■	■
A	N	G	S	T	■	P	A	W	N	■	T	I	N	S
B	E	H	I	N	D	T	H	E	S	C	E	N	E	S
E	T	T	E	■	R	A	I	D	■	E	L	T	O	N
■	■	S	P	A	■	■	D	O	L	E	■	■	■	■
B	O	T	T	O	M	L	I	N	E	■	A	R	A	L
E	N	E	■	R	A	I	N	O	U	T	■	F	D	A
A	S	S	E	T	■	B	U	T	T	H	E	A	D	S
D	E	L	L	A	■	R	I	M	■	U	N	C	L	E
S	T	A	L	L	■	A	T	E	■	S	T	E	E	R

40

L	P	S	■	A	L	T	O	■	■	R	E	F	E	R
I	R	K	■	B	A	R	N	■	S	O	M	A	L	I
M	A	I	N	S	T	A	Y	■	E	G	O	I	S	M
I	D	E	E	■	K	I	X	■	M	E	T	R	E	S
T	A	R	H	E	E	L	■	F	I	R	E	S	■	■
■	■	R	L	S	■	L	O	P	■	S	H	E	D	■
A	R	G	U	E	■	B	E	R	R	A	■	A	V	E
R	O	O	■	G	O	O	D	D	O	G	■	K	E	N
I	D	O	■	Y	U	R	T	S	■	L	E	E	R	Y
D	E	S	K	■	T	A	O	■	C	O	M	■	■	■
■	■	E	N	A	C	T	■	H	O	W	C	O	M	E
M	E	D	I	N	A	■	P	O	L	■	E	R	A	S
C	L	O	V	I	S	■	H	O	U	S	E	S	I	T
A	L	W	E	S	T	■	D	E	M	I	■	O	N	E
T	E	N	S	E	■	S	Y	N	C	■	N	E	E	■

41

L	E	T	S	■	A	M	A	J	■	S	K	U	N	K
A	U	R	A	■	T	A	L	E	■	A	N	N	O	Y
I	R	O	N	■	E	T	A	T	■	L	I	B	E	L
C	O	N	S	U	M	E	R	P	R	O	F	I	L	E
■	■	■	A	P	P	■	M	O	A	N	E	R	■	■
N	A	M	■	O	O	F	■	W	T	S	■	T	E	D
A	V	I	A	N	■	A	G	E	S	■	O	H	I	O
C	O	N	T	E	N	T	P	R	O	V	I	D	E	R
H	I	D	E	■	E	A	S	E	■	C	L	A	I	M
O	R	B	■	D	H	L	■	D	A	H	■	Y	O	S
■	■	E	M	E	R	I	L	■	M	I	C	■	■	■
C	O	N	C	L	U	S	I	V	E	P	R	O	O	F
O	L	D	I	E	■	T	M	A	N	■	A	M	S	O
A	G	E	N	T	■	I	B	I	D	■	M	A	L	E
L	A	R	G	E	■	C	O	N	S	■	P	R	O	S

42

S	E	W	S	■	T	A	X	I	■	E	C	L	A	T
O	A	H	U	■	I	V	A	N	■	S	H	A	P	E
D	R	A	M	A	T	I	C	L	I	C	E	N	S	E
A	T	M	■	T	A	S	T	E	D	■	E	D	E	N
S	H	O	O	I	N	■	O	T	T	E	R	■	■	■
■	■	■	A	L	I	T	■	A	N	Y	H	O	W	■
S	H	I	F	T	C	H	A	N	G	E	■	O	N	O
L	I	D	S	■	E	P	A	■	■	O	S	L	O	■
U	R	L	■	F	L	O	R	I	D	A	K	E	Y	S
E	E	Y	O	R	E	■	R	O	L	E	■	■	■	■
■	■	F	O	A	L	S	■	G	O	D	E	E	P	■
P	I	A	F	■	V	A	N	I	S	H	■	G	R	U
S	A	N	D	I	E	G	O	C	H	A	R	G	E	R
A	G	O	A	T	■	O	R	E	O	■	D	O	C	S
T	O	N	Y	S	■	S	T	E	W	■	A	N	T	E

43

NALA BORE AJAR
ADAM UTES IRULE
NOWORRIES SALON
CIRCLEOFLIFE
INTOTO SFO ETE
NAH ESSO FRAT
DIETS ELLE SALT
ILLS REAIR EYER
ASIA AMFM SAMOA
ORBS SACK ONS
OWN ATE RAHRAH
HAKUNAMATATA
AGING PRIDEROCK
RENTS TELL ERIE
ARGO YALE SCAR

44

SCRUB SLAM MOS
PRUNES LOBE AAH
FUNINTHESUN CSI
SET GOODS ONAIR
MALT AROUSE
ICICLE SPLAT
MADEINTHESHADE
ORES ION CRAW
BACKINTHEBLACK
HIRES LAUGHS
TERESA BENE
USERS EPICS OOH
PIC EYEINTHESKY
AGO RENT SEALED
CNN SAYS ERODE

45

LABS HARSH CRAP
IDVE AKITA LIRE
BEINGMCCOY IDEA
TEA KID POET
SACRIFICEMCFLY
SUMATRA NIL
AMI HARTS TOPAZ
FONT SEWON PINE
ESSAY DONUT PIE
PAM IMAMESS
RUNAWAYMCBRIDE
OTIS RUE ISR
BEEB ICEMCQUEEN
ORCA ACTOR SALE
TIER HASTY EMIT

46

RASPS SCREW WIT
ELTON ELUDE HMO
BEATLEMANIA APU
EXIT MID TVSTAR
LADYDI WEANS
MARCHMADNESS
MINOR LAIR TRIO
ISOUT ERS SAVOR
FLIT JADE ILENE
FASHIONCRAZE
MEETS GETSAT
BALDIE MOO TARA
ABA SPRINGFEVER
JAW SHINE DRESS
ADS OSAKA ASDOI

47

ACTS CUBAN DEJA
NYET ASIAN EVEL
NASL FENCE LETS
ENTER DDE PINTO
POINTILLISM
ANI FOO LAT ONT
SOLDTO CHERIE
TROI RAISE LEND
RATES INE POSED
ODS NFLSTAR ORY
LOOM ATOB
GEORGESSEURAT
PRINT NUI DAFOE
JENGA TED OVARY
SWEET STE FORTE

Title spelled by the dotted letters: "A Sunday Afternoon on the Island of La Grande Jatte"

48

HDTVS USOFA NIL
AEIOU LEAST ORE
HARUMSCARUM SOD
ALEC HEM FLING
HEARYEHEARYE
CAL DQS LOEWE
ASADA DSL FEEL
MAKEMINEADOUBLE
OPEL OOF GLOMS
GUSTO CAR BOT
ALEXVANHALEN
DONEE OVA AGAR
ONE LOGGINGINTO
REV TREAT AVAIL
ERA EBONY BETTE

49

```
A T E A M ■ O L D I E ■ L A M
T I A R A ■ F E E D S ■ I W O
M A R K R U F F A L O ■ Z A P
■ ■ S I N ■ T R Y ■ B A K E
T A J ■ T W I S T ■ A I M E D
A S A L A R K ■ H O P K I N S
T I M E L I N E ■ T E E N ■
A D E S ■ T O R C H ■ R N A
■ E S S ■ T W I N E ■ B E R G
■ S T Y E ■ N O R M A L C Y
A N T H O N Y ■ T W I R L E R
I B E A M ■ A T E I N ■ I D O
S A W N ■ S C I ■ S G T ■
L E A ■ J O H N B E L U S H I
E R R ■ A S T E R ■ E T H I C
S S T ■ B O S S A ■ S U E M E
```

50

```
C A P P ■ I M I N G ■ S C A M
L U L U ■ N O L I E ■ T O G A
A R A B ■ P O I N T G U A R D
P A Y G R A D E ■ G O A L I E
S E A A I R ■ ■ B O O R ■
■ M D T ■ P A I N T G U N
H O S E S ■ B E N N Y ■ R N A
A R T S ■ P A N D G ■ P A I N
S E E ■ P R I U S ■ S A N T A
P O P G R O U P ■ F U N ■
■ H I L L ■ E N G E L S
S A F E C O ■ P E A G R E E N
P A R T Y G I R L S ■ A N N A
A B E T ■ U B O L T ■ V I D I
M A Y O ■ E M M Y S ■ Y E L L
```

51

```
A S Y E T ■ B E B O P ■ E S T
S E E M E ■ O T O E S ■ N T H
P A S T H I S T O R Y ■ D E I
E C O ■ E N S U E ■ I W I N
C O R D E D ■ R A T F I N K
T O N I ■ Y I N ■ M A S S E S
S K O S H ■ N O Y E S ■ E M O
■ C A S H M O N E Y ■
B O T ■ V E D A Y ■ S E G A R
I N A F O G ■ D O G ■ A R I E
T A X I C A B ■ E S H A R P
E L S E ■ Y U B A N ■ B T U
S I C ■ B U N N Y R A B B I T
A N A ■ I S O U T ■ F R A M E
T E M ■ N E W M E ■ U R G E D
```

52

```
C A L F ■ R O S Y ■ R A I D S
A R I E ■ O P I E ■ E P C O T
B U Z Z W O R D S ■ P R E G O
■ G A Z A ■ Y E N T A ■ A B U
P U R E S T ■ B O B S A G E T
O L D S A W S ■ S T B E D E
W A S ■ B I L G E ■ U S S R
■ P I X I E D U S T ■
O A T H ■ T O A S T ■ F U M
R E H E A T ■ M E R G I N G
C R E W N E C K ■ R E E S E S
H A M ■ G L O A T ■ E L S A ■
A T A L L ■ S H O R T C U T S
R O G U E ■ E L I E ■ A R E A
D R I V E ■ C O L A ■ P E N D
```

53

```
A B R A ■ A ■ A B L E
L A O S ■ A V A ■ M A I D
T T O P ■ A C E L A ■ A T O I
A T F ■ A M E R I C A ■ T N T
R E G A L E D ■ A D S A L E S
■ D A N E S ■ A ■ C A M E L
J A R T S ■ A L A ■ P A D M E
A N D I ■ A R E N A ■ T R E S
N E E ■ A N T E N N A ■ E S T
D Y N A S T Y ■ E N M A S S E
J E S S I E ■ E E N S I E
■ F A C E P L A N T ■
A F R A M E B U I L D I N G S
B R O S ■ D A N C E ■ C O O K
S O O T ■ E N T E R ■ S W A Y
```

54

```
C A P ■ D E E R ■ D O D G E D
R I O ■ I D L E ■ O R I O L E
E S P ■ R U M M A G E S A L E
E L U D E ■ U R N ■ C L A P
P E L I C A N S T A T E ■
■ A E T N A ■ P E R I L S
R A T S ■ A D O S ■ E N D O W
A L I ■ S T I L T O N ■ I R A
S T O V E ■ R E U P ■ P O E M
P O N I E D ■ D E B I T ■
■ S K I N N Y D I P P E R
A U D I ■ S A O ■ S E R T A
W H A T S M Y N A M E ■ O U T
E U R O P A ■ O P E C ■ O D E
S H E R Y L ■ S E N T ■ F E D
```

55

```
A B S E N T █ S W A L L O W
D O O D A H █ K A R A O K E
E X C U S E S E X C U S E S
N Y C █ M E D █ R E D █ █
█ E S T E R █ D Y E █ █
M A R C U S A U R E L I U S
A T B A T █ N A P █ C H E
C R A M █ G R O W █ H E H E
A I L █ B A A █ S E D U M
W A L R U S M U S T A C H E
█ A M P █ N E U R O █
█ S A P █ P I G █ F D A
J U S T T H E T W O O F U S
U P T O N O W █ A S L E E P
G E O R G E S █ Y O D E L S
```

56

```
B I G I F █ S K I N █ W E S T
A R E S O █ T A C O █ E X P O
B A L L P L A Y E R █ R E I N
A N T E █ E R A █ T E R R E
█ P A R K V I S I T O R █
G E T B U S Y █ E B A N █
A T A L L █ H E E █ L E A K
T R I A L C O U R T J U D G E
E E L S █ A S H █ I C A R E
█ T O N S █ M I L K M A N
J A Z Z P I A N I S T █
A D I O S █ U S E █ B A A S
P E N N █ O N T H E B E N C H
A L E E █ R O S A █ B A N T U
N E S S █ S T O P █ Q U E S T
```

57

```
S L O T █ A X I S █ B A S K S
T A S E █ P I T T █ D I N A H
R U I N █ R I G A M A R O L E
I R E N E █ I S A Y █ W E D
P A R I S H P R I E S T S █
█ S T O O L S █ A U T O
C A B █ A R M S █ F O X I E R
S T A R T U P █ C A P I T A L
I M B U E S █ D E N T █ S L Y
S O Y S █ P R O T I P █
█ B E R N I E S A N D E R S
F L U █ H O L A █ G I N U P
R O M E O R O M E O █ D E L A
A M P E D █ T O T O █ D R E D
T E S L A █ S N A P █ Y O R E
```

58

```
C A S T █ L A T H █ C L A S P
A S H E █ A C H Y █ H U M O R
S T A N █ T E E M █ E M P T Y
H U D D L E █ G N O M E █
I T O █ A R G O █ W I N D U P
N E W T S █ R O S E S █ O N E
█ B A E █ O D I S T █ W I G
S C O U R █ U S E █ R U N T S
P O X █ P A T H S █ Y A W
A R E █ O N S E T █ L E A F S
S P R A I N █ P A P A █ R E A
█ G N A S H █ A B I D E S
C A R A T █ H E W N █ O D D S
P R I M E █ O R E S █ T O M E
A M B E R █ E D D Y █ A G E D
```

59

```
C C T V █ C A S C A █ J O S H
O H O H █ U S U A L █ A L L A
M E W S █ B A B Y P O W D E R
P E N █ V I S █ H O S T E D
A R C T I C O C E A N █ I V E
Q U A I D █ N H L █ A D M E N
S P R E E S █ E A R █ R E D S
█ R O Y A L N A V Y █
L A D E █ D R S █ J E R K E D
E V A D E █ A E C █ R O L L E
G O T █ C O B A L T S T E E L
I N S I T U █ A W E █ E V E
B L U E O N B L U E █ A N A T
L E N S █ C A U S E █ J E T E
E A S T █ E D G E D █ A X E D
```

60

```
F L A T █ L O C A █ S A G A S
L U S H █ O V I D █ A L I B I
O B I E A W A R D █ P I T O N
P E N P A L █ C O S █ E M M A
█ O B I W A N K E N O B I █
A C T U A T E █ I L S █
T U R N █ E S T E E █ T L C
O B E D I E N C E S C H O O L
M A X █ C R Y I N █ O R S O
█ B O O █ E M I T T E D
O B G Y N D O C T O R S █
S L A G █ E C O █ P A T E N T
C A P O N █ O H B E Q U I E T
A R E N A █ M E A D █ F R A Y
R E S E T █ E N D S █ F E L L
```

61

```
ROSS . TONTO . . MET
OSLO . SPOON . LODE
CHILDPROOF . ERIE
KATIE . ANTI . ANTS
. . DASH . . RAVI .
SILENT . PREVENTS
ACER . ALOE . INGOT
BEA . CROSSED . DNA
LASSO . GETS . MEAT
EXTERIOR . TRAWLS
. . OXEN . . GAIN .
WIFI . KEEL . SALSA
IRAS . STRIKEGOLD
FILM . INANE . ENID
ESL . NASTY . DEMS
```

62

```
. PLATO . SLUR . PTAS
DIALOG . PISA . ORNE
RECTOR . IBET . SATE
ATE . TEETERTOTTER
BADPR . GEL . EDIT .
. . EURO . . TROTOUT
BORNEO . STARR . RPI
OMEN . TAHINI . TION
ANI . DOVES . ETHANE
RITAORA . . BRRR .
. ERNO . BIO . EULER
TORATORATORA . EVE
ADAM . TOGA . ATWOOD
CITI . EVEL . REINKS
ONES . RELY . ARTIE
```

63

```
PTA . AWE . . OHSTOP
ART . CELS . NAPOLI
TEESHIRT . TIRADE
HAUL . ROUGHRIDER
STPADDY . REST .
. . CUE . RID . ZITS
BUNKERHILL . DYE
FROST . ESL . ACORN
FDR . GREENSALAD
SUMS . LES . AIR .
. . NEAT . MTADAMS
CUPOFCOCOA . ISEE
AVICII . GOLFBALL
REGALE . INIT . DOM
EASTER . SEC . ANA
```

64

```
CASTS . BIBS . LAUDE
ONEUP . ALOE . ESSEX
BAABAABLACKSHEEP
RIM . RUE . TAB . MMA
ASSERT . . NICEST
. . BOOBOOBEAR . .
IKNOW . LILO . NICKI
OREO . SENDON . BONA
TICK . TAKETO . SMOG
ASK . SUR . LIE . OXO
. . BYEBYEBIRDIE . .
DROOL . ERIC . INSTA
RANGE . YOLK . TATUM
ATEIN . EDGE . ENACT
TESSA . DEER . DESKS
```

65

```
DORAG . THEOC . EVA
AROMA . ORTHO . VIS
MELISSASAIMLESS
POE . BUD . OPENTO
. . FIRSTS . ATBAR
TOWEL . RIBS . EST
STELLASALLSET
POLL . UTILE . UTNE
. LAURENSUNREAL
TAS . NAME . FORTY
OFFER . SEPALS .
PLANES . ORG . AHI
DARLENESLEARNED
OMG . LAPEL . MENLO
GEO . SPACY . EXAMS
```

66

```
SPA . . AHA . OHARE
TENS . EGAD . MADAM
RACK . GORDONJUMP
ICHING . TRI . LIT
PHOTOSHOOT . ETSY
. . SCOUR . HEWS .
AMS . ANTI . ONEWAY
BENIN . UGG . CRIME
SHONDA . AUTO . MAP
. WOOS . MAORI .
RAFT . CHICKENRUN
IRE . KOI . ESCAPE
PENTATHLON . ANTS
INCUR . AIDS . SCOT
TAEBO . TEE . HPS
```

67

```
O H F U N   A R T     C L I P
L E A F S   R A M A   A O N E
M A K O C L I N I C   L O L A
O D E S   E A U   C A V I A R
S S N   K E L P R E V I E W S
  P A R I S     E D E N
J A M A L   T H E E   B L O W
I C E I T   Y 2 K   W A I V E
F E S S   D I O S   E L V E S
  E V E N     P A L E R
F I N D I N G D O R K   A L P
A L O H A S   A D O   S L O E
M U L E   E N D O F S T O R K
E V I L   R E A R   R A N D O
D U E L     A S S   O B E S E
```

68

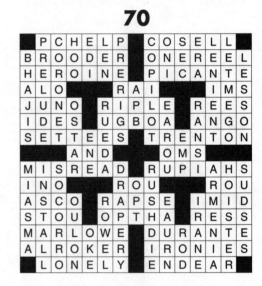

```
S E A L   S C O N E S   L E T
P L I E   E F F E C T   A L E
A F R A I D O F T H E   M A N
  S P C A   S T O P G A P S
W A I T U N T I L   H O R S E
O R N O   I T E M   P R E S
M I A   A C M E   U A R
B E I N T H E   N S T O R M Y
  A V E   J A K E   E E O
C A S K   Z I O N   A G A R
A F T E R   C H O C O L A T E
T R A D E S I N   U R A L
N I T   T H E D A R K S I D E
A C E   R E S O R B   K N E W
P A N   O A T E R S   A G E E
```

69

```
I S H   M R T O A D   F E T A
M O E   M O R R I E   A M A N
A L A R M B E L L S   V I C E
C O L O M B O   S O R R O W
  A G E   A D E L E
  A U R O R A B O R E A L I S
B A S S O   M A T T   U L N A
R N A   D A B   E S C   A S P
E D G E   R I A L   A G N U S
A W E S O M E B L O S S O M
  S T Y N E   C T U
E T C E T C   H A L I B U T
Y A R N   A B P O S I T I V E
E X E C   M A R L I N   R E N
S I D E   P H O T O G   D A N
```

70

```
  P C H E L P   C O S E L L
B R O O D E R   O N E R E E L
H E R O I N E   P I C A N T E
A L O   R A I   I M S
J U N O   R I P L E   R E E S
I D E S   U G B O A   A N G O
S E T T E E S   T R E N T O N
  A N D   O M S
M I S R E A D   R U P I A H S
I N O   R O U   R O U
A S C O   R A P S E   I M I D
S T O U   O P T H A   R E S S
M A R L O W E   D U R A N T E
A L R O K E R   I R O N I E S
  L O N E L Y   E N D E A R
```

71

```
S C O T   A C E R   S P I E D
C H A I   L O W E   M A C E D
H I T B E L O W T H E B E L T
U M B E R       A A A S
S P A R R I N G P A R T N E R
S S R   D O L E S     A N O
  E R I T U   A N N U L
T H E G L O V E S A R E O F F
H A N G S     P A N S Y
A T T   K I O S K   T M C
T H R O W I N T H E T O W E L
  L O L L     E N O L A
P U L L O N E S P U N C H E S
A V O I D   T H U G   U I E S
C A G E Y   S E T H   E T S Y
```

72

```
F E T A   S P R I G S   C H A I
A A R P   T O E T A P   R O D S
U T E P   A N G O R A   O R A L
N I A L O N G   B R O W N I E
A T T E N D     E L D E R S
  J O U R N E Y M A N
M E G A   P E E W E E   O T I S
E X E C S   S T O W   P I A N O
L A N K A   T S K S   A S K U P
  M E S S Y     G R E E K
E T A   H O N E Y B E E   A T L
B A L T   D I R E L Y   O K I E
O B O E   U N I T A S   A N T E
O L G A   D E C I D E   F E U D
K E Y S   E R A S E R   S E T S
```

73

```
SNOB  RIPS  RACED
ABEL  ORGY  ELATE
CARIBBEAN  CORAL
  NEON  CHINA
ADRIATIC  UPENN
LEE  NICOISE  TIP
BALTIC  ICK  WEAR
ILENE  GNU  TINGE
NEAT  LAO  REINAS
ORS  CASPIAN  ARE
  SENOR  SNIPESAT
  DIODE  EMIT
BLACK  SEVENSEAS
LATHE  OMEN  EDNA
TWEED  SORT  QUAY
```

74

```
OCULAR  ETA  SAP
SONORA  YURT  ILE
TRICEP  ERGO  LGA
ROCKSTHEBOWTIE
INOUT  AXIS  ICBM
CARP  BRAN  AMORE
HEN  GIMMEASINAI
  ARK  LTD
THEGOODWIFI  CPA
MAMAS  RARA  SHAM
CLIP  EIRE  LAILA
 FREEVERSAILLES
TWA  SIDE  STILTS
EAT  STUN  SENATE
AYE  EPS  TREXES
```

75

```
BFF  GASCAP  LIMB
ELI  IDEALS  ARIA
LONGFORNIA  BANK
LEER  RID  TOQUE
  PINEFORCHRIS
 SOLES  IOU
PHILS  POOL  GRAB
JONESFORJANUARY
SOTS  IKEA  AMIGA
  ODE  IAMSO
 YENFORDONNIE
TAROT  EPA  EAST
OHIO  HOPEFORBOB
MOCK  ULTRON  EFS
BOAS  HASAGO  TAP
```

76

```
IT COUPLE  GATEWAY
SUBTLER  ONELOVE
ARIZONA [COLD] SHOWER
JAW  DISS  EEN
ORAL  NETTLE  COD
BENIN  DAY  SMOKE
  BE [COOL] TRE  AVIS
PLAYHIDEANDSEEK
LIMA  OAF  DOC
OMENS  MAG  NONPC
WON  ASPIRE  TARO
 [WARM] UP  RED [HOT] GOV
PARSNIP  TITRATE
AGITATE  ELEANOR
LEGOSET  LEANON [ME]
```

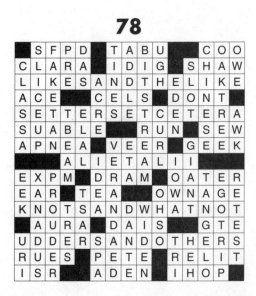

77

```
RAMADA  ATM  WHAM
EXITED  CATCHAIR
POMONA  COWLINGS
ONENIGHTSTAND
  EEO  FREED
PIPER  TMC  ORDER
WORKSOFART  ORE
ALOE  ROMEO  AVID
VAC  DOBEDOBEDO
ENEWS  TAP  PARES
 IDAHO  EAT
 USEDFURNITURE
TARHEELS  ICEBOX
SLAMPOET  TALESE
KALE  NWA  ALLRED
```

78

```
 SFPD  TABU  COO
CLARA  IDIG  SHAW
LIKESANDTHELIKE
ACE  CELS  DONT
SETTERSETCETERA
SUABLE  RUN  SEW
APNEA  VEER  GEEK
  ALIETALII
EXPM  DRAM  OATER
EAR  TEA  OWNAGE
KNOTSANDWHATNOT
 AURA  DAIS  GTE
UDDERSANDOTHERS
RUES  PETE  RELIT
ISR  ADEN  IHOP
```

79

```
O K R A ■ A T E ■ T H R E E S
S N O C O N E S ■ H E A V E N
L O V E C O N Q U E R S A L L
O W E ■ H I T ■ P O M P ■
■ ■ S O N S ■ O L E ■ E M O
■ D E A T H A N D T A X E S
■ D O W ■ S O X ■ S I X E R S
R E I N S ■ W E B ■ C I R C A
A L T O I D ■ L A B ■ O T S
T H U N D E R S T O R M S
S I P ■ E P I ■ G T O S ■
■ ■ A L L A ■ U T A ■ G P S
W A R T O E N D A L L W A R S
I M E A N T ■ O N E D O Z E N
N O O D G E ■ G O D ■ K E Y S
```

80

```
C C S ■ H E R B ■ S T A G E
H A I ■ E A V E ■ O C E L O T
O R G ■ I N S E R V I D A Y S
O W N E D ■ F I E F ■ N A Y
S A U C I S H ■ P R I M A ■
E X P O ■ E I N E ■ B E L A Y
■ ■ A U D I ■ N O I D E A
R E V E R S E C T I O N A R Y
G R A T I S ■ E I N K ■
S A L T S ■ F R E T ■ E P I C
■ H A T H A ■ S H A V E D E
E T A ■ O A T H ■ L E T I N
R O L L T H E D I C E ■ A D S
M A L A L A ■ T R O U ■ L I U
A D A G E ■ V E S T ■ S T S
```

81

```
■ F I S H ■ E T R E ■ P E R O T
B A N T U ■ L A O S ■ G R A P E
R I C E S ■ L Y F T D R I V E R
B L U E S T E E L ■ R A C E R S
■ S P A R ■ T A T ■ N A E
T O T ■ R E U P ■ I N I T
A T O M ■ K N I C K K N A C K S
S O D A S ■ S P A T ■ G R O A N
K E Y S T O N E K O P ■ P O L O
■ H A N A ■ E K E S ■ K E G
I D S ■ R A P ■ R E F I
N E P A L I ■ S W I P E L E F T
S W I P E R I G H T ■ K O J A K
E A R P S ■ I T I S ■ E R A T O
T R E S S ■ I S P Y ■ R A R E
```

82

```
B A R ■ O B A M A ■ R S V P
O L E G ■ A L I A S ■ I C E E
U P L 8 ■ H U N C H ■ P H E W
T H E F O U R T H E S T 8 ■
S A T U P ■ ■ P O L L S
■ P A T T I ■ P A R D O N
P A W ■ H 8 R S G O N N A H 8
I S H ■ S A L U T ■ Z A P
T A I L G 8 P A R T Y ■ E N S
A D R I A N ■ M U S I C ■
S A L E M ■ ■ P L O W S
■ P I E C E S O F E I G H T
X R 8 D ■ O N A D 8 ■ C R 8 R
F I L L ■ V I G I L ■ K E P I
L O S E ■ E D E N S ■ S I P
```

83

```
G R A M M Y ■ O N K P ■ K A T
R A D I O S ■ R O A R ■ O N O
A T O N A L ■ A T T E S T T O
B E G U N ■ P L A Y M O B I L
■ S E G A ■ I D I D ■
H I P S D O N T L I E ■ S K I
E S A I ■ P A W ■ D R A P E D
L E I G H ■ M O D ■ S U R L Y
P E R N O D ■ P E P ■ T E L L
S M S ■ T R O M P E L O E I L
■ A F A R ■ T R O T ■
A S Y O U W I S H ■ R U S S O
G O A N D S E E ■ B E N H U R
O A K ■ G I N A ■ O N E A L L
G P S ■ E N T S ■ B A D G U Y
```

84

```
■ B A S S ■ L S A T ■ R U N
W O R T H ■ A C L U ■ C A P E
H O M E R ■ T H E B O R D E R
O[MS] ■ M I N E R S ■ P O I N T
■ N E R O ■ M A S O N S
A N D R E W ■ D I A L S ■
W E R E ■ B R I A R S ■ F[EM]
L A O S ■ L I N G O ■ M A A M
T[OP] ■ G O O G O O ■ A S I A
■ I L O S E ■ N E T T L E
L E A N E D ■ R V E R ■
A L L E N ■ B S I D E S ■ T[WO]
S O M E S P A C E ■ C A R E W
I P A D ■ C L A W ■ T R U E S
K E Y ■ P I T S ■ S I G N
```

In each shaded space, the middle letter can alternatively go in the first square — creating 16 possible combinations of solutions to the puzzle.

85

```
VAPOR  GEAR  FOIL
AGAME  ANDY  LIME
CONGA ZO DEFENSE
   MIELE  BAKER
 SSE  GIANTS  STY
SWANSON  DATA
HOWOARTH  CARESS
ALEUT  OOH  TONKA
WEDGIE  TATUMOAL
  HAMA  MISACTS
PAT  TUNEIN  SHE
AGILE  INLET
CLAUDEMOT  WRENS
TORN  MAKO  ONEUP
SWAG  OLIN  SALTY
```

86

```
DEFACES  WEBSTER
OCANADA  AMILATE
NOTABIT  GIGOLOS
NRA   ETC   OWEN
APLUS   ESTATE
   SESSION  DRAW
 CLARET  OTB  ERA
STIFFS   LADIES
ARC  SAD  SELINA
CLEF  METHREE
   AMELIA  RUBIN
 ALDI  ORD   ESO
STAINED  PANGRAM
TOWNCAR  EMPORIA
LINGERS  INROADS
```

87

```
PECAN  HEAT  COBRA
ARUBA  ALTO  IDEAS
LETUP  TELE  TEENS
MAI  EYECANDY  FLU
EDEN  ASTRAY  SCAM
REPO  PORGIE  TAPE
 RICA  NOEL  ARKS
  EARP    ALOE
  STUDMUFFIN
BLAH  MEANER  GAGS
OAR  ANGELO  RAT
UTEP  STEALS  HIYA
GINUP  INTO  MIAMI
INTRO  STEW  INNER
EXILE  TANS  STARS
```

88

```
CANASTA  SPILLED
ABORTED  HEROINE
FORSALE  RAISEUP
 SOIL  GUTS  SRO
UPENN  BABYSHOES
RUM  SPARS  CONDE
GRAS  ITD  MAA
ERNESTHEMINGWAY
  ICY  NOD  YETI
ASANA  LEOIX  NIP
NEVERWORN  BUTTE
SRI  LAOS  TONS
WEASELS  SIXWORD
ENTITLE  KNEELER
REENTER  ITSDONE
```

89

```
USOPEN  IMIN  PEZ
MORALE  NERO  AMI
PLAYFULDEAD  NIP
EAT  TOOT  OUSTS
DREAMED  CAUSE
  CAREFULBEARS
DANTE  ATAT  RAH
ARES  OFTEN  AERO
FEW  DORA  ENDED
TASTEFULTEST
 FONSI  EXCELAT
GOLEM  THAI  ONA
AKA  AWFULSHUCKS
IRS  ROLE  TAMALE
NAH  KEYS  STALER
```

90

```
ICES  SHAPE  BBS
MAME  TUGON  CLAW
ASIA  AMOOD  TOME
CTRLCRIGHT  ROBE
  RED  BALLPIT
PENNED  REBOX
AVOID  HALLOWED
NARC  STORE  FETA
ENMESHED  CFLAT
 CRONY  EASTLA
DISTORT  STL
ODOR  TOOTHCTRLV
DILL  COBRA  WOOD
GOOF  UNION  OKRA
ETS  TEEMS  SUEY
```

91

```
RACE  CAPO   BRAG
PLUM  ROMANS REDO
MARMEEMARCH  IMHO
 LARVA TAUTENED
TESSA  FILCH  ARP
ICU  APRILKEPNER
COPAPLEA   TATS
  MELINDAMAY
 LEIA   IMISSYOU
JUNECLEAVER  UPS
INT  HORSE  MALIA
CARRYOUT  EAGLE
ABAT  SPRINGROLLS
MANE  ETALIA  NOEL
ARTS  SLED  EGGY
```

92

```
LESS  ERR  ORATOR
ALAN  YOU  PEARCE
WNBATEAM  ISSUES
FIERO  ROGUE  ELI
UNREPS  ROMANGOD
LOS  GUM  ASTARTE
  EURAIL   KISS
  INNERPLANET
OHNO  COINED
SOAKAGE  NYE  BBS
MUSICIAN  ADVERT
ODE  CLUES  TAHOE
SINGED  AUTOMAKE
INSIDE  RIO  OVAL
SIEGED  STY  SEWS
```

93

```
CLAY  ITEM  SWEDE
LOGO  CARA  WANED
AREYOUKIDDINGME
WIDOW  ENDUP  ION
  SLIT  FERN
REB  INHALF  VENI
ATLAST  MOE  IRES
WHOTHEHELLKNOWS
ENOS  NON  BOGOTA
RODE  TUSCAN  MOD
  SARI  AGIN
BAT  HOPON  CABLE
IHAVENTGOTACLUE
GEIST  ARLO  HILL
AMNOT  SEAN  OPUS
```

94

```
MAP  SNOOT  [NOTE]PADS
ORE  TORTE  LINES
ICE [BUCK]ETCHALLENGE
 OKAPI  ELAM
 ROTFL  HORN[BILL]
[SINGLE]TON  ELS  TRAM
ISAO  BRONZESTAR
NBC [CLAM]OR  AIL  AHA
TAKECREDIT  PLED
 ROTH  TIL  NEER
 SNOOP  MSDOS
 WRAP  ARTOO
FIVEDOLLARWORDS
ADORE  FELLA  ZOO
BOXER  ASSAY  ORB
```

95

```
GODARK   CLANCY
OBERON   DRUMPAD
BIERCE  BOOBIRDS
STRIKEFORCES
 BYLAWS  SHEEP
RAFA  BLEU  RYE
AHA  SPLITSCREEN
NINETEEN  IOTA
 MAYA  GUNNEDIT
SPARECHANGE  ECO
ARI  HOLD  BREW
COLAS  CLAIRE
 TURKEYBASTER
PULLAUEY  AVIATE
IMSAVED  REDTAG
PAUSED  SLEETS
```

96

```
UNO  LAURA  ASANA
MAP  ASSAD  REMIX
PUTONHOLD  TEACH
ITINA  PIN  ZOE
RIME  SCHNOZZOLA
ELI  PLO  STAINED
DISCOERA  SNL
 MADEACHOICE
 RIP  LIFEHACK
MYFAULT  TAR  TIE
ROADMARKER  MACY
TUT  BUN  LALAW
OLIVE  MORSECODE
AIMAT  PLUOT  NAS
DEANS  SLEDS  EST
```

97

```
N P R . S I N . . R A S P E D
A R I . T O O . C O N Q U E R
V I N C E N T . O C T U P L E
I M G U R . O L D . Z A P .
. E S T E . R E Y . . R E S T
. . L O U I E . S E E T H E
W I F E . S E R I A L . E U R
E D I T O U T . N U M B E R S
L A B . D R Y E S T . E R I E
S H O D D Y . V I E W S . .
H O N E . L E D . A T O P
. A F T . O N E . S I L O S
P U C C I N I . O T H E L L O
E N C O R E S . U S E . I L L
C O I N E D . . T A R . E Y E
```

98

```
R A C I S T . V I P . T B A R
A L L N E W . E M U . H O R A
S T A G E A C T O R . A J A R
P E S O . H O N E S T A B E .
. [RED] S T A T E . . B O S N .
. . S P E C S . [RED] D O G S .
C O G . B A K E S . A D L I B
U N O S . T E R P S . D E C O
[RED] M E A T . [RED] F L A G . S K Y
. E S T A S . S O S A D . .
. U S M C . . T H R U M S .
D O N T P A N I C . N A T E
A N D I . R I G H T O N R E D
R E E L . A N G . O P E N E D
K A R L . B A Y . W I D E L Y
```

99

```
N A Y . S A G G E D . . T L C
O N E . A D R A T E . T I E R
V I T A L O R G A N . O K A Y
A M I G A . A L A . K I D .
S E S A M E S . I D L E .
. V I D A L I A O N I O N
A M I E . G T O . A S T R O
V A N . V E E R O F F . Z A P
I H O P E . E L O . M A L E
V I N O R D I N A I R E . .
. M A R M . F L A T C A P
E P A . O P S . M O O L A
G R A D . V A C U U M O V E N
O G R E . E L A P S E . E R S
V O 5 . S E N S O R . S T Y
```

100

```
. G L A N D . I G O R . A W E D
Q U I N O A . S O N Y . R A G U
U P T O W N . S A L E M S L O T
I T E M . G A U D Y . C O L B Y
P A R A S I T E . C A N S O .
. . L A T H . E L A N . P O L
A T H O S . E F L A T . P A S A
T H E U S U A L S U S P E C T S
I R A S . P R E E N . I D E S T
T E D . R O T E . D A L I .
. E G G O N . T R U E G R I T
P S A L M . M E R Y L . R A M A
H O M E A L O N E . A R E N A S
A M E N . A N D Y . I C E A G E
T E S S . B O S S . T A S T E
```

101

```
. B I G B A N G . T R E A D S
S A F E A R E A . H E A L U P
P A S T O N E S B E D T I M E
A S O F . D P L U S . B B L
. A G E . T S E L I O T
W H E R E A M I . A A A .
O U T . A V E D A . M O B S
N E T P R E S E N T V A L U E
T S A R . H A N O I . D N A
. E T C . S E S A M E S T
P E N Z I A S . S L O
A L A . T R A W L . P C B S
B A C K T O T H E F U T U R E
S T R O L L . E A R L O B E S
T E E P E E . W H I M P E R
```

102

```
E N I D . M O I S T . A W L S
L I F E . A L I C E . L I O N
M A Y A . I D I O T . E L L A
E P O N Y M S . R E G U L A R
R E U S E . A S S . S T I F F
S E C . S I X F E E T . A A S
. P A P . C O P S E . S M L
A L T A . U N D E R . C H A T
D E C R Y . . . F I O N A
A S H T R E E . S P Y S W A P
. M I S T Y . E L I S A .
B R Y N . S E A M Y . O R Z O
S E D G E . S C I . O R D E R
A A R G H . L E S . A L T A R
. R I I S . E S O . R I A L .
```

FT FT   FT   FT   FT FT

103

```
A F R O . P A L A U . O G R E
L A I T . H B O M B . C R A G
B U S I N E S S M E E T I N G
U N I S O N . T O R M E N T S
M A N . R O D . . N E T . . .
. . G Y M M E M B E R S H I P
B A S E S . F E R R Y . A D O
R I T A . S O L I D . O I L S
A D A . P A R E D . I N L E T
G E R M A N M E A S L E S . .
. . E S T . . L E I . A V A
I G L E S I A S . C A S T E R
S E E M E A F T E R C L A S S
I N G A . G A U G E . E X P O
S T O W . O R N O T . D I A N
```

104

```
S P A S . A G O . . C R E S S
T A M P . T A C T . H O N K S
U R B A N M Y T H . A D D I N
P A L M E . . A R M R E S T .
O D E . W O R D O F M O U T H
R E D T A P E . W A S . P I E
. . . A G E N T . . G A S X
. M O M E N T O F T R U T H .
A C H E . . W I R E S . .
L E I . M I A . J O S H I N G
I N G O O D F A I T H . N O N
. T E N U O U S . . O M A H A
C I T E S . S Y L V E S T E R
A R I A S . S E G A . R I L L
L E T M E . . T A T . P E P S
```

105

```
H E A D . B I R T H . G E M .
E A S T . E V E R Y . E R I C
A S P S . L I N U S . T O S H
R Y E . G L E E . T I S S U E
T O R C H E S . F E N . I S R
H U S H E S . B A R K . O E R
. T E E N . S E T I . A N D Y
. . S T O N E W A L L . .
C R A T . P I T A . L A S T
O A S . R E D S . H O M E E C
R N C . O N E . Y E S O R N O
N A R I T A . O K R A . R U B
E M I T . T O N N E . B A R B
R O B S . A R T O O . O N E L
. K E Y . B R O W N . L O D E
```

106

```
A(DD) S . A C A . C A B . B(OO) T
N(AA) N . L O B . E C O S A(VV) Y
O T T O M A N S . L I T E B(EE) R
D(EE) R E . J A D E D . T E(RR) A
E(SS) E N E . L O S S E S .
. T A P O U T . P I N T A
A Y C A R A M B A . S N A R F
R E A L L Y . L S D . G A L
G A P . A L E . O A X A C A
U S E M E . I D I O M A T I C
S T R A Y . C O M M O N .
. R E S E W S . S A L(AA) M
A(TT) I C . O N N O W . D O(GG) O
A(RR) A I G N S . R E F U G(EE) S
R(EE) M E R G E . R N A . I(NN) S
P(EE) S . U S D . Y T D . A(TT) Y
```

107

```
C A M S . G A S U P . V A P E
A D A M . A R O S E . E L O N
R I C O . T I R E D B L O O D
B A C K S E A T D R I V E R .
. . H E P . . . O L E . .
I R I D E S C E S . B E B O P
L O A . C O U C H P O T A T O
O U T S . A R I E L . A R T S
S T O O L P I G E O N . B E E
T E S L A . E S P Y A W A R D
. . E T C . . . S I R . .
. A R M C H A I R E X P E R T
L I O N H U N T E R . E L I E
I D O L . G A M E R . U L N A
L A D Y . S L E D S . P A D S
```

108

```
H T T P S . K A R T . S A C K
I H A D N O I D E A . A L L E
R E N A I S S A N C E F O U R
E S T . P I S M O . A F T E R
D E A R E R . . A C R . .
. M U S I C A L C H O R E S
S O O N . S A L U T . N U D E
T H U . . R A G . . . B I T
A I N T . J A M E S . A B E S
N O T I M E T O S P O R E .
. . E A T . . A N T R U M
S P R A Y . A W A R E . T S A
T H E B A D N E W S B O R E S
D I D O . N O N R E A D E R S
S L O W . A N D Y . G E E S E
```

109

B	R	A	S	■	P	S	Y	C	H	O	■	A	B	B	A
L	A	M	E	■	U	T	E	R	U	S	■	T	R	I	M
A	P	E	X	■	M	Y	R	I	G	H	T	F	O	O	T
N	A	N	■	D	A	M	■	T	H	E	E	■	N	P	R
K	N	I	V	E	S	I	N	■	■	A	C	A	C	I	A
C	U	T	I	E	■	E	U	R	O	■	S	T	O	C	K
D	I	Y	E	R	S	■	T	I	N	A	■	A	S	S	■
■	■	W	E	S	T	O	F	E	D	E	N	■	■	■	■
■	S	K	I	■	N	E	I	L	■	D	R	E	V	I	L
C	H	I	N	A	■	A	L	E	S	■	U	N	I	T	E
H	A	N	G	U	L	■	■	S	T	E	P	D	O	W	N
I	K	E	■	D	U	M	B	■	B	L	T	■	L	O	G
M	I	S	D	I	R	E	C	T	E	D	■	B	E	R	T
P	R	I	M	■	E	N	C	O	D	E	■	A	N	K	H
S	A	S	S	■	D	U	S	T	E	R	■	E	T	S	Y

110

F	R	O	G	■	D	A	M	■	G	I	S	H
I	O	W	A	■	S	I	S	A	L	■	O	S	S	O
S	T	E	M	■	M	A	P	L	E	■	L	E	N	O
H	I	D	E	O	U	S	■	L	A	P	D	E	S	K
■	C	A	T	P	E	O	P	L	E	■
L	A	B	O	R	■	O	R	R	■	I	N	S	T	A
I	S	B	N	S	■	R	I	C	■	E	S	T	E	S
S	P	A	(S)	■	M	A	C	A	U	■	(P)	A	P	A
P	(E)	L	O	S	I	■	P	A	I	R	(E)	D
S	N	(L)	■	A	L	A	S	K	A	N	■	(K)	E	A
■	I	N	K	S	T	A	N	D	S	■
P	E	R	M	■	S	T	Y	L	I	■	T	S	A	R
A	R	A	P	A	H	(O)	■	(E)	S	Q	U	I	R	E
C	A	M	(E)	R	A	■	(H)	U	D	S	O	N
S	T	A	L	(K)	■	(A)	S	I	D	E

111

V	A	M	P	S	■	T	O	O	■	A	F	R	O
I	D	I	O	T	■	R	U	M	I	■	S	(L)	A	W
R	A	C	E	R	■	U	T	A	H	S	T	(A)	T	E
U	G	H	■	O	P	S	■	N	A	T	I	V	(E)
S	E	A	G	L	A	S	S	■	V	I	N	(O)
■	(E)	E	L	S	■	H	E	E	(L)	■	R	O	B
U	N	L	(E)	S	S	■	A	R	N	E	■	O	N	O
R	O	C	K	■	T	Y	P	E	(O)	■	R	F	I	D
N	O	(R)	■	S	H	O	E	■	(C)	H	A	T	T	Y
S	K	(I)	■	M	(E)	N	U	■	L	U	S	H
(C)	R	I	B	■	P	L	U	M	P	E	S	T
■	S	H	U	T	(U)	P	■	O	E	D	■	W	O	E
H	O	T	S	E	(C)	O	N	D	■	R	E	E	F	S
A	L	O	E	■	K	N	E	E	■	U	S	E	I	T
D	E	N	S	■	Y	E	S	■	M	C	K	A	Y

112

P	I	E	T	A	■	I	N	F	O	■	D	A	M	P
I	D	L	E	D	■	M	O	O	N	R	I	V	E	R
N	O	M	A	D	■	P	E	R	S	E	V	E	R	E
[HEAD]	S	O	R	T	A	I	L	S	■	D	I	C	E	Y
■	O	O	P	S	■	A	V	O	N	■
G	A	T	O	■	S	H	A	K	I	N	G	M	Y	[HEAD]
O	R	O	M	E	O	■	L	E	V	I	■	C	O	W
T	A	N	S	Y	■	B	I	N	■	O	N	C	U	E
A	B	O	■	E	M	I	T	■	S	N	O	O	D	S
[HEAD]	S	W	I	L	L	R	O	L	L	■	T	O	O	T
■	N	I	K	I	■	A	A	A	S	■
A	S	W	A	N	■	Y	O	U	B	L	O	C	K	[HEAD]
S	T	A	G	E	H	A	N	D	■	O	B	O	E	S
T	O	L	E	R	A	N	C	E	■	H	A	L	L	E
O	P	T	S	■	T	I	E	D	■	A	D	A	P	T

113

S	C	R	I	P	T	■	H	A	B	I	T	A	T
T	H	E	S	O	U	P	■	I	S	O	M	E	R	S
E	I	G	H	T	B	I	T	■	S	I	X	P	A	C	K
W	A	R	M	■	E	G	O	S	■	D	I	A	L	■
S	N	E	A	K	S	■	S	E	V	E	N	S	E	A	S
■	G	W	E	N	■	I	S	L	E	■	S	O	L	O
■	L	I	E	N	■	I	N	N	U	E	N	D	O
S	H	E	■	F	I	V	E	G	U	Y	S	■	I	O	N
P	U	N	T	E	D	O	N	■	E	M	T	S	■
A	N	E	W	■	K	I	S	S	■	O	H	M	S
T	H	R	E	E	P	E	A	T	■	J	O	Y	O	U	S
■	V	E	V	O	■	C	U	T	E	■	A	R	I	A
O	C	A	N	A	D	A	■	N	I	N	E	W	E	S	T
H	A	T	E	D	I	T	■	E	N	M	A	S	S	E
O	V	E	R	E	A	T	■	Y	O	Y	O	E	D

114

S	T	A	T	S	■	G	P	S	■	H	A	R	M
O	W	L	E	T	■	R	E	E	F	■	O	R	E	O
S	O	L	A	R	P	A	N	E	L	■	W	O	N	T
■	M	E	A	N	D	M	Y	M	O	U	T	H
N	O	S	■	G	I	T	S	■	R	I	N	S	E	S
E	A	T	S	I	N	■	N	O	N	E	E	D
W	H	A	T	S	T	H	E	I	D	E	A
T	U	B	A	■	O	W	N	■	R	B	I	S
■	Y	O	U	O	W	E	M	E	T	I	M	E
■	A	B	O	U	N	D	■	E	T	H	A	N	E
S	T	E	N	T	S	■	H	O	R	A	■	S	O	D
T	H	A	T	S	A	V	E	R	Y	I	F
R	O	M	A	■	I	L	L	A	L	L	O	W	I	T
A	M	E	S	■	D	O	L	L	■	E	C	O	L	I
P	E	R	K	■	G	O	B	■	R	I	N	K	S

115

```
T A D A   O H M     B R E R
S L O P   B E A U   R A V E L
A P O P   S A D R   O M E G A
      R E F   T A K E S A N A P
D E B A R     M E L     S I S
U S E L E S S   L E G B O N E
G A L     E C T O   C R O
  S L O W A N D S T E A D Y
    R A P   D O R M   I O C
O H D R Y U P   P A L O O K A
N B A     L A G   I N N E R
L O S E S A B E T     N A Y
S N A G S     S T E P   P S A S
D O N O T   T A C O   A I R E
  W I N S     T H E   R A C E
```

116

```
B O O B O O     B I O S     O R B
E N F O L D     O B I E     V E E
A L A M O D E   W E L L W E L L
C O I N S       T I A R I A
O A K     A N N S     E A G L E
N N E   L E O T A R D     O V A
      S T A T U S     E R R E D
T H A I   R A D I O     A D D S
W O R T H     T E A B A G
A T E     A V E N G E R   W O W
  P A U L A     T O R T   O U R
M A M M I A         S O L T I
I N A P A N I C   Y O G A T
S T P   S E R A   E N L A C E
S S S     T R E Y   A G E N T S
```

117

```
O F F S     R A V E S     S I P
C A R T E   E T A I L     E S L
C R Y I N G W O L F E     A A A
A G E N D A   L I F E B O A T
M O R K   W I L D E P I T C H
      E L K S     L S A T
W H E R E E L S E     S E G A
H E X   E R E A D E R   R E D
O N T O     Y O G A P O S E S
    R I P S     E R M A
T O O L E C H E S T   K A R A
U S V S T H E M   H O L D I T
T H E   P E A C H Y K E E N E
O E R   I M P E I   S A L S A
R A T   G A S E S     F E E T
```

118

```
Y U M Y U M     I M T O O     T I P
C O C O A   C A R O B     R I C A
C O K E S   B L A M E   I D O L
A R F   T I M E S P I C A Y U N E
    A F R O   L H A S A A P S O
L A C R O S S E   H A M
A L T O     N A S   N E S T L E
Y U K O N G O L D P O T A T O E S
P A R D O N   S E W     A M O S
    P A L   E N E R G Y U S E
O T H E R H A N D   S E E M
W H Y Y O U L I T T L E   S K A
L O D E   N A C R E   D R O I D
E R R S   C L E A N   Y O U T H
T A O   H A R P S     O P E D
```

119

```
K O B E     A M I S H     D O D O
G R I Z Z L E D V E T E R A N
B A R R E L H O U S E J A Z Z
  N C A A         R E T E E
U G H   L A P A Z   A C E D
N E B   S M O G   S O T
P L A T   I K E   W H I M S
C O R R O D E   R A M O N E S
  S K I N S   C O T   N E A T
    P V T   O A H U   M B A
  D A L I   Z O N E S   O R B
B O N E D         U T N E
O Z Z I E A N D H A R R I E T
N E A P O L I T A N P I Z Z A
O R C A   P A S T Y   P E E P
```

120

```
R A T   O P E N   W I D G E T
E R E   T R U E   E N R A G E
H I P S T E R S   I C E B O X
H I P P O P O T A M U S E S
A S I A     S C A B S
B E D T I M E   C R U S A D E
    C O X A E   S I L E X
P A R T Y W H I P S   Z E S T
I D E A   S H I P W R E C K S
K H A K I   A R T I E
A D R E N A L   S M A S H E D
    S A G E T     P O L O
  J O I N E D A T T H E H I P
D E A D E N   P I T A C H I P
D E T E S T   E D Y S   U T E
T R Y S T S   D E L T   M E D
```

121

B	F	F	S		P	E	P	S	I		S	U	M	P
O	R	E	O		A	V	I	L	A		E	P	E	E
P	E	T	U	N	I	A	P	I	G		A	T	R	A
S	E	A	S	O	N		P	O	L	L	O	C	K	
		E	V	E	R	S	O		I	P	A			
D	O	T	S		O	W	N		S	U	P	E	R	
I	R	E		A	C	T	A		O	P	P	O	S	E
S	I	N		D	R	I	B	B	L	E		I	T	E
C	O	N	R	O	Y		B	O	A	R		N	E	D
O	N	I	O	N		O	I	L		I	T	R	Y	
		S	C	I		R	E	D	B	U	D			
J	A	C	K	S	O	N		A	R	I	O	S	O	
E	V	A	C		P	A	D	D	I	N	G	T	O	N
L	I	M	O		A	T	E	I	T		I	T	A	L
L	A	P	D		L	E	A	P	S		T	O	R	Y

122

U	S	S	R		P	O	S	T		W	H	I	Z	
H	U	T	U		O	N	T	O		H	Y	D	E	
S	E	R	B		G	E	R	I		A	P	E	D	
	D	I	S	P	O	S	A	L	A	R	E	A		
	P	R	E	S	I	D	E	N	T	S				
	A	T	T	E	S	T	T	O						
W	E	I	W	E	I		R	E	N	T	E	D		
O	A	R		C	I	T	I		O	L	E			
E	R	O	S		K	N	E	E		N	U	M	B	
	N	E	W	S	C	A	S	T	E	R				
O	S	C	A	R			A	I	D	E	S			
F	I	L	L	I	N	T	H	E	B	L	A	N	K	
U	M	A		S	E	R	I	A	L		T	O	E	
S	O	D		T	W	E	L	V	E		E	K	E	
E	N	S		S	T	Y	L	E	D		S	I	T	

123

N	A	T	O		A	S	P	I	R	E		B	A	T
A	N	O	N		C	L	O	S	E	T		A	P	E
M	O	N	S	T	E	R	M	A	S	H		R	T	E
	M	E	A	D			B	E	I	G	N	E	T	
W	A	L	L	S	T	R	E	E	T	C	R	A	S	H
A	L	O	E		W	I	L	L	S		A	R	T	E
N	Y	C		F	I	F	E		O	D	D	S		
			C	O	N	T	A	C	T	U	S			
	T	B	A	R		N	A	I	R		B	E	E	
P	H	A	T		G	R	O	P	E		A	I	M	S
R	U	S	H	H	O	U	R	T	R	A	F	F	I	C
O	N	M	Y	O	W	N		I	R	O	N			
A	D	A		F	I	L	M	S	P	L	I	C	E	R
M	E	T		F	L	O	T	U	S		C	A	N	I
S	R	I		A	D	W	A	R	S		A	L	T	O

124

M	E	G	A		H	I	M	O	M		O	T	I	S
A	L	E	S		O	P	E	R	A		T	R	A	P
O	F	T	H	E	W	O	R	L	D		S	E	G	A
	A	B	E	L		M	E	D	I		B	R	R	
A	P	R	I	L		B	A	A		S	K	E	E	T
L	I	O	N		D	R	I	N	K	L	I	K	E	A
E	S	O		B	R	A	D	S	H	A	W			
C	A	M	E	R	A			A	N	I	M	A	L	
		W	E	N	T	C	O	L	D		A	X	E	
H	O	L	E	C	O	V	E	R	S		O	M	I	T
A	P	I	S	H		G	N	C		G	L	A	S	S
R	E	N		T	O	U	T		I	M	D	B		
I	N	K	Y		B	E	A	T	S	A	D	E	A	D
B	E	T	A		I	S	U	Z	U		O	A	H	U
O	D	O	R		S	T	R	E	P		G	R	I	D

125

M	I	D									M	O	I	
A	G	A		A	L	C	O	P	O	P		A	I	R
T	O	T		V	E	R	M	O	N	T		M	L	K
S	T	A	R	E	D	I	N	T	O	S	P	A	C	E
U	C	L	A		M	I	A		I	B	I	D		
	H	O	M	B	R	E		T	A	B	L	E	T	
	A	S	S	E	E	N		O	D	E	L	A	Y	
	S	E	R	V	O		S	W	E	A	R			
	S	T	E	V	E	K	E	R	R					
	R	E	T	I	E									
	H	A	D	A	B	L	A	N	K	L	O	O	K	
T	I	G	E	R			B	U	R	R	O			
S	H	O	W	E	D	N	O	E	M	O	T	I	O	N
P	A	R	E		V	O	L	V	O		R	E	N	T
S	T	A	Y		D	W	E	E	B		E	L	E	V

126

H	O	H	O		D	E	L	T		R	A	C	E	D
E	P	I	C		A	Q	U	A		E	B	O	N	Y
H	U	G	H		F	U	N	N	Y	N	E	R	V	E
	S	H	O	O	T	I	N	G	M	E	T	E	O	R
	H	A	R			E	C	G		S	Y	S		
O	N	E		B	U	D		N	A	A	N			
R	E	E	F		R	I	O	T		D	E	A	L	T
C	A	L	L	S	I	T	L	I	K	E	I	T	I	S
A	T	S	E	A		T	E	A	M		L	A	M	P
	A	L	L	O		L	S	D		G	A	S		
A	C	T		V	I	M		I	L	L				
K	O	A	L	A	M	A	R	S	U	P	I	A	L	
E	C	U	A	D	O	R	H	A	T		C	N	E	T
R	O	N	D	O		K	E	K	E		I	C	O	N
S	A	T	Y	R		S	A	S	S		T	E	S	T

127

P	A	R	M			E	G	A	D			O	B	O	E
O	R	E	O		S	A	R	G	E			F	L	U	S
P	I	N	T	H	E	T	A	I	L			F	A	T	S
		H	O	E		P	L	U	M		N	S	A		
F	E	B		O	N	T	H	E	D	O	N	K	E	Y	
W	H	A	T	F	O	R			E	R	E	C	T	S	
D	O	D	O		T	E	E			P	G	A			
	W	H	I	T	E	E	L	E	P	H	A	N	T		
	A	L	A		F	D	A		T	V	A	D			
O	R	I	E	N	T			A	P	P	E	A	S	E	
P	A	R	T	Y	A	N	I	M	A	L		S	K	I	
I	T	D		A	T	O	N		Y	U	K				
N	E	A	T		T	H	O	M	A	S	N	A	S	T	
E	D	Y	S		L	O	N	G	S		O	H	N	O	
D	E	S	K		E	W	E	S		T	A	L	E		

128

E	C	I	G		L	O	G	A	N		D	R	U	M
Y	U	M	A		C	R	OAT	I	A		N	I	N	A
E	T	A	L		D	E	E	D	S		C	O	D	Y
	T	R	O	D		C	E	A	S	E		L	E	B
T	H	E	R	O	C	K			A	L	G	O	R	E
O	R	T	E	G	A		H	O	U	S	E	B	OAT	S
M	OAT	S		I	R	R	E	G		N	O	H	O	
		C	E	R	E	A	L	B	O	X				
A	L	F	A		A	T	E	A	M		B	U	M	
C	OAT	O	F	A	R	M	S		R	I	A	L	T	O
T	H	R	E	S	H		F	I	T	T	OAT	E	E	
E	S	T		K	Y	O	T	O		S	O	W	N	
D	O	U	G		T	H	E	G	OAT		N	A	S	A
U	M	N	O		H	I	R	E	E		C	R	I	B
P	E	E	T		M	O	I	L	S		E	E	L	S

129

H	E	R	D	S		I	S	B	N		A	B	L	E
O	X	E	Y	E		N	E	R	F		S	L	O	W
M	A	S	S	A	P	P	E	A	L		C	U	R	E
E	M	I	T		I	A	M	S		H	E	E	D	S
	S	N	O	R	E	R		T	E	E	N	S		
		P	I	T	T	E	R	P	A	T	T	E	R	
M	O	D	I	F	Y		S	A	I	D		A	G	E
A	N	N	A	L		A	S	P		H	I	T	O	N
Y	E	A		E	L	L	A		R	U	D	E	S	T
A	S	S	E	M	B	L	Y	L	I	N	E			
	A	V	A	S	T		I	D	T	A	G	S		
R	A	M	E	N		H	I	K	E		L	O	U	T
E	S	P	N		F	E	V	E	R	P	I	T	C	H
V	A	L	E		E	R	A	S		A	Z	U	R	E
S	P	E	D		Z	E	N	O		T	E	P	E	E

130

C	O	S	M	O		J	A	G		N	O	R	W	A	Y
A	S	C	A	P		A	T	E		I	N	W	A	R	D
S	C	A	L	E		M	H	O		C	O	A	S	T	S
S	U	R	I	N	A	M	E		H	O	R	N			
I	L	E		S	T	E	N	C	I	L		D	C	O	N
N	A	T	S		T	R	A	I	N		M	A	A	C	O
I	R	A	I	S	E		A	D	U	E		N	T	H	
	C	R	O	S	S	C	O	U	N	T	R	Y			
O	F	T		O	T	T	O		T	H	R	O	E	S	
A	L	I	S	T		A	L	I	B	I		R	U	L	Y
F	A	C	T		T	H	E	B	E	E	B		D	E	N
	I	D	O	L		M	A	D	E	T	I	M	E		
M	A	R	G	I	N		A	P	T		N	I	G	E	R
O	N	E	M	E	G		S	C	I		I	D	I	N	G
P	A	N	A	M	A		P	S	T		N	E	T	T	Y

131

A	S	H		A	B	S		B	U	M	D	E	A	L
S	I	A		N	Y	U		E	S	S	E	N	C	E
A	P	B		D	O	N	T	Y	O	U	F	R	E	T
H	O	A	G	Y		R	H	O				I	D	S
I	N	N	I	E		I	A	N		F	A	Q		
	E	F	T		S	T	D		E	L	U	D	E	
E	A	R	T	H		E	S	O		B	L	E	A	T
S	C	O	R	E		M	A	N		F	I	N	S	
P	A	P	E	R		O	B	E		Z	I	G	G	Y
N	I	E	C	E		V	I	S		A	X	L		
	P	E	W		E	G	G		N	E	E	D	S	
A	S	P	I	E		M	I	R		I	D	S	A	Y
T	H	E	P	A	L	E	F	A	C	E		I	N	K
A	I	R	T	R	A	N		S	O	S		A	D	E
B	A	S	S	E	T	T		P	O	T		S	Y	S

132

A	D	D	E	D		O	D	D		S	A	M	P	L	E
D	R	O	N	E		L	I	E		O	B	E	R	O	N
Z	E	N	G	A	R	D	E	N		W	I	D	E	S	T
	A	K	A		A	S	T	I	N		D	I	N	E	R
I	M	I	G	H	T		P	R	O	S	E	C	U	T	E
C	O	N	E	Y		F	I	O	N	A		I	P	O	
E	N	G		A	W	O	L		G	I	N	S			
	S	T	A	B	L	E	M	A	T	E					
J	O	T	S		V	I	N	G		S	R	O			
Y	E	R		T	P	A	I	N		U	P	T	O	N	
W	E	A	T	H	E	R	E	D		A	Y	E	A	Y	E
H	O	N	D	A		O	N	E	A	L		T	S	A	
I	M	L	A	T	E		E	N	D	L	E	S	S	L	Y
N	E	U	T	E	R		A	C	E		S	P	E	W	S
E	N	C	A	S	E		S	E	N		P	A	N	E	L

133

```
. L H A S A . S U M O . F E Z
M A I S E L . O P A L . A L E
O N T H E D O U B L E . T A R
W A T T . A N T E . . C A T O
. . H O B . S H A K E A L E G
G R E N A D E . T I M E . . .
R I G . R I T A . G E N I E S
I P A . B E S T M A N . M R I
T E S L A S . M E L D . W I N
. . I R E S . T I E T A C K
L O O K A L I V E . D O I .
A C H E . . L I O N . O T I S
Y E A . G E T C R A C K I N G
E A R . A G U E . S P I N E T
R N A . P O P S . H A N G S .
```

134

```
C L A D . . T I M . P R O A M
H I L O . S I N E . R A N D O
I N C H . L E A D G U I T A R
N E O . Y O U L I E D T O M E
O N W H A T P L A N E T . . .
. . L O L S . B I N . S E T
K R I L L . S O L E T I T G O
I O N S . D I N O S . L O G O
W A G T H E D O G . M A R O N
I D S . E S E . O O N A .
. . C L O S E U P M A G I C
A P R I L T H E S E S . E W E
B E E R C O O L E R . A F A R
U T I C A . W E R E . W E N T
T E N E T . S R S . W E T S
```

135

```
C O M E Q U I C K . A C C R A
O V E R U N D E R . S H O A L
P A R S I M O N Y . Y O U N G
T L C . T E N T P O L I N G .
O S H A . M T E T N A . T E T
. . L E B A R O N . R E L O
L I S T L E S S . A B A D A N
O N A L A R K . B R E W I N G
G A M I N S . H A C I E N D A
I M E T . H A I L I N G .
C O T . F I N A L S . G A D S
. M O N O P O L I S T . P E T
M E Y E R . D E S I R A B L E
S N O R T . E A T S A L I V E
S T U D Y . S H A M P O O E D
```

136

```
D A T A B R E A C H . S K E W
E X T R A E X T R A . H A V E
M E Y E R L E M O N . O M A N
I L L O G I C . P E R C E N T
. . L E T U S . S I K H .
G O N A D . T O W . D E A L S
R U B E . P A R A N O R M A L
E T A . D E B R I E F . E S E
A I R Q U A L I T Y . P H E W
T E E U P . E E L . T E A R S
. . F I R S . R I S E R .
T H E B E A N . S C R E W I T
V E R B . W I N T E R T I M E
P E E L . A L I E N A T I O N
G L E E . S E T D E S I G N S
```

137

```
. B U R G L A R . C H A D
R U N A R A C E . T R A L A
I T S M A G I C . C O E D I T
S T A B B E D . G A U T A M A
K E V L A R . S O P R A N O S
. D E E S . E L I E . N I N E
. . D O E S L U N C H . N Y T
. . N A H I M G O O D .
R E A . T A X D O D G E S .
A C M E . D I O N . H A N S
T H U N B E R G . S E D A T E
P E S T E R S . S T A N C E S
A L E R T S . S L O V A K I A
C O M E S . F I L E M E N U
K N E E . O P E N E R S .
```

138

```
. M O H I C A N S . A L S O
. L E G O M O V I E . T U T U
W A L L T O W A L L . T S A R
R I T E S . T E A C H I N S
I D I D . B R A S S H A T .
S S N . T O U R . S I T A R S
T I G . R A G . B I C . N E A
P E P P E R . S T E A D I E S
A G O R A . P E W . G O A L S
D E T A C H E S . E O N .
. . G L I T T E R B O M B S
S T R E E T . I N R E T U R N
L I O N S M A N E . A E R I E
I R O C . E D A M . R A S T A
D E F Y . N O S Y . S T E A K
```

139

AMTS · AJAR · NCAA
COEN · MEGACHURCH
LMAO · ATAPREMIUM
· BRONZERPALETTE
OLDPRO · · EMPTIED
KOREANWAR · SAC
IGOR · PAL · TIL
ESP · GAYPORN · TMI
· FOY · HAO · OVEN
· ART · PARLORCAR
IMPASSE · LIBATE
WENTOUTONALIMB
ICEBREAKER · TEAM
SHAREDROOM · ERGO
HALO · · DKNY · RASP

140

BETENOIRE · EPSON
ICELANDER · NACRE
BOXBRAIDS · CRUDE
INTERIOR · HOTBED
· ARMOREDCARS
SPLAT · SCALE
ELOPED · KIM · HAIL
LEAPDAY · LEMONDE
LADS · TUG · TURTLE
· FILET · LASER
IMAGINETHAT
MAKING · SEMIPROS
AFIRE · MONOPLANE
MINOR · AMBULANCE
SASSY · REARENDED

141

BARON · MARIGOLD
UTERO · GREATSOUL
SEVEN · MNEMOSYNE
KAISER · LBS · AGA
ESE · WUSSES · CLAN
REWATCHED · THIRD
· CAKED · AHISEE
CHICXULUBCRATER
HEROES · COTES
ALOSS · MEDIAMAIL
LINT · RODENT · NNE
UPS · OOH · GENEVA
PAINTBALL · NOMAD
ADDITIVES · ELIDE
· SETONEND · DICER

142

KEG · ELDEST · LOST
ITO · LANDHO · ONTO
WAYNEMANOR · NCIS
ISAAC · AVENGERS
· ITS · ERAT
MADRONA · LORETTA
ATE · RADARSCREEN
CRAPSGAME · MATT
RIDE · MBAS · MRI
OASES · IDOS · MIC
· IKEA · GYMCLASS
SOLARCAR · MIGS
THEBATCAVE · BCCS
ANNO · ELMER · TOGA
TOTO · DUSTS · QTIP

143

SESAMES · DOSAGE
ONLYONCE · RAISON
GREENTAX · ASLANT
LAD · DORISMILLER
AGGIE · TEAS · WPA
DEEM · OBIES · CAAN
· SEDANS · TRYST
COULDNTRESIST
SOURS · DEEPEN
ERTE · CARDS · GMOS
ANY · SHIV · MEANT
CHECKEDINTO · MRI
ROLLIE · ECONOMIC
ALLIES · WINERACK
BESORE · SETTLES

144

AHAMOMENTS · PLED
TOMATOSOUP · AERO
IMPROBABLE · PTAS
LILIES · ACCESS
TEEN · TANKARD
· FORCE · THING
ROCKIDOL · SEAGAL
INHERIT · MARTINI
TEIGEN · WINESNOB
AGASP · SOLED
· STIPEND · TSPS
· TEATAX · DMITRI
WHEN · ITSMEAGAIN
MADD · GOTOETOTOE
DISS · EYEOPENERS

145

```
VISA  ITSWAR  FAM
ALEC  CANADA  ECO
CLAUDEMONET   ACL
CEDRIC  BESEATED
IGUANAS     MUSS
NATS  SPLITTERS
ELY  STRIKEONE
   ALLABOARD
   TRUECRIME  NTH
  FAIRSHAKE  LORE
PLIE   OVOIDAL
LOLLIPOP  EMERIL
OOF  BOWLINGLANE
TRI  ORIENT  OMEN
SSN  STEAKS  WARE
```

146

```
AMEN  MASS  TAMPS
FORESIGHT  ARIAL
GROWINGUP  DINGY
HOTSTART  WADDED
ANI  JOYCE  GOO
NICHE  ORB  PANG
   EXSQUEEZEME
   BIGSURPRISE
   GODIHOPENOT
JONI  ARI  NOBEL
ETA  PAEAN  ENO
TOFFEE  HEADINTO
SPILL  WORKINGIT
KODAK  ALIENRACE
ITEMS  NEED  EYED
```

147

```
SKA  STIR  NOVAS
CRIB  NONAPOLOGY
RIRI  ITSHANDLED
ESCORT  ERIE  CNN
WHOSE  SCAN  WADE
UNO  FILTH  CONEY
PALMEDOR  FLOOR
   AREWEGOOD
  NINES  PLUSSIGN
HINGE  BEALE  COO
ECHO  WELD  INERT
YEA  FALL  UNIPOD
NOSPOILERS  TOGO
ONTHEFENCE  SPUN
WEEDS  STAR  SEE
```

148

```
AMPLE  ELLA  THU
RELAX  LEAS  TAOS
NAILPOLISH  OKRA
INEARNEST  EYES
ETS  EON  LASSES
  MSN  HEAT  AMY
   CASEDISMISSED
   LETTHATSINKIN
GENERATIONGAP
EFT  ANAT  AFT
STUPID  ITO  CHO
  TRON  POKERCHIP
SOIL  GOONSTRIKE
EWOK  OUZO  WOVEN
ANN  DREW  OPEDS
```

149

```
POPQUIZ  EMIRATI
GROUCHY  MASALAS
FIRELOG  OILGLUT
INK  APOSTLE  SRI
LORE  ETHICS  TIN
MCING  EACH  TANK
SOBEIT  DOIDARE
   RSVP  NMEX
  PIGTAIL  PRICES
DENY  NEUF  ENACT
ATE  ITCLUB  GROK
TUX  DEALERS  TRI
INAWINK  LEADACT
NICEONE  UVLIGHT
GATEMAN  PETFEES
```

150

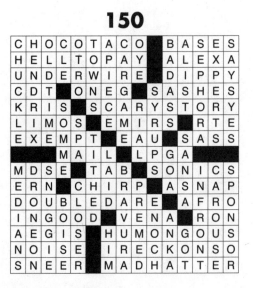

```
CHOCOTACO  BASES
HELLTOPAY  ALEXA
UNDERWIRE  DIPPY
CDT  ONEG  SASHES
KRIS  SCARYSTORY
LIMOS  EMIRS  RTE
EXEMPT  EAU  SASS
  MAIL  LPGA
MDSE  TAB  SONICS
ERN  CHIRP  ASNAP
DOUBLEDARE  AFRO
INGOOD  VENA  RON
AEGIS  HUMONGOUS
NOISE  IRECKONSO
SNEER  MADHATTER
```

151

```
VOCAB   SATE   ODDS
IVORYTOWER   NOAH
SEATFILLER   ANTE
ANT  ASE  HEARTED
     TRACKEDDOWN
 HAS  PIPE  SLAIN
LUMPFISH  LALIGA
ALB ATM GAL  THY
BLURRY  HIDEOUTS
SALEM  CARY  PPS
 BASEBALLBAT
CATERER  TIM  TOE
ELIA  EDGARAWARD
COOL  FIELDHOUSE
EONS  YOLK  LETON
```

152

```
STARDOM   SPOUSE
MINORCA  CHURROS
ODDDUCK  AUTOBOT
GAS  GUESSTIMATE
 LOS  PLUS  TEN
  LAYOPEN  OHSO
FLUID  VETTE  IOU
DONTOVERTHINKIT
ICI  SENSE  NOELS
CHOO  GOTPAST
 NAT  TALL  ABC
TURKEYWRAPS  AHH
OPENSEA  YALELAW
POPULAR  ECONOMY
ONSTAR  RAGTOPS
```

153

```
 SLAM  ACID  SULA
STOREBRAND  ANEW
WERERABBIT  LIFE
IVE  CRUST  TEXTS
GENDERS  OHM
  ODE  PONE  APP
PROPELLERBEANIE
TAKESFORGRANTED
STARBUCKSORDERS
DEY  ELKS  ALE
  INS  ODYSSEY
GLITZ  FLOWS  EMU
LAGS  PLAZAHOTEL
ATOM  IOWEYOUONE
MERE  TEND  WIND
```

154

```
GAYMECCA  IMBIBE
OVERLORD  FORCED
RETAINER  SCREED
PRIZE  PICAS  MRI
   LETFLY  FAKE
RIPE  PITA  TACO
ONANDON  WARTHOG
MATRIX   BELIZE
ACRONYM  BIKINIS
 COLT  BARD  PEET
CULL  VALUES
ARC  TESTS  KEMPT
MAALOX  EQUALPAY
ETRADE  RUSTLEUP
LESBOS  SEAEAGLE
```

155

```
GOPRO  DILI  GDAY
AVIAN  URAL  REPO
EERIE  REYKJAVIK
ARAL  KANE  OZONE
 STRANGERTHINGS
OLEOLE  CINE
DEBATETEAMS  BBS
DEAD  DARKO  NEAT
SPY  SECRETSANTA
  SEEK  HEIGHT
CLEANPLATECLUB
HALLS  EDIE  CROP
IREMEMBER  RAIMI
NANO  MOLE  PROBS
OMAN  AXED  MENSA
```

156

```
SHIVERMETIMBERS
HOTELCALIFORNIA
ETHNICRELATIONS
ETAT  ORAL  HARKS
POP  LYN  TERMS
  PICA  ODORS
STEPH  DRUGS  SAX
FUNSIZE  DADJOKE
OTS  LEVIS  AQUAS
  NIKON  RYAN
 GLOVE  GTA  DRE
WHINE  AROD  SWAB
HATERSGONNAHATE
INEEDAHUGEFAVOR
GARDENAPARTMENT
```

163

```
A I R . G P A . . S T E P T O
P R E Q U E L S . H A T E R S
T A Q U E R I A . A L A N I S
. Q U E S T . W I K I . C O O
. . I S S U E . S U S H I . .
A G R A . R U M O R M I L L .
B L E D . B R A T . A T S E A
L E D I N . O R O . N O H O W
E A R L E . Z I N E . P A N E
. M E L A T O N I N . F R E D
. A A R O N . C H E A P . . .
D O D . S E E M . A R D E N .
O R I S I T . L E N I E N C Y
D E N A D A . B A C K S E A T
D O G L E G . . T E A . R A D
```

164

```
B I B I M B A P . V I S A G E
O R A T O R I O . I M P R O V
B E S T R O D E . S O L U T E
A S S Y R I A . M I N I B A R
. . B I L . J O G . T A T S .
S E M I S . G E N O A . . . .
I C E T . H O T S T R E A K S
T H A T H I T S T H E S P O T
H O L Y S M O K E S . T O F U
. . T A P I R . S A P I D . .
A P R S . L E S . L E T . . .
F R E E G A N . L I N E M A N
L O V E L Y . S A B O T A G E
A N E M I A . A V E R A G E S
C E L E B S . G A L A X I E S
```

165

```
A C T S . R A N T S . A D D S
R A V E . A L O H A . T O O T
I N S T A N T W I N . A T T A
. W E L L D A M N . B L I N I
P E R I O D . O K B O O M E R
A N I S E . T R A I N S E T S
P O E T . B E E G E E S . . .
I T S . N O S T A R S . C P A
. . D I G T H I S . B R A Y .
F R Y I N G P A N . S U I T E
L E A V E S I N . B E G E T S
E T H E R . L E M O N A D E .
T I E R . C O V E R S T O R Y
C R A G . S T E R E . T U N A
H E R E . I S R E D . I T S Y
```

166

```
D R E W B A C K . . O M I T
N E U R A L N E T . M E M E
A F R I K A N E R S . A T O N
L I E G E S . P A T . N A V Y
A N K H S . L A C E S . D E E
B E A T . B O C K . T I A R A
. . C O W L S . A S T I R .
. Y E A H A B O U T T H A T .
P O S S E . A S I D E . . .
H U C K S . L E T S . G A S P
S A O . S O L E S . T O S C A
T W O S . R E Y . T A S S E L
R A T E . G R E W A S P I N E
I K E A . S O I L T E S T S .
P E R M . . N I C E L I S T
```

167

```
. . P H O T O A P P S .
. T H E N E W B L A C K .
. S H O R T S W E A T H E R .
P L I N T H S . T S E L I O T
I O N I Z E . . T S E T S E
T A L C . R A I M I . P E E N
A N Y . J A M P A C K . L S D
. . G O D F O R B I D .
. O O H I M S C A R E D .
. R H I N O . . G I V E S
T E E N S . M A P . N I C A D
A T M S . M O M O A . A L L Y
M E G A C O R P O R A T I O N
E L E N A D E L L E D O N N E
S L E E V E L E S S D R E S S
```

168

```
F R U I T T A R T . G A S P S
O O M P A H P A H . A D O R E
T U N A M E L T S . R U B O N
O X O . A P A T . O R L E S S
. . X R A Y L A B . T R E E
A P P E A L . E L S A S .
B E E R . E A S I E R . V I M
L E T S T H I N G S S L I D E
E R A . W O M A N S . A N N A
. . B A R A K . E L W O O D
J O E L . S T E P D A D .
I N R O M E . B L O T . F E W
L E I C A . V I A V E N E T O
T A C K Y . A T T E N U A T E
S L A Y S . R E A R T I R E S
```

169

```
WINNER     PLANBS
WHOOPI   MAOSUIT
IAMBIC DOUGHBOY
  TOUCHSENSOR
CERTS  WAKE  APPT
LIES  SITE  SMORE
ATF  CATHY  ASTIN
WHO  ZXCVBNM  ADD
SERTA HARES  TEA
ARMOR  BLEW  COPY
TEES  LALA  CASAS
   PEACEDOLLAR
CLEARSKY  PILLAR
SEARATS  UNMADE
IGUESS    SEEDED
```

170

```
ACNE  GAME  RUSTS
THOR  OPEN  IDAHO
TONI  THATSSOYOU
ICANDOIT  CENSUS
COP  END  SRA
  HORSE  COINFLIP
SOLOS  WARPDRIVE
ELOPE  ERR  SIMON
TIGERLILY  HAIRS
ICYSTARE  DIRTY
   WMD  TON  ECO
ANEMIA  SHEEPDOG
DOZENROSES  URAL
AGREE  UNTO  MUSE
MOATS  ISAK  ANTS
```

171

```
PASCALSTRIANGLE
INTIMATEAPPAREL
TOOTIREDTOTHINK
SSN  SCREEDS  MGM
AMID  HOURS  FATE
WINES  IMS  SACHA
SAGCARDS  PHTEST
   IPOS  MART
AIMLOW  TAKEACAB
TRUER  SIR  WILLA
LESS  PARIS  LULL
APE  ARMANIS  BEL
SETAGOODEXAMPLE
EATDESSERTFIRST
STEADYASSHEGOES
```

172

```
   BANDMATE   CST
   MOUSEOVER  CHAR
TEATASTING  RIMA
OTTO  KHAN  RULED
GUESTS  INEXILE
OPRAH  OASIS  DOW
   VERBIAGE  OVA
WIRELESSCHARGER
ADE  OMELETTE
RAD  RISES  EARLS
CRAVATS  ADDOIL
RELAX  OPER  UPTO
AYES  EVILEMPIRE
FORT  TELLNOONE
TUT  CREATING
```

173

```
SMACKDAB  ASLANT
EAGLEOWL  MOOCOW
IHEARYOU  ENTIRE
ZOOMBOMBING  DIE
EMUS  GABS  WRIST
SET  PANELTRUCKS
  SOHO  REOIL
  FETED  TOTEM
  ATEIT  ERAS
SWIVELCHAIR  KTS
MINER  TENT  NEAP
USB  MOUNTSHASTA
REEBOK  OHBOTHER
FUTURA  REALTALK
SPACEY  MMDDYYYY
```

174

```
AMPUP  GALA  MAGS
RAISEHAVOC  AURA
EATENALIVE  GDAY
AMY  SUEDE  BIRDS
   BITS  BRACE
SHROVE  BEARCLAW
TRADE  BLACKHOLE
ARTY  SEEDY  ARIA
GETSALLAS  ARDEN
SPECIALK  LUMENS
  RANGY  CONS
TURNT  AFOOT  ADA
GRIN  SCRAPMETAL
ISEE  THATSAMORE
FARR  YETI  YIPES
```

175

BASAL ADDLED
PARADE FREEGAN
HORCRUX LONGORIA
OUCHIE MOLTOBENE
TREES MEAL HODOR
COLD PAST SOO
OVO VINS SLUSHIE
MENTALGYMNASTICS
BRAILLE EASE REP
MES MACH SECT
SALON KINK PADRE
PLOTTWIST SINGES
FASHIONS THEGOAT
SEENOTE BOTTOM
REELED SPYON

176

HITUP ORSO QIN
INAPT POOL ANO
JAKES LADLE TAB
ATEN SIRED PASO
BRADPITT FEARED
SAC HMM SOSPICY
PAJAMAPARTY
BASEJUMPERS
ZEROGRAVITY
FUZZIER ARE ROT
ABOUND RITZBITS
COOP DOOMS ICEE
IAM CONDI GOTAT
ATE OWIE ITEMS
LSD ONTO FAROE

177

SPAT IGA ALOHA
ARIA GOLDMEDALS
HORN LOADEDDICE
APB COUNTS RAN
REARLOT HULLS
ALGAE FREERIDE
CARPOOLLANE
MINEALLMINE
NANCYPELOSI
SOYOUSAY TURBO
AVAST ISOMERS
RIN SENDUP BOP
ICANRELATE DOOR
SERENASLAM ROME
STEAM AGE ETSY

178

AKA LIESTO SWUM
VERMONSTER UHNO
LIFEONMARS MADD
AREAS ENRON TEE
BADREP DONOHARM
AYESIR TADS
OMB GOON STREET
REASONS TOOTALL
LACHOY MIRO LLC
SKIS RIPEST
TURNEVIL RHOMBI
ORO YIPES ATEAT
TINT SPACEBALLS
ENYA ALGALBLOOM
MGMT SEEMLY NOE

179

CONRAD AREPAS
AREARUG NERUDA
BIBIMBAP DEADLY
LOUSY TASED DIY
ELLE PERPS BYTE
SEA LOWER BETES
BANANACREAM
PETTYTYRANT
PACKEDHOUSE
PRICE RENDS DIN
LENA BUSTS FAST
ACT LOGIA CANOE
NOGGIN SNOOKUMS
EDUARD SUREBET
TENSES RYDERS

180

YEOFLITTLEFAITH
AGREETODISAGREE
LOCHNESSMONSTER
ESS TMC ABA
GAIA BERMUDA
BENZ GESTURES
GARDE LAO TALE
LITHO WIN SANTA
AREA BEN DENIS
MTARARAT ETTA
SHUDDER ALAS
EAT AUG DIE
READSTHERIOTACT
ISNOTHINGSACRED
BETWEENTHELINES

181

C	O	M	B	O	█	C	L	A	P	T	R	A	P	█
A	P	E	R	Y	█	H	E	S	A	R	E	B	E	L
M	E	T	A	L	█	E	T	H	N	I	C	I	T	Y
E	R	R	S	█	L	E	I	█	S	P	A	D	E	R
L	A	O	█	L	A	T	T	E	█	█	P	E	R	E
S	T	A	C	E	Y	A	B	R	A	M	S	█	█	█
P	I	R	O	G	I	█	E	A	S	E	█	B	A	S
I	C	E	B	A	T	H	█	S	C	R	O	O	G	E
N	S	A	█	T	O	A	D	█	E	L	M	O	R	E
█	█	C	O	N	T	E	X	T	I	S	K	E	Y	█
A	B	B	A	█	E	L	G	I	N	█	D	E	A	█
P	R	A	N	C	E	█	T	A	C	█	P	E	A	S
P	E	N	T	A	G	R	A	M	█	P	E	A	B	O
S	A	T	E	S	A	U	C	E	█	H	E	L	L	O
█	D	U	R	A	N	G	O	S	█	O	L	S	E	N

182

D	A	P	S	█	R	A	S	P	█	█	H	U	F	F	Y
E	R	I	E	█	A	L	T	O	█	A	D	O	R	E	
B	R	A	I	N	F	A	R	T	█	L	O	R	E	N	
T	O	N	K	A	T	S	U	█	C	O	N	E	S	█	
S	W	O	O	N	█	█	T	S	O	█	█	N	C	R	
█	█	O	S	H	█	H	I	R	E	S	O	N	█	█	
█	B	I	T	T	E	R	E	N	E	M	I	E	S	█	
█	W	A	T	E	R	A	E	R	O	B	I	C	S	█	
B	O	D	I	C	E	R	I	P	P	E	R	S	█	█	
T	R	A	S	H	E	S	█	A	S	L	█	█	█	█	
S	E	P	█	█	T	E	A	█	█	L	E	A	S	H	
█	D	P	L	U	S	█	N	A	K	E	D	L	I	E	
H	O	L	E	S	█	B	O	X	E	D	W	I	N	E	
O	W	E	N	S	█	I	D	L	E	█	I	C	E	D	
E	N	S	O	R	█	B	E	E	N	█	N	E	W	S	

183

A	W	R	A	T	S	█	S	C	O	R	E	S
B	E	A	R	H	U	G	█	C	H	R	O	M	E
R	E	V	E	A	L	E	D	█	R	I	B	B	E	D
U	Z	I	█	I	K	N	E	W	I	T	█	B	R	A
P	E	N	D	█	S	I	G	E	P	█	C	L	A	N
T	R	E	E	D	█	U	R	N	█	T	O	I	L	S
█	█	B	A	S	S	E	T	H	O	U	N	D	█	█
█	█	P	A	R	O	L	E	B	O	A	R	D	█	█
█	█	M	A	K	E	D	E	M	A	N	D	S	█	█
H	I	R	E	S	█	V	I	N	█	S	E	R	V	E
O	L	A	Y	█	R	E	L	A	Y	█	S	O	I	L
H	E	S	█	W	E	L	L	N	O	W	█	U	S	E
O	R	I	G	I	N	█	S	A	D	I	S	T	I	C
H	U	T	O	N	E	█	S	E	R	P	E	N	T	
O	N	E	D	G	E	█	L	E	A	S	E	S	

184

I	Q	S	█	S	M	E	L	L	█	A	N	D	E	S
S	U	E	█	C	I	L	I	A	█	M	E	A	D	E
M	E	D	█	A	C	I	N	G	█	O	W	N	E	D
█	B	U	T	T	H	A	T	S	J	U	S	T	M	E
B	E	C	A	M	E	█	█	E	N	D	E	A	R	█
A	C	T	U	A	L	S	█	A	N	T	E	█	█	█
M	O	I	█	N	A	T	I	V	E	█	S	W	A	P
B	I	O	S	█	N	O	D	E	S	█	K	I	L	L
I	S	N	T	█	G	O	O	D	A	T	█	K	O	I
█	█	A	P	E	D	█	A	I	R	L	I	N	E	█
S	P	I	R	A	L	█	█	S	O	A	P	E	D	█
W	I	L	L	Y	O	U	B	E	Q	U	I	E	T	█
A	L	L	I	E	█	P	O	T	U	S	█	D	I	D
T	A	B	L	E	█	C	A	N	O	E	█	I	M	O
H	U	E	Y	S	█	S	T	A	I	R	█	A	E	C

185

E	G	R	E	T	█	U	B	E	R	█	B	C	C	S
C	L	A	R	A	█	S	L	A	Y	█	L	E	A	H
O	U	T	E	R	S	P	A	C	E	█	E	L	L	A
L	E	T	█	P	O	A	C	H	█	S	A	L	T	Y
A	T	A	D	█	T	S	K	█	B	A	T	M	E	N
B	O	N	O	B	O	S	█	S	U	B	█	A	C	E
█	█	G	O	S	P	E	L	T	R	U	T	H	█	█
█	█	S	E	X	P	O	S	I	T	I	V	E	█	█
█	█	D	E	S	S	E	R	T	M	E	N	U	█	█
K	I	A	█	T	A	T	█	T	R	A	L	A	L	A
A	D	W	E	E	K	█	D	O	C	█	A	L	A	N
S	T	A	M	P	█	R	U	N	U	P	█	L	U	G
B	I	T	E	█	E	Y	E	O	P	E	N	E	R	S
A	M	E	N	█	V	A	I	N	█	S	A	G	E	T
H	E	R	D	█	A	N	N	E	█	T	E	E	N	Y

186

A	B	L	E	R	█	D	O	C	U	S	O	A	P
P	R	E	G	O	█	R	E	V	E	R	E	N	C	E
P	I	G	G	Y	█	I	C	E	D	L	A	T	T	E
L	E	A	S	█	S	T	A	R	R	█	T	O	I	L
E	L	L	█	S	E	A	L	S	I	N	█	█	█	█
█	A	I	S	L	E	█	█	E	C	O	T	A	G	E
M	R	S	M	A	I	S	E	L	█	B	A	S	R	A
E	S	S	E	N	T	I	A	L	W	O	R	K	E	R
M	O	U	L	D	█	M	R	S	A	N	D	M	A	N
O	N	E	T	E	R	M	█	R	E	Y	E	S	█	█
█	█	█	R	E	E	D	I	T	S	█	L	E	D	█
A	Z	U	L	█	T	R	A	N	S	█	C	A	F	E
L	O	S	E	F	A	I	T	H	█	K	A	T	I	E
T	R	E	E	L	I	N	E	D	█	A	L	E	R	T
S	A	D	S	O	N	G	S	█	█	T	I	R	E	S

187

| M O S S | P R O V E I T |
| C O N E O F S I L E N C E |
| F R I E N D L Y B A N T E R |
M O E	S T O I C	F A R C E
A R M S	R I G H T	L E A S
I G E T B Y	H O Y A	E P A
M E D I A	S T U R D Y
T E L L O N	T A M A L E S
D A L L O W A Y	N I K O L A
A B A	O N P O I N T	V I P
M O C K	S A G G Y	M E S S
A U R A S	T A U	P A P I
S T E P I N	M A D E R O O M
K I M O N O	A N D S C E N E
S T E W E D	T A R T	M S G

188

P A B S T	F I C A	M B A S
I H A V E T O R U N	E R I E
T A B U L A R A S A	L I M E
A B E	K E N T	O D E S
W O E S	O R A N G E
D E F I N I T E M A Y B E
O V I N E	R E V E A L E D
G E N T	A T A R I	L O C I
G R E E N L I T	A L A R M
D R O P D O W N M E N U S
B I G T O E	R O A R
R O N A	P L A N	F E W
S W I M	C O U P O N C O D E
V I N E	B O N U S R O U N D
P E G S	S L A P	A T L A S

189

| B R I B E D | P A C T |
| C A E S U R A | A P H I D |
| N O N D A I R Y C R E A M E R |
O R D E A L S	H I D	E C O
I N S E C T	T A P	J L A W
S E A M S	P A R A G U A Y
Y A W	T H O N G S O N G
B E A U G E S T E
B O R N T O R U N	A S H
F L U N K I E S	O L L I E
P R A T	A N D	T W E E Z E
B I Z	M A E	B E H A V E D
J E E P E R S C R E E P E R S
D R A N O	P A T R O L S
S T U N	A T H E N S

190

A V O N	D I S A P P E A R
M A N O	B E S T C H A N C E
B L T S	O N E A T A T I M E
E V I L	U S E R	S I D E D
R E P O S T	T H E O
P U T	I C E E	S W A G
J O Y C E	C A R R Y	A G O
O N T H E B A C K B U R N E R
S L O	L A N A I	C A N D Y
E Y E S	T R O T	K I A
H O S E	S Y S T E M
A T R I A	L I P A	E R G O
P O I N T T A K E N	S A G A
P R O T E S T E R S	U D O N
S O T O S P E A K	P E N S

191

A B U	M E W	S P I C Y
L I S S O M E	C L O T H E
L O V E D I T	L O O K S O N
O L I V E R	P O N T I A C
T A S E R	B U N C H E D U P
B A R N D A N C E	R U L E
S A F A R I H A T	D A N
L I V E S A L I E
I C E	T E C H N E R D S
P A N T	C H E E R E D U P
A R T I L L E R Y	T Y P O S
W E E L A S S	G R I P P E
S A N D A R T	S E E N O T E
I S T U N K	A N A G R A M
T H E P O	M E D	T B S

192

| I T E M I Z E | R E C I P E S |
| L O V E C O N Q U E R S A L L |
| L E A D A D O U B L E L I F E |
S T L	N I S I	E E N I E
O U T T A	C R U D	T S P
U T A H	C A K E S	A S H Y
M O T E L	I Q T E S T
S E E M E	R U E	S H E D S
E N A M E L	T A X I S
A B E D	T E S L A	N C A A
N E D	C E N T	M A D A M
C H I N A	I S I S	V E G
H A T E R S G O N N A H A T E
O V E R O P I N I O N A T E D
R E D F L A G	P R A Y E R S

193

```
. B R A N D I S H . O R A L B
S E E D O U B L E . L A N A I
M R S A N D M A N . D I T T O
O L E . P E S T . R E L I E F
K I N D A . . F E N . G R U .
E N T I R E . P A W . T O M E
. . R E A L O R I G I N A L .
. C A N I G E T A N A M E N .
C U D D L E P U D D L E . . .
H T M L . R E S . S A L A D S
E L I . S L R . . P Y L O N .
M O T L E Y . F I F A . S T A
L O O I E . A L L I G A T O R
A S N A P . S A Y N O M O R E
B E E R S . S W A N S O N G .
```

194

```
E B A Y . T I K I . B E G E T
M O L E . O N U S . A M O R E
M O U T H W A S H . H I T O N
A T M . E A C H . . . G O D S
. . A I W A . S L U R P E E .
H A N D S A N I T I Z E R . .
T W E E T Y . K Y L O . I S U
M E W S . E N E . . P S A S .
L D S . R E D O . C R E O L E
. W I N D O W C L E A N E R .
O P O S S U M . H U N T . . .
A I R S . . L A T E . S P A .
S E T U P . S A L T W A T E R
E T H E R . T Y K E . H A R M
S A Y S O . U S S R . A R T Y
```

195

```
C O N S U L . I N S P I R I T
A P O L L O . S E T A D A T E
R E C A N T . F A R C I C A L
D R A M A . S A T E . D E L L
T A M S . S C H L E P . D Y S
A G E . S P R A Y T A N . . .
B O R D E R O N . S P I C E D
L E A R N E D . O M A K A S E
E R S A T Z . P L A C E N T A
. W I Z A R D R Y . N A T .
P G A . N A M E I T . R O T H
A R U M . T O M E . M I N E R
S U R E S U R E . M A S A L A
T E A S E R A D . O N E D A Y
A L L H E A L S . S I N E W S
```

196

```
G I T M O . P A L . . G A H
A S W A N . I D I G . E R G O
G H O S T . C A M E C L E A N
. P E A S . M A T H L E T E
S C O R P I O . R A I D E D
A R I A . S U N S E T S . .
M A N T A . T A P A S . S H O
O P T I C A L I L L U S I O N
A S S . C R A V E . P E R S E
. R E T W E E T . M E T A
R E W I N D . N O M I N A L
A L I S T E R S . P O T S .
N U D E S C E N E . L O O S E
O D O R . O V A L . A N N I E
N E W . . S P F . R E G A L
```

197

```
M U S T B E N I C E . A P B S
O B A M A B I D E N . C H A T
N E W Z E A L A N D . T O D O
I R E . R Y E . S I L E N T O
C E R A . C U T A D E A L .
A D S L O G A N S . T U T S I
. G E R U N D S . P A T E
R I D . R A T P A C K . G E S
O B I T . F O O T A G E . .
B E R R A . C L A M B A K E S
A F T E R A L L . T A L C
B O B A T E A . Y A M . F D A
A R I D . T V R E P O R T E R
N E K O . N E X T P L E A S E
K E E N . A S S I S T A N T S
```

198

```
X R A Y E Y E S . A R A F A T
X O X O X O X O . R E L A T E
X Y L O P H O N E M A L L E T
. . H O O T . C Y R I L . .
I P S O . H I T O N . N E S T
S H O O . O C A L A . A Q U A
A O L . R E V . L U R K
I B A R . P A T S Y . L I V E
D I R E . E R A . . N I T
N A P S . T E R S E . C O V E
O S L O . S T E A L . O X E N
. E R A T O . F I N N . .
T E X T B O O K E X A M P L E
R O U T E R . O L I V E O Y L
I N S O L E . P Y R E N E E S
```

199

D	C	B	A	S	E	D	■	■	K	E	E	P	T	O
A	L	I	S	T	E	R	S	■	O	R	L	E	A	N
G	O	T	T	A	C	A	T	C	H	E	M	A	L	L
A	V	E	R	Y	■	G	I	R	L	S	■	S	K	A
M	E	M	O	■	T	I	C	O	S	■	C	A	I	N
A	R	E	■	R	I	N	K	S	■	C	A	N	E	D
■	■	B	O	O	T	Y	S	H	O	R	T	S	■	■
■	K	I	N	G	O	F	B	E	E	R	S	■	■	■
■	M	E	D	I	A	C	I	R	C	U	S	■	■	■
G	O	T	O	N	■	O	N	E	H	R	■	B	E	T
O	V	E	N	■	P	U	G	E	T	■	M	A	L	E
O	I	L	■	B	A	R	E	D	■	D	A	M	N	S
G	E	O	C	E	N	T	R	I	C	O	R	B	I	T
L	A	N	C	E	D	■	S	N	O	W	C	O	N	E
E	D	E	S	S	A	■	G	O	D	H	O	O	D	■

200

L	I	F	E	H	A	C	K	■	L	E	A	N	O	N
I	M	A	M	O	R	O	N	■	A	R	C	A	N	E
B	A	R	E	N	E	C	E	S	S	I	T	I	E	S
I	R	O	N	S	■	K	E	A	T	S	■	L	O	T
D	E	E	D	■	C	E	L	T	S	■	G	E	N	E
O	T	S	■	P	A	R	E	S	■	Y	O	D	O	G
■	■	A	I	M	E	D	■	T	U	B	I	N	G	■
O	L	D	S	O	U	L	■	D	I	L	A	T	E	S
H	A	I	K	U	S	■	F	I	N	E	D	■	■	■
S	T	E	M	S	■	B	O	G	G	S	■	N	Y	U
T	E	T	E	■	M	O	R	S	E	■	M	I	E	N
O	S	S	■	S	O	D	O	I	■	R	O	G	E	R
P	H	O	T	O	S	Y	N	T	H	E	S	I	Z	E
I	O	D	I	N	E	■	C	E	R	B	E	R	U	S
T	W	A	N	G	S	■	E	S	S	A	Y	I	S	T